Child Care &
Development

6th edition

Pamela Minett

HODDER
EDUCATION
AN HACHETTE UK COMPANY

Orders: please contact Bookpoint Ltd, 130 Milton Park, Abingdon, Oxon OX14 4SB. Telephone: +(44) 01235 827720. Fax: +(44) 01235 400454. Lines are open from 9.00 to 5.00, Monday to Saturday, with a 24-hour message answering service. You can also order through our website www.hoddereducation.co.uk.

British Library Cataloguing in Publication Data
A catalogue record for this title is available from the British Library

ISBN: 978 1 444 11713 4
First Published 2010
Impression number 10 9 8 7 6 5 4 3 2 1
Year 2014 2013 2012 2011 2010

Cover photo Marc Rimmer/Corbis
Illustrations by Kathy Baxendale, Dawn Brend, Chris Forsey, Jenny Mumford, Pat Tourret, Philip Wilson and Oxford Designers and Illustrators

Typeset by Fakenham Photosetting Ltd, Fakenham Norfolk
Printed in Italy for Hodder Education, an Hachette UK Company, 338 Euston Road, London NW1 3BH

Contents

Preface to the sixth edition

The five previous editions of **Child Care & Development** have been gratifyingly well received and have proved very popular in schools and colleges, and also with private students. Since the publication of previous editions there have been a considerable number of changes in the child-care field. These have taken place in legislation, medicine and approaches to the subject, and to the specifications for examinations. Producing a new edition has provided the opportunity to carry out a thorough review of the text and illustrations, and to update the book to reflect changing conditions and terminology. Publication is in full colour, enhancing student appeal.

Each of the 76 topics ends with a bank of questions to reinforce knowledge, and further activities to broaden the subject. These include guidelines for Child Study – an important element in almost any course of child care and development, investigations and discussions.

The book continues to be intended primarily as a textbook for students of subjects involving child care and development. In particular, it covers the knowledge and understanding requirements of the GCSE Examining Groups and BTEC Level 2. It will also be useful for lower level Council for Awards in Children's Care and Education (CACHE) courses as well as those parts of Social Studies and Community Studies which are concerned with children and with aspects of Health and Social Care.

Courses in child care and development are not always followed by an examination. The subject covers an area of study which has a strong appeal to many young people and can, therefore, provide an excellent vehicle for the encouragement of a wide range of related educational activities. In addition, it provides useful guidelines for the parents of the future, helping young people to understand what is involved in bringing up children. Awareness of the effects of the care of children on their development can lead to a greater understanding of a person's own behaviour – and, it is hoped, to a greater tolerance of the behaviour of others.

Students of this subject in schools and colleges are mainly young people who are not yet parents, nor even contemplating parenthood. The book has therefore been written at this level and with this approach. A broad outline of the subject has been presented in a simple, straightforward manner. Technical terms have been explained or an everyday alternative given. Where controversy exists, I have attempted to give a balanced view. Although written primarily for students, it is hoped that the book will be of interest to the many parents and others who are concerned with the care of children.

I have received much help and advice in preparing the sixth edition and would like to thank all those who have contributed in any way, not least those teachers who have taken the trouble to write to me or discuss various aspects of the book, and those who answered the questionnaire. Help from those who have experience of using the book in the classroom has been invaluable.

I particularly wish to acknowledge the contributions made to this edition by Dr David Wayne (Consultant Physician), Elizabeth Ramsden (Senior Sister, Guy's Hospital), Jill Purkis (Practice Nurse, Lewisham) and Judith Harvey (Specialist Consultant).

I continue to be indebted to all who helped me in any way with previous editions. I remain particularly grateful to the late Professor Robert Illingworth, an internationally recognised authority in paediatrics, for his considerable guidance during the preparation of the first edition.

P.M.

Tips on website research and Credits

TIPS ON WEBSITE RESEARCH

During your course you will need to demonstrate that you are able to use the internet for research. The weblink boxes in this book provide tips on useful websites that could be used for internet research. To start, enter the website address from the weblink box in your internet browser. Then use the website's search box to look for the particular page within the website by using the search hints in the book. The most suitable page will usually be the first search result. For websites without a search box we have provided 'direction' hints to the particular page within the website.

CREDITS

SECTION 1

Family and home

CHAPTER 1

The family

The family is the basic unit of society. It is a group of people of various ages who are usually related by birth, marriage or adoption.

FUNCTIONS OF THE FAMILY

One of the most important functions of a family is to provide for a child's needs, because children are unable to care for themselves. These needs include:

- food and drink
- care and training
- shelter
- a secure environment in which they can develop into young adults
- warmth and clothing
- love and companionship
- boundaries for behaviour
- protection and support
- encouragement with their education.

Family ties

The members of a family usually feel that they have a special relationship with each other based on some or all of the following:

- blood – knowing that they have the same ancestors
- affection
- duty – due to a traditional sense of obligation
- shared experiences
- common interests.

VARIETY OF FAMILY STRUCTURE

Extended family

The extended family is a large family group which includes grandparents, parents, brothers, sisters, aunts, uncles and cousins.

Such a family is the basis for the traditional pattern of family life in many countries. When the members of an extended family are closely connected by affection, duty, common interest, or daily acquaintance, they may help and support each other in a number of ways such as:

An extended family at home

- providing comfort at times of distress
- helping the parents to bring up their children
- looking after the children in an emergency or when the parents are working
- giving advice on problems
- helping financially.

In recent years, changes to the traditional pattern of family life have been taking place in some countries, particularly the countries of western Europe and the USA:

- Effective methods of contraception have led to families with fewer children.
- Moving away from the family base is common in a changing industrial and technological society.
- Many grandparents are living longer and are more independent.
- Many mothers go out to work.
- Parents may choose not to marry.

These changes have led to weakening of links between members of the extended family, and to the nuclear family becoming the most common family unit.

Nuclear family

A nuclear family consists of parents and their children. They form a self-contained family unit living in a separate household. Life in a nuclear family differs from that in an extended family:

A nuclear family at home

- Nuclear families can be separated by long distances from other members of the extended family.
- Parents may bring up their children with little or no help and support from grandparents and other relations.
- Grandparents and grandchildren may be deprived of each other's company.
- Contact with other relatives is a matter of choice.
- Often, both parents have jobs and the children may be cared for by adults who are not part of the family.

A nuclear family becomes an extended family when, for example:

- Grandparents come to live with the family.

- A teenager in the family becomes pregnant and both the new parent(s) and baby continue to live in the family home.

One parent families (lone parent families; single parent families)

In this type of family the children are brought up by only one parent. Usually the parent is the mother, but sometimes it is the father.

The one parent has to do everything that is usually shared by two parents – provide food, shelter, clothes, a sense of security, daily care and training. This is very hard work for one parent and, as in any other family, this work continues for many years until the children have grown up.

One parent families can vary as widely as two parent families in terms of health, wealth, happiness and security. The family situation can also change, with a one parent family becoming a two parent family or the other way round.

Reasons for families being 'one parent' include:

- divorce or separation of the parents
- death of one parent
- births to single women
- one of the parents being away from home for a long time through work, illness or imprisonment.

One parent families

Step-families

A step-family is one in which there is a child (or children) who is the natural child of one partner in a marriage (or partnership) but not both.

Such a family is usually the result of divorce, or the death of a parent, followed by re-marriage. Since the step-child will not have grown up with the step-parent from birth, it may often (but not always) take some time for them to adjust to living together, and resentments can arise. This may be further complicated when there are other children from the step-parent's previous marriage to get used to.

Example of a step-family

Shared-care families

These are families where the parents live in separate homes and the children spend part of the week living with one parent and the rest of the week with the other. Both parents are equally responsible for looking after their children's needs. The main reasons for shared arrangements are either divorce or separation of the parents.

Foster families

These are families who care for children who are not related to them. Sometimes there are a number of children from different families living in the same foster home.

Same-sex families

These are families with same-sex parents – homosexual couples who are either gay or lesbian.

Residential children's home

Children without families, or whose families are unable or unwilling to look after them may live (reside) in a residential home. Usually, the adults who care for the children try to make life in the home as much like normal family life as possible.

Questions

1 a What is a family?

  b List nine needs of a child which are provided for by the family.

  c The members of a family usually feel that they have a special relationship.

    Give reasons for this.

2 a Describe briefly the difference between an extended family and a nuclear family.

  b Give five ways in which members of an extended family can help and support each other.

  c Give five changes to the traditional pattern of family life which have taken place in some countries.

  d List five differences between life in extended families and nuclear families.

3 a (i)   What is a one parent family?

    (ii) Name some of the tasks that the one parent has to do which are normally shared by two parents.

  b Give four reasons for one parent families.

4 a What is a step-family?

  b What problems may possibly occur when a step-family is formed?

5 Describe (i) a shared-care family, (ii) a foster family.

Further activities

 Discussion

Discuss possible factors which may complicate life in a step-family, and the ways in which such situations might be eased.

 Child study

Begin a long-term study of one child, or a group of children, or of a particular aspect of development by:

● obtaining the parents' permission
● recording general information
  ∗ first name (if the study is to be confidential, the name should be fictitious)
  ∗ age
● describing physical appearance
  ∗ height (in cm)
  ∗ weight (in kg)
  ∗ colouring
  ∗ special features, e.g. glasses
● describing personality, e.g. lively, shy with strangers

Use a computer to present your work.

Suggestions for Child Study activities are given at the end of many of the topics throughout this book.

Weblink

Visit the Quote Garden website:

www.quotegarden.com

Search for 'family quotes' and select at least three quotations that reflect your views of family life.

CHAPTER 2

Family lifestyles

FACTORS WHICH HAVE BROUGHT CHANGES TO FAMILY LIFE

The general pattern of family life in the UK has changed during the last century due to many factors:

- Laws have been introduced which give women much more independence – votes, property rights, equal opportunities.
- Education and career choices are similar for boys and girls.
- Women can opt out of marriage because they do not need to rely on a husband for financial support.
- Labour-saving devices in the home have made domestic work less exhausting and have given women more free time for outings with the children, a job outside the home, more social life, hobbies etc.
- State benefits have eased financial problems to some extent.
- Reliable methods of contraception allow couples to choose not to become parents or to have fewer children.
- There are more single parent families and step-families.
- Divorce is easier and has become more socially acceptable.

ROLES WITHIN THE FAMILY

Traditional roles

At the beginning of the 20th century in the UK, the roles of husband and wife within the family were distinct. The traditional role of the husband was to be the 'breadwinner' and to make the important decisions, whilst that of the wife was to care for her home, husband and children.

During the course of the century these roles have become blurred in many families. Many women have paid jobs and many of the household jobs are shared by both sexes. The two World Wars have been major causes of this change.

This change in society has been reflected in legislation. Employers must offer equal terms of employment to men and women doing the same or similar jobs (*Equal Pay Act* 1970). Also it is illegal to discriminate against a person on grounds of sex or marital status (*Sex Discrimination Act* 1975, *Amendment Regulations* 2008).

Shared roles

In some families, mother and father do not have distinct roles. Each parent may have a job (perhaps part-time) and each contributes to the family finances, and shares the household jobs and child care. The advantages claimed are:

- Fathers have a closer relationship with their children.
- Mothers have more time to enjoy their children and to follow other interests.
- Children benefit from greater variety.
- The quality of the marriage improves.

Role reversal

When 'role reversal' takes place, the father cares for the home and children while the mother earns the money.

Trends in family life in Britain

At the beginning of the 20th century …

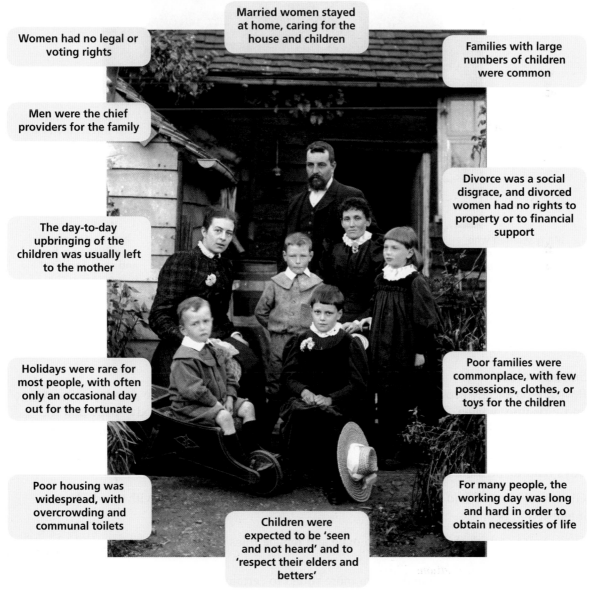

Married women stayed at home, caring for the house and children

Women had no legal or voting rights

Families with large numbers of children were common

Men were the chief providers for the family

Divorce was a social disgrace, and divorced women had no rights to property or to financial support

The day-to-day upbringing of the children was usually left to the mother

Holidays were rare for most people, with often only an occasional day out for the fortunate

Poor families were commonplace, with few possessions, clothes, or toys for the children

Poor housing was widespread, with overcrowding and communal toilets

For many people, the working day was long and hard in order to obtain necessities of life

Children were expected to be 'seen and not heard' and to 'respect their elders and betters'

Victorian family life

At the beginning of the 21st century ...

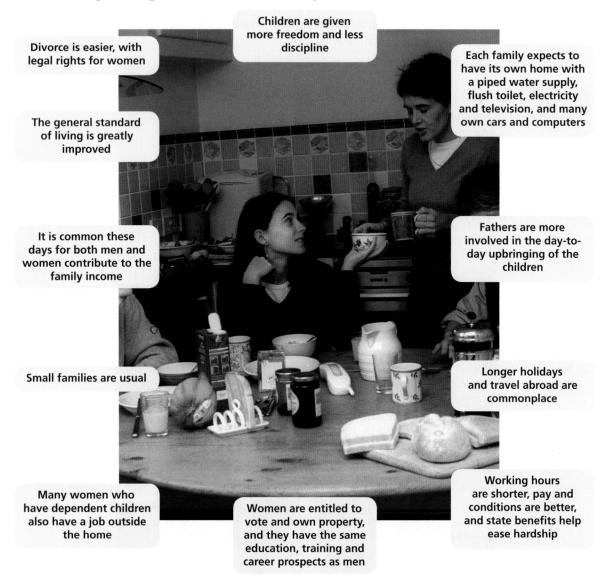

Divorce is easier, with legal rights for women

Children are given more freedom and less discipline

Each family expects to have its own home with a piped water supply, flush toilet, electricity and television, and many own cars and computers

The general standard of living is greatly improved

It is common these days for both men and women contribute to the family income

Fathers are more involved in the day-to-day upbringing of the children

Small families are usual

Longer holidays and travel abroad are commonplace

Many women who have dependent children also have a job outside the home

Women are entitled to vote and own property, and they have the same education, training and career prospects as men

Working hours are shorter, pay and conditions are better, and state benefits help ease hardship

Modern family life

Sexual roles

Boys are physically programmed by their genes (p. 128) and hormones to develop into men, and girls into women. Their sex hormones control the development of body shape and the activities of the sex organs. Differences in behaviour are often noticeable from the age of three months.

Boys tend to: be more active and energetic, aggressive, competitive, keen to explore.

Girls tend to: walk and talk earlier, control the bladder earlier, be better with words, be more interested in people.

The extent to which children develop male and female roles as they grow into adults is due to two main reasons:

1. **Physical factors**, which make them more suited to certain activities; for example, men usually have larger muscles and greater strength, and women bear children.

2. **The encouragement or discouragement of distinct male and female roles in childhood** by:
   - **the expectations of adults** – boys are usually expected to be brave, and girls expected to cry
   - **toys** – girls and boys are often given different types of toys
   - **clothes** – girls and boys are usually dressed differently
   - **the child's own observations** of how men and women behave inside and outside the home, and how they are portrayed in books, newspapers, television etc.

Questions

1 Study the pictures on pp. 7 and 8. Place the labels in appropriate pairs in a table like the one below (there are 11 pairs).

Typical of family life at the beginning of 20th century	Typical of family life today

2 Name eight factors which have brought changes to family life.

3 a Compare the traditional roles of husband and wife at the beginning of the 20th century.

   b What has happened to these roles since then?

   c What is the difference between shared roles and role reversal?

   d List four advantages claimed by those who practice shared roles.

4 a Give examples of differences in behaviour between boys and girls that are often noticeable at an early age.

   b Name four factors which can affect the development of distinct male and female roles.

Weblink

For more information about poverty and families in the Victorian era visit:

www.hiddenlives.org.uk

Further activities

 Investigation

Interview one or more people aged 70 or over and try to list 20 ways in which they think that family life has changed since they were children. Use the information to give a short talk to your class about what you discovered from your interviews.

 Discussion

Do mothers and fathers play differently with their children?

 Extension

a From your experience, list five jobs in the family which are usually part of (i) a father's role, (ii) a mother's role.

b (i) For each item in your lists state why you think it is usually part of the father's or the mother's role – is it habit, tradition, preference, physical strength, or what? (ii) What effect do you think it would have on the family if all the jobs were shared between them?

 Child study

Give a brief history of the child up to the date of starting the study.

CHAPTER 3

Variation between families

There is no such thing as a typical family. Families differ from each other as much as individuals differ from each other, and they change with time.

Some of the ways in which families vary

Size   from two people .... to many people

Age range of the members   from very young .... to very old

Location of the family home   from urban (town, city) .... to rural (country)

Health   from generally healthy .... to generally unhealthy

Wealth   from rich .... to poor

Feelings

The feelings of members of a family towards one another can vary from:

- care   ⟶   to indifference
- respect   ⟶   to contempt
- love   ⟶   to hate
- trust   ⟶   to fear

Attitudes of parents to their children

- The children may be:
  wanted   ⟶   tolerated   ⟶   unwanted
- Parents may:
  over-indulge their children ⟶ act responsibly ⟶ neglect them
- Parents may enforce:
  strict discipline ⟶ moderate discipline ⟶ no discipline

CULTURE

Culture means the way of life of a group of people, for example a family or people living in the same country, and is passed on from adults to children. Aspects of culture include:

- language
- food, diet and eating habits
- religion
- music, songs, drama, literature and art
- traditions
- leisure activities
- education
- style of dress
- hygiene.

A

B

C

Varieties of cultural life

Influence of religion on culture

The cultural life of any family will be influenced by the religious background of the country in which the family lives, as well as by any religious group to which the family belongs. Religion may:

- provide a set of rules for behaviour
- set special times for worship and festivals
- affect style of dress, diet, leisure activities etc.

A christening

Multicultural societies

Britain is a multicultural society. This means it contains people of many different **ethnic groups** – people of differing races or countries of origin. Each ethnic group will have its own particular culture, for example, customs and language. This makes for much greater variety of lifestyles, and also brings about social changes:

- The ethnic groups have to adapt to life in a country which has a different culture.
- The native population has to accept people of various cultures as equal members of the community.

There is a cultural mix when people of different ethnic origins marry, also when children of one culture attend a school where most pupils are of another culture. Children often adapt to a new culture more quickly than their parents, and this may result in children living in two cultural styles – one at school and another at home.

The *Race Relations (Amendment) Act* 2000 makes racial discrimination unlawful in employment, training, housing, education, and the provision of goods, facilities and services. The Commission for Racial Equality has the power to enforce this Act, which gives everyone an equal chance to learn, work and live free from discrimination and prejudice, and from the fear of racial discrimination and violence.

Questions

1 **a** How do families differ in (i) size, (ii) age range, (iii) location, (iv) health, (v) wealth?

  b Give examples of ways in which feelings towards other members of the family can vary.

  c Give examples of variation in attitudes of parents to children.

2 **a** What is meant by culture?

  b (i) Give nine examples of aspects of culture. (ii) Suggest aspects of culture shown by each of the photographs on p. 11. Give reasons for your suggestions.

  c Give ways in which religion may influence culture.

3 **a** What is meant by ethnic groups?

  b Give two ways in which people living in multicultural society need to change.

  c Give two examples of a cultural mix.

4 Give the function of the Race Relations Act.

Further activities

 Investigation

People of different ethnic groups and ways of life celebrate different festivals – special days of celebration. Find the names and dates of at least two traditional festivals celebrated by each of five groups, e.g. Christians, Jews, Hindus, Sikhs, Muslims.

Write a short article for a local newspaper comparing two different festivals.

 Child study

Describe the child's family. Make a family tree. If this is not possible, make a family tree of your own family.

CHAPTER 4

The home

The home provides a base in which babies develop into young adults. Different aspects of a child's development are encouraged when the home provides the facilities and opportunities shown below and on page 14.

the child is encouraged to improve skills

A Praise and encouragement

lighting adequate for playing and reading

space to display pictures and posters

shelves and cupboards for toys, books and clothes

B A place which the child can call his or her own and where possessions can be kept

vocabulary increases

bonds between parent and child develop

listening and understanding are encouraged

C Opportunities for parent and child to play or read together

easy-to-clean floor and furniture

furniture can be moved easily

D Space for play

EFFECTS OF THE HOME ENVIRONMENT ON DEVELOPMENT

The **home environment** – the conditions in the home – affects all aspects of a child's development:

- **physical** – development of the body (p. 141)
- **speech** – learning to talk (p. 155)
- **social** – learning to interact with people (p. 161)
- **emotional** – learning to control feelings (p. 165)
- **intellectual** – development of the mind (p. 188)
- **cultural** – acquiring knowledge of the society in which the child is growing up.

interests can be shared

questions can be answered

plans can be made

E Opportunities for conversation

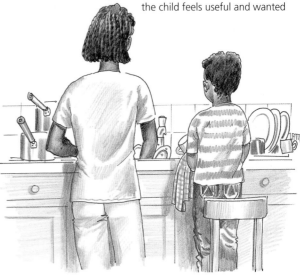

the child feels useful and wanted

F Opportunities to help

self-confidence develops

G Opportunities to meet other adults

co-operation and sharing are learnt

H Opportunities to play with other children

Television in the home

Nearly all homes have one or more televisions and many have video recorders or DVD players, computers and games consoles, and they are very much part of most children's lives. Even babies are fascinated by movement on a television screen and they will stare at it for quite a long while – but they will not understand what they see. Gradually children become able to understand, particularly those programmes made especially for them. When they watch with adults and talk about what they have seen they will more quickly increase their understanding of the world in which they live.

Television is beneficial for children when it:

- stimulates curiosity
- increases knowledge
- enlarges vocabulary
- encourages family discussions and conversation
- entertains.

Television is harmful for children when:

- it is on continuously – because it makes conversation difficult
- too much time is spent watching – because this reduces opportunities for talking, playing, reading and drawing
- children watch unsuitable programmes or videos which may frighten them or encourage them to behave in an antisocial way
- it prevents them having sufficient fresh air and exercise
- they are tired in the morning from late-night viewing.

Questions

1 List six aspects of a child's development, briefly explaining what each means.
2 Under the heading 'Development is encouraged when the home provides', list the facilities and opportunities shown in pictures A–H in this topic.
3 a Give five benefits of television for children.
  b Give five harmful effects of television on children.

Further activities

Extension

For each of pictures A–H, state which aspect(s) of development (p. 14) are being encouraged.

Design

Use a graphics program to design a layout for a 5-year-old's bedroom. (i) Draw a floor plan. (ii) Design wall-to-wall storage units 3 m long, 2 m high and 40 cm deep, to hold a child's clothes, toys, books etc.

Child study

1 Describe the child's home.

2 How much time does the child spend watching television or videos, or using a computer or games console? What type of programmes or videos are watched? What reactions have you observed?

3 Watch a suitable programme with a young child, talking about what is happening on the screen, wondering what will happen next, and answering any questions. In what ways did the child gain from watching the programme with you that would not happen if the child watched the programme alone?

Weblink

For information on the effect of television on children, visit:

www.kidshealth.org and search for 'tv effects'.

CHAPTER 5

Parenthood

Couples who hope to start a family should be reasonably happy together and fairly self-confident, because child-rearing is a long and demanding job. This is why it is often considered undesirable for young people still in their teens to become parents. They themselves have not finished growing up, and they may not be sufficiently mature to cope with the demands of parenthood and the changes it will bring to their lives.

HOW PARENTS' LIVES CHANGE

Having children changes the lives of the parents in many ways:

- **Children are hard work**. When young, they are by nature neither clean nor tidy. Also, they have to be cared for seven days a week and at nights as well.
- **They are a long-lasting responsibility**. Children require years of care as they grow from 'dear little babies' into adolescents who can be much more difficult to manage.
- **They require sacrifices from the parents** of both time and money.
- **They restrict the parents' freedom,** but at the same time, provide a new and continuing interest.
- **They bring the parents much pleasure and satisfaction** if the parents are prepared to give time and energy to bringing them up.

PREPARATION FOR PARENTHOOD

Preparation for parenthood begins in childhood. As children and teenagers, the parents-to-be will have been influenced by:

- the way in which they themselves were brought up
- experience gained through helping with younger brothers, sisters or cousins, or neighbours' children
- baby-sitting or experience of working with young children
- the study at school or college of subjects such as Child Care and Development or Nursery Nursing.

Children are hard work ...

... but they bring much pleasure

NEW PARENTS

In these days of smaller families, it is quite possible that new parents will have very little knowledge of how to bring up children. If they live far away from their own families, then the grandparents will not be at hand to give help and advice.

Sources from which the parents of today can get information, advice and support include:

▪ other members of their families and friends
▪ preparation classes at the antenatal clinic
▪ the health visitor, at the Child Health Clinic (baby clinic) or on home visits
▪ the National Childbirth Trust – see p. 372
▪ television programmes and videos produced for parents
▪ pamphlets issued by the local Health Promotion Service and many other organisations – a list of some of them is given on pp. 371–3
▪ books – there are many to choose from which have been written by parents or doctors.

Child Health Clinic

Suggestions for parents

1. **Love your baby** to give your baby the security of feeling wanted.
2. **Cuddle your baby**.
3. **Speak to your baby** – so that your baby can learn how to talk.
4. **Listen to your baby** as well as talking to your baby and you will learn how to communicate with each other.
5. **Play with your baby** – your baby will enjoy it, and it will enable a far closer relationship to develop between you.
6. **Keep your baby clean** and comfortable, but do not be over-fussy.
7. **Be firm with your child** when your baby is old enough to understand what is wanted. Boundaries for behaviour help a child to be socially acceptable to other children and adults.
8. **Praise is more effective than punishment** in the training of children.
9. **Do not over-protect** – children must gradually learn to be responsible for their own lives.
10. **Do not spend all your time and energy on your child**. If you do not leave time for yourselves and your own interests, you will become very dull people. When the child has grown up and left home there will be the danger that you will be lonely and bored.

HAPPY FAMILY LIFE

When parents set up home and have a family, they naturally hope to create a happy environment in which the children can grow up. Some of the factors which can help to make a home happy are given below.

Children are more important than the housework

- **Parents who love and respect each other and their children.** This helps to give all the members of the family a sense of security.
- **Parents who consider that children are more important than the housework.** Worrying too much about tidiness or the state or appearance of the house can make for a great deal of nagging and unpleasantness. Children would rather have happy, contented parents who have time to do things with them than a spotlessly clean and tidy home.
- **Parents who realise they themselves are not perfect.** No parents are perfect. There are days when they are cross and irritable, particularly when they are tired, unwell or worried. It happens in all families.
- **Parents who realise that no child is perfect.** All children go through phases of good and bad behaviour.
- **Parents who do not expect too much of their children.** Children enjoy life more when they are praised and loved for what they can do, rather than criticised for what they are unable to do.

Questions

1 Name five ways in which having children changes the lives of their parents.

2 a Name four ways in which preparation for parenthood can begin in childhood.

   b Name seven ways in which new parents can obtain information, advice and support.

3 List ten suggestions which may be of help to new parents.

4 Name five factors which can help to make home a happy place.

Further activities

 Extension

List your daily routine on a typical school day or day at college (from midnight to midnight). Compare this routine with that of a parent who has a home and a young baby to care for. Remember that a baby needs to be cuddled and played with, kept clean, fed about five times a day, and the nappy changed about eight times a day. Write a pamphlet for new parents explaining how their lives might change. Include illustrations.

 Investigation

Compare two books written for parents which deal with the care and development of young children.

Points to be compared could include topics covered (contents list), the illustrations, and the usefulness of the index. Write a report on your findings.

CHAPTER 6

Family planning and sexual health

Family planning (birth control) means taking action so that only wanted babies are born. When sexually active women or their partners do not use some form of contraception, 80–90 per cent of the women will become pregnant within a year. This shows that for most women, pregnancy is very likely to occur unless action is taken to prevent it.

UNPLANNED PREGNANCIES

It is estimated that at least one in three pregnancies is unplanned. Although many babies that result from unplanned pregnancies become wanted babies, some are unwanted, and may be terminated. **Termination of pregnancy** (abortion) means the removal of the fetus (developing baby) from the womb. The current legal limit for an abortion is 24 weeks after conception although cases of abortion at this stage of pregnancy are very rare. Unplanned pregnancies can happen to girls and young women because either they have been given the wrong advice, or they have ignored good advice. A girl who does not wish to become pregnant should remember the following facts:

- pregnancy can follow first intercourse
- pregnancy can occur even if the penis does not enter the vagina (sperm can swim)
- pregnancy sometimes occurs when intercourse takes place during a period
- pregnancy can occur even when the woman does not 'come' (have an orgasm)
- intercourse in any position can result in pregnancy
- withdrawal ('being careful') can result in pregnancy
- douching (washing out the vagina) will never prevent pregnancy, however soon after intercourse
- breast-feeding does not prevent pregnancy, although it may make it less likely.

CONTRACEPTION

Contraception (contra = against, ception = conceiving) is the deliberate prevention of pregnancy.

It is natural for men and women in relationships to have intercourse. But if they do not want a baby, they need to know about the various methods of contraception. Using this knowledge, they are able to plan their family and start a baby only when they want one.

The following table lists the different methods of contraception and explains briefly how they work, and how effective they are at preventing pregnancy:

Method	How it works	How effective it is in preventing pregnancy
Abstention – saying 'No' (not having intercourse)	Because intercourse does not take place there is no danger of an unwanted baby.	100%.
Male sterilisation* (vasectomy)	A simple operation in which the sperm ducts (vas deferens) are cut or blocked to prevent semen from containing sperm.	More than 99.5%.
Female sterilisation*	An operation in which the Fallopian tubes from the ovaries are blocked so that the egg and sperm cannot meet.	99.5%.
Combined pill*	This type of pill contains two hormones – oestrogen and progestogen – which stop ovulation (stop the ovaries from producing eggs). Progestogen is similar to progesterone made by the ovaries.	More than 99% if taken according to instructions and at a similar time each day. Missed pills may make the method less reliable depending on when and how many have been forgotten. Condoms must be used if there is vomiting and/or severe diarrhoea or during antibiotic treatment.
Contraceptive patch* (an alternative to the combined pill)	A small thin, beige plastic patch that releases oestrogen and progestogen is placed on the skin of the buttocks, abdomen, back or upper arm once a week for 3 out of 4 weeks. No patch is used in the 4th week.	99% if used according to instructions. Not affected by vomiting, diarrhoea or antibiotics.
Vaginal ring* (an alternative to the combined pill)	A flexible transparent ring about 5 cm in diameter is inserted in the vagina. Low doses of oestrogen and progestogen are slowly released. After 3 weeks, the ring is removed for a 1 week break.	99% if used according to instructions. Not affected by vomiting, diarrhoea or antibiotics.
Progestogen-only pill* (mini-pill)	This type of pill contains one hormone – progestogen – which causes changes to the lining of the womb. This makes it very difficult for sperm to enter the uterus or for an egg to settle there.	99% effective if taken at the same time each day. Not reliable if taken 3 hours late (or 12 hours for the pill Cerazette). An extra method, such as condoms, must be used if there has been vomiting, or severe diarrhoea or during antibiotic treatment.

Method	How it works	How effective it is in preventing pregnancy
Contraceptive injections*	An injection of progestogen is given every 8 or 12 weeks. The hormone it contains is slowly absorbed into the body and works in a similar way to the progestogen-only pill.	More than 99%.
Contraceptive implant*	A small flexible tube 40 mm × 2 mm containing progestogen is inserted just under the skin on the inside of the upper arm. The hormone is slowly released into the blood stream, and works by stopping ovulation. The implant is effective for up to 3 years. If a pregnancy is desired, the implant can be removed, and fertility returns immediately.	More than 99%.
Withdrawal ('being careful'; coitus interruptus)	The penis is withdrawn from the vagina before the semen is ejaculated.	Very unreliable because a little semen can escape from the erect penis before the main amount is released.
Intra-uterine system (IUS)* (Mirena)	A small T-shaped plastic device is placed in the womb. It contains progestogen, which is slowly released. This stops sperm from meeting an egg. The IUS can be left in place for 5 years, but can be taken out at any time.	More than 99%.
Diaphragm or cap with spermicide*	A diaphragm is a flexible rubber dome which covers the cervix (the entrance to the womb). A cap is smaller and fits neatly over the cervix. Used with spermicide, these devices form a barrier which helps to prevent the sperm from meeting an egg and must stay in place for at least 6 hours after intercourse. Spermicide (jelly or cream) makes sperm inactive.	92–96% if used carefully and according to instructions.
Male condom	Made of very thin rubber, it is put over the erect penis before intercourse takes place. It prevents sperm from entering the woman's vagina. Using a condom also helps to protect against sexually transmitted diseases, including HIV infections.	98% if used carefully and according to instructions.

Method	How it works	How effective it is in preventing pregnancy
Female condom	A soft polyurethane sheath lines the vagina and the area just outside. It is placed in position before intercourse takes place and prevents the sperm from entering the vagina. Using a condom also helps to protect against sexually transmitted diseases, including HIV infections.	95% if used carefully and according to instructions.
Natural methods (sympto-thermal method; temperature method; cervical mucus method; calendar method; urine analysis)	These methods allow a woman to recognise the days when she is fertile and can become pregnant. This is done by noting and recording the different natural signs, such as changes in temperature and cervical mucus that happen during the menstrual cycle. Sperm can live inside a woman for 3–7 days, so intercourse a week before an egg is released may result in pregnancy. To avoid pregnancy, intercourse should not take place during the fertile days unless another method of contraception is used.	98% for sympto-thermal methods if used according to instructions. Very unreliable when periods are irregular, during illness, when travelling, and unless very careful records are kept. Instruction from a teacher who has been specially trained in natural methods of family planning is recommended.
IUD*(intra-uterine device; coil; loop)	A small plastic and copper device is put into the womb. It stops sperm meeting an egg or may stop a fertilised egg from settling in the womb. Depending on the type, it can stay in place for 5–10 years, but can be taken out at any time.	More than 99%.

*These methods require medical advice or treatment from a doctor or at a Sexual Health and Reproductive Clinic (Family Planning Clinic).

WHICH METHOD OF CONTRACEPTION TO USE

Deciding which of the methods of contraception to use depends on a number of factors, including:

- individual preference
- religious beliefs
- age
- whether a short- or long-term method is wanted.

The **reliability** of any of the methods of birth control depends on using that method correctly. Many of the failures which result in pregnancy are due to incorrect use. The advantage of attending a Sexual and Reproductive Health Clinic is that advice is given in choosing a suitable method, and instructions are given to help make that method as safe as possible.

EMERGENCY CONTRACEPTION

When intercourse has taken place without using contraception, or when any precautions which were taken might have failed, for example a condom failure or forgetting to take the contraceptive pill, there are two emergency methods of contraception which can be used. It is important to contact a pharmacy, sexual health clinic, NHS walk-in centre or doctor as soon as possible because pregnancy can usually be prevented by:

- emergency contraceptive pills (previously known as 'morning after' pills) containing hormones which are taken within 72 hours; the sooner the pills are taken, the more effective they are likely to be
- an IUD (coil) fitted within five days of intercourse.

TERMINATION OF PREGNANCY (ABORTION)

If a baby is found to be developing abnormally, or the mother has emotional or other problems which the birth of a baby will (according to at least two doctors) worsen to a harmful degree, a pregnancy can be terminated (aborted) before the end of the 24th week, but is safer and easier in the first 12 weeks. In Northern Ireland, abortion is only legal in very exceptional circumstances.

OBTAINING ADVICE

Advice on contraception and sexually transmitted infections is provided free by the National Health Service (NHS). It can be obtained by people of all ages, married or single, male or female, from the following sources:

- **Sexual and Reproductive Health Clinics**, which advise on family planning, contraception and sexually transmitted infections.
- **Leaflets**, which can often be obtained from Health Centres, where doctors (GPs) and nurses can advise.
- Special confidential **telephone helplines** are available.
- **Websites** are another helpful source of information.

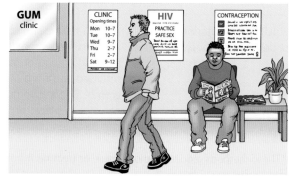

Sexual and Reproductive Health Clinic

SEXUALLY TRANSMITTED INFECTIONS (STIs)

These diseases are so-called because the usual way in which they spread from one person to another is by sexual contact. Examples are:

Chlamydia   This is one of the most common sexually transmitted infections in the UK, especially in young people. Often there are no symptoms, so the infected person may not seek medical help. If left untreated, chlamydia can cause long-term problems such as pelvic inflammatory disease in women, and infertility in both men and women.

Gonorrhoea   Again, symptoms may not be present but, if left untreated, the infection can lead to pelvic inflammatory disease in women and infertility in both men and women.

Genital warts   These are caused by a virus (HPV – Human papilloma virus) which infects the skin of the genitals and anus. Fleshy growths or bumps are produced which may itch. The infection can be treated but is not harmful to health if left untreated.

Genital herpes   The herpes virus causes blisters and pain around the genitals which may develop into sores or ulcers and pain on passing urine. It can take months or years for the symptoms to appear, so an infected person will not know they have the condition.

Syphilis   The symptoms of this bacterial infection appear in three stages. A few weeks after catching the infection, a painless sore or spot appears on or around the genital area. A few weeks later a rash may develop. It may take several years for the third stage to develop, causing serious health problems for the heart and brain.

Hepatitis B   This liver disease is caused by a virus. It spreads through contact with an infected person's blood, semen or other fluids.

HIV (human immunodeficiency virus)

This virus will be present in many of the body fluids of an infected person, including sexual fluid from the penis in males and the vagina in females. **It can be caught**:

- during unprotected sexual contact with an infected person
- during pregnancy, from an infected mother to her unborn baby
- from the breast milk of an infected woman
- by contact with infected blood, for example when using the same needle for drug injections.

The virus is very delicate and dies quickly outside the body, so **HIV is *not* caught**:

- by shaking hands, touching and cuddling someone who is infected with the virus
- from using the same towel, cups, cutlery or lavatory seats
- from swimming pools.

HIV testing

When a person becomes infected with HIV, the virus remains in the body for life and produces HIV antibodies, which can be detected by a blood test. If HIV antibodies are found, that person is HIV positive. When HIV is detected early, the person may look and feel healthy, and treatment can be given which delays or prevents AIDS.

AIDS (Acquired Immune Deficiency Syndrome) develops when HIV attacks the immune system. The body then loses its resistance to infections such as pneumonia and tuberculosis (TB).

Questions

1 What is (i) contraception, (ii) the chance of a woman becoming pregnant if no form of contraception is used?

2 Match each of these methods of birth control with one of the statements a–i: vasectomy; cap; abstention; male condom; withdrawal; combined pill; natural methods; IUS; female sterilisation

   a stops the ovaries from producing eggs

   b stops sperm entering the vagina

   c covers the entrance to the womb

   d blocks the Fallopian tubes

   e prevents semen from containing sperm

   f intercourse avoided on fertile days

   g intercourse does not take place

   h does not deposit semen in the vagina

   i stops sperm from meeting an egg

Questions (continued)

3 a List the different methods of birth control in order of their effectiveness in preventing pregnancy.

b (i) Name one method which requires the use of a spermicide. (ii) What does the spermicide do?

c Why is withdrawal an unreliable method of contraception?

d (i) What do natural methods depend on? (ii) When are natural methods unreliable?

4 a Name twelve methods of contraception which depend particularly on the woman.

b Name two effective methods of contraception available to men.

c Which methods of contraception require medical advice or treatment?

d (i) When deciding which method of contraception to use, give four factors which may be taken into account. (ii) What does the reliability of any method depend on? (iii) Give two advantages of attending a Reproduction and Sexual Health Clinic.

5 Give the meaning of: (i) IUS, (ii) IUD, (iii) AIDS.

6 a To prevent an unwanted pregnancy, list eight facts which it might be useful to know.

b Describe two methods of emergency contraception.

c What is meant by termination of pregnancy?

7 a What is an STI?

b Name two STIs that can cause infertility.

c Name three STIs caused by a virus.

d In what ways can HIV pass from an infected person to another person?

e Describe types of contact in which HIV is not caught. Explain why.

f What is the purpose of an HIV test?

g When does AIDS develop?

Weblinks

For more information about contraception and sexual health, visit:

www.nhs.uk

and search for 'sex: worth talking about'.

For Sexually Transmitted Disease statistics in the UK, visit:

www.avert.org/stdstatisticuk.htm

Exercises

Exercises relevant to Section 1 can be found on p. 380.

SECTION 2

Becoming a parent

CHAPTER 7

How a baby is conceived

A baby starts life with two parents – a mother and a father. When the couple make love and have sexual intercourse ('have sex'), a baby begins to develop if a sperm from the father **fertilises** (joins with) the mother's egg (ovum). 'A baby has been conceived' or 'conception has taken place' means that an egg has been fertilised and a baby is developing – the mother is pregnant. How does this happen?

Puberty is the stage during which the sex organs mature and start to produce sperm or eggs and also to secrete sex hormones. The male sex hormone **testosterone** causes the penis to enlarge, shoulders to broaden, the voice to deepen, and body hair to grow. The female sex hormones **oestrogen** and **progesterone** cause periods to start, breasts to enlarge, and body hair to grow.

MALE REPRODUCTIVE SYSTEM

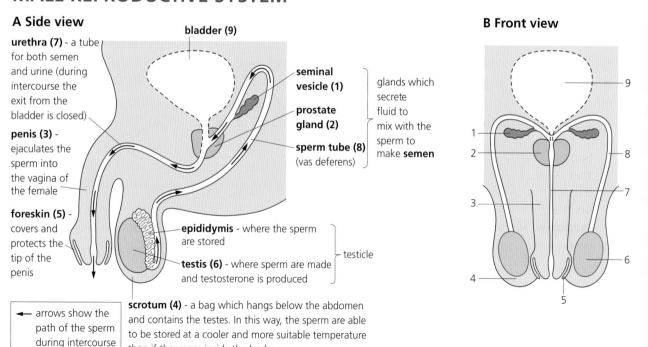

A Side view

urethra (7) - a tube for both semen and urine (during intercourse the exit from the bladder is closed)

penis (3) - ejaculates the sperm into the vagina of the female

foreskin (5) - covers and protects the tip of the penis

bladder (9)

seminal vesicle (1)
prostate gland (2)

glands which secrete fluid to mix with the sperm to make **semen**

sperm tube (8) (vas deferens)

epididymis - where the sperm are stored

testis (6) - where sperm are made and testosterone is produced

testicle

scrotum (4) - a bag which hangs below the abdomen and contains the testes. In this way, the sperm are able to be stored at a cooler and more suitable temperature than if they were inside the body

⬅ arrows show the path of the sperm during intercourse

B Front view

Diagrams of the male reproductive organs
(The numbers in the side view refer to numbers 1–9 in the front view)

A man has two testes (each is a testis) where sperm are made, and a penis which is used to deposit the sperm inside the woman's body.

The foreskin of the penis will be absent in males who have been circumcised. **Circumcision** is the removal of the foreskin by surgery. It is rarely necessary for medical reasons although it is widely carried out amongst some religious groups.

FEMALE REPRODUCTIVE SYSTEM

The female reproductive system is more complicated than that of the male because it has more things to do. It has to produce eggs (ova), receive sperm, protect and feed the unborn child, and then give birth.

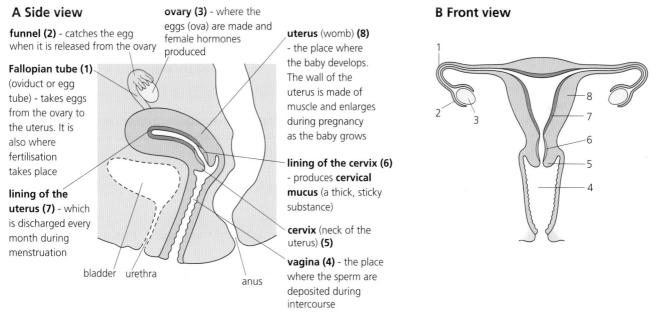

A Side view

funnel (2) - catches the egg when it is released from the ovary

Fallopian tube (1) (oviduct or egg tube) - takes eggs from the ovary to the uterus. It is also where fertilisation takes place

lining of the uterus (7) - which is discharged every month during menstruation

bladder   urethra

anus

ovary (3) - where the eggs (ova) are made and female hormones produced

uterus (womb) **(8)** - the place where the baby develops. The wall of the uterus is made of muscle and enlarges during pregnancy as the baby grows

lining of the cervix (6) - produces **cervical mucus** (a thick, sticky substance)

cervix (neck of the uterus) **(5)**

vagina (4) - the place where the sperm are deposited during intercourse

B Front view

Diagrams of the female reproductive organs
(The numbers in the side view refer to numbers 1–8 in the front view)

MENSTRUATION

Sometime between the ages of 10 and 17, girls begin to menstruate – have periods. This shows that the reproductive organs are getting into working order. It is usual for the periods to be irregular and scanty at first. It is not uncommon for a year or more to elapse between the first and second period, and for months to elapse between periods in the second year. The periods gradually become regular, although they may stop for a while during illness, poor diet or emotional upsets.

MENSTRUAL CYCLE

The menstrual cycle is sometimes called the monthly cycle as it takes about 28 days to complete. The purpose of the cycle is to produce an egg and prepare the uterus to receive the egg if it becomes fertilised.

During the first part of the cycle, the lining of the uterus is built up into the right state to receive the egg. If the egg is not fertilised, then the lining breaks down, and is removed from the body in a flow of blood called a **period** or **menstruation**.

Sometime between the ages of about 45 and 55, the menstrual cycle and periods cease. This stage is called the **menopause**, and the woman can then no longer conceive a baby.

Although the cycle, on average, takes about 28 days to complete, it is normal for it to vary between 21 and 35 days. The cycle continues over and over again until such time as an egg is fertilised. It then stops during pregnancy and does not start again until several months afterwards.

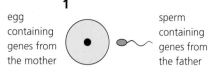

ovulation takes place about day 14

repair phase – a new uterus lining grows

receptive phase – the uterus is ready to receive a fertilised egg

menstruation – blood and fragments of uterus lining leave the body

premenstrual phase – the uterus lining begins to break up

Diagram of a typical menstrual cycle

OVULATION

Generally, an egg is released every month from one or other of the ovaries. This usually happens about half-way through the menstrual cycle, that is, about the 14th or 15th day. After being released from the ovary, the egg is moved slowly along the Fallopian tube (oviduct).

CONCEPTION

Conception is the start of pregnancy.

Sexual intercourse (coitus)

Before intercourse, the man's penis enlarges and becomes hard and erect. It is now able to penetrate the vagina of the woman and semen is ejaculated there. **Semen** is a thick, milky-white substance containing millions of sperm. Once inside the vagina, the sperm use their tails to swim in all directions. Some may find their way into the uterus and along the Fallopian tubes.

Fertilisation

If intercourse takes place at about the time that an egg has been released from the ovary, then the egg has a chance of meeting sperm in the Fallopian tube. If this happens, the egg will be fertilised by one of the sperm.

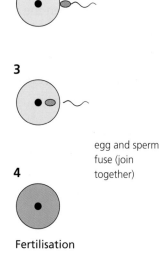

1
egg containing genes from the mother

sperm containing genes from the father

2

3

egg and sperm fuse (join together)

4

Fertilisation

After fertilisation, the egg continues to be moved along the Fallopian tube towards the uterus. By the time it gets there, the uterus lining will be ready to receive it.

Implantation

This means the embedding of the fertilised egg in the uterus wall. The fertilised egg becomes attached to the uterus wall about six days after conception. The mother is now able to supply it with food and oxygen so that it can grow and develop into a baby.

Conception occurs when an egg in the Fallopian tube is fertilised by a sperm, and the fertilised egg then becomes implanted in the uterus

HORMONES

Hormones play a very important part in controlling the menstrual cycle, pregnancy, birth and breast-feeding. They are substances which act as chemical messengers. They are produced in glands called **endocrine glands** and then circulate in the bloodstream, carrying messages to various parts of the body. There are many different hormones and they help control the way the body works. Examples are:

- **oestrogen** (female sex hormone) – responsible for the development and functioning of the female sex organs
- **progesterone** (pregnancy hormone) – helps to prepare the uterus to receive the fertilised egg and maintain a state of pregnancy; it also interacts with oestrogen and other hormones to control the menstrual cycle
- **oxytocin** – stimulates the uterus to contract during childbirth
- **prolactin** – controls milk production.

INFERTILITY

Sometimes couples plan to have a family and find, to their disappointment, that they are unable to produce children. Being unable to conceive is known as **infertility**.

There are many reasons for infertility and couples can obtain advice from their doctor or Family Planning Clinic. With some couples the right advice soon solves the problem. Other cases need treatment from a doctor who specialises in the problems of infertility.

Some causes of infertility:

- **too few sperm being produced** – at least 20 million sperm need to be ejaculated at any one time to ensure that one fertilises the egg
- **failure to ovulate** – the ovaries are not producing eggs
- **blocked Fallopian tubes** – the eggs cannot be fertilised or pass down the tubes
- **the cervical mucus in the neck of the uterus (womb) is too thick** – so sperm are unable to enter
- **sexually transmitted infections** – chlamydia and gonorrhoea.

FERTILITY TREATMENTS

Once infertility has been diagnosed, fertility treatment may be tried to increase the chances of conception. Treatment is available from the NHS and from private clinics. To be eligible to receive free NHS treatment, couples have to meet certain criteria. These vary from area to area and waiting lists can be long. Private treatment is costly but there are no long waiting lists. UK clinics that carry out fertility treatment are licensed by the Human Fertilisation and Embryology Authority (HFEA). Fertility treatment can involve the use of surgery, medicines and assisted conception.

Surgery

- **In women** – to obtain eggs from the ovaries or to unblock the Fallopian tubes.
- **In men** – to unblock the vas deferens (sperm tubes), usually to reverse a previous vasectomy.

Medicines

Fertility medicines are used to stimulate the ovaries to produce eggs for assisted conception.

Assisted conception

Intra-uterine insemination (IUI)

The woman is given fertility medicines to produce eggs, and sperm are then placed in her uterus at the time of ovulation. The sperm which are used come from the woman's partner or from a donor. If IUI does not work, other methods can be tried including those describe below.

In vitro fertilisation (IVF)

With IVF, fertilisation takes place outside the woman's body in a glass dish ('in vitro' means 'in glass'). With this technique, the woman takes fertility medicines to stimulate the ovaries to make more eggs than usual. These eggs are removed from the ovary, mixed with sperms from the partner or donor, then left for a while for fertilisation to take place and embryos to develop. One or two embryos are then placed in the woman's uterus.

Intra-cytoplasmic sperm injection (ICSI)

An individual sperm is injected directly into an egg that has been removed from the ovary. The fertilised egg is then placed into the woman's uterus. This method bypasses any barriers that may have prevented natural fertilisation from taking place.

Gamete intra-fallopian transfer (GIFT)

A fertilised egg is placed into the woman's Fallopian tubes.

Surrogacy

Eggs are obtained from one woman and fertilised using IVF with sperm from the woman's partner. An embryo is then transferred to the uterus of another woman – the **surrogate mother** – who will eventually give birth to a baby. In UK law, the birth mother is the legal parent and the couple who donated the eggs and sperm need to adopt their own genetic child. Surrogacy may be used for a woman who has no uterus or is unable to carry a child.

Sperm and egg donation

Males can donate (give) their sperm and females donate their eggs for use in IVF. Since 2005, donors may not remain anonymous. After a child reaches the age of 18 years, the donor's name must be supplied if the child requests it.

Questions

1 a What is puberty?

b What are the effects of testosterone?

c Name the female sex hormones and give their effects.

2 a What is conception?

b Where does fertilisation take place?

c Copy the diagrams showing fertilisation (p. 30).

3 a Where are sperm made?

b What is the scrotum?

c Where are the sperm stored?

d What is the technical name for the sperm tube?

e Name the central tube to which both sperm tubes join.

4 a Where are eggs made?

b How often are eggs usually released?

5 a What is the function of the penis in reproduction?

b (i) Name the substance which is deposited by the penis in the vagina.

(ii) About how many sperm does it contain?

c If an egg is in a Fallopian tube, how can the sperm reach it?

d After fertilisation, where does the egg move to?

6 a What is the purpose of the menstrual cycle?

b What happens to the uterus lining during menstruation?

c What happens to the uterus lining after menstruation?

d Give four reasons why menstruation may stop for a while.

7 a (i) What are hormones? (ii) In which glands are they produced? (iii) How do they reach the various parts of the body?

b (i) Name four hormones important in controlling the menstrual cycle, pregnancy, birth and breast-feeding, and give a function of each. (ii) Which two hormones help to control the menstrual cycle?

8 a (i) What is infertility? (ii) Give five causes of infertility.

b (i) What is the purpose of fertility treatment? (ii) Why are medicines used? (ii) Why may surgery be used?

c Describe IVF.

d How does ICIS differ from IVF?

e Explain how a couple can have a baby with the help of a surrogate mother.

Further activities

1 a Copy diagram B on p. 28 showing the front view of the male reproductive system. Use the information in diagram A to add the correct labels for 1–9 on your diagram.

b Add arrows to your diagram to show the path of the sperm during intercourse.

2 a Copy diagram B on p. 29 of the female reproductive system, front view.

b Complete your diagram by adding the correct labels 1–8.

c Add arrows to show the path of an egg from ovary to uterus.

d Colour in red the part called 'uterus lining'. (This is the part which is shed every month during menstruation.)

3 Copy and complete the chart below using information from the diagram of the menstrual cycle.

Days	Phase	What happens
	menstruation	
28		

Alternatively, use a graphics program to copy the diagram at the top of p. 30.

Weblink

For an overview of the main treatment options for infertility, visit:

www.patient.co.uk

and search for 'infertility summary of treatments'.

CHAPTER 8

Growth and development before birth

A human egg is just large enough to be seen – about the size of a full stop. After being fertilised, the egg soon starts to divide, first into two cells, then into four, then eight and so on until it is a mass of cells. By this time it has become attached to the wall of the uterus. The number of cells continues to increase and gradually a tiny **embryo** forms.

Besides producing the embryo, the fertilised egg also gives rise to the placenta, umbilical cord and amnion. These structures are developed for the support of the baby, and they are expelled from the uterus at birth.

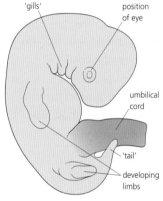

Embryo at 6 weeks (enlarged)

THE TIMING OF PREGNANCY

Pregnancy is timed from the first day of the last menstrual cycle, not from conception. So what is called 'week 6' or 'six weeks pregnant' is actually about four weeks after conception. Pregnancy normally lasts for 37–42 weeks from the first day of the last menstrual cycle, the average being 40 weeks.

Week 6

At this stage a human embryo looks rather like the embryo of a fish or frog (tadpole). It is possible to see a tail, and parts which look as though they might develop into gills. The actual size of the embryo at this stage is shown in diagram **A**.

A Week 6 (actual size)

Week 9

The embryo has grown to look more human-like and it is now called a **fetus** (or foetus): see diagram **B**. The main organs of the body are developing and the heart can be seen beating on an ultrasound scan.

B Week 9 (actual size)

Week 14

During weeks 10–14 the nerves and muscles develop rapidly and by the end of this time, the fetus can swallow, frown, clench the fist, and move by turning the head and kicking. The mother does not feel the movements at this stage. The fetus is now about the size of a mouse and weighs about 55 g, diagram **C**.

C Week 14 (actual size)

Week 20

About this time the mother is able to feel the movements inside the uterus as the baby practises using its muscles. The heartbeat can be heard, and very fine hair (lanugo) covers the skin. The fetus weighs about 350 g.

Week 28

Development is almost complete. The baby will spend the remaining time in the uterus growing larger and stronger. It will become more plump as a layer of fat is stored under the skin. The length will be doubled and the weight increased three times. By about week 32 the baby is usually lying head downwards and ready for birth. The **fetal position** is shown in diagram **B** below – the back is curved, head forwards, knees bent, and arms crossed over the chest.

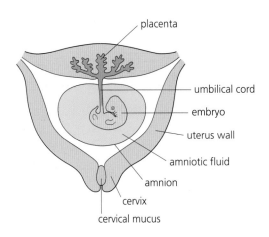

A Embryo in the uterus

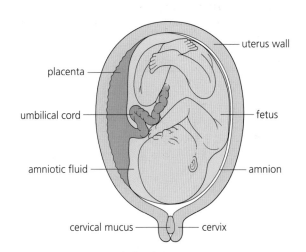

B Fetus just before birth

INSIDE THE UTERUS

In the uterus, the baby develops in a 'bag of water' (amniotic fluid) which remains at a constant temperature of about 37 °C. The drawings above show two stages of development inside the uterus and the following parts are labelled:

- **Uterus wall** – this is made of muscle. During pregnancy the muscle tissue expands as the embryo grows. It becomes greatly enlarged – for example, a uterus weighing 30 g at the start of pregnancy may weigh about 1 kg at the end.
- **Cervix** – a ring of muscle which surrounds the outlet of the uterus. It is able to expand widely during childbirth.

- **Amnion** – the bag which contains the amniotic fluid.
- **Amniotic fluid** – the fluid in which the baby grows before birth. It acts as a cushion against shocks and so helps to protect the baby from being damaged.
- **Umbilical cord** – this cord links the baby with the placenta. It grows to be about 50 cm long and 2 cm in width. The cord contains blood vessels.
- **Placenta** – a large, thick, disc-like structure firmly attached to the wall of the uterus. It is fully formed at about 12 weeks and then grows steadily to keep pace with the baby. When fully grown it is about 15 cm across and weighs about 500 g. When twins are developing, non-identical twins each have their own placenta. Identical twins share the same placenta.
- **Cervical mucus** – the mucus forms a plug which seals the uterus during pregnancy.

FUNCTION OF THE PLACENTA

The placenta is the organ through which the baby feeds, breathes and excretes waste matter while in the uterus. Blood from the baby flows continuously to and from the placenta through the umbilical cord. In the placenta, the baby's blood comes very close to the mother's blood, but they do not mix. However, they are close enough for food and oxygen to pass from mother to baby, and for carbon dioxide and other waste products to pass in the other direction.

Viruses, alcohol, antibodies, and chemicals from smoke and medicines can cross the placenta from the blood of the mother to the blood of the baby. Some of these substances may damage the developing baby, especially in the early months of pregnancy.

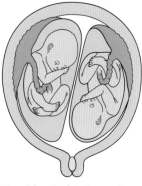

Non-identical twins each have their own placenta

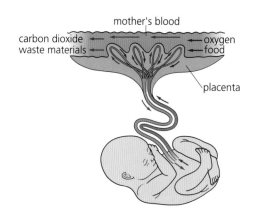

The baby feeds, breathes and excretes waste matter through the placenta

PREMATURE BABIES

Babies born between 38–41 weeks of pregnancy are called **full-term**. **Premature (pre-term)** babies are those born before 38 weeks. A baby born before 37 weeks will probably be a little slow to feed. Those born before 33 weeks will have more serious problems, possibly including immature lungs. Birth before 28 weeks causes very significant problems but the survival rate is quite remarkable. If born before 24 weeks, the baby has little chance of surviving. The lungs have not yet finished developing and the baby will not be able to breathe properly.

Most premature babies weigh less than 2500 g (2.5 kg) and, being very small and weak, may need special care. Frequently they have difficulties with breathing, sucking and keeping warm, and need to be kept in a hot-cot or **incubator** for the first few days or weeks. An incubator acts as a half-way house between the uterus and the outside world. The baby is kept isolated, protected and in a controlled environment. The temperature is kept constant, so is the humidity. The baby can be fed through a tube or dropper until it has the strength to suck. If necessary, extra oxygen can be supplied to help with breathing. A **hot-cot** is a crib for a premature baby to be kept warm.

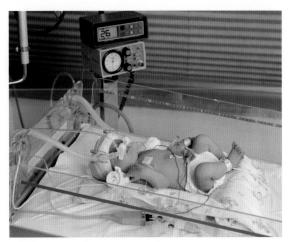

A pre-term baby in an incubator

Neonatal care

Neonatal care takes place in special units (wards) for newborn babies who are born prematurely, are ill or need extra care. The type of care depends on the baby's needs.

- **Intensive care** (Neonatal intensive care; NICU) – for the most seriously ill babies.
- **High dependency care** (HDU) – for babies who are not critically ill but still need special care, for example who are slow to feed, need help with keeping warm or are jaundiced.
- **Special care** (SCBU) – for well babies who are catching up on growth and development after a premature birth, or those who are getting better after more complex treatment.

MISCARRIAGE

A miscarriage is the loss of pregnancy sometime during the first 23 weeks. The baby comes out of the uterus accidentally and too early to survive on its own. The first sign of a miscarriage is bleeding, sometimes with pain. Miscarriages are quite common, the majority occurring in the first three months of pregnancy. The usual reasons are that there is something wrong with the baby's development or the cervix (neck of the uterus).

ECTOPIC PREGNANCY

An **ectopic** pregnancy occurs when a fertilised egg becomes implanted in a Fallopian tube instead of the uterus. An operation is needed to remove the embryo and repair the damage.

Questions

1 **a** Describe the appearance of the embryo at 6 weeks.

  b (i) By what age after conception does the embryo look human-like?

  (ii) What is it now called?

  c (i) What parts develop rapidly during weeks 10–14? (ii) Give five examples of the movements the fetus is able to make at 14 weeks. (iii) When should the mother be able to feel those movements?

  d By how many weeks is (i) the heart beating, (ii) the skin covered with hair, (iii) development almost complete?

2 **a** Draw a diagram to show the fetus in the uterus just before birth.

  b Label and describe the following parts – uterus wall; amnion; amniotic fluid; umbilical cord; placenta.

  c Describe the fetal position.

3 **a** Name the organ through which a baby feeds, breathes and excretes while in the uterus.

  b In the placenta, does the mother's blood mix with the baby's blood?

  c Name one waste product which passes from baby to mother.

  d Name six substances which may pass from mother to baby.

4 (i) What is a premature baby? (ii) Why may a hot cot be used?

5 (i) What is the purpose of neonatal care? (ii) Describe three types.

6 Explain the meaning of (i) miscarriage, (ii) ectopic pregnancy.

Further activities

 Extension

1 Why can an incubator be thought of as a half-way house? Name ways in which the incubator resembles:

  a the uterus

  b the outside world.

2 Study the photograph below of a fetus at 7 weeks of pregnancy. What parts of the body can you identify?

 Investigation

Carry out a survey of the resources available to help parents explain human reproduction to their young children. Use the information to prepare and give a short talk to your class on different ways of explaining human reproduction to children at Key Stage 2.

Weblink

For a conception to birth slide show, search for 'pregnancy development slideshow' on the NHS website:

www.nhs.uk

CHAPTER 9

Pregnancy

Pregnancy is the process that occurs between conception and birth.

PRE-CONCEPTION CARE

Pre-conception care aims at ensuring that the parents are fit and healthy at the time of conception as this increases the chance of having a healthier baby. They are advised to:

- have a healthy diet.
- exercise regularly.
- not be overweight.
- not smoke.
- not use recreational drugs.
- reduce intake of alcohol to a little or none.
- women should check that their immunisations for rubella and varicella are up-to-date. Varicella is the virus that causes chickenpox and shingles. If immunisation is necessary, pregnancy should be delayed for one month afterwards for rubella and three months for varicella.
- take a daily dose of folic acid tablets, and continue to do so until three months into pregnancy. Folic acid (one of the B vitamins) is particularly important in the baby's early development and helps to prevent defects such as spina bifida (p. 352). When folic acid is taken the incidence of spina bifida in babies is greatly reduced.

Foods containing folic acid

SIGNS OF PREGNANCY

For a woman whose periods are regular, and who has had intercourse recently, the first sign that a baby is on the way is usually a missed period. (Adolescent girls may miss periods for other reasons, see p. 29.)

By the time a second period has been missed, other signs of pregnancy may be noticeable. For example, enlarged breasts, darkening of the skin around the nipples, more frequent passing of urine, constipation, and possibly feelings of nausea (sickness).

When the mother is four months pregnant, it will begin to show as her waistline enlarges. At this stage, the baby is still very tiny, and the increase in size is due to the uterus becoming much bigger.

Pregnancy tests

HCG (human chorionic gonadotrophin) is present in the urine of pregnant women, and reaches its highest level at the 8th week of pregnancy. It can usually be detected from 10 days to 16 weeks after conception, but this varies in different women and with different brands of pregnancy test.

INFECTIOUS DISEASES

Most minor infections, such as colds, do no harm to the unborn baby, but a few infectious diseases can cause problems and action should be taken to avoid them during pregnancy.

The earlier in pregnancy that infection occurs, the more serious the possible effects on the fetus.

Rubella (German measles)

This disease is dangerous in the first four months of pregnancy. The mother will not be very ill, but the baby may be harmed. If it survives, it may be born deaf, blind, have heart disease or a learning disability. Most women have immunity against the disease because they had rubella as a child or have been vaccinated against it. A blood test early in pregnancy will check to see if the mother is immune. If she is not, she will be advised to avoid children with rashes and to keep well away from any known cases of rubella.

A

Chicken pox (Varicella)

Most people are immune to this disease as they had it in childhood. The virus may become active again in adults and cause **shingles**. Pregnant women are therefore advised to avoid children with rashes or who are known to have chicken pox. They should also avoid adults with shingles as this is caused by the same virus. If chickenpox is caught during pregnancy, the mother may become quite ill and the unborn baby could be affected with brain damage as well as severe skin problems.

I've got shingles

B

Parvovirus

This virus often causes a mild flu-like illness sometimes called 'slapped cheek' disease because it produces a blotchy red rash on one or both sides of the face. Infection with parvovirus B19 during the first 20 weeks of pregnancy increases the risk of miscarriage. If it occurs during weeks 9–20, there is a low risk of serious disease in the baby.

C

Animal-borne diseases

A rare disease called **toxoplasmosis** can be caught from cat faeces and soil contaminated by faeces. The disease is usually harmless in a pregnant woman with perhaps a mild flu-like illness, but if it passes to her unborn baby it can damage the nervous system, particularly the eyes. To prevent toxoplasmosis, pregnant women are advised to wash their hands thoroughly after handling cats and kittens and to wear gloves when cleaning out the litter tray and when gardening. This disease can also be caught from handling raw meat.

D

Pregnant women are also advised not to help with lambing or come into close contact with newborn lambs or with sheep that have recently given birth. If they do so, they may be at risk from **chlamydiosis** (a lambing disease) which could cause them to miscarry.

E

Milk-borne infections

Drinking unpasteurised milk should be avoided during pregnancy because it may contain bacteria or other organisms which can cause illness. Only milk which has been heat-treated, i.e. pasteurised, sterilised, or UHT (ultra-heat-treated) is recommended. This advice also applies to milk from goats and sheep.

F

Listeriosis

This is a rare disease which, in its mild form, resembles influenza. It is caused by a species of bacteria (*Listeria monocytogenes*) which is able to grow in certain foods at normal refrigerator temperatures. It is important to avoid this disease during pregnancy because even a mild attack in the mother can result in miscarriage, stillbirth, or severe illness in the newborn baby. Pregnant women should therefore avoid:

- soft cheeses, e.g. Brie, Camembert, and blue-veined cheese
- pâté
- 'cook-chill' meals, unless they have been heated until piping hot throughout
- meat which is not cooked thoroughly, particularly chicken.

G

HIV and AIDS

Current evidence suggests that an HIV positive mother in good health and without symptoms of the disease is unlikely to be adversely affected by pregnancy. However, one in four children born to HIV positive mothers is likely to be infected. HIV positive mothers may also pass on the virus through breast milk.

MEDICINES, DRUGS AND ALCOHOL

In a strictly technical sense, medicines are drugs – a drug being any substance which has an effect on the working of the body. However, in general conversation the words tend to be used rather differently – medicines are used for the treatment of disease and drugs are taken for their effect on the mind, and we shall use the words in this sense.

Medicines

When medicines are taken by a pregnant woman, they are likely to cross the placenta and reach the baby. There is a chance that the medicine will interfere with the baby's normal pattern of development. If this happens the baby will develop abnormally. There is a greater chance of this occurring during the first three months after conception than later. To be on the safe side, no medicines should be taken during pregnancy, except on the advice of a doctor.

Drugs

When the word 'drug' is used, it usually refers to a habit-forming (addictive) substance which affects the mind. Examples are cannabis, LSD, ecstasy, crack, cocaine, heroin and the fumes from some solvents and glues. If taken by a pregnant woman these drugs almost always cross the placenta and can affect the babies development. For example, studies show a link between cannabis and premature birth and low birthweight. Taking ecstasy during pregnancy increases the risk of the baby being born with abnormalities. Babies born to drug addicts can suffer withdrawal symptoms shortly after birth, in the same way that an adult addict suffers, and may suffer severe long-term damage. The advice given to pregnant women is not to use any recreational drugs at all.

Alcohol

This may be thought of as a tonic or a pleasure, but it is also a drug. Like the substances mentioned above, it can be both habit-forming and affect the mind.

When a pregnant mother has an alcoholic drink, the alcohol crosses the placenta and the baby takes in alcohol as well. It is unlikely that an occasional drink will harm the developing baby, but regular drinking of even moderate amounts of alcohol could interfere with the growth and development of the unborn baby. A pregnant mother who is an alcoholic can give birth to a baby who is also addicted to alcohol and who may suffer severe long-term damage (fetal alcohol syndrome).

SMOKING

When a pregnant woman smokes, some of the chemical substances in the smoke pass from her lungs into the bloodstream, and soon reach the uterus. At the placenta, the chemicals cross from the mother's blood into the baby's bloodstream. They are then carried to all parts of the baby's body.

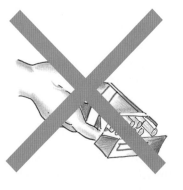

Two of the harmful chemicals in smoke that reach the baby's bloodstream are:

- nicotine – makes the baby's heart beat too fast
- carbon monoxide (the same poison as in car fumes) – takes the place of oxygen in blood. The baby receives less oxygen and does not grow as well as expected.

Effects of smoking

Pregnant women who smoke have an increased risk of having:

- a miscarriage
- a stillborn baby
- a premature baby
- a low birthweight baby.

Pre-term and low birthweight babies are more prone to illness and infections.

Passive smoking

After babies are born:

- Those exposed to tobacco smoke are more at risk of cot death (see p. 76).
- Children who regularly inhale smoke are more likely to suffer from asthma, bronchitis, pneumonia or other chest infections, ear infections and glue ear. About 17,000 children under 5 years old in England and Wales are admitted to hospital each year due to illnesses caused by their parents smoking.
- Children who live in a home where there is a smoker are more likely than average to become smokers themselves when older.

To protect the baby

Pregnant mothers are advised to give up smoking because every cigarette can harm the baby. If help and support are needed to stop the craving, it can be obtained free from the NHS Stop Smoking Service. Nicotine Replacement Therapy (NRT) replaces cigarettes with skin patches or chewing gum. These contain smaller amounts of nicotine that is released slowly and without the toxic chemicals in smoke like tar and carbon monoxide.

Questions

1 a (i) What is pre-conception care? (ii) What advice is given to a woman who hopes to become pregnant?

b (i) What foods containing folic acid should be part of a healthy diet? (ii) Why is folic acid recommended?

2 a How does a woman know she is pregnant? Name six signs which may be present.

b At what stage can pregnancy be detected by a pregnancy test?

c What can be expected to happen to the mother's figure when four months pregnant?

3 a (i) When is rubella a dangerous disease to catch? (ii) What damage may it do? (iii) Why are most women immune? (iv) If a pregnant woman is not immune, what advice will she be given?

b Explain why a pregnant woman should avoid each of the situations shown in the drawings A–G on pp. 40–1.

c (i) What causes listeriosis? (ii) Why is it dangerous during pregnancy? (iii) Which foods should pregnant women avoid?

4 a (i) Why are pregnant women advised not to take medicines?

b (i) Name seven substances which are used as drugs. (ii) Name three effects which drugs of this type can have on the baby in the uterus.

c Name two characteristics which drugs and alcohol have in common.

d Name two effects which alcohol can have on the baby in the uterus.

5 a Name two harmful chemicals in smoke and say why each is harmful.

b Use these words to complete the sentences below: body, chemicals, uterus, lungs, placenta, bloodstream

'When a pregnant woman has a cigarette, – – – from the smoke in her – – – pass into the bloodstream. They soon reach the – – –, cross the – – –, enter the baby's – – – and are then carried to all parts of the baby's – – –.'

c Give four increased risks to the baby when the mother smokes during pregnancy.

d What is the cause for concern when babies are smaller than they ought to be?

Further activities

 Extension

1 If the unborn child in the drawing on page XX could understand the effects that his mother's smoking might be having on him, why would he say 'lucky you'? How does smoking affect birthweight, brain development and health? When the child gets older, what may encourage him to become a smoker? Make a list of your suggestions.

2 What help to give up smoking can be found on the NHS Stop Smoking Service: smokefree.nhs.uk/?

 Investigation

Carry out a survey of the following facilities in your district:

- antenatal clinics
- maternity hospitals
- dentists
- child health clinics
- parent and toddler groups
- playgroups
- health centres
- parks
- playgrounds.

Use a computer and graphics program to produce an information leaflet for new parents. Include a map of the district showing the positions of the various facilities. Comment on the ease of access to these places (are they near bus routes, car parks etc.).

Weblinks

For preconception care, go to the NHS website and search for 'pregnancy care planner':

www.nhs.uk

For information on alcohol and smoking in pregnancy, visit:

www.direct.gov.uk

and search for 'having a baby'.

For stop smoking support and advice, visit:

http://smokefree.nhs.uk/

CHAPTER 10

The expectant mother

Pregnancy is a normal and natural process, and necessary for the survival of the human race. It is not an illness, and the expectant mother does not need to be treated like an invalid. Nevertheless, she does need to keep healthy for the sake of her unborn baby and herself. Also, she has to adjust to the various changes that take place in her body as the pregnancy proceeds.

Changes will take place in the mother's:

- **size, shape and weight**
- **hormones** (substances which help to regulate the way the body works)
- **emotions** (she will feel different)
- **way of life** (at least in the latter part of pregnancy).

SICKNESS

Hormone changes are responsible for the **nausea** (feeling sick) and **vomiting** (being sick) from which many women suffer during the early stages of pregnancy. Although often called 'morning sickness' it can occur at any time of the day or night. It may be experienced on only a few occasions or at the same time every day, but rarely lasts beyond the 15th week of pregnancy.

DIET

When a woman is pregnant, she does not need to eat much more than usual. The developing baby will take what food it requires, and the mother will suffer if she eats too much or too little.

It is what the mother eats that is important. Her diet needs to contain extra protein, vitamins (particularly folic acid – see p. 39) and minerals for the baby, also extra fibre because expectant mothers are prone to constipation. She does not need extra carbohydrate and fat. Fried foods and spicy foods should be avoided if they lead to indigestion. Also, foods which could cause listeriosis should be avoided (see p. 41).

Odd tastes and cravings

It is quite common during pregnancy for a mother's tastes in food to change. She may have the urge to eat the oddest foods at the most unusual times, especially in the early months. Often she dislikes things she used to enjoy such as tea and coffee.

Heartburn

This is a strong burning sensation in the chest due to stomach acid passing up into the oesophagus (gullet). It is common in later pregnancy due to relaxation of the valve at the entrance to the stomach. Large meals, particularly late in the evening, should be avoided. Heartburn may be eased at night by lying propped up or even sitting up.

EXERCISE

Regular exercise is good for everyone, including expectant mothers. It keeps the muscles in a healthy condition, and helps to bring restful sleep at night. The right type of exercise during pregnancy is the sort the mother wants to do: maybe walking, swimming, cycling, dancing. But, like everything else at this time, it should be done in moderation.

Pelvic floor exercises

The pelvic floor (the floor of the abdomen) is composed of muscles which surround the vagina and the openings from the bowel and bladder. These muscles come under great strain in pregnancy and childbirth, and special exercises can help to strengthen them. Slack pelvic muscles are one of the main reasons for the leaky bladder which some women suffer from after pregnancy.

POSTURE

The increase in weight in the abdominal ('tummy') region alters the normal balance of the body. When walking there will be a tendency to hollow the back and to waddle and plod along. To avoid this, the spine needs to be kept upright and the head erect. It is particularly important at this time to bend the knees and not the back when lifting a heavy weight.

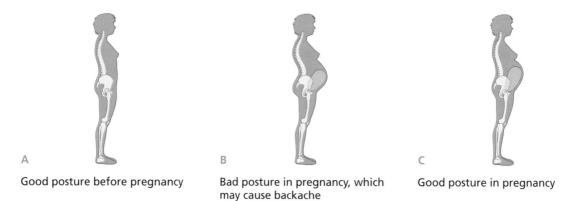

A

Good posture before pregnancy

B

Bad posture in pregnancy, which may cause backache

C

Good posture in pregnancy

REST

During the latter part of pregnancy, the increase in weight puts more strain on the legs, feet and back. A rest in the middle of the day helps to prevent problems like backache, varicose veins and over-tiredness.

Varicose veins

These are veins which have become stretched and swollen. This may sometimes happen to veins in the legs during pregnancy. The legs may then ache. This condition is made worse by standing still for long periods of time.

Resting now and again with the feet up takes the pressure off the veins, reduces the swelling, and makes the legs feel better. If the veins are uncomfortable or painful then it may be helpful to wear elastic tights (support tights) or support stockings. Support stockings need to be specially measured to suit the individual. They will not cure varicose veins but they may relieve the discomfort.

The condition of the veins almost always improves after the baby is born, although they may not completely disappear.

VISITING THE DENTIST

Contrary to popular belief, teeth do not lose calcium during pregnancy, even when the mother's diet is short of calcium. However, they are more prone to decay and the gums may become a little swollen and spongy and may bleed more easily than usual. A visit to the dentist for a check-up at an early stage is advisable, and again after the baby is born. Dental treatment is free during pregnancy and for one year after the birth.

MATERNITY CLOTHES

During pregnancy, the breasts enlarge and the abdomen expands greatly. The mother will therefore need clothes which are expandable or loose around the waist, and a larger, properly fitted bra with good support and a cup that does not squeeze the nipple. The bra should have wide straps and adjustable fastenings.

A good support bra, loose clothing and flat shoes are comfortable during pregnancy

Feet may ache or swell slightly in pregnancy, so it helps to wear shoes which are comfortable. They should also be designed to give support to the foot, and have low or medium heels. Shoes of this type help the mother to keep her balance as well as helping to prevent backache.

Questions

1 a Nausea is common in the early weeks of pregnancy. What is the cause?

b Does it always occur in the morning?

c Is it likely to occur throughout pregnancy?

d Explain what is meant by heartburn.

2 a Does an expectant mother need to eat for two?

b What substances should she make sure she eats enough of?

c What substances should be avoided?

d Do some mothers have cravings for odd foods at this time?

3 a Give two reasons why regular exercise is good for expectant mothers.

b Give examples of the types of exercise that an expectant mother can do if she wants to.

c Explain why pelvic floor exercises are recommended for pregnant women.

4 a Which parts of the body are particularly affected by the increasing weight?

b What problems does a daily rest help to prevent?

5 a What are varicose veins?

b What can make varicose veins worse?

c What is the advantage of resting with the feet up?

d What may also help to relieve the discomfort?

6 a Why should an expectant mother have a dental check-up?

b When should she visit the dentist?

c For how long is dental treatment free?

7 Describe types of clothing suitable during pregnancy.

Further activities

 Extension

1 Study the posture drawings on p. 46. Describe the difference between 'good' and 'bad' posture. How does posture affect walking?

2 Use a computer and a desk-top publishing program to prepare an information sheet for expectant mothers about some aspects of good practice during pregnancy. This could be done as a group exercise or by students individually.

3 Use a spreadsheet to analyse the cost of a maternity bra, trousers, shirt, and dress by comparing prices from four different sources.

 Design

Collect some pictures of clothes and shoes suitable for wearing during pregnancy. Design some styles yourself and comment on their suitability.

CHAPTER 11

Antenatal care

Antenatal (*ante* = before, *natal* = birth) care is given throughout pregnancy, either at an antenatal clinic, or with the mother's own doctor (GP) or community midwife. This is to make sure that the baby is developing properly and to prevent things going wrong during pregnancy or the birth. The mother also has the opportunity to ask questions and talk about any worries.

The first antenatal visit takes place between the 8th and 12th week of pregnancy. Further check-ups usually take place once a month until about the 30th week. Then more frequent check-ups are needed. Employers are required by law to allow women to receive paid time off from work for antenatal care.

WHAT HAPPENS AT THE CLINIC

On the first visit to the antenatal clinic, a medical history is taken to discover any relevant information which may affect the health of the mother or her baby. The mother will have a general physical examination including a check on her heart and lungs.

Weight check

Women are weighed on their first visit to the clinic and again at the end of pregnancy. They may be weighed in between if there is too much, or too little, weight gain. Apart from the first few months, a pregnant woman gains, on average, about 450 g in weight per week. In total she puts on about 12 kg. The increased weight is due to the baby plus the greatly enlarged uterus, the placenta, umbilical cord, and amniotic fluid. In addition, extra fat may be stored in the layer under the skin. This fat will be used in milk production after the baby is born. If the mother puts on too much weight, she will be advised to adjust her diet.

Blood tests

It is routine for a small sample of blood to be taken from the mother to check for the following:

1. **Anaemia** – this condition is common in pregnancy and makes the mother feel tired and weak. The usual treatment is to take iron and folic acid (iron-folate) tablets.
2. **Blood group** – this is essential information if a blood transfusion should be needed in an emergency.
3. **Rhesus factor** – most people have this factor in the blood, and the blood is termed Rhesus positive. Those who do not have it are Rhesus negative. The Rhesus (Rh) factor is inherited

and problems can arise in families when the father is Rh positive and the mother is Rh negative. If the children are Rh negative like their mother there is no problem. The first Rh positive baby will usually be all right. But a second Rh positive baby may have anaemia and jaundice, may be mentally handicapped, or may even die. Further Rh positive babies would also be affected. The problem can nowadays be avoided. Rh negative mothers can be given an injection when 28 weeks pregnant, and again after birth, to prevent the build-up of harmful substances in her blood which could damage her babies.

4. **Immunity to rubella (German measles)** – if the blood test shows that there are no antibodies against rubella, it means the mother is not immune to the disease. After the baby is born, she will be offered a rubella vaccination for long-term protection.

5. **Hepatitis B** – this liver disease can infect the baby unless special care is taken.

6. **HIV** – pregnant mothers are recommended to have this test as it is the only way to tell if they may be infected with this virus. It is important to know if the mother is infected because she can then receive treatment for HIV. The birth will then be managed in a particular way to reduce the risk of the baby being infected. Without treatment one baby in six born to HIV infected mothers is likely to be infected.

Blood pressure check

The mother's blood pressure is checked at every visit to the clinic. If it rises too high then she must rest, possibly in hospital. High blood pressure (**hypertension**) may be a sign of **pre-eclampsia** (pregnancy-induced hypertension). This condition occurs only during pregnancy and disappears six weeks afterwards. As well as high blood pressure, symptoms include swollen ankles and the gaining of too much weight. One of the benefits of regular attendance at the antenatal clinic is that pre-eclampsia will be diagnosed in the early stages. Steps can then be taken to prevent it from becoming worse. Should the condition

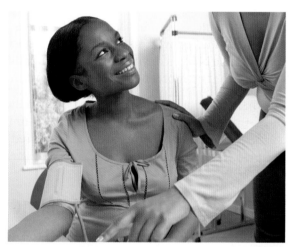

Blood pressure check

be allowed to continue, the mother may develop a kind of epilepsy (eclampsia) at the end of the pregnancy. This can be fatal to the baby and also to the mother.

Urine test

At every antenatal visit a sample of urine is tested for:

- sugar (glucose) – if present it may indicate diabetes
- protein (albumin) – if present may be an early sign of pre-eclampsia or infection
- bacteria (germs) – during pregnancy the mother may have an infection without any symptoms. Treating the infection with antibiotics prevents the risk of problems later in pregnancy, for example, premature birth.

Vaginal examination

On the first visit to the antenatal clinic, the mother's vagina may be examined:

- **to check that there is no infection**, for example, thrush
- **to obtain a cervical smear**, in order to detect early warning signs of cancer of the cervix (rare in pregnant women, but more common in later life).

Towards the end of pregnancy, a vaginal examination may be performed to check that the pelvic outlet will be big enough for the baby's head to pass through.

Examination of the uterus

By gently feeling the outside of the abdomen, it is possible for the doctor to get some idea of the baby's size and position in the uterus. The uterus expands as the baby grows at the rate of about 1 cm per week. The size of the baby can therefore be assessed by using a tape to measure from the top of the enlarging uterus to the bone at the bottom of the abdomen. At 28 weeks it will be about 28 cm. Towards the end of pregnancy, it is important to know if the baby is in the best position to be born, that is, with the head downwards so that it comes out first. Should the baby be in the 'breech' position (p. 62), the doctor may try to turn it so that the head points downwards.

Baby's heartbeat

In the second half of pregnancy, the baby's heartbeat can be heard through a stethoscope, pinard or Doppler machine placed on the mother's abdomen. It will be beating between 120 and 160 times per minute, which is about twice as fast as the mother's heart.

Doppler – a hand-held ultrasound machine

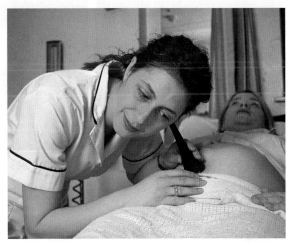

Pinard – a type of ear trumpet that magnifies sounds made by the baby's heart

SCREENING AND DIAGNOSTIC TESTS

A **screening test** is a routine test carried out on a large number of people to find those individuals who have a particular disease or are at risk of developing that disease. A **diagnostic test** is carried out to find out (diagnose) whether a person has a disease or not.

Screening tests on unborn babies

Ultrasound scan

In an ultrasound scan, sound waves are used to produce pictures of the baby in the uterus. A routine ultrasound scan is usually offered at:

- 10–14 weeks of pregnancy to estimate the age of the unborn baby and find out whether twins or more are present
- 18–20 weeks of pregnancy to check the position of the placenta and look for any physical abnormalities of the unborn baby.

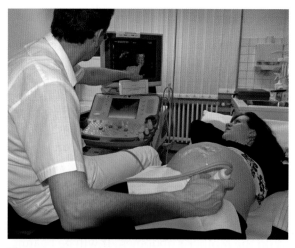

Ultrasound scan

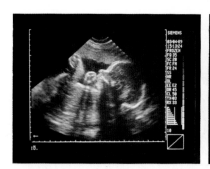
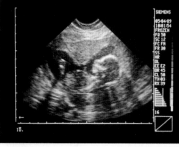
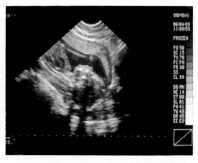

A **At 12 weeks**
Note the
- placenta
- head
- body
- lower limb
- amniotic fluid
- uterus wall

B **At 19 weeks**
Note the
- face
- heart
- spine

C **At 28 weeks**
Note the
- ear
- neck
- upper limb
- lower limb

Ultrasound images

Nuchal translucency scan

This scan is carried out at 10–13 weeks of pregnancy to measure the thickness of the fold of skin at the back of the baby's neck (*nucha* – the nape of the neck). The thicker the fold the higher the risk of the baby having a chromosome defect.

Serum screening (quadruple test)

This special blood test is carried out around 15 to 19 weeks. It cannot tell whether the baby does or does not have Down's syndrome or spina bifida. However, it can tell which women are at a greater risk of their baby having either of these conditions.

Diagnostic tests on unborn babies

Amniocentesis

This test may be carried out when the serum screening test or the ultrasound scan indicate that there could be a problem with the baby's development. A hollow needle is inserted through the mother's abdominal wall and into the uterus to obtain a sample of amniotic fluid (the liquid surrounding the baby). By examining this liquid and the cells from the baby which it contains, it is possible to detect spina bifida and chromosome disorders such as Down's syndrome. Amniocentesis is usually carried out at 16 to 18 weeks of pregnancy.

Chorionic villus sampling (CVS)

With this test, a small piece of the placenta is removed and the cells examined. It is carried out from 11 weeks of pregnancy on women whose babies are at high risk of having Down's syndrome or certain inherited diseases, e.g. sickle cell anaemia or thalassemia.

PREPARATION CLASSES

Many hospitals and clinics hold preparation classes. They are especially useful for mothers who are expecting their first baby. At these classes they find out about:

- diet and health in pregnancy
- how the baby develops
- how it will be born, and how to prepare for labour
- different types of pain relief available during labour
- breast-feeding
- how to look after the new baby.

The mothers may also be taught special exercises to help with breathing and relaxation, for use when in labour. Controlling the breathing during a contraction and being able to relax between the contractions helps to make the birth easier.

Fathers are welcome at many of these classes. The father is often the person who can give the greatest help and encouragement to the expectant mother. Understanding the progress of pregnancy will enable him to be even more interested and helpful. If he plans to be present at the birth, he needs to be prepared for what is going to happen and know how he can be of support.

Preparation for breast-feeding

Mothers are encouraged to breast-feed because breast milk is the natural food for babies. They should certainly do so for the first two weeks (the baby will receive colostrum, see p. 85), and ideally for several months. There are very few mothers who do not produce enough milk to breast-feed, but some may need advice and encouragement, especially if they come from families where breast-feeding is not popular.

Questions

1 a What is the meaning of the word 'antenatal'?

b (i) What is the purpose of antenatal care? (ii) How often should check-ups take place?

2 a (i) What is the average total weight gain in pregnancy? (ii) What is the average weekly gain?

b Name six factors which contribute to this increase in weight.

3 a Name six tests which are routinely carried out on the mother's blood, and give a reason for each.

b Why is it important for a pregnant mother to have an HIV test?

c (i) Name three symptoms of pre-eclampsia. (ii) Why is this condition dangerous?

d Name three tests which are carried out on the mother's urine, and give reasons.

e Why do vaginal examinations take place?

f Why is the uterus examined?

4 a How can the doctor tell the difference between the baby's and mother's heartbeats?

b Compare the doppler machine with the pinard and describe how each is used.

5 a Explain the difference between a screening and diagnostic test. Give three examples of screening tests and two examples of diagnostic tests.

b What information can be obtained from an ultrasound scan? (ii) What happens in a nuchal translucency scan?

c (i) What is the purpose of serum screening?

d (i) What part inside the uterus is tested in (i) chorionic villus sampling, (ii) amniocentesis?

6 a How may preparation classes be useful to the mother of a first baby?

b Why may breathing and relaxation exercises be taught at these classes?

c Why are fathers welcomed at these classes?

d Give reasons why mothers are encouraged to breast-feed.

Further activities

 Investigation

1 Find out more about

a Antenatal clinics in your area.

b Preparation classes.

c Rhesus problems in pregnancy and what can be done to prevent them.

d The ultrasound scan and its uses.

2 Attendance at antenatal clinics

Prepare a questionnaire and use it to find out from mothers of young children in your area:
(i) Whether they attended an antenatal clinic (Yes or No).

If they attended the clinic: **(ii)** The month of pregnancy in which they first attended (2nd–9th).
(iii) How convenient it was to attend (a scale of 1–5). **(iv)** How worthwhile the visits were (a scale of 1–5).

If they did not attend the clinic: **(v)** The reason for not attending. **(vi)** Did they receive any other type of antenatal care or advice?

Enter your survey answers into a database file and use it to analyse the results.

Weblinks

For more information on antenatal care, visit:
www.bbc.co.uk/parenting
and search for 'antenatal care'.
For general information on fatherhood, visit:
www.dad.info

CHAPTER 12

Arrangements for the birth

Pregnant women may have the choice of where to give birth – in hospital, a birth centre or at home. If a mother wishes to have her baby at home, midwives are required by law to care for her there. If any help is needed, the midwife will send for an ambulance to transfer the mother to hospital.

HOSPITAL DELIVERY

Advantages of a hospital delivery:

- Trained staff are present all the time.
- Special monitoring equipment is there to check the baby's health and safety throughout labour.
- Other equipment is immediately available in the event of an emergency.
- The mother is free from domestic responsibilities and worries.
- The mother is protected from too many visitors.
- There are other mothers to talk to and share experiences with.

Delivery in hospital is definitely advised for higher-risk mothers who:

- are expecting multiple births
- have already had a Caesarian section
- have medical problems
- began labour prematurely before 37 weeks.

BIRTH CENTRES

Birth centres are small maternity units staffed by midwives. They may be called midwife-led units (MLU), birthing centres, maternity hospitals or GP units. They are a kind of halfway house between home and hospital. They offer a homely, relaxed atmosphere with facilities which may not be available in a hospital, such as family accommodation, water pools, complementary therapies and comfortable, low-tech birthing rooms. Many birth centres are able to offer antenatal and post-natal care.

Birth centres are not hospitals and do not have the high-tech facilities needed for caesarian births or for special neonatal care. Epidural pain relief is unlikely to be available, or assisted delivery with forceps or ventouse. Despite the lack of these medical facilities, evidence shows that giving birth in a birth centre is just as safe as a hospital for the mother and baby. Midwives are skilled in life-support and resuscitation techniques and in managing emergency situations. If difficulties arise during labour, the mother will be transferred to hospital by ambulance with a midwife.

HOME DELIVERY

Advantages of a home delivery:

- The mother will be attended by a midwife, often one she knows.
- She is in familiar surroundings, amongst family and friends.
- Any other children in the family can be involved in the exciting event.
- She will have more privacy than in a ward with other women.
- She will be able to choose the conditions in which she gives birth.
- She will not have to keep to the hospital routine of meals etc.
- She will be able to look after her baby in her own way.

Having a baby at home

The room in which the birth will take place should have:

- a bed for the mother
- a plastic or polythene cover over the mattress
- a cot for the baby
- a table for the equipment of the midwife and doctor
- adequate light and heating
- a cover over the carpet for protection
- a wash basin or bowl and jugs of hot and cold water
- towels and toiletries
- a bucket for used dressings.

The midwife will bring her own delivery pack containing item necessary for home births.

DOMINO SCHEME

The **domino scheme** (domicilliary scheme) combines home and hospital and may be an option. The mother is visited at home by one of a small group of midwives who goes to hospital with her and delivers the baby. If both mother and baby are well, they return home after a few hours with the midwife, who continues to care for them until the health visitor takes over.

BIRTH PLAN

A birth plan is a document completed by the mother that tells the midwives and doctors the kind of labour she would like to have. Information for completing the birth plan can be obtained from midwives, antenatal classes, talking to women who have already given birth, and discussions with the person who will be the birth companion Although during the birth, things may not go according to the plan, writing it gives the mother a chance to make decisions in advance and record the things that matter to her.

A birth plan includes information such as:

- where to give birth – home, hospital or birth centre
- who is to be present at the birth – husband, partner, mother, friend
- what kind of delivery – in bed, in water, a Caesarean section
- pain relief methods preferred – relaxation and breathing, gas and air (Entonox®), diamorphine, epidural
- the delivery position – sitting, standing, squatting
- delivery of the placenta – natural or an injection to speed it up
- if necessary – assisted birth or caesarean section
- feeding the baby – breast-fed or bottle fed
- any special diet or religious needs
- whether students could observe the birth.

MEDICAL STAFF

Midwife

A midwife is a nurse who is specially trained in the care of pregnancy and childbirth. Besides being present during labour, midwives undertake the antenatal care of a normal pregnancy, and also the postnatal care if necessary. They either work in the maternity department of a hospital, in a birth centre, or in the community looking after mothers and babies in their own homes.

Obstetrician

An obstetrician is a doctor who specialises in pregnancy and childbirth. Obstetricians attend antenatal clinics to check the health of expectant mothers. They also attend the births of babies born in hospital when there are likely to be any complications such as a breech birth or Caesarian section.

Gynaecologist

A gynaecologist is a doctor who specialises in the functions and diseases of the female reproductive system. Gynaecologists are usually also obstetricians.

Paediatrician

A paediatrician is a doctor who specialises in the care of children from the time they are born. The medical check-up given to babies born in hospital is usually carried out by a paediatrician.

Questions

1 a Give six advantages of a hospital delivery.

   b Give seven advantages of a home delivery.

   c (i) What are other names for birth centres? (ii) Why is a birth centre regarded as halfway between a hospital and home? (iii) What is the domino scheme?

   d Name four groups of women for whom a hospital delivery is definitely advised.

2 How should a room be prepared for a home delivery?

3 (i) What is a birth plan? (ii) What is its purpose?

4 a What is the job of a midwife?

   b What is the difference between an obstetrician and a gynaecologist?

   c What is a paediatrician?

   d Which type of hospital doctor would you expect to find (i) in an antenatal clinic? (ii) Carrying out a check-up on a newborn baby?

Further activities

 Investigation

What are the aims of the National Childbirth Trust? There are branches in different parts of the country. Where is your nearest branch? Find out about the branch and the activities it organises (see www.nctpregnancyandbabycare.com).

 Extension

Use the figures in the table below to construct a bar chart comparing home and hospital births in the 40 years between 1959 and 1999.

Percentage of births by place of delivery in England and Wales					
	1959	1969	1979	1989	1999
Hospital	64	84	98	99	98
Home	36	16	2	1	2

What changes do you think took place during these years to allow nearly all births to take place in a hospital? Give at least three suggestions.

CHAPTER 13

Birth

HOW TO ESTIMATE THE DATE OF DELIVERY

Delivery is another name for childbirth. Pregnancy lasts on average 38 weeks from the date of conception. The actual date of conception is often unknown, but is likely to have been about two weeks after the first day of the last period. The estimated date of delivery (**EDD**) can be worked out in two ways:

1. By adding 40 weeks to the first day of the mother's last period.
2. By adding nine calendar months and one week to the first day of the mother's last period.

However, the baby often arrives a little earlier or later than the estimated date.

A placenta (afterbirth)
B uterus (womb)
C backbone
D amniotic fluid
E cervix (neck of uterus)
F vagina
G pelvis (hip bone)
H plug of mucus

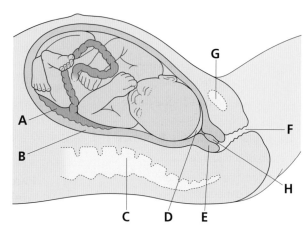

Ready to be born

THE THREE STAGES OF LABOUR

Stage 1: The neck of the uterus opens

When the mother notices one or more of the following signs she will know that labour has started:

■ **A show** – this is a small discharge of mucus mixed with blood. It has come away from the cervix where it formed a plug.
■ **Rupture of the membranes (breaking of the waters)** – the amniotic fluid (bag of water) in which the baby has been developing breaks, and the fluid is released.

▪ **Regular and strong contractions occur** – these contractions of the uterus start very slowly, perhaps every 20–30 minutes. They then become stronger, regular and more frequent.

During the first stage of labour, contractions of the muscles in the wall of the uterus gradually open the cervix. The membranes rupture at some time during this stage, either at the very beginning of labour, or later on. The first stage is the longest stage of labour and it comes to an end when the cervix has opened wide enough for the baby's head to pass through.

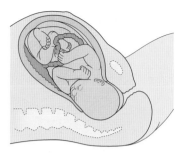

The first stage of labour

Different women will find different positions the most comfortable for labour. Some lie on their back, sometimes propped up by pillows, some lie on their side, some prefer to crouch or kneel for at least part of labour.

Stage 2: The baby passes through the birth canal

The uterus, cervix and vagina have by now become one continuous **birth canal**. The contractions are very strong and they push the baby head-first through the birth canal. The mother must help to push. When the baby's head emerges from the vagina it is called **crowning**.

When the baby's head has emerged, the midwife clears mucus from the nose and mouth. The baby may then start to breathe, and even to cry, before the rest of the body comes out.

The midwife or doctor now eases the shoulders through the birth canal and the baby slides out into the world.

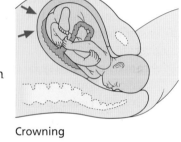

Crowning

Sometimes the opening to the vagina will not stretch enough for the head to pass through. A small cut is then made to widen the opening and prevent the skin from tearing. This minor operation is called an **episiotomy**.

Stage 3: The baby becomes a separate person

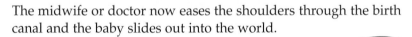

End of stage 2

Once the baby is breathing, the umbilical cord is clamped in two places and a cut is made between them. This separates the baby from the mother. Clamping the cord prevents bleeding. Cutting the cord does not hurt either the mother or the baby.

When the baby first appears, the skin is a bluish colour. As soon as breathing starts, the skin quickly turns pink (this shows that oxygen is being obtained from the air).

The contractions continue until the placenta (**afterbirth**) becomes separated from the wall of the uterus and has been pushed out through the vagina. The mother may be given an injection of **syntometrine** to speed up the process and to prevent excessive loss of blood. Labour is now completed.

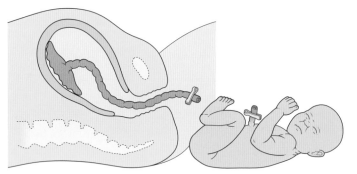

The baby is separated from the mother

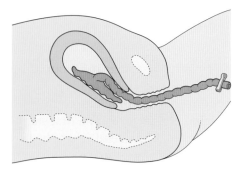

The placenta is pushed out

PAIN RELIEF

Labour is usually painful. There are a number of ways in which the pain can be relieved:

- **Relaxation and breathing exercises** (taught in antenatal classes) help to make labour easier for many women, especially during the first stage.
- **Aromatherapy** may be of help in the first stage of labour. A few drops of certain oils such as lavender or camomile can help to relieve anxiety, fear and pain.
- **Gas-and-air** (Entonox®) is often offered to the mother towards the end of the first stage of labour, when the contractions are very strong. A gas called nitrous oxide ('laughing' gas) is mixed with oxygen. The mother inhales the mixture through a mouthpiece attached to the gas supply.
- **Pethidine** – an injection of this pain-killer may be given if the contractions become very uncomfortable.
- **Epidural anaesthetic** – this is injected into the lower part of the spine. It stops the pain by blocking the nerves that carry painful sensations from the abdomen to the brain (all pain is felt in the brain).
- **TENS** (Transcutaneous Electrical Nerve Stimulation) is a method of relieving pain in labour. It works by reducing the intensity of the pain messages which the body sends from the uterus, cervix and vagina to the brain. At the same time, it increases the amount of a hormone (called endorphin) which the body produces as its own natural response for dealing with pain. Four pads are strapped to the mother's back at the start of labour. These are connected to a hand-held device which the mother operates as necessary during contractions.

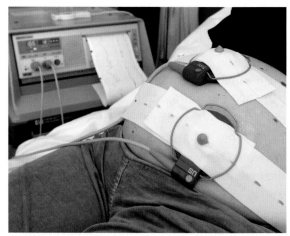

This woman in labour has been linked to a monitor which keeps a continuous check of the baby's heartbeat, and the time and strength of the contractions. This information is valuable in helping to make labour as safe as possible for the baby

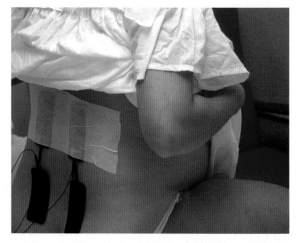

A woman in labour using a TENS machine

AFTER THE BIRTH

The baby

The newly born baby is handed to the mother so that she can hold the baby closely to her. If she wants, she can put the baby to her breast. It is comforting for the baby to be cuddled and loved, and it gives the mother her first opportunity to begin to get to know her new baby. The APGAR score is carried out (see the table below), and the baby is also given a dose of vitamin K to prevent a rare bleeding disorder (see pp. 65 and 255). After being weighed and measured, the baby will spend much of the first day sleeping.

APGAR Score

This is used to assess the health of a new-born baby by evaluating 5 vital signs:

Appearance – assessed by the colour of the baby's skin

Pulse – assessed by the rate of heartbeat

Grimace (distressed facial expression) – assessed by a reflex response to a stimulus such as being touched; the response might be a grimace, cry or cough

Activity – assessed by amount of movement

Respiration – assessed by the ability to breathe.

Score	0	1	2
Appearance	Blue, pale	Body pink, toes/fingers blue	Completely pink
Pulse	Absent	Slow – below 100/min	Fast – above 100/min
Grimace	No response	Grimace	Crying/cough
Activity	Limp	Some movement	Active movement
Respiration	Absent	Slow-irregular	Good, crying

- A high score of 8, 9 or 10 indicates a healthy baby.
- A score between 5 and 7 indicates that the baby may need some help with breathing (the midwife may vigorously rub the baby's skin or give oxygen).
- A low score of under 5 warns that urgent attention is needed and a paediatrician would be called to assist the midwife.

The test is generally done at one minute and again at five minutes after birth, and may be repeated later if the score is low.

The mother

Giving birth is hard work. After it is all over, the mother will want to rest and sleep for a while to recover. The uterus shrinks back to size in the days following the birth, and this is speeded up by breast-feeding. Eventually the uterus will be almost the same size as it was before the baby was conceived. Bleeding from the place in the uterus to which the placenta was attached continues until the wound has healed. It may take up to 6 weeks to heal completely.

OTHER WAYS OF BEING BORN

Assisted delivery

Assisted delivery by forceps or ventouse may be necessary if the baby becomes distressed or the mother is exhausted. Perhaps the contractions are not strong enough to push the baby out, or the baby is lying in an awkward position, or there are other difficulties. A **forceps delivery** uses special forceps (like large tongs) that fit over the baby's head and are used to ease the baby through the birth canal. A **ventouse delivery** (vacuum extraction) uses a rubber suction cup that is attached to the baby's head and gently pulled. The baby's head may look a little bruised after an assisted delivery but it soon returns to normal.

Breech birth

Babies are usually born head first but occasionally they are born bottom or feet first, and this is called a breech birth. Breech births are more difficult and often require caesarian section.

Caesarian section

This is an operation to remove the baby from the uterus. It is carried out when the birth canal is too narrow, the umbilical cord is around the baby's neck, the baby is very late, or the health of the baby or mother makes immediate delivery necessary. An incision is made through the abdominal wall and into the uterus so that the baby can be removed. The umbilical cord is cut, the placenta is then removed and the uterus and abdominal wall are sewn up. The operation takes about 20 minutes.

Epidural anaesthetic is commonly given for this operation. The mother remains conscious and the father can be present at the birth to support her. When the mother is given a general anaesthetic she will be unconscious while the baby is being delivered.

Induction

Induction means that the process of labour is started artificially. It may be possible to do this by breaking the waters. A 'drip' may also be given to the mother through a vein in her arm. The drip contains the hormone **oxytocin** which stimulates the uterus to start contracting. The birth may be induced when the baby is very late, or when the health of the mother or baby is at risk.

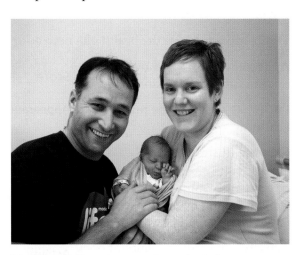

Most hospitals are happy to have the father present at the birth. When this happens, the mother, father and baby are all together as a family from the very first moment

Questions

1 **a** Give another word which means childbirth.

  b What is meant by EDD?

  c If the first day of the mother's last period was 9th December, work out the EDD using both methods mentioned in this topic.

  d What is the process of giving birth called?

  e What three signs indicate that labour has started?

2 **a** List briefly the three stages of labour.

  b (i) Which is the longest stage? (ii) When does it come to an end?

  c Name the three parts that together make the birth canal?

  d What is crowning?

  e At what stage may the baby start to breathe?

  f How is the baby separated from the mother?

  g When is labour complete?

3 Describe ways in which the pain of childbirth can be relieved.

4 **a** What is the purpose of the APGAR score?

  b Describe five signs shown by a healthy baby.

5 What is meant by (i) assisted delivery?(ii) forceps delivery,?(iii) ventouse delivery? (iv) breech birth? (v) caesarian section? (vi) induction?

Further activities

 Extension

a Copy the diagram of the birth position on p. 58. Add the correct labels for A–H.

b Study the diagrams on pp. 59 and 60. Describe what is happening in each of the diagrams.

 Investigation

A drug-free childbirth is ideal from the baby's point of view. On the other hand, drugs ease the pain for the mother. Find out more about the advantages and disadvantages of the use in childbirth of:

a pethidine

b epidural anaesthetic

c TENS.

CHAPTER 14

Postnatal care

The word **postnatal** refers to the first days and weeks after the baby is born (*post* = after, *natal* = birth).

MIDWIFE

The mother will have help from a midwife for the first ten days after the birth. If she is in hospital, she will be looked after by the midwives there. If she is at home, a midwife will call daily.

HEALTH VISITOR

The health visitor will call to see the mother and baby at home about ten days after the birth. She will call from time to time after that. The purpose of her visits is to:

- advise the mother on how to keep herself and her baby healthy
- check that the baby is making normal progress
- advise on feeding
- advise the mother to attend a baby clinic
- discuss a timetable for immunisation
- give help and guidance on any emotional problems
- put the mother in touch with other mothers locally and with postnatal groups.

She will also tell the mother how she can be reached when the parents want advice, for example because the baby will not feed, or will not stop crying, or is vomiting, or has a sore bottom, or spots, or if there is any other matter which is worrying the parents. Health visitors are trained nurses with some experience in midwifery and extra training in family health and child development.

FORMALITIES AFTER THE BIRTH

Notification of the birth

The local Health Authority must be notified of every birth within 36 hours. This is usually done by the doctor or midwife present at the birth.

Registration

All babies must be registered with the local Registrar of Births within 42 days of the date of the birth (21 days in Scotland). The Registrar will need to know the name under which the child is to be brought up, its sex and the parents' details. A **birth certificate** will then be issued. If the parents are married to each other, either of them can register the child. If they are not married to each other:

- Both parents can together register the child, and details of both parents will be entered on the birth certificate.
- The mother or father can register the child on her or his own. Details of the other parent can be entered on the birth certificate provided the correct documents (declarations, court orders etc.) are given to the Registrar.
- The mother can register the birth on her own, but not give any details of the father. It is possible for the child to be re-registered at a later date and the father's details entered on the birth certificate.

Some hospitals arrange for the local Registrar of Births to visit the hospital so that the baby can be registered before going home. Otherwise, the parents must visit the office of the Registrar of Births.

Parental Responsibility (PR)

All mothers automatically have parental responsibility, which gives them full legal responsibility for their child. If the father is married to the mother, he will also automatically have parental responsibility. If the parents are not married, the father will not have parental responsibility and will not legally be allowed to make important decisions about the child. To change this situation he must specifically request parental responsibility from the Registrar.

Medical card

When a baby is registered, the parents are given a card to take to their family doctor. This enables the baby to be registered with the doctor and to receive an NHS medical card.

THE BABY

Examination of the baby

Every newborn baby is given a routine examination, usually the day after birth and in the presence of the mother. A paediatrician, or midwife who is trained in the examination of the newborn, checks that the facial features and proportions of the body are normal, examines the baby's eyes, checks the mouth for cleft palate, listens to the heart, and looks to see if an extra finger or toe is present. Other checks include testing the movement of the hip joints for **congenital dislocation of the hip**. If a dislocated hip is discovered, the baby will require hospital treatment to correct the hip joint to prevent the development of a permanent limp. The genitalia of a male baby are also checked.

PKU test (Guthrie test)

When babies are 7 to 9 days old, they are tested for a rare disorder called PKU (phenyl ketonuria). The test involves pricking the baby's heel and collecting a few drops of blood on a test card. If PKU is discovered, the baby is put on a special diet and will then be able to develop normally. When PKU is left untreated, the brain becomes damaged and the child will have learning difficulties.

PKU test

(PKU is a metabolic disorder – the baby is unable to metabolise a chemical called phenylalanine which is present in milk and other foods.)

Thyroid function test

This test is carried out at the same time and in the same way as the PKU test. The object is to check that the thyroid gland is producing the hormone thyroxine. This hormone is needed for normal growth and development. A child who lacks thyroxine will be undersized and have learning difficulties. This condition can be prevented by giving the child regular doses of the hormone from an early age. The photographs on the left show a baby aged 3 months just before thyroxine treatment began, and aged 6 months, now normal and healthy.

Vitamin K

It is recommended that breast-fed babies are given a second dose of vitamin K at 10 days and a further dose at 6 weeks. This is unnecessary for bottle-fed babies as vitamin K is added to baby milk.

Umbilical cord

During the week to ten days following the birth, the stump of the umbilical cord attached to the baby dries and shrivels. It then drops off to leave the **navel** (belly button).

Before and after thyroxine treatment

THE MOTHER

Besides looking after the baby, the mother also needs to care for herself. The baby needs a healthy, happy mother who:

- has a suitable diet
- does not get over-tired
- does not worry too much about domestic chores
- is able to relax for a while each day
- has the energy to play with and talk to her baby and to take him or her out for outings.

Postnatal exercises

Pregnancy greatly stretches the muscles of the abdomen and afterwards they are very loose and floppy. The muscles of the pelvic floor (muscles that help to hold the bladder, uterus and bowel in place) are also loosened and stretched during delivery. All these muscles will gradually improve and tighten. Special postnatal exercises will help them to regain their shape more quickly.

Postnatal examination

This takes place when the baby is about 6 weeks old and is carried out either at the hospital or by the family doctor. The baby is examined to make sure he or she is healthy and making normal progress. The mother is examined to make sure she is healthy and that the uterus has returned to its normal state.

Re-starting the menstrual cycle

The time at which periods start again varies considerably, and may be six months or longer after the birth if the mother is breast-feeding. It is possible to become pregnant before the periods return. It is also possible to become pregnant while still breast-feeding, although conception is less likely.

Baby blues and postnatal depression

During the week following the birth, commonly between the third and fifth day, it is quite usual for the mother to feel miserable and depressed without knowing why. This period of mild depression is often called the 'baby blues'. Reasons for it include:

1. **Hormones** which controlled pregnancy and childbirth have not yet settled back into their normal pattern of activity and they are making the mother feel 'out of sorts'.
2. Tiredness due to disturbed nights and busy days.
3. Reaction to the excitement of the birth – now it is all over, life seems to be a constant round of feeding, changing nappies and washing.

It helps the mother:

- if she can talk to someone about how she feels
- to know who to ask for advice
- to know that these feelings are quite common in new mothers
- if she can get plenty of rest.

An attack of the 'baby blues' should pass in a few days. If it develops into long-term depression (**postnatal depression**) then this is something rather different and needs the help of a doctor.

THE FATHER

The father can play an important role in supporting the mother in the days immediately following the birth. He may wish to take **paternity leave** (time off from work for fathers of newborn babies). He will then be able to spend more time in helping with the care of the mother and baby, and general household tasks.

CHILD HEALTH CLINICS

These are usually referred to as **baby clinics**. They are run by the local Health Authority or general practitioners (GPs – family doctors) and are held at regular times every week. Parents can please themselves whether they go or not, but clinics do have the following advantages:

- A doctor and health visitor will be present to examine the baby and check that normal progress is being made.
- A record will be kept of the baby's progress and weight.
- Advice can be obtained about any problems such as feeding, weaning and skin rashes (but the family doctor is still the person to consult when the baby is ill).
- Advice is given about immunisation.
- Developmental checks are usually given at about 6 weeks, 8 months, 18 months and 3½ years.
- It is a good place for parents to meet and get to know other parents with children of the same age.
- It may be possible to buy baby foods at a lower price, also second-hand clothes and equipment.

Parent-held records

New parents are given a **Personal Child Health Record** (PCHR) in which they can keep a record of their child's health, growth and development. The parents fill in details about the child (address, name of family doctor, progress etc.). Doctors and other health staff fill in medical details (about immunisation, height and weight records, hearing tests, health problems etc.). The book also contains information and advice which parents could find useful (when to call a doctor, feeding a baby, teeth care etc.).

Questions

1 a Why does a health visitor come to see the mother and baby?

b The health visitor is likely to suggest that the baby is taken to the baby clinic. What are the advantages of going to the clinic?

2 (i) Who carries out an examination of a newborn baby? **(ii)** Who else is also present? **(iii)** What checks are made on the baby? **(iv)** If a dislocated hip is discovered, why is treatment necessary?

3 a (i) Describe a PKU test. **(ii)** How can PKU be treated?

b Why is it important that PKU should be treated?

c Two photographs of the same baby are shown on p. 65. Explain the baby's condition at **(i)** 3 months **(ii)** 6 months.

d Why is a dose of vitamin K recommended for breast-fed babies at ten days old but not for those who are bottle-fed?

4 a Name five ways a mother can help care for herself.

b In what way will the baby benefit from having a healthy, happy mother?

c Which two sets of muscles regain their shape with the help of exercises?

d Give three reasons why a mother may suffer from 'baby blues'.

5 a When does the postnatal check-up take place?

b When will the mother's periods return?

c Is it possible to become pregnant before the periods return?

d Is it possible to become pregnant while still breast-feeding?

6 a By what age does a baby's birth have to be registered?

b What information has to be given to the Registrar of Births?

c Who has parental responsibility for the child?

d What two items will be issued for the baby?

7 a (i) What do the initials PCHR stand for? **(ii)** Who holds this record?

b Give six examples of the type of details the record will include.

8 (i) Who is entitled to parental leave? **(ii)** How long is it? **(iii)** When can it be taken?

Further activities

Investigation

Arrange a visit to a Child Health Clinic. Make a list of all the activities that take place there.

Discussion

In your opinion, what are the points for and against (i) an expectant mother working up to the seventh month of pregnancy; (ii) a mother returning to employment a few months after the birth? Contribute to a class discussion on this topic.

Design

Draw a plan of a room which is to be used as a nursery for a young baby. Mark in the position of the cot and heater. What other equipment and furniture would you have in the room? Give reasons for your decisions.

Weblinks

For information on postnatal care:
www.mothersbliss.com/life/mother.asp
For more information on dads and babies, visit:
www.dad.info
and search for 'newborn babies'.

Exercises

Exercises relevant to Section 2 can be found on p. 381.

SECTION 3

Caring for babies

CHAPTER 15

The new baby

Until two hours ago, the baby on this page had spent all his life inside his mother. She had provided him with food, breathed for him, removed (excreted) his waste products, kept him warm and protected him from damage and disease. Suddenly, at the moment of birth, the baby is on his own. He is now a separate person who can move freely and has to breathe, feed and excrete for himself.

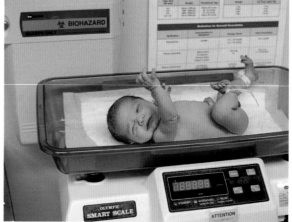

Weighing a newborn baby

SIZE OF A NEWBORN BABY

People who are not used to looking at newborn babies are always surprised at their smallness. Three measurements are taken immediately after birth – weight, length and head circumference. They are used as the starting points for measuring the child's growth.

1. **Weight** – the birth-weight of **full-term** babies (those born at the full term of 38–42 weeks) varies considerably around the average of about 3.5 kg for boys and a little less for girls. Full-term babies may weigh as little as 2.25 kg, or as much as 6.5 kg. (Birth-weight is discussed further on pp. 70–3.) Babies usually lose weight in the first few days of life and do not regain their birthweight until the second week.

Measuring the length of a baby

2. **Length (height)** – the average length of a full-term baby is about 50 cm.
3. **Head circumference** – the average head circumference of a full-term baby is about 35 cm.

Reasons for the variations in size of full-term babies include the following:

Taking a head measurement

░ small parents tend to have smaller babies and large parents tend to have larger babies

- first babies tend to weigh less that brothers and sisters born later
- boys are usually larger than girls.

SHAPE

This drawing shows the shape of a newborn baby. The head is very big compared to other parts of the body. The legs are very short. The abdomen (tummy) is large. A layer of fat under the skin of full-term babies gives the legs, arms and body a plump appearance.

The clamp on the stump of the umbilical cord can be seen. As the stump dries out, it should shrink and drop off within a week to ten days after birth.

When resting on his back, a newborn baby lies with his head to one side. Often, the arm and leg on the face side are out-stretched and the opposite arm and leg are bent. The soles of the feet are turned inwards.

HEAD

Hair
The amount and colour of the hair on the head at birth varies from baby to baby. Often the hair which the baby is born with falls out in a few weeks or months. The new hair which grows to replace it may be a different colour.

Eyes
Most Caucasian (light- or white-skinned) babies have blue or grey eyes at birth. They may stay blue or grey or turn green, hazel, or brown. Babies of African and Asian parentage are usually born with brown eyes that stay brown. Babies of mixed parentage can have a variety of different eye colours.

Soft spot
There is a soft spot, **fontanelle**, on the top of the head where the four pieces of bone which make up that part of the skull have not yet joined together. Parents may notice that the soft spot pulsates (moves up and down) with the beat of the heart. This is normal and is caused by the blood being pumped through the artery underneath. There is no need to worry about touching the soft spot when washing the baby's head. It is covered by a very tough membrane which protects the brain underneath.

SKIN

Vernix
At birth, the baby's body is sometimes covered with a greasy, whitish substance called vernix, which protects the skin while the baby is in the uterus. Most babies are not bathed immediately after birth to protect the skin from infections.

Lanugo

If the baby arrives early, the skin may be covered by a fine layer of hair called lanugo, which is normally shed during the last two weeks in the uterus. It will come off by itself soon after birth.

Milia

Many newborn babies have small, whitish-yellow spots on the face, particularly the nose. They are known as milia or milk spots and are the blocked openings of the oil glands in the skin. They are not harmful and usually disappear by the end of the first week of life.

Jaundice

About half of all newborn babies develop jaundice on the second or third day after birth. The skin and eyes become tinged with yellow and remain yellow for three to four days. It is usually harmless and no treatment is necessary.

Birth marks

There are different kinds of birth mark. Most are harmless, need no treatment, and disappear with time. **Red blotches** on the skin of the upper eyelid, on the middle of the forehead, and on the back of the neck, will disappear in a few years. They are often called **stork bites**. (The old wives' tale is that this is the place where the stork's beak gripped the baby when it was being delivered to the mother.) **Strawberry marks** are another type of birth mark. They appear a few days after birth as bright red raised areas, and may get bigger for up to six months. They gradually fade and are likely to be gone by 5 to 10 years of age.

BIRTHWEIGHT

Babies born at	Average birthweight
28 weeks	1.5 kg
32 weeks	2.0 kg
36 weeks	2.6 kg
40 weeks	3.5 kg

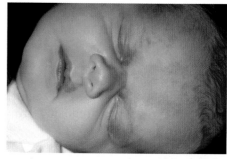
Newborns may have a stork bite birthmark

Low birthweight babies are those who weigh 2.5 kg (2500 g) or less at birth. The reason is likely to be one or more of the following:

- **the baby inherits a small size**, probably because one or both of the parents are small – these babies are perfectly normal
- **the baby is born prematurely** and therefore has not had time in the uterus to grow to full size
- **shortage of food while in the uterus**, which prevents the baby from growing at the normal rate.

Low birthweight babies in the last two groups need special care. They will be weaker and less able to cope with the stress of being born, and then of living an independent existence outside the uterus. These babies may therefore need to be kept for a while in an incubator.

A baby who grows more slowly in the uterus than is normal is said to be '**small for dates**' or '**light for dates**'. This may be due to:

- a multiple birth – twins, triplets
- the mother being poorly fed during pregnancy
- the mother smoking during pregnancy (see pp. 42–3)

- pre-eclampsia (see p. 50)
- the mother regularly drinking alcohol in large quantities
- drug addiction
- a problem with the baby's development in the uterus, e.g. rubella infection or a malfunctioning placenta.

AGE STAGES

When the following terms are used, they usually relate to children of the age range indicated:

- **perinatal** – from about the 28th week of pregnancy to 1 month after birth
- **neonatal** – from birth to 4 weeks
- **infant** – from 4 weeks to 1 year
- **young baby** – the first 6 months
- **older baby** – from 6 months to 1 year
- **toddler** – from 1 year to 2½ years
- **pre-school** – from 2½ to 5 years.

Questions

1 a What does 'full-term' mean?

b For what period of a child's life does the term neonatal apply?

Describe what is meant by the following: (i) fontanelle, (ii) vernix, (iii) lanugo, (iv) milia.

2 a What measurements are taken at birth?

b What are the average measurements of full-term babies?

c What factors may account for the variations in size of full-term babies?

3 Need parents be alarmed if their new baby:

a is covered with a fine layer of hair

b is not bathed immediately after birth

c has red blotches on the skin of the eyelids, forehead or back of the neck

d develops jaundice a day or two after birth

e develops milk spots

f develops a strawberry mark?

Explain why in each case.

4 a What is a 'low birthweight' baby?

b Give three main reasons for low birthweight.

c Give six possible reasons why a baby is 'small for dates'.

Further activities

 Extension

1 Draw a diagram of a newborn baby and describe its shape.

2 Find pictures of newborn babies to accompany your notes. Study them and make a note of any differences between the babies.

3 Use the conversion data below to convert the five metric measurements on p. 70 and the average birthweights on p. 72 into imperial measurements.

1 kilogram (kg) = 2.2046 lb

1 centimetre (cm) = 0.3937 in

 Investigation

Carry out a survey of the birthweights of at least 20 children to find out how closely your results agree with the average birthweights given on p. 72.

 Child study

If possible, ask the parents what the child was like when born and record the information.

Weblink

For a great deal of information on the care of newborn babies search for 'newborn' at:

www.babycentre.co.uk

CHAPTER 16

What a new baby can do

Although basically helpless, newborn babies are able to do many things besides cry. There are times when they sleep and times when they are awake. They can move their arms, legs and head. They can stretch, yawn, hiccup, sneeze and make many other movements. They are also able to receive a certain amount of information from the world around them through their senses – sight, hearing, taste, smell and touch.

A Sucking and swallowing

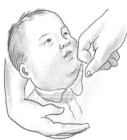

B Rooting

MOVEMENTS

Babies display a number of movements called **reflexes** or **reflex actions**. Movements of this kind are inborn and made automatically without thinking. The diagrams illustrate five reflexes shown by newborn babies.

C Grasping

Sucking reflex (A)
When anything is put in the mouth, the baby immediately sucks. Some babies even make their fingers sore by sucking them while still in the uterus.

Rooting reflex (B)
When gently touched on the cheek, the baby's head turns as if in search of its mother's nipple.

D Walking

Grasp reflex (C)
When an object is put in the baby hand, it is automatically grasped.

Walking reflex (D)
When held upright with the feet touching a hard surface, the baby will make walking movements.

Startle (Moro) reflex (E)

When the baby feels it is falling, the arms are flung back with the hands open, the arms are then together as if to clutch hold of something.

E Startled

Some of these reflexes are necessary for a baby to survive, for example, sucking. Others might have been more useful at an earlier stage of human evolution. For example, it is thought that the grasp reflex dates back millions of years to the time when our ancestors lived in trees. Grasping would have enabled the young animal to cling to its mother's fur or to a branch of a tree.

These reflexes mainly disappear by the age of 3 months and are replaced by actions which the baby has to learn. For example, the walking reflex disappears long before the baby learns to walk.

THE SENSES

Sight

Newborn babies are able to see. Their eyes can focus at a distance of about 20 cm, so they are short-sighted. They see most clearly those things which are near to them, for example, the mother's face when she is holding or feeding her baby. They also notice brightness, e.g. they will look towards a brightly lit window, or shut their eyes when a bright light is suddenly turned on. Sight is discussed in Topic 30.

Hearing

Newborn babies can hear. They respond to sounds by blinking, jerking their limbs, or drawing in breath. They may stop feeding at the sound of a sudden noise. If crying, a baby may become quiet and appear to listen when someone speaks to her, and soon learns to recognise her mother's voice. Hearing is discussed further in Topic 31.

Smell and taste

Babies are sensitive to smell and taste. An unpleasant smell makes a baby turn her head away. The baby will also indicate if she finds a taste pleasant or unpleasant. When near her mother's breast, she smells the milk and may try to get her mouth to it.

Touch

New babies are sensitive to touch and pain and change of position. They will cry if the bath water is too hot or too cold. They will be comforted by contact with another human being, as happens when they are held close and cuddled.

SLEEP

Many newborn babies spend most of their time asleep, waking at intervals to be fed. The amount of sleep varies from baby to baby, and often from day to day. Some sleep 20 out of 24 hours, whilst others spend much more time awake. It is impossible to say how long a baby should sleep at any one time. It could be for five hours, or perhaps only for an hour.

Very young babies cannot help falling off to sleep, and it can be difficult or impossible to wake them. But by 9 months old, sleep has become more of a voluntary process, and they have some control over whether they stay awake or not.

Pattern of sleep

At first, newborn babies do not have a regular pattern of sleep. Gradually, as they become aware of daylight and the sounds of movement around them, sleep starts to fall into a pattern. They begin to sleep less during the day and more at night, although some babies decide that night-time begins at 10 p.m. or later. Many babies are sleeping through the night by the age of 3 months. They will still have one or more naps during the day, and may continue to need sleep in the daytime for several years.

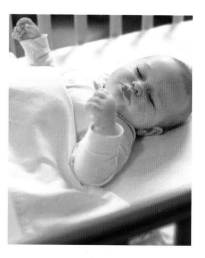

Sleeping position

It is recommended that young babies are placed on their backs for sleeping and with their feet close to the foot of the cot (see p. 116). The sleeping position is only important until babies are able to turn over and move around in the cot. They can then take whichever position they choose.

COT DEATH (SUDDEN INFANT DEATH SYNDROME; SIDS)

Cot death is the sudden and unexpected death of an infant for no apparent reason. Fortunately cot deaths are rare and, since recommendations to reduce the risk in 1991, cot deaths have been reduced by 75 per cent. These recommendations are:

- **Lay babies on their backs to sleep**. Babies put to sleep face downwards are more at risk of cot death. Pillows are not recommended.
- **Place the baby with their feet to the foot of the cot**. The baby cannot then wriggle down under the covers.
- **Keep babies away from tobacco smoke**. Babies whose parents smoke before and after birth are more at risk of cot death.
- **Do not let babies become too hot** with a room temperature that is too high (see p. 76) or too much bedding or clothing. Ensure that the baby's head remains uncovered while sleeping.
- **Breast-feed if possible**, because breast milk contains antibodies which help to protect the baby against infections.
- **Seek medical advice** quickly if the baby seems unwell.

Questions

1 a What is the name given to movements which are inborn and automatic?

  b Name five such movements shown by newborn babies.

2 a Name the five senses.

  b For each of these senses, give an example which indicates that it is already functioning in a newborn baby.

3 a How much time does a newborn baby spend asleep?

  b Does a newborn baby have a regular pattern of sleeping?

  c By what age is a baby likely to (i) be sleeping through the night, (ii) have some control over whether she sleeps or stays awake?

4 a (i) Which is the recommended sleeping position for young babies? (ii) Why should babies not be placed on their fronts for sleeping?

  b What other advice is given to help reduce the risk of cot death?

  c What does the acronym SIDS stand for?

Further activities

 Extension

1 What is a newborn baby able to do? Make a list of as many things as you can think of. Add drawings or photographs to show some of these.

2 A reflex action can be defined as an automatic response to a stimulus. Continue the table below, describing the reflexes mentioned in this topic.

Reflex action	Stimulus (cause of movement)	Response (movement which follows)
Grasp reflex	Something is placed in the hand	It is automatically grasped

 Investigation

Record the sleep patterns of one or more babies and/or young children over several weeks. Present the information as a diagram and compare it to information in another source such as a textbook.

 Child study

Find an opportunity to look at a very young baby. Describe the appearance and movements of the baby. If possible, compare this baby with other babies of about the same age.

CHAPTER 17

The needs of a baby

Every baby has certain needs. Some of these are essential for the baby to survive and to grow and develop physically. Others provide favourable conditions in which the child can thrive emotionally, socially and intellectually. Table 1 lists the needs of a baby and the main chapters of this book in which they are discussed.

Table 1

The needs of a baby	Topic number
Warmth	17
Food	19–21, 52, 55
Shelter	4
Clothing	24
Protection from illness and injury	60, 67–70
Fresh air and sunlight	17
Exercise and rest	16
Love and comfort	34
Continuity of care	17
Security to make the baby feel safe	35
Training in habits and skills	33, 37
Stimulation from play to help in learning	40, 41
Praise and opportunities to develop self-confidence	4

As the child gets older, the needs increase. The additional needs of an older child are given in Table 2.

Table 2

Additional needs of an older child	Topic number
Discipline which is firm but kind	36
Companions to play with	33
The opportunity to gain self-esteem	34
The opportunity to become independent	–
The opportunity to be useful to others	–
The opportunity to be successful in some way	–
The opportunity to take responsibility	–

WARMTH

Normal body temperature of both adults and children can be about 36 to 37 °C (97 to 99 °F). It varies slightly throughout the day, generally being higher in the evening than in the morning. It is also affected by the temperature of the surroundings and by exercise. Crying, too, makes a baby hot and raises the body temperature slightly. The stomach or back are a more reliable guide to the baby's temperature than the hands or feet.

A nursery thermometer enables a quick check of the temperature of the baby's room

While in the uterus, the baby is kept at the right temperature. After birth, the baby is dependent on the parents and carers for protection against becoming too hot or too cold. For the first month of life, babies should be kept in a room temperature of 16–20 °C, day and night; this is a comfortable temperature for a lightly clothed adult. As babies grow larger and stronger, they gradually become more able to keep themselves warm when in a cold place, but the room in which a baby sleeps should continue to be kept about 16–20 °C until the baby is several months old.

Effects of cold

Full-term babies have some protection against losing warmth from the body, as they are born with a layer of fat under the skin. This fat helps to keep the warmth in, and can also be used as fuel to supply extra heat when necessary. However, if babies are kept in a cold place for too long, they lose more heat than they can generate, and will suffer from **hypothermia** (low body heat). This condition may cause a baby to suffer from **cold injury** and can even cause death. The smaller the baby, the more quickly heat will be lost from the body.

Effects of heat

If young babies get too hot, they are not able to move away from the heat or kick off the covers. In a very warm room, or in hot weather, a young baby who is covered by too many clothes or blankets will become very uncomfortable and irritable and may develop a **heat rash** (see p. 300).

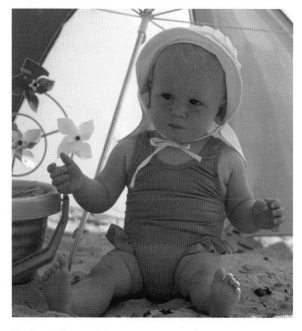

Molly at the seaside

In hot weather, water is lost from the body by sweating. Excessive water loss leads to drying out – **dehydration** – of the body. This dangerous condition is prevented by ensuring that children, particularly babies, take in sufficient water in food and drinks. A very important sign of dehydration is when the soft spot (fontanelle) on the baby's head becomes sunken.

FRESH AIR AND SUNLIGHT

Babies benefit from being out of doors for a while each day, as long as they do not become too hot or too cold. Being in the fresh air helps to make them lively, improves the appetite, puts a healthy colour into the cheeks, and helps them to sleep soundly at night.

Sunlight contains ultraviolet rays which kill many bacteria and also makes the skin produce vitamin D. As these rays cannot pass through glass, children need to be out of doors to benefit in this way.

Too much hot sun can easily burn a baby's delicate skin, and cause overheating. It is therefore best to protect babies and young children from a hot sun by keeping them in the shade. When in direct sunlight, a sun-hat will protect the baby's head, and sun-protection cream should be used on all exposed skin.

Air pollution

Smoke from factories and fumes from vehicles pollute the air and may cause or worsen breathing problems such as asthma. The use of catalytic converters in cars has helped reduce this problem as their purpose is to change harmful exhaust gases into less harmful ones. Now that petrol no longer contains lead, there are no lead particles in vehicles fumes. This has been of particular benefit to young children as they are most at risk from brain damage caused by lead poisoning. Lead is occasionally found in toys made in other countries.

Baby Tina in a busy street

CONTINUITY OF CARE

It is better for a baby to be cared for by a small number of people who are familiar, rather than by strangers. These carers provide a constant centre to the baby's life, giving a sense of **security** – making the baby feel safe. A baby cannot cope with meeting many new people at the same time but needs to get to know them one by one.

The mother is usually the main person who looks after the baby, but the more the father is involved the happier life can be for all. He can help the mother with the continuous and tiring day-and-night care of their new baby. At the same time, he can share the fun and interest of watching the baby develop.

ROUTINE

Most young babies soon fall into a pattern of times for sleeping, being awake, and wanting to be fed. The pattern varies from baby to baby and may change quite often as the baby gets older.

The new mother may sometimes be told that it is important to have a routine – that is, set times for feeding and changing the baby and for bath time, bedtime and so on. This is sound advice if the mother fits the routine around the baby's natural pattern of behaviour. When a mother tries to make her baby feed and sleep at set times, the result can be an irritable and uncooperative baby and an exhausted mother.

When a baby becomes old enough to understand what is wanted, which will probably not be until at least the age of 1 year, then a suitable routine can be very helpful to family life and give the child a sense of security.

Questions

1 a What are the needs of a baby?

  b What additional needs does an older child have?

2 Compare the photographs on pp. 79 and 80:

  a Name five possible advantages to Molly of being in the fresh air and sunshine.

  b (i) What substance is more likely to be in the air being breathed by Tina than by Molly. (ii) Why has the removal of lead from petrol been an advantage to children?

  c If the body temperatures of Molly and Tina were both normal, within what range would you expect them to be?

  d The body temperature of these two babies will vary throughout the day. Name four causes of such variations.

  e How may Molly behave if she gets too hot?

  f What may happen to Tina if she remains outside in the cold for too long?

3 a From the section on p. 80 'Continuity of care', describe a situation which helps to give a baby a sense of security.

  b When does a routine give a baby a sense of security?

Further activities

 Extension

Table 1 on p. 78 lists the needs of a baby. Taking each item in turn, give a reason why it is necessary. Do the same with the list of the additional needs of an older child, Table 2.

 Child study

How many people help to look after the child? How does the child react to them? How does he or she react to strangers?

CHAPTER 18

Crying

All babies cry – it is the only way they have of telling other people that they are hungry, lonely, bored, uncomfortable or in pain. A short cry does not harm a baby, but crying for a longer time is distressing to the baby and may worry the parents.

Babies vary in the amount they cry. Placid ones are often content to wait for quite a long time before crying for attention, whereas others scream the moment they wake up. During the first three months, some babies have a regular time of the day at which they cry, often in the evenings.

It is impossible to teach young babies to be patient by letting them cry for a long while before attending to them. At this stage they are too young to learn, and only become more distressed. During the first few months, parents need not worry about 'spoiling' their baby by picking her up when she cries. An older baby can be 'spoilt' by always getting what she wants the moment she cries for it. The baby will then begin to cry just to get her own way.

Tears are not usually shed until the baby is 3–4 weeks old. Sometimes older babies cry without producing tears and when this happens the baby is really shouting for attention.

WHY BABIES CRY

Although it is not always possible to tell why a baby is crying, parents soon learn that there are a number of reasons:

- **Hunger** – babies vary considerably in the amount of food they need and how often they get hungry. It is usual to feed a baby 'on demand', that is at any time from about two to five hours after the last feed, whenever the baby cries and seems hungry.
- **Thirst** – bottle-fed babies are likely to get more thirsty than those who are breast-fed. In hot weather or a centrally heated house, they may need a drink of water (boiled and then cooled) between feeds.
- **Discomfort** – babies cry when they are uncomfortable, perhaps because of a wet or soiled nappy, or if they are too hot or too cold, or when a bright light is shining in their eyes, or when they have wind or are teething.
- **Pain** – a baby in pain will cry, maybe loudly or just a continuous whimper. When a baby cries for no apparent reason and behaves in an unusual way, a doctor should be consulted.
- **Tiredness** – a tired baby becomes cross and irritable (like an adult) and, in addition, shows her feelings by crying. It may be possible to soothe the baby and rock her to sleep. If left alone to cry, the baby will continue to do so until she falls asleep through exhaustion.

- **Dislike of the dark** – some babies cry when they are put in a room to sleep and the light is turned out. It may help to leave a dim light on, but this should be discontinued when it becomes unnecessary.
- **Loneliness** – a common cause of crying in babies is loneliness. They want to be picked up and cuddled and to feel close to another person. In many cultures, babies are carried in a sling on the back of their mother or elder sister. These babies cry much less than babies who spend a long time on their own in a cot or pram. Baby carriers or slings are becoming increasingly popular.
- **Colic** – an abdominal pain which comes and goes is a common cause of crying in the first three months. It occurs mainly in the evenings. The baby appears to be in pain and screams for up to 20 minutes with her legs drawn up. She then stops and is just about to go off to sleep when another attack occurs. Fortunately, the colic does not seem to do the baby much harm. These crying sessions have usually stopped by the time the baby is 3 months old – to the great relief of the parents.
- **Boredom** – a baby will cry with boredom if she is put in her pram or cot to sleep when she would much rather be watching what is going on in the family, or playing with a toy. The extent to which a baby is liable to suffer from boredom depends on her personality. An alert and interested baby will want to be propped up in the pram, put in a bouncing cradle or carried round more than a placid and contented baby.
- **Noise** – a sudden noise may make a baby cry.

A cotlight may comfort the baby at night

Baby Alice is comforted by closeness to her mother

SOOTHING A BABY

Parents can try to stop their baby from crying by rocking her up and down and making soothing noises in a low tone of voice. Low noises have a more soothing effect than high-pitched sounds. A rhythm of sounds similar to that of the adult heartbeat (about 60 times per minute) has a particularly soothing effect. The repetitive sounds and movements will help to send the baby to sleep. Audio tapes of soft music or 'whooshing' noises (similar to repetitive sounds the baby heard in the uterus) help to soothe some babies.

A bouncing cradle enables the baby to see what's going on

Baby massage

Baby massage is another way of soothing fretful or distressed babies, for example those in pain from colic or when teething. Babies are very aware of being touched, and can be calmed by the gentle, stroking hand movements of parents or carers. Guidance and advice can be obtained from health visitors, and there may also be a baby massage group in your area.

Questions

1 **a** Look at the photograph on p. 83 of baby Alice crying. Why is she crying? Make a list of at least ten suggestions.

  b (i) Will leaving her to cry teach her to be patient? (ii) Why?

  c (i) Will it spoil Alice to pick her up every time she cries? (ii) Might it spoil her when she gets older?

  d What is meant by 'feeding on demand'?

2 **a** Can you see any tears in the photograph?

  b Was Alice able to produce tears at birth?

  c When she gets older and cries without producing tears, what will this tell her parents?

3 Perhaps Alice is crying because she has colic.

  a What is colic?

  b Describe how babies with colic behave.

  c By what age is it usual for 'evening colic' to stop being a problem?

4 **a** Suggest what Alice's mother or father can do to try to soothe her and stop the crying.

  b What helps to send a baby off to sleep?

  c Why can massage help to soothe a baby?

Further activities

 Investigation

1. Spend a weekend helping to care for a real baby or caring for a 'virtual baby' (infant simulator).

  Record:

  * the number of times the baby cries
  * the amount of time spent on each of the activities of feeding, nappy-changing, bathing or comforting
  * the total amount of time per day (24 hours) that the baby required attention.

2. Describe how looking after a baby affects the carer's lifestyle.

 Discussion

How does caring for a baby affect the lifestyle of teenage parents?

 Media search

Carry out a media search to find out what advice is given to parents whose babies cry a great deal. Summarise the information given, saying from which source it was obtained.

 Child study

How often does the child cry? What are the reasons for crying? What will stop the crying?

CHAPTER 19

Feeding a new baby

Sucking comes naturally to babies. If put to the breast immediately after birth, they will usually start to suck.

At this stage there will be no milk but a yellowish liquid called **colostrum**. Besides containing water, colostrum is rich in protein. It also contains **antibodies** to protect the baby against disease. Colostrum continues to be produced in small quantities until, two or three days after the birth, it is replaced by milk. This is the right time for the baby as the appetite develops slowly. Very little food is needed in the first few days and this is supplied by colostrum.

A baby who is to be bottle-fed is usually given a bottle of baby milk soon after birth.

MILK

Milk contains all the necessary food ingredients that a new baby needs. It is about 90 per cent water and 10 per cent food substances: sugar, fat, protein, vitamins and minerals (including salt). The sugar in milk is a type called **lactose** (milk sugar). Lactose is much less sweet than the ordinary type of sugar (**sucrose** – from sugar cane or sugar beet).

BREAST MILK

Breast milk is the natural milk for babies.

- **It contains the right amounts of all the necessary food substances**. As the baby grows, the amounts of the various ingredients alter to meet the changing needs of the baby. This helps the baby to grow at the right pace.
- **It contains antibodies** to help protect the baby against infections.
- **The milk is at the right temperature** – not too hot to burn the baby's mouth, nor too cold to make the baby cold.
- **It is easy for the baby to digest and absorb**.
- **It is clean and safe**. Fully breast-fed babies almost never get gastro-enteritis (sickness and diarrhoea).

A mother breast-feeding her baby provides comfort as well as food

COW'S MILK

Cow's milk is the natural milk for calves but is not suitable for human babies unless specially treated. It differs from human milk in having:

- different types of fat and protein
- more protein
- more salt and other minerals
- less sugar
- antibodies which help to protect a calf against disease but are no use to babies.

Cow's milk is difficult for young babies to digest. Besides having more protein, it also has a much higher amount of a particular protein called **casein**. Casein forms curds in the baby's stomach and is difficult to digest. Little white lumps (curds) of undigested protein may be seen in the baby's stools (faeces).

Fat is present in milk in the form of droplets. Although the fat content of cow's milk and breast milk is about the same, the fat droplets in cow's milk are larger and more difficult to digest.

Cow's milk has a higher salt content. The amount of salt in the body needs to be kept at a more or less constant level and this is normally done by the kidneys. However, the kidneys of a young baby are unable to remove excess salt, so if the baby takes in too much salt he or she will become very ill. This can happen if the baby is fed on undiluted cow's milk or given strong feeds, see p. 95. Salt (sodium chloride) is a compound of two elements – sodium and chlorine. It is the **sodium** which is so dangerous for young babies in large amounts.

BABY MILK (INFANT FORMULA MILK)

Baby milk is made from cow's milk and altered (modified) to make it more like human milk. Additional vitamins and iron are added. Two types of baby milk are 'first milk' and 'follow-on milk'.

First milk
This is a substitute for breast milk and intended as a complete source of nourishment for the first six months of life. First milk suits nearly all babies. If they appear to dislike it, or suffer from constipation, this is most likely to be due to how the bottle of milk was prepared (e.g. with too much milk powder). Changing the baby's milk to a soya-based product should only be done after consulting a doctor, as it can be harmful to some babies, especially when under six months.

A baby held while being bottle-fed also receives comfort

Follow-on milk
This type of milk is recommended for use from 6 months onwards. When weaning starts, milk is still an important item in the diet, even though the baby will be having a variety of other foods. Bottle-fed babies should be given follow-on milk to drink until 12 months of age to prevent any risk of anaemia.

QUESTIONS PARENTS ASK

Is the baby getting enough food?
If the baby is gaining weight satisfactorily, then he is getting enough food.

Are extra vitamins required?

The doctor or health visitor may recommend that babies over 1 month old be given vitamins in the form of vitamin drops or fruit juices.

- **Vitamin drops** contain vitamins A, C and D. They may be recommended for breast-fed babies. Bottle-fed babies normally obtain enough of these vitamins in baby milk.
- **Fruit juice** contains vitamin C. Unsweetened well-diluted orange juice, apple juice and blackcurrant juice are suitable for babies. Fruit juices and squashes that contain additives (sweetners and colourings) should not be given to babies.

Are extra minerals required?

Milk contains all the minerals a baby needs for the first few months of life. Although milk is low in iron, a baby is born with several months' supply stored in the liver.

When can cow's milk be introduced?

Cow's milk should not replace baby milk or breast milk until the age of 12 months, but it can be introduced in small quantities (e.g. on breakfast cereals, in sauces and custards) from 6 months. Milk used should be pasteurised whole (not skimmed) milk.

Is extra water needed?

Breast milk contains all the water a baby needs. Unless the weather is extremely hot, and provided the baby is allowed to feed as often as he wants, there should be no need to give extra water between the feeds. Giving water between feeds may cause the baby to suck less well on the breast and therefore to receive less food. In the case of bottle-fed babies, the baby can be given water between feeds. All water given to young babies should first be boiled.

Questions

1 a Name the main substance in milk.

   b Name five other substances in milk.

2 Comparison of breast milk and cow's milk (grams per 100 ml):

	Sugar	Fat	Protein	Minerals	Water
Breast milk	7	4	1.2	0.4	90
Cow's milk	4.7	4	3.3	0.75	88

   a (i) Which type of milk is sweeter? (ii) How does milk sugar differ in taste from ordinary sugar?

   b (i) Is the fat content the same for both milks? (ii) Why is the fat in cow's milk less easy for a young baby to digest?

   c (i) Which type of milk has the most protein? (ii) Why is the protein in cow's milk less suitable for young babies?

   d (i) Which type of milk has a higher mineral content? (ii) Which particular mineral can be dangerous for young babies in large amounts?

   e (i) What is baby milk? (ii) Give the two main types of baby milk and say for what age group each is intended.

3 Give five reasons why breast milk is the natural milk for babies.

4 When a baby is held close while being fed, what else is being provided besides food?

5 a How does a mother know if her baby is getting enough food?

   b Should babies be given water between feeds if they are (i) breast-fed (ii) bottle-fed?

   c Milk has a low iron content; does a baby need to be given iron or other minerals?

   d Which vitamins are contained in vitamin drops?

   e What types of fruit juice should not be given to babies?

   f At what age can cow's milk replace baby milk or breast milk?

Further activities

 Discussion

What extra problems are involved in feeding twins? How may these problems be overcome? Is it possible for a mother to breast-feed both babies?

 Investigation

Note the contents of two or more different brands of baby milk. Compare them, and also compare them with breast milk and cow's milk (see question 2).

CHAPTER 20

Breast-feeding

Breast-feeding is the natural way to feed a baby. Early on in pregnancy, the breasts enlarge and start to prepare for the job of supplying the baby with milk. In the last 12 weeks or so of pregnancy they may secrete colostrum. When colostrum is first secreted it is clear and colourless; later on it becomes a yellow colour.

The baby's birth is the signal for the breasts to begin producing milk and two or three days later it starts to flow. Breast milk tends to look watery and bluish at the beginning of a feed and creamy towards the end.

HOW MANY FEEDS A DAY?

Babies should be put to the breast regularly in the first few days. They will not need or get much food, but they will enjoy sucking.

Between the third and the sixth day, babies become much more hungry and may want to be fed ten or twelve times a day (a day being 24 hours). This may be inconvenient for the mother, but it helps to establish a good supply of milk – because the more the baby sucks, the more the breasts are stimulated to produce milk.

Frequent 'demand-feeding' may continue for several weeks. After that, babies settle down to a pattern, which varies from baby to baby, but most will want to be fed about six times a day with the intervals varying from three to five hours. Gradually the interval between feeds in the night gets longer until the night feed is given up altogether. This may have happened by the time the baby is 3 months old but some babies take longer.

Breast milk contains traces of the food and drink taken by the mother. Babies are thought to enjoy the variation in the flavour of the milk caused by the day-to-day changes in the mother's diet. Occasionally, the milk may unsettle the baby if, for example, the mother's diet contains too much fruit or there is a certain item that irritates the baby's digestive system.

STRUCTURE OF THE BREASTS

Each breast contains about 20 sections (lobes) in which milk is produced from milk glands. Each section has a duct which opens on the surface of the nipple; the milk therefore comes from about 20 tiny openings. The dark area around the nipple is called the **areola**.

The size of the breasts before pregnancy depends on the amount of fat tissue and not the number of milk-producing glands. So women with naturally small breasts will be able to breast-feed just as well as those with larger breasts.

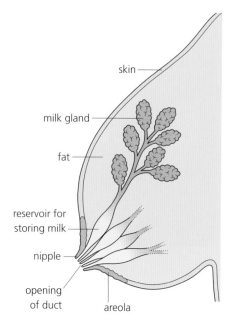

ADVANTAGES OF BREAST-FEEDING

1. It is **safe**.
2. It is **easy** for most mothers – there are no bottles to sterilise, or feeds to mix and get to the right temperature.
3. Breast milk **very rarely causes indigestion**.
4. Breast milk **contains antibodies**. In the first few months of life, and especially when newborn, babies do not have very much resistance to infections such as coughs, colds and diarrhoea. They are likely to become more ill at this age than when older, and complications are more likely to follow. Compared with bottle-fed babies, breast-fed babies get fewer infections, are less prone to severe infections, and almost never get gastro-enteritis.
5. The baby **is less likely to become overweight**.
6. The baby **is less likely to be constipated**.
7. The baby **is less likely to develop nappy rash**.
8. The baby **is less likely to develop allergies such as asthma and eczema**.
9. It is **cheaper**.
10. Breast-feeding gives time for a **bond of attachment** to develop between mother and baby. A mother who breast-feeds spends a long time each day in very close contact with her baby. This gives the opportunity for a close and loving relationship to develop between them which is very important for the future wellbeing of the child.

Benefits for the mother

Besides giving the child a good start in life, breast-feeding also benefits the mother. Her uterus will shrink back to size more quickly. Her periods will take longer to return, so she may be more relaxed and contented for not being bothered by the irritable feelings often linked with menstruation. A mother who enjoys breast-feeding feels especially close to her baby. It also reduces the risk of breast and ovarian cancer.

HOW LONG SHOULD BREAST-FEEDING CONTINUE?

Many doctors advise mothers to try to breast-feed at least for the first two weeks, and ideally for six months. In the latter case, the babies are then at the right age to be weaned gradually from breast milk to a mixture of other foods. As the amount of nourishment from other foods increases, the need for breast milk decreases. Breast-feeds become fewer and smaller until either the supply of milk fails or the baby refuses to feed from the breast any more. Some mothers continue to breast-feed for a year or longer, perhaps for only one feed a day with older babies.

A baby who is fed entirely on milk beyond the age of about 6 months may find it difficult to take to new foods. If weaning (p. 268) has not started before 9 to 10 months, there is a danger of anaemia due to the shortage of iron in breast milk. The baby is born with a store of iron in the liver, which is gradually used up as the baby grows.

REASONS FOR NOT BREAST-FEEDING

A few mothers do not have enough milk to breast-feed and a few more are unable to breast-feed for medical reasons. But although nearly all mothers are able to breast-feed their babies, many choose to bottle-feed. Those who could breast-feed, but decide not to do so, give reasons which include:

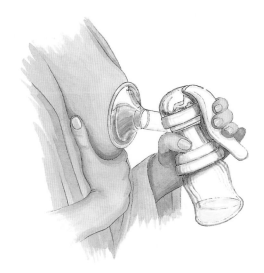

Hand-operated breast-pump

- *'Breast-feeding will spoil my figure'*
- Breast-feeding helps a mother to regain her pre-pregnancy shape more quickly as fat stored in the body during pregnancy can be used to produce breast milk.

- *'My baby may not get enough milk'*
- Regular weighing of the baby will show whether the baby is getting enough milk.

- *'I feel embarrassed about feeding my baby on the breast'*
- It may help to overcome embarrassment to realise that breast-feeding is nature's way to feed a baby. When the right clothing is worn, it can be done discretely. Many shops and public buildings now provide breast-feeding facilities.

- *'It is impossible to breast-feed if I need to go out for long intervals in order to go to work'*
- A compromise would be for the mother to breast-feed for the first few weeks, then change to bottle-feeding when she needs more freedom. Some mothers overcome the problem by using a breast pump to express their milk into bottles. A baby-minder can then give the breast milk to the baby while the mother is at work.

Questions

1 It is usual for a mother to start breast-feeding her baby within a few hours of birth. At this stage there is no milk but a yellowish liquid.

   a Name this liquid.

   b Name three substances which the liquid contains (see previous topic).

   c When do the breasts begin to produce milk?

   d What helps to establish a good supply of milk?

   e Between 3 and 6 days old, how often may a baby want to be fed?

   f About how many times a day will the baby want to be fed when he settles down into a pattern?

   g Why does a breast-feeding mother need to be aware of her diet?

2 a Draw a diagram to show the structure of the breast.

   b Whereabouts in the breast is the milk produced?

   c Does milk leave the breast from one opening or many?

   d Before pregnancy, what does the size of the breasts depend on?

Questions (continued)

3 Give ten advantages of breast-feeding.

4 a Give ways in which a mother can benefit from breast-feeding.

  b What is considered to be an ideal length of time for a baby to be breast-fed?

  c Name two possible effects of breast-feeding for a longer time.

Further activities

 Extension

What reasons do mothers give for deciding not to breast-feed? Suggest a solution in each case.

 Investigation

Carry out a survey to find out what proportion of children were breast-fed and for how long. Present your findings in either a pie chart or a bar chart.

 Child study

Find out if the child is/was breast-fed or bottle-fed. If the mother had any problems with feeding, how did she overcome them?

Weblink

For more information on breastfeeding, visit:
www.mothersbliss.com/life/breast.asp

CHAPTER 21

Bottle-feeding

Not all mothers wish to breast-feed their babies and in a few cases they are unable to do so no matter how hard they try. The babies will then be bottle-fed. Babies will also need to be bottle-fed if a mother returns to work and the baby is being looked after by a carer. If properly bottle-fed, there is no reason why the babies should not thrive, grow and develop in the same way as breast-fed babies.

ESSENTIAL RULES OF BOTTLE-FEEDING

1. Use the right type of milk for a young baby.
2. Keep every piece of equipment scrupulously clean.
3. Follow the instructions on the container for making up the feed.
4. Give the baby similar cuddling and attention to that which he would receive in breast-feeding.

ADVANTAGES OF BOTTLE-FEEDING

Bottle-feeding has some advantages over breast-feeding:

- The mother knows how much milk the baby is taking.
- The baby can be fed anywhere. This is an advantage to mothers who would be embarrassed to breast-feed in public.
- Other people are able to feed the baby besides the mother. When the father takes a turn in giving the feed, it provides him with an opportunity to cuddle and bond with his baby.
- When the mother does not have to be present at feeding times, it means that she can return to work before the baby has been weaned.

EQUIPMENT FOR BOTTLE-FEEDING

Feeding bottle

A suitable feeding bottle is one which has the features shown in the diagram.

a wide neck for easy cleaning

made of clear material — to check that it is clean inside

graduated measurements on the side — in millilitres or fluid ounces

a cap to keep the teat clean

designed so that the teat can be placed upside down in the bottle for storage or travelling

sealing disc placed in the bottle to prevent spillage of milk

A   B

Teat

The most important thing about the teat is the size of the hole. A hole of the right size allows the milk to drip out rapidly without having to shake or squeeze the bottle. The hole readily becomes blocked by dried milk and should be tested before every feed.

When the hole is too large, it may cause the baby to choke as he tries to swallow the milk. When the hole is too small, the baby will suck so hard and for so long that a great deal of air will be swallowed. The baby will then have trouble with wind.

C

CLEANING AND STERILISING

Equipment used for bottle-feeding must be sterile to prevent germs getting into the milk and then into the baby. It can be sterilised in various ways, but first it must be cleaned.

1. Wash your hands thoroughly.
2. Clean the bottle, the teat and the cap using hot water, detergent and a bottle brush. Special care should be taken to ensure that the teat is cleaned well. A 'teat cleaner' can be used. Rinse off the detergent. Bottles and teats are easier to clean if they have been rinsed out with cold water immediately after use.
3. Sterilise the equipment in one of the following ways:
   - **Chemical sterilisation** – place in a sterilising solution and leave for at least 30 minutes. Make sure that everything is completely covered by the solution and that there are no air bubbles. Metal spoons or other metal objects should not be put in the sterilising solution because they will corrode. Fresh solution needs to be made up every day.
   - **Steam sterilising** – using a steamer specially designed for bottle-feeding equipment.
   - In a microwave oven, by creating steam in a **microwave steriliser**.
   - By **boiling** for at least 10 minutes. This is not recommended as regular treatment for plastic bottles. They soon become rough and cloudy and may crack, and the teats become sticky.
4. Wash your hands again. Remove the bottle and teat from the steriliser. Make up milk in the bottle, put the teat on, and protect with the cap.

Bottle brush

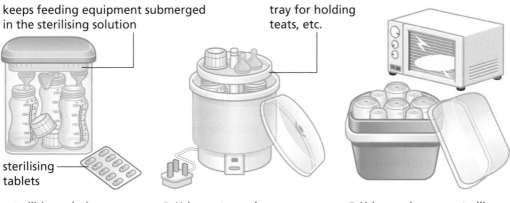

keeps feeding equipment submerged in the sterilising solution

tray for holding teats, etc.

sterilising tablets

A Using sterilising solution

B Using a steam cleaner

C Using a microwave steriliser

PREPARING FEEDS

Follow the instructions on the container. Tins of baby milk carry detailed instructions on how to mix the feeds – and they should be followed exactly. The amount of milk powder and water has been carefully worked out to make the feed just right for the baby. Even if the milk seems tasteless to you, do not add extra sugar and **never** add salt.

The water used for making the feeds must be boiled and then cooled to the temperature recommended in the instructions. Too much water will make a poor feed. Too little water will make the feed too strong. It is important to measure the necessary amount of boiled water into the bottle before adding the milk powder, not to put the powder in first.

Measuring milk powder

The scoop provided with the milk powder is an accurate measure when used correctly. To obtain the exact quantity, fill the scoop, then gently level off the powder with the back of a plastic knife. Do not pack the powder down, or heap it up.

Harmful effects of making the feed too strong

When using milk powder there may be a tendency to think that it is 'good for the baby' to add more powder than the instructions say. This results in a strong feed which contains too much protein and salt. A baby who is given a strong feed is likely to become thirsty and cry. The baby may then be given another feed instead of boiled water because the mother thinks that he is still hungry. If this happens often, the baby may become too fat. A worse danger is that the extra salt in strong feeds may make the baby very ill, possibly causing convulsions, coma and permanent brain damage.

GIVING A BOTTLE

When giving a bottle feed:

1. Make sure that the milk is at a suitable temperature for the baby. If the milk has come out of the fridge, it will need to be warmed up before being given to the baby. This can be done by placing the bottle in a jug of hot water or in an electric bottle warmer. To check that the milk is not too hot, sprinkle a few drops onto your wrist.

2. Check that the hole in the teat is not blocked.
3. Hold the baby in a comfortable position. Tilt the bottle so that the teat is kept full of milk, otherwise the baby will suck in air as well as milk.
4. From time to time, remove the teat from the baby's mouth to let air get into the bottle, otherwise a vacuum is created. When this happens the teat goes flat and no milk can pass through. If the baby continues to suck on a flattened teat he will take in air – and this will result in wind.
5. After a feed, help the baby to bring up any wind.

WIND

'**Wind**' is air which has been swallowed. All babies suck in air when feeding. An air bubble which forms in the stomach may cause the baby to cry with discomfort until it has been brought up.

Electric bottle warmer

When a baby takes too long on a feed, air will be swallowed instead of milk. If being bottle-fed, the baby may take in air because the hole in the teat is too small, or if breast-fed, because there is too little milk present.

Bringing up wind (burping the baby)

When breast- or bottle-feeding, it is usual to give the baby the chance to bring up wind. Whether this is done once or twice during the feed, or at the end, depends on what seems to suit the baby. There is no good reason for interrupting the feed while the baby continues to suck happily. Babies do not need to 'burp' with every feed – it depends on how much air they swallow.

Helping the baby to bring up wind

The wind can escape more easily when the baby is held against the shoulder (a cloth on the shoulder helps to catch any milk which comes up with the wind). Gently patting the baby's back may help. Some mothers prefer to use one hand to hold the baby in a sitting position and leaning slightly forwards, the other hand gently rubs the baby's back.

Normally wind is brought up without much trouble. If the baby cries a great deal after a meal, it is likely to be due to reasons other than discomfort from wind, for example for any of the reasons mentioned on pp. 82–3.

An alternative way of helping to bring up wind

GIVING THE BABY PLENTY OF CUDDLING AND ATTENTION

When a mother holds her baby close to her and talks and smiles at him as she feeds him from the bottle, she can feel just as loving towards her baby as a mother who breast-feeds.

Care needs to be taken to give bottle-fed babies the same amount of time to develop a bond of attachment with the mother as when breast-feeding. This will not happen if a variety of people hold the baby when he is being fed, or if the bottle is propped up so that the baby feeds himself.

The mother will feel more comfortable if she chooses a chair which supports her back and arms. If she also takes the opportunity to relax as she feeds, she will enjoy the contact with her baby as much as the baby enjoys being held close and fed.

If the baby is left to feed himself:

- there is a danger the baby might choke
- the baby is deprived of the comfort of being held close and of feeling loved and wanted
- there is no one to notice that the baby is taking in air by sucking on a flattened teat or an empty bottle
- there will be no one to help the baby bring up wind.

GASTRO-ENTERITIS

Gastro-enteritis is inflammation of the stomach and intestines. Illness of this type is rare in breast-fed babies but far too common in those who are bottle-fed. Many cases of this illness could be prevented with better hygiene, particularly when preparing bottles or dealing with nappies.

Germs which cause gastro-enteritis live in the bowel and also thrive in warm, moist food. These germs can be given accidentally to the baby when:

- the equipment used for bottle-feeding is not sterilised properly
- the water used to mix with the milk powder is unboiled
- the feed is stored in a warm place before being given to the baby
- dirty hands contaminate the teat or milk.

The symptoms of gastro-enteritis are vomiting, diarrhoea and abdominal pain, and their effect is that the baby loses too much water from the body too quickly. The body cannot function properly when it is **dehydrated** (short of water). Babies who show indications of possible dehydration – the soft spot on the baby's head is sunken, the eyes look glazed and sunken and the mouth is dry – need urgent medical attention.

Questions

1 a Suggest four advantages of bottle-feeding over breast-feeding.
  b Give four essential rules to follow when bottle-feeding.
2 a What features would you expect a suitable feeding bottle to have?
  b Why does the hole in the teat need to be the right size?
  c What test can be done to find out if the hole in the teat is the right size?
  d Describe how to sterilise feeding bottles.
3 a How should the scoop be used to obtain the correct amount of milk powder?
  b Name two substances which should not be added to a milk feed.
  c Why is a strong feed likely to make a baby thirsty?
  d What should a thirsty baby be given?
  e What is the danger of giving a baby too much salt?
4 a Describe how to give a bottle-feed.
  b Describe, in words or pictures, two ways to 'wind' a baby.

Questions (continued)

5 a Name four disadvantages of leaving a baby to feed himself from a bottle.

 b Give one reason why a baby might swallow air instead of milk while (i) breast-feeding, (ii) bottle-feeding.

6 a What are the symptoms of gastro-enteritis?

 b Why is this a dangerous illness in babies?

 c Are babies who suffer from gastro-enteritis likely to be breast- or bottle-fed?

 d Name four ways in which gastro-enteritis germs can be given to a baby.

Further activities

 Discussion

Should a mother who does not breast-feed her baby feel guilty?

Weblinks

For a good introduction to bottle-feeding, visit: www.nhs.uk and search for 'bottle-feeding'.

For more information on formula feeding, visit: www.babycentre.co.uk

CHAPTER 22

Keeping a baby clean

It is almost impossible to keep a baby spotlessly clean all the time, nor indeed is it necessary. After a feed, babies often bring up a little milk (a posset). They frequently wet and soil their nappies. When they start to feed themselves they make a great deal of mess. This is all part of babyhood, and parents would be far too busy if they changed the baby's clothes every time they were a little soiled. There is evidence that keeping a baby too clean can prevent the baby from coming into contact with enough germs to build up immunity against disease.

The aim of parents and carers should be to keep the baby's skin, feeding bottles, clothes, bedding and other equipment sufficiently clean so as not to become a breeding ground for germs. Some of the germs which can harm a baby live in the bowel and are present in the stools. Other types of germs grow and multiply in urine. They can also thrive in milk and other foods.

PROTECTION BY CLEANLINESS

The parents and carers can protect the baby against germs by:

- keeping their own hands and nails clean – hands should be washed after visiting the toilet, changing a nappy, and before giving a feed
- careful disposal of disposable nappies
- washing terry nappies thoroughly
- regularly washing clothes and bedding
- regularly cleaning nursery equipment and toys
- not giving the baby stale food, or food which has been kept in a warm place for several hours.

CHANGING THE NAPPY

The nappy will need to be changed several times a day. Points to note are:

- The job can be done more quickly when the equipment needed is collected together first.
- The job is easier when the baby is placed on a flat surface rather than the lap – both hands are then free for nappy changing. The safest place to change the nappy is on the floor.
- Placing the baby on a changing mat or plastic sheet helps to prevent dirtying objects underneath.
- There is no need to wash the baby's bottom every time a wet nappy is removed, although wiping with wet cotton wool or a 'baby wipe' will help to prevent nappy rash. 'Baby wipes' are ready-moistened with a special solution which neutralises the ammonia from urine.

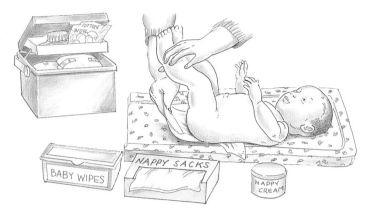

- When the nappy has been soiled, any solid matter on the baby's skin should be gently removed with cotton wool or tissues. (When the baby gets older, a corner of the nappy can be used.) The skin can then be cleaned with cotton wool and warm water, or with baby wipes.
- Make sure the skin is dry. A little 'nappy cream' may then be smoothed over the skin before the clean nappy is put on. The cream may be zinc and castor oil cream, or another type of cream, lotion or

This type of changing mat with PVC coating is an ideal surface to clean and change a baby

oil made for the purpose. It helps to prevent nappy rash by forming a protective layer over the surface of the skin. Cream does not need to be used at every nappy change.

DISPOSAL OF DISPOSABLE NAPPIES

Cotton wool, wipes or tissues which have been used to clean the baby's skin can be placed inside the used nappy. This is then rolled up and taped into a 'parcel' and disposed of. Special deodorising 'nappy sacks' can be bought to wrap the dirty nappy in; these are particularly useful if away from home.

CARE OF RE-USABLE NAPPIES

Re-usable nappies need to be kept clean and free from germs. After being removed from the baby, it is usual for them to be stored in a bucket with a lid while waiting to be washed. This keeps in smells and keeps out flies.

1. **Remove any solid matter** from nappies before placing in the bucket. One way of doing this is to hold the nappy under the flushing water in the lavatory. This may be unnecessary if a nappy liner has been used; remove the nappy liner and flush it away.
2. **Wash nappies** in hot water with soap or mild detergent. The water should be at least 60°C. Boiling helps to whiten nappies, but it is not necessary every time they are washed. 'Biological' detergents should be avoided as they may irritate the baby's skin.

Nappy bucket

3. **Rinse thoroughly**. All traces of soap or detergent should be removed by rinsing in several changes of clean water. Nappy softener can be added to the last rinsing water, but this is unnecessary unless the nappies have become hard, as it makes the nappies less absorbent and may irritate the baby's skin.
4. **Dry**. Drying outside in the open air helps to keep nappies soft. Sunlight whitens them and also helps to destroy germs. Drying nappies on radiators or hot pipes makes them stiff.

NAPPY RASH (AMMONIA DERMATITIS)

All babies will get nappy rash from time to time. The first sign is when the skin becomes red and sore in the nappy area. If the rash is not promptly treated, the skin becomes rough and septic spots may appear.

Nappy rash is caused by ammonia, and a strong smell of ammonia may be noticed when the nappy is changed. The ammonia is produced from urine when the urine comes into contact with bacteria in the stools (faeces). The same type of germs may also be present in a nappy which has not been properly washed. The longer the baby lies in a wet, dirty nappy the more time there will be for the germs to produce ammonia. The ammonia irritates the skin and a rash appears.

Breast-fed babies are less likely to suffer from nappy rash because their stools are more acidic. The acid discourages the activity of the germs which produce ammonia.

Prevention of nappy rash

Nappy rash cannot always be avoided, but much can be done to prevent it. The rules to observe are:

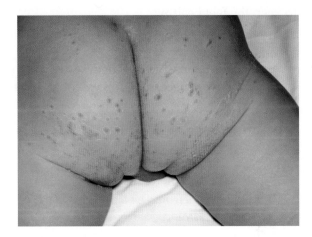
Nappy rash

- do not let a wet, dirty nappy remain on the baby for longer than is necessary
- apply a protective layer of a suitable cream or lotion to the baby's bottom
- leave off the nappy whenever possible
- wash cotton nappies thoroughly after they are removed from the baby
- use 'one-way' liners
- do not use tightly fitting plastic pants more than is necessary – they keep warmth and moisture in and encourage nappy rash.

Treatment of nappy rash

When a baby develops nappy rash, the bottom needs to be kept as clean and dry as possible to allow the skin to recover. It is best to leave the nappy off altogether, but this is not always practical. Alternatively:

- leave the nappy off as often as possible
- use only sterilised nappies
- change the nappy as soon as it becomes wet or soiled during the daytime
- change the nappy at least once during the night
- use nappy liners
- do not use plastic pants
- apply cream every time the nappy is changed
- seek medical advice if the rash becomes wet and oozing.

OTHER CAUSES OF SORENESS

A baby's skin is very delicate and it is quite common for the bottom to become sore, however well the baby is cared for. There are a number of causes besides nappy rash. For example, a rash similar to nappy rash can develop if the soap, detergent or sterilising solution is not removed from the nappies by thorough rinsing. Nappy softener and other fabric conditioners have also been known to be the cause of such a rash.

Soreness around the anus is caused by the skin being in contact with the wet stools. It is common in very young babies and at times of diarrhoea when older. The chances of it happening are increased by not changing the nappy frequently. For treatment follow the guidelines for nappy rash.

THE NOSE

It is necessary to wipe a baby's nose to prevent soreness or blockage of the nostrils. By the age of 2 years, children should be able to do this for themselves. It is often very difficult to get them to blow the nose, but it is a useful skill for them to learn before starting school.

THE FEET

To keep the feet healthy:

- dry thoroughly between the toes after washing
- put on clean socks every day
- cut toenails regularly – cut them straight across, but not too short nor down into the corners
- when shoes are necessary, it is essential that they should fit well (see pp. 246–7).

Questions

1 a Name six ways in which cleanliness by parents helps to protect their baby.

   b Explain why there may be a danger in keeping a baby too clean.

2 Give one reason for doing each of the following when changing a baby's nappy:

   a collecting the equipment needed first

   b placing the baby on a flat surface

   c using a changing mat

   d using cream.

3 Describe how to:

   (i) dispose of disposable nappies

   (ii) wash nappies.

4 a What is ammonia dermatitis?

   b Where does the ammonia come from?

   c Name two places where germs which cause nappy rash may be found.

   d Describe what nappy rash looks like.

   e Give six rules that help to prevent nappy rash.

   f Give eight suggestions for the treatment of nappy rash.

5 Name other causes of a sore bottom apart from nappy rash. What treatment would you recommend in each case?

6 a Give two reasons for wiping a baby's nose.

   b By what age should children be able to wipe their own noses?

   c How can feet be kept healthy?

Further activities

 Investigation

1 Compare the information which accompanies two brands of nappy steriliser. List the similarities and the differences.

2 a Devise experiments to find out (i) which of at least three brands of disposable nappy is able to absorb most liquid, (ii) whether a terry nappy or a disposable nappy can absorb the most liquid, (iii) the effect of a nappy liner.

   b Carry out the experiments and use the numerical data collected to support your findings.

Weblink

For an interesting discussion of whether society is too concerned with hygiene, and if this could be damaging children's health, go to askbaby.com and search for 'how clean is too clean':

www.askbaby.com

CHAPTER 23

Bathtime

When babies get used to the idea, they enjoy being bathed and this makes bathtime fun. Some parents prefer to give an evening bath as they find the activities of bathtime help the baby to sleep more soundly. Others find it more convenient to bath the baby in the morning. It does not matter which.

PREPARATIONS FOR BATHTIME

A warm room

Young babies lose body heat very quickly and easily become chilled. Therefore it is important that the room in which the baby is to be bathed is draught-free and warm – at least 20 °C.

Warm water

The bath water should be warm but not hot – about body temperature, i.e. about 37 °C. A bath thermometer is useful for taking the temperature of the water. If this is not available, the water can be tested by using the elbow – the elbow is more sensitive to heat than the hands. Another thing to remember is always to put the cold water in the bath before the hot water, because if hot water goes in first, the bottom of the bath may be too hot for the baby.

Equipment

Before putting the baby in the bath collect everything needed for washing, drying and dressing the baby. Place them where they can be reached easily.

Bathtime equipment

BATHTIME ROUTINE

The following routine, or one very similar, is often recommended for bathing young babies.

1. Collect everything needed for washing, drying and dressing the baby and make sure the room is warm.
2. After washing your hands, undress the baby apart from the nappy and wrap her in a warm towel (**A**).
3. Test the temperature of the bath water with a bath thermometer or your elbow to check that it warm but not hot (**B**).
4. Gently wash the baby's face with wet cotton wool. Soap should not be used. The eyes should only be cleaned if infected or sticky. If it is necessary, wipe each eye from the inside corner outwards, using a clean piece of damp cotton wool for each eye.
5. Wash the scalp with water (**C**). Soap or shampoo only needs to be used once or twice a week. The hair must then be well rinsed, using a jug of clean, warm water for the final rinse.
6. Take off the nappy and clean the bottom with wet cotton wool (**D**). Do not try to force back (retract) the foreskin of a little boy's penis. This action is likely to tear the foreskin and make it bleed. The foreskin will gradually become able to retract, usually completely so by the age of 3 years. Wipe the bottom of girls from front to back to avoid spreading germs from the bottom to the vagina.
7. Add some baby bath lotion (liquid soap) to the water before placing the baby in the bath. The baby needs to be held securely (**E**): note how one of the mother's hands holds the baby's shoulder, while the baby's head rests on her arm. This allows the baby to enjoy splashing and kicking.
8. Lift the baby out and wrap in a towel. Dry by patting gently (**F**) not by rubbing. Pay particular attention to the creases of the neck, the back of the ears, the armpits, groin, back of the knees and in between the toes. If the creases are not dried, they easily become sore. When turning the baby over to dry the back, the safest way is to turn the baby towards rather than away from you.
9. Apply nappy cream to the bottom and into creases in the skin to prevent soreness.

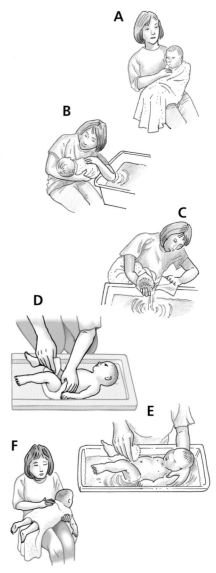

Bathtime routine

Cleaning the ears

Wax can be cleaned away from the end of the ear canal (ear hole), but the inside of the canal should never be cleaned. The wax is there for protection. Cotton wool buds can be useful for cleaning outside and behind the ears, but should never be poked inside. Anything which is poked into the ear canal may damage the ear drum.

Cradle cap

This is the name given to the greasy scales or crusts which form on the scalp of many young babies. It first appears around 4 weeks of age and usually clears up by itself after about 6 months. It is harmless. If it is considered to be unsightly, it can be removed by the use of a special cream made for the purpose.

Cutting the nails

The fingernails of very young babies grow quickly and need to be cut every few days. This is best done while the baby is asleep. If the nails are left to grow too long, the baby will scratch herself. With an older baby, the nails can be cut immediately after a bath and, because they are softer, it is easier.

Rounded ends for safety

'TOPPING AND TAILING'

It is not necessary to bath the baby every day as long as the face, hands and bottom are kept clean by 'topping and tailing':

1. Clean the baby's face and hands with warm water and cotton wool, and then dry.
2. Clean the bottom using warm water with a little 'baby bath', baby lotion or soap and more cotton wool. Dry and then apply a nappy cream.

OLDER BABIES

When a baby is bathed in the family bath it is desirable to put a non-slip mat on the bottom of the bath. **Never leave the baby unattended** for a moment, even if she can sit steadily. Babies can drown in a few centimetres of water.

Toys such as plastic cups will make bathtime fun for an older baby

Questions

1 a (i) What is a suitable room temperature for bathing a baby? (ii) Why does the room need to be at this temperature?

  b (i) What is a suitable temperature for the bath water? (ii) Give two ways of testing the temperature.

  c Why should cold water be put into the bath before hot water?

2 List the items in the drawing on p. 103 which have been collected together in preparation for bathtime.

3 When bathing a young baby:

  a (i) Do the eyes need to be cleaned? (ii) If so, how?

  b Should soap be put on the face?

  c How often does shampoo need to be used on the scalp?

  d Why should a boy's foreskin not be forced back?

Questions (continued)

   e When a baby being held on the knees is turned over, in which direction is it safest to turn her?

   f How should a baby be held when in the bath?

   g Why should the creases in the skin be thoroughly dried?

4 a Why is it dangerous to poke anything into the ear canal?

   b What is cradle cap and how can it be removed?

   c Is it necessary to bath a baby every day?

   d Describe how to 'top and tail' a baby.

Further activities

 Extension

1 Describe the bathtime routine using illustrations and/or words.

2 Use a life-size doll to practise bathing a baby.

 Child study

Help to bath the child. Describe the bathtime routine and the child's behaviour when being bathed.

Weblinks

Two websites that show how to bath a baby as a video clip are:

www.howto.tv

www.newdadssurvivalguide.com

Search for 'bathing a baby'.

CHAPTER 24

Baby's first clothes

The baby's first set of clothes may be referred to as the layette. A new baby does not need many clothes, just enough to keep warm, but they will need to be washed frequently. In addition to nappies, the items shown in the photograph should be sufficient.

Expectant mothers often enjoy collecting items for the new baby. They may be tempted by pretty or attractive clothing. This may give the mothers pleasure, but it is not of importance to their babies. The requirements of the babies are rather different.

Layette

Requirements for baby clothes
Baby clothes should be:

- loose and comfortable
- easy to put on and take off
- easy to wash and dry
- lightweight, soft and warm
- non-irritant (will not scratch or otherwise irritate the skin)
- porous (so that moisture can escape)
- flame-resistant (will not easily catch fire).

Points to remember
1. Clothing should not be tight, especially round the neck and feet. When young feet are cramped for a long while they can become deformed.
2. Avoid drawstrings and ribbons near the baby's neck – they could pull too tight and strangle the baby.
3. Avoid loosely knitted or open-weave garments – a strand of wool or nylon caught round a baby's finger or toe can cut off the blood supply.
4. Babies grow quickly and sleepsuits will not stretch indefinitely.

5. Several layers of lightweight clothing are warmer than one thick, bulky layer.
6. The amount of clothing a baby needs to wear depends on the temperature. There are cold days in summer and it is very warm in an over-heated house in winter. In hot conditions, the minimum of clothes is required, and when very hot, a nappy is all that is necessary.
7. All clothes for babies up to 3 months old must carry a permanent label showing whether or not the garment passes the low flammability test for slow burning (see p. 323).
8. Most new parents have a limited amount of money to spend. Therefore it is sensible to buy only the essential items required for the baby. The money can be saved until later when the baby needs more clothes:
    - in larger and more expensive sizes
    - for daytime and night-time
    - because they will get damaged and dirty more easily and more often.

MATERIALS USED FOR BABY CLOTHES

Both natural and synthetic materials are used for baby clothes.

Natural materials
Two natural materials used for baby clothes are:

- **wool** – warm to wear and therefore more suitable for cold weather. Wool garments should not be placed next to a baby's skin as they are likely to cause irritation.
- **cotton** (e.g. terry towelling, muslin) – absorbent and therefore more comfortable to wear next to the skin when the body is hot, as it can absorb sweat.

Synthetic materials
These are easier to wash and dry than natural materials. In general, they are cold to wear in winter because they do not retain body heat, and hot and clammy in summer because they do not absorb sweat. There are exceptions: acrylic gives warmth and viscose is absorbent. Synthetic materials include:

- **acrylic** (e.g. Acrilan®) – soft and warm to the touch, lightweight, crease-resistant and non-irritating to the skin; used as an alternative to wool as it retains its shape and does not shrink.
- **polyester** (e.g. Terylene®) – crease-resistant and does not catch fire easily; used as a light-weight alternative to cotton
- **viscose** (rayon) – absorbent, retains whiteness, pleasant to handle but lacks strength
- **nylon** – very strong and does not shrink.

Many baby clothes are made of mixtures of different types of material. In this way, the advantages of different materials can be combined.

WASHING BABY CLOTHES

Most ready-made garments are machine washable. A label on each garment gives instructions about washing or dry-cleaning, bleaching, ironing and other necessary information.

Woollen garments
Wool is a very useful fabric for children's clothes when warmth is required, but it needs careful washing, preferably by hand. If the water is too hot, the garments shrink. They can easily be pulled out of shape when being dried.

Cotton garments

Cotton can be washed in hot water, although the colour may fade. The advantage of white cotton is that it has no colour to lose and it can be boiled or bleached when necessary to remove stains and to whiten it. See p. 100 for washing of nappies.

Synthetic materials and mixtures

Follow the instructions that accompany the garments. The charts on these pages show the meanings of some of the symbols used on garment labels.

Fabric conditioners

These may irritate the baby's skin.

Fabric care symbols

Washing

60	Maximum temperature of the water
	Bar indicates reduced machine action for synthetics
	Broken bar indicates much reduced machine action for wool
	Handwash only
	Do not wash

Bleaching

△	Any bleach allowed	⧅	Do not bleach

Tumble drying

⊡	May be tumble dried	⊙	With low heat setting
⊙⊙	With high heat setting	⊠	Do not tumble dry

Ironing

⌁	One dot – cool temperature	⌁	Three dots – hot temperature
⌁	Two dots – warm temperature	⌁	Do not iron

Dry cleaning

Ⓟ	Can be dry cleaned (the letter indicates the solvent to be used)
⊠	Unsuitable for dry cleaning

NAPPIES

Disposable nappies

These are commonly used because:

- changing the baby's nappy is quick and easy
- nappies are available in various sizes to suit the baby's increasing weight
- there are different types for boys and girls
- there are nappies for daytime and for night-time use
- stretch waistbands and sides ensure a comfortable fit
- the fastening tapes are easy to use
- the nappies are designed to keep moisture away from the baby's skin to help prevent a sore bottom
- a waterproof outer covering prevents moisture escaping from the nappy
- being disposable, the nappies are thrown away after use.

Disposable nappy

One disadvantage of disposable nappies is the cost. They work out more expensive than terry nappies, even when allowing for the cost of nappy liners and of washing and drying the terry nappies. There is also the environmental problem for Local Authorities of disposing of the vast numbers of nappies that are put into rubbish bins.

Re-usable nappies

There are three main types and they need to be washed after use:

- **Traditional terry nappies.** Each is a square of terry towelling that is folded into shape and then fastened with a curved safety pin (**A**) or a **Nappi Nippa** (**B**). They come in one size and are worn with waterproof pants.

A 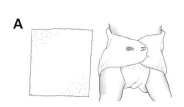   B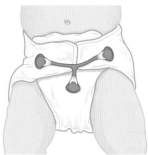

- **Shaped terry nappies.** These are shaped to fit neatly around the baby's bottom with easy fastening tabs (**C**). They come in different sizes, can be made from bamboo, muslin and cotton, and are worn with waterproof pants.
- **All-in-one nappies.** These are padded pants with absorbent cotton inside and an outer waterproof cover. They are sold in a variety of styles and sizes.

C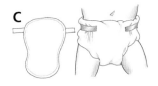

Terry nappy

Muslin squares

Because they are not as bulky as terry towelling, muslin squares may be used as nappies for very small babies. They may also be used to line terry nappies for babies with sensitive skins.

Nappy liners

A nappy liner placed inside a terry nappy helps to prevent soreness by acting as a barrier between the baby's skin and a wet nappy. Liners are made of material which allows moisture to pass through but does not absorb it. So, when a liner is placed inside a terry nappy, the urine passes through to be absorbed by the nappy while the lining itself keeps dry.

Nappy pins

These are large, curved and have a safety catch which is removed in order to open the pin. When putting the pin in a nappy, one hand should be kept under the nappy to prevent the baby from being pricked accidentally.

Nappy pin

Waterproof pants

These are worn over terry nappies to keep the clothes and bedding dry, and by doing so, reduce the amount of washing. But because the urine remains inside the pants, the baby's skin is kept damp and this encourages nappy rash (p. 100).

Trainer pants

These are useful for older toddlers who are being potty-trained. They are made to look like real pants, are easy to pull down, and yet are absorbent like nappies. They have a waterproof covering and are ideal for use at night-time, at playgroup, and when travelling. Trainer pants can be re-usable or disposable.

Swim nappy

Swim nappies

These are waterproof nappies for babies to wear in the swimming pool or for playing in the sea.

Nappy washing services

These are a fee-based services for laundering reusable nappies. Each week fresh nappies are delivered to the customer and soiled nappies are taken away. Between collections, soiled nappies are kept in a bin with a deodorised liner provided by the service.

Nappy service

BABY CLOTHES

Bodysuits

A bodysuit is an all-in-one vest and pants which is worn over the nappy. Being worn next to the skin, it needs to be made of material which is soft and non-irritating, for example cotton. Many bodysuits have wide 'envelope-type' stretch necklines which are easy to pull on and off over the baby's head. 'Poppers' at the crotch hold the garment in position and allow the nappies to be changed easily.

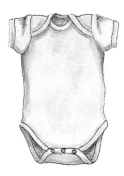

Bodysuit

Sleepsuits

These cover the baby well, are easy to wash, and need no ironing. As the feet are covered, there is no need for bootees except in cold conditions. They must be loose-fitting to allow plenty of room for the baby to move. Sleepsuits are designed with poppers down the front and in the crotch. This makes them easy to put on and take off, and convenient for quick nappy changing.

Sleepsuit

Cardigan

A cardigan is worn when an extra layer is required for warmth.

Cardigan

Bootees

These are useful in cold weather. They can be worn outside a sleepsuit, or inside if there is plenty of room.

Bootees

Mittens

Warm mittens are essential when the baby is outside in cold weather. **'Scratch' mittens** are thin mittens which are sometimes put on to prevent the baby from scratching himself.

Mittens

Hat or bonnet

This is necessary in cool or cold weather. If the baby is out in hot sun then a cotton sun-hat is necessary with a flap to protect the neck.

Hat   Sun-hat

Shawl

A shawl needs to be lightweight and warm. A cellular blanket makes a good shawl. The holes in a blanket of this type make it lightweight, and air trapped in the holes will hold the baby's body heat.

Pramsuits or snowsuits

These are fleecy or padded, all-in-one jacket and trousers for outdoors on cold days. They usually have a hood and bootees attached.

Snowsuit

Bibs

Paper tissues or paper towels may be used as bibs and thrown away afterwards. Bibs made of terry towelling are absorbent but need frequent washing if they are to remain hygienic. Bibs made of soft plastic or plastic backed material must be securely tied around the waist as well as the neck or held in place by velcro fastenings. This will prevent the plastic from flapping over the face and causing suffocation. For the same reason, any bib should always be removed before the baby is put in his cot or pram. Bibs made of stiff plastic with a 'catch-all' pocket are for older babies (p. 274).

Bib

Questions

1 List the items for a baby's first set of clothes shown in the photograph on p. 107.

2 a What are the requirements for baby clothes?

  b What points are useful to remember when choosing clothes for a new baby?

3 a Name two natural materials used for baby clothes.

  b Name four synthetic materials used for baby clothes.

  c Name two types of material suitable for wearing in cold weather.

  d Name two absorbent materials suitable for wearing in hot weather.

  e Why are baby clothes often made of a mixture of different materials?

  f Draw and describe the symbols used for washing instructions.

4 a Describe three different types of nappy. Give one advantage of each.

  b How is a nappy liner able to act as a barrier between the baby's skin and a wet nappy?

  c Describe (i) a nappy pin and how to use it, (ii) Nappi Nippa, (iii) training pants, (iv) swim nappies.

  d Why does the use of waterproof pants encourage nappy rash?

5 a Why are bodysuits and sleepsuits useful garments for babies?

  b What are scratch mittens?

  c When is a pramsuit useful?

  d Give an advantage and a disadvantage of using a towelling bib.

  e (i) How should a soft plastic bib be secured on a baby? (ii) Why is this necessary?

  f When should a bib always be removed?

Further activities

Extension

1 Make a list of the items (apart from nappies and waterproof pants) you consider to be essential for a new baby. Find the cost of these items, and calculate their total cost.

2 Collect different labels from clothes, showing fabric care instructions. Describe how you would wash, dry and iron each garment.

Investigation

1 Compare at least three different brands of disposable nappy. (They could be the same brands which were used in the absorbency experiment on p. 102).

Use a spreadsheet to record your findings. Set up the spreadsheet like this:

	A	B	C	D	E	F
00	Brand	Shape	Faste- ning	Pack cost	No. in pack	Unit cost
01						

2 Estimate and compare the costs of using towelling and disposable nappies for one year, with six nappy changes per day. Use middle-priced disposable and towelling nappies, liners, plastic pants, steriliser, washing powders etc. for your comparison. Assume that two dozen towelling nappies are used, and that they will last for two years.

Experiment

Devise and, if possible, carry out an experiment on the washability of different types of materials used for baby clothes, in relation to one or more of the following: (i) temperature of water, (ii) stain removal, (iii) washing powders, (iv) fabric conditioner. Use at least one synthetic material and one natural material.

Weblinks

For information on how to change a baby's nappy, visit:

www.howto.tv

For a comprehensive guide to buying a baby's layette, visit:

www.babycentre.co.uk

CHAPTER 25

Nursery equipment

Besides needing clothing, a baby also needs somewhere to sleep, to be bathed, to sit and to play. It is also essential to have some equipment for keeping the baby safe when necessary, and for taking the baby out to the shops or park. Some of the equipment designed for these purposes is discussed in this topic.

FOR SLEEPING

Cot

A cot of the type shown in the drawing is suitable for all babies, even when newborn. The space and safety of a cot of this type is essential after the age of about 6 months. Another advantage is that the slatted sides allow the baby to see out. The safety features to check for in a cot are:

Cot

▥ The bars should be between 45–65 mm apart, to prevent the baby's head being caught between them.
▥ The mattress should fit so that there is just enough room for the bedclothes to be tucked in. There should be no gap more than 4 cm anywhere round the mattress in which the baby's head, arms or legs can become trapped.
▥ Cots usually have one side which drops down, with catches to hold the drop-side in the upper position. The catch needs to be too difficult to be undone by the baby or a young brother or sister. When the baby can climb out of the cot it is time for a bed.

Cot bumper

This is a foam-padded screen which fits around the sides of the cot. It protects the baby from draughts, and from knocking his head on the sides. They are not recommended for babies who can sit unaided, and should not have loops or ties in which the baby can become entangled.

Carry-cot

A carry-cot makes a suitable first bed. It is useful for the first 6 months or so, until the baby becomes too big and active to be left in it safely. The sides and hood keep out draughts, and it can be carried from room to room. If made of weatherproof material and fitted with hood, apron and wheels, a carry-cot has the added advantage of being a pram as well as a bed.

If there are cats around, a **cat net** over the carry-cot or pram will prevent one from snuggling against the baby's face for warmth and comfort.

Carry-cot

Travel cot

This is a folding cot with fabric sides, meant for temporary use when travelling or on holiday. Some are large enough for use by toddlers, and some double as a play-pen when the mattress is removed.

'Moses basket'

This can be used as a bed for a young baby. Being light-weight and with grab handles, it can be moved easily without disturbing the baby.

Mattresses

These are needed for the cot, carry-cot and pram. The baby will spend much time lying on a mattress, so it should be comfortable. A firm mattress is safer than a soft one because the baby cannot

Moses basket

bury his head in it and suffocate. A waterproof covering on the mattress allows it to be sponged clean.

Ventilated mattresses are available which have a part with ventilation holes through which air can flow and so help to prevent any risk of suffocation. When a baby is put in the cot, the head should be placed on the part of the mattress which has the ventilation holes.

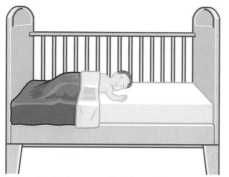

Place the baby near the foot of the cot for sleeping. This prevents the baby from wriggling down under the covers and becoming too hot or suffocating

Blankets and sheets

It is better for these to be made of materials which are easy to wash and dry. Babies often dribble milk on them, or are sick, and they can also become very damp and smelly with urine after a night's sleep.

Sheets are needed to cover the mattress of both cot and pram. A minimum supply of three is required, although more will be useful as they need to be washed regularly. The material which is usually recommended when warmth is required is flannelette (brushed cotton).

Acrylic blankets, particularly the cellular ones, are lightweight, reasonably warm, and easily washable. Woollen blankets are warmer, but they do not wash so well and take much longer to dry.

Duvets and cot quilts are not recommended for use for babies under 12 months because of the risk of over-heating or suffocation.

Pillow

A baby does not need a pillow for sleeping. It is safer without one because of the danger of suffocation. When a pillow is used to prop up the baby in a chair or pram, it should be firm and not soft.

If a baby needs to sleep with the head raised higher than the feet, for example if the baby has breathing difficulties due to a cold, a pillow can be placed under the mattress.

Baby monitors

These are devices which enable a baby to be monitored by the parents or carers when they are not in the same room. The device is in two parts, the **transmitter** which transmits information from the baby's room and the **receiver** which receives the information. Some monitors can be plugged into the electricity system in the home. Others are battery operated and can transmit baby noises by radio to a receiver up to 100 metres away, and so can be used both in the home or out in the garden. Monitors are also available which keep a check on the temperature of the baby's room and the baby's breathing rhythms. TV monitors enable carers to look in and listen to the baby from another room.

Baby monitor

FOR GOING OUT

Prams and pushchairs

Whatever type of pram or pushchair is used, or whether it is new or second-hand, it should:

- have efficient brakes
- be stable – should not tip over easily
- be easy to steer
- have anchor points for a safety harness – which needs to be used as soon as the baby can sit up
- have a basket which fits underneath where heavy shopping will not cause the pram to overbalance
- be the right height for the parent to be able to push easily without stooping and yet still be able to see where she or he is going.

A Pram

Until a baby can sit up unaided for a reasonably long time a pram or pushchair which allows the baby to lie flat or almost flat will be needed, preferably one in which the baby can be placed facing the mother. This can be a traditional pram (**A**), a carry-cot which fits onto a wheel base to form a pram (**B**), or a baby car seat which clips onto a wheel base (**C**). The pushchair shown in **D** is suitable for older babies and toddlers. Which is most suitable depends on the age of the child, parents' way of life and their budget.

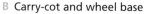

B Carry-cot and wheel base   C Baby car seat on wheel base   D Pushchair

Points to consider when deciding which pram or pushchair to choose include:

- weight – will it need to be carried very far, upstairs, or very often?
- size – will it be used in busy streets, narrow passages or lifts?
- comfort – will the child be spending much time in it?
- where it is to be stored – does it need to fold up?
- outings – will they be on foot, by car, or by public transport?
- is a combined pram and pushchair required?
- is it needed for one baby or two?
- is good suspension important – for a more comfortable ride?
- swivel front wheels – for easier pushing in difficult conditions or crowded spaces
- should the seat be detachable – for use as a car seat or baby seat?
- the family budget – new or second-hand?

The pushchair can be fitted with additional items, such as hood and apron to protect the child against bad weather, and a canopy or parasol to protect against strong sunlight.

Safety harness

A baby or child in a pushchair needs to be secured by a safety harness with shoulder, waist and crotch straps.

Baby nest

This looks like a tiny sleeping bag, with or without handles. It is designed to keep a young baby warm while being carried. The baby will only be safe when lying on his back, otherwise the face may become buried in the soft surface and the baby may suffocate. A baby should never be left alone when in a baby nest, nor should the nest be used for sleeping. Some babies have died while sleeping in a baby nest, either by suffocation or because they have become too hot.

Baby nest

Baby carriers

These enable parents to carry their babies about with them, leaving their hands free for other tasks. At the same time, the babies have the comfort and security of being close to a parent.

A carrier for a young baby needs to have a head support

An older baby in a back-carrier can see all around

Walking rein

A walking rein attached to a harness gives a toddler freedom of movement while remaining in the control of an adult. This can be replaced by a wrist strap when the child has outgrown the rein.

FOR SITTING

Bouncing cradle or rocker

From the age of a month or two the baby can be put in a 'bouncing cradle' or 'rocker'. This makes a change for the baby from lying on his back in the cot or pram, and the baby will enjoy the bouncing or rocking movement and being able to look around. When a bouncing cradle or rocker is used, it must be placed on the floor, not on a table. Babies can wriggle quite a lot and may cause the bouncing cradle or rocker to move and fall off the table. They can be used until the baby is able to sit up unaided, but should only be used for short periods of time and the baby must not be left unattended.

Bouncing cradle

Baby chair

When the baby is able to sit upright, at the age of about 6 months, a baby chair can be used. High chairs have the advantage that the baby is at table level and can be part of the family at mealtimes, but they are not recommended for babies under one year. Low chairs are safer because, being less top-heavy, they do not topple over so easily.

Whichever type of chair is used, it needs to have a broad base and be very stable so that it will not easily topple over. The baby needs to be firmly harnessed to the chair so that he cannot fall or slip out.

Baby chairs often have trays in front which can be used at mealtimes or for toys. The best type of tray is large with rounded corners which are easy to clean.

Car seats

In many parts of the country, it is possible to rent an infant car seat so that a newborn baby leaving hospital can travel home safely. It is illegal for a child to travel in the front seat of a car on an adult's lap. Child car seats are dealt with more fully on pp. 331–2.

FOR BATHING

Baby bath

This is not an essential item of equipment because a young baby can be bathed in the wash basin. Care must then be taken to ensure that the baby does not knock himself on the taps. There is also the danger that the baby could receive burns from touching the hot tap. Some parents therefore prefer to use a baby bath.

After a few months, babies reach the stage when they love to splash the water. The best place then is the ordinary adult bath. A rubber bath mat in the bottom of the bath will help prevent the baby from slipping.

FOR PLAYING

Bouncers and exercisers

Although not essential, these are popular with babies, and provide exercise for the legs, which helps to strengthen them. They are recommended for babies at 8–10 months who have learnt to take their weight on their legs and are starting to stand. They should stop being used as soon as the child can walk unaided.

Bouncer

Exerciser – the wheels are hidden by the bumper

Door bouncers can be suspended from most doorways and can be used for babies when they are able to hold their heads steady. The babies bounce gently up and down and are able to move their legs and arms freely. Baby bouncers are controversial and are banned in some countries. The important thing is that babies must never be left unsupervised in a baby bouncer.

Exercisers of the type shown here have a wide base which gives them stability, speed-restricting wheels which prevent the baby from going too fast, and a tray on which toys can be placed. This toy is recommended for babies who can sit unaided and are learning to walk.

Play-pen

A play-pen is useful when the baby begins to move around. It will keep the baby safe while the parent is busy or out of the room for a short time. Most babies will play happily in a play-pen until they start to object to their freedom being restricted. A baby in a play-pen can learn to pull himself into a standing position and to walk while holding on to the edge for support. Accidents may happen with play-pens if a child climbs out and falls, or gets trapped in the bars.

Play-pens

BUYING EQUIPMENT: CONSUMER LAW

The *Sale and Supply of Goods Act* 1994 gives customers (consumers of goods and services) certain rights. Any goods which you buy must be:

- **of satisfactory quality** – this means they must be fit for their normal purpose, bearing in mind the price which was paid
- **as described** on the package, on a display sign or by the seller
- **fit for any particular purpose** made known to the seller.

If these conditions are not met, the customer may be entitled to a refund.

The *Consumer Protection Act* 1987 covers:

- **product liability** – if damage or injury has been caused by faulty goods, the consumer can claim compensation
- **misleading price indications** – it is an offence to give any misleading indications to consumers about the price of goods or services.

The *General Product Safety Regulations* 2005 make it an offence to sell unsafe goods.

If you wish to make a complaint:

- stop using the item
- tell the shop at once
- take the item back with the receipt

Advice on consumer matters can be obtained from your local Trading Standards or Consumer Protection Department.

Questions

1 a Name two advantages of using a carry-cot as a bed for a young baby.

b Give three advantages of a cot when the baby reaches the age of about 6 months.

c Name three safety features to check when choosing a cot.

d Why is a firm mattress safer than a soft one?

e Give an advantage of (i) a ventilated mattress, (ii) acrylic blankets.

f When are cot quilts not recommended?

g How should a baby be placed in a cot for sleeping?

h (i) Should a baby have a pillow for sleeping?

(ii) Give a reason.

2 (i) What is the function of a baby monitor? (ii) Why is the device in two parts?

3 a List six points to check when choosing a pram or pushchair.

b From the list 'Points to consider' when choosing a pram or pushchair, give the three points which you think are most relevant for each of the types A–D. Give your reasons.

c At what stage does a baby require a safety harness?

d When is a walking rein or wrist strap useful?

4 a Describe a baby nest.

b For what purpose is a baby nest designed?

c Why should a baby never be left alone to sleep in a baby nest?

5 Describe two types of baby carrier.

6 a Name some safety features desirable in a baby chair.

b Name one advantage of a high chair and one advantage of a low chair.

c Why should a bouncing cradle or a rocker not be placed on a table when in use?

7 a (i) When may a play-pen be useful?

(ii) Suggest an advantage and disadvantage of each of the two types shown.

b (i) For what stage of development are bouncers and exercisers recommended?

(ii) When should they not be used?

c (i) What can be used instead of a baby bath?

(ii) What care has to be taken?

d What helps to stop a baby from slipping when in the bath?

8 a Name three Acts or Regulations which give consumers certain rights.

b When may customers be entitled to a refund?

Further activities

 Extension

1 Find photographs of the pieces of equipment mentioned in this topic to accompany your notes.

2 Make a concept keyboard overlay of pieces of nursery equipment. Provide data about the cost of each of them, its use and safety features.

 Investigation

What other equipment can be bought for young children? For each item, say what age group it is designed for, and whether you consider it to be useful or unnecessary.

 Design

Design and, if possible, make a cover suitable for a cot, pram or young child's bed. Use a graphics program to design the item. Experiment with different colours to find those you think will look best. Present your design to your class, giving information on the materials you will use and why you chose them.

 Child study

Discuss with the child's mother or father the items of nursery equipment mentioned in this topic. Which were used, and were these found useful, well-designed or a waste of money?

Weblink

Search for 'nursery safety' at askbaby.com for further tips and information:

www.askbaby.com

Exercises

Exercises relevant to Section 3 can be found on p. 382.

SECTION 4

Development

CHAPTER 26

Why each child is different

No two children are exactly alike, and each can be recognised as an individual with his or her own unique appearance and character (personality). The way a child grows and develops depends on three main factors:

- the **genes** inherited from the parents (p. 128)
- the **environment** in which the child grows up
- the child's **health**.

Each child differs from all others because each (except identical twins) has a different set of genes, each has a different environment, and each has a different health record. From the moment of conception onwards, these factors interact continuously to produce a person who is unlike anyone else.

Identical twins have identical genes. Nevertheless, they will develop differently because the environmental factors will differ. For example, they will be in different positions in the womb and are likely to have different birthweights; they will have different friends, different accidents and illnesses, and so on.

EFFECTS OF ENVIRONMENT ON DEVELOPMENT

Environment means surrounding conditions. Environmental factors which affect a child's development include the following:

Home conditions

The influences of family and home on a child's development include:

- the place where the child lives
- who looks after the child
- whether or not the child is loved and wanted
- the child's companions

whether the child is encouraged to learn, or is ignored, or is prevented from learning by over-protection.

The results of these influences are unpredictable, and they help to produce a rich variety of personalities.

Culture

The cultural life of the family to which a child belongs will affect his or her upbringing. So too will the national culture of the country in which the family is living, and the ethnic group to which it belongs (see pp. 11–12).

Education

Development will be affected by the family's attitude towards education, the availability and use made of different types of pre-school groups, and the teachers and pupils the child meets throughout school life.

EFFECTS OF HEALTH ON GROWTH AND DEVELOPMENT

Health is physical and emotional well-being. Good health helps to ensure proper development of a child. The following factors affect a child's health.

Food

A child needs a balanced diet in order to grow properly.

Malnutrition (poor diet) stunts growth, and may be the result of poverty, famine, or simply lack of parental care or knowledge. The brain grows fastest during the last weeks of development in the uterus and the first three years of life, and malnutrition during this time may affect brain development and reduce the level of intelligence. On the other hand, over-feeding a child leads to obesity (fatness) and the possibility of health problems.

Illness

Severe long-term illness may slow down growth, and the younger the child, the greater the risk of illness having a permanent effect. If a child's rate of growth is only temporarily slowed down by illness, he or she will afterwards adapt with a period of 'catch up' growth. Severe or prolonged illness may also affect emotional development.

Exercise

Exercise strengthens and develops muscles. Lack of exercise makes muscles flabby and, when coupled with over-feeding, encourages the growth of fatty tissue.

Stress

Happy healthy children flourish. But those who are under severe stress for a long period of time may not grow to reach their potential height and often become very thin, or over-eat and get fat. Stress may result from unhappiness, worry, loneliness, illness or abuse.

Parents and carers who smoke

There is evidence that heavy smoking by parents and carers may slow down their children's rate of growth and development both before and after birth. One investigation found that 7-year-old children whose mothers were smokers were, on average, shorter in height and three to seven months behind in reading ability when compared with children of non-smoking mothers.

Children who spend much time in a smoky atmosphere may be more prone to lung disorders (such as asthma and bronchitis) than children who do not live in a smoky environment.

POSITION IN THE FAMILY

The position of a child in the family may have an effect on the development of his or her character.

Children in a large family

These children are likely to be influenced by:

- learning to share and 'give and take' at an early age
- having little privacy
- in the case of the older children, being involved in the care of the younger ones
- in the case of the younger children, receiving less individual attention from parents
- having fewer material benefits because the family income has to support more people, possibly resulting in hand-me-down clothes and toys
- always having someone to play with
- interaction with siblings (brothers and sisters).

An only child

The only child in a family is likely to have:

- less opportunities for sharing
- considerable privacy
- little involvement in the care of younger children
- a great deal of adult attention
- a greater proportion of material goods
- a lot of time in which he or she plays alone
- no siblings to interact with.

The middle child of three or more

Such a child lacks the status of being the eldest, and any special treatment of being the youngest. How a middle child reacts will vary greatly, and may be a factor in the development of character.

Twins

Twins may have to fight to be recognised as individuals, especially if they look alike, are dressed alike, treated the same, and are always referred to as 'the twins'. The early language development of twins can sometimes be slower than that of other children because they may develop their own private means of communicating with each other which does not require real words. Also, there may be less individual attention from adults.

DEVELOPMENT OF SELF-IMAGE (SELF-CONCEPT)

As a baby grows and develops, she gradually becomes conscious (aware) of her:

- own name
- own home
- own body
- age, and of growing up.
- own family.

The child gradually forms a mental image (concept) of herself and becomes aware that she is unlike anyone else. As the child begins to relate to a wider environment, she comes to understand her:

- physical capabilities and limitations
- intellectual (mental) capabilities and limitations
- dependence on others – and to realise that others depend on her
- place in the family and community – where she 'fits in'.

By the time adulthood is reached the child should:

- know how to receive and give love
- have learnt self-discipline
- be self-reliant and feel confident to take charge of her life
- have experience of coping with success and failure. These are both part of life. Being successful enhances self-esteem. Being unable to cope with failure can lower self-esteem.

Questions

1 **a** Name the three main factors on which a child's development depends.

  b Give examples of environmental factors which enable identical twins to develop into different individuals.

2 **a** What does the term 'environment' mean?

  b Give examples of environmental factors which affect a child's development.

3 Give five factors which affect the health of a child, and say what effect these have on the child's development.

4 **a** Compare, using a table with two columns, the effects of being a child in a large family with those of being an only child.

  b Give two reasons why the early language of twins can sometimes be slower than that of other children.

5 Describe the development of self-image.

Weblink

For an interesting article on how depriving children of a loving environment can damage intelligence, visit:

www.guardian.co.uk/science and search for 'environment intelligence'.

Further activities

 Extension

1 Suggest ten situations, both in and outside the home, which could give rise to stress in a child.

2 How do you see yourself? Using the section 'Development of self-image' as a guide, describe your own self-image.

 Discussion

Discuss ways in which environmental influences can affect development. Give examples of environmental influences on physical, social, emotional, and intellectual aspects of development.

Child study

1 Look back at your description of the child's appearance and personality. Can you add anything now that you know the child better? What influences do you think have been important in the child's development?

2 In what ways do you think that the child's own self-image is developing?

CHAPTER 27

Genetics

Genetics is the study of genes and their effects. **Genes** are units of **DNA** (deoxyribonucleic acid) and they are linked together to form threadlike structures called **chromosomes**. Children inherit genes from their parents and this is why they resemble their parents, their brothers and sisters, grandparents and other relatives.

CHROMOSOMES

The human body is composed of vast numbers of tiny cells, each normally containing 46 chromosomes. Of the 46, 23 are exact copies of the chromosomes which came from the mother (in the egg); the other 23 are exact copies of the chromosomes which came from the father (in the sperm). They can be matched together in 23 pairs.

The only cells in the body which do not contain 46 chromosomes are the sex cells (eggs and sperm) – which contain only 23.

Sex chromosomes

The sex of a baby is determined by one pair of chromosomes – the sex chromosomes. One of the sex chromosomes is called **X** and the other is called **Y**. A body cell in a female has two **X** chromosomes (**XX**); a body cell in a male has an **X** and a Y chromosome (**XY**).

Boy or girl?

Every egg contains an **X** chromosome. Half of the sperm contain an **X** and the other half have a **Y**. Whether the child is a boy or a girl depends on whether the egg is fertilised by a sperm containing an **X** or a **Y** chromosome.

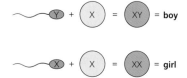

GENES

Each chromosome contains thousands of genes. Each gene contains an instruction that affects a part of the body. Together, the genes provide a set of instructions for growth and development of the whole body. For example, the baby's genes decide:

▓ the shape of the body

- the colour of skin, hair and eyes
- the blood group
- the age at which teeth appear
- the size of hands and feet
- the way the muscles function
- the maximum height to which the child will grow.

Dominant and recessive genes

Genes can be dominant (strong) or recessive (weak). Dominant genes mask the presence of recessive genes. For example, if a child inherits a gene for black hair from the father and a gene for blonde hair from the mother, the child will have black hair because the gene for black hair is dominant to that for blonde hair. However, the child will be a 'carrier' for blonde hair and may pass the recessive gene on to his or her own children. **Recessive genes** can only have an effect when they are inherited from both parents; for example, two genes for blonde hair are necessary to produce a blonde-haired child.

INHERITED DISEASES

Genetic disorders

A few diseases are caused by abnormal genes which can be passed from one generation to the next. Examples are:

- **cystic fibrosis** – abnormally thick mucus is produced which blocks the air passages of the lungs and is very difficult to cough up.
- **haemophilia** – the blood is unable to clot properly and this results in severe bleeding from minor wounds. This disease only affects boys, although girls can be carriers for the faulty gene.
- **thalassaemia** – A disorder of the red blood cells; this type of anaemia is found mainly in countries bordering the eastern Mediterranean, the Middle East, India and Asia, or in people who have originated from these areas.
- **sickle-cell anaemia** – the red blood cells change to a sickle shape when there is a shortage of oxygen; this type of anaemia is more common in West Africa and in people of West African descent, such as Caribbean people.
- **muscular dystrophy** – See p. 352.
- **PKU** (phenylketonuria) – See pp. 64–5.

Chromosome disorders

These occur when the chromosomes fail to divide properly during cell division. If this happens when eggs or sperm are being formed, it can produce an individual with more, or less, chromosomes than is normal. For example, a person with **Down's syndrome** (p. 351) has 47 chromosomes instead of the normal 46. **Turner's syndrome** develops in girls whose cells contain only 45 chromosomes because one of the **X** chromosomes is missing. Girls with Turner's syndrome fail to grow normally in height.

GENETIC COUNSELLING

Genetic counselling is the giving of expert advice on the likelihood of disease being passed from parents to children by inheritance. People may ask for genetic counselling:

- when there is a history of inherited illness or abnormality in their family when the father and mother are closely related – for example, cousins – because if there are harmful recessive genes in the family, both may be carriers. Any children they have may then inherit a recessive gene for the same disease from each parent, allowing these genes to become effective and cause disease

when there is a possibility of an abnormal condition affecting an unborn child and the parents are considering terminating the pregnancy by abortion.

Embryo screening for inherited diseases

Couples who want to have children but know that they are may be carriers of an inherited disease may opt for **embryo screening** (PGD – Pre-implementation Genetic Diagnosis). This procedure involves testing embryos produced by IVF (see p. 32). A single cell is removed from an embryo at the eight-cell stage of development (around three days old), leaving the embryo undamaged and unaffected. The DNA from the removed cell is then analysed to find out, for example:

the sex of the child – only boys can inherit Duchenne muscular dystrophy

the presence of disease-causing genes – such as the abnormal gene that causes cystic fibrosis.

In practice a large number of embryos are usually created by IVF and each embryo is then tested by PGD. A decision can then be made to select one or more unaffected embryos for insertion into the mother's uterus.

DETECTING DISORDERS IN UNBORN CHILDREN

When there is a chance that a fetus may have a genetic disorder, tests such as amniocentesis or chorionic villus sampling may be carried out (see pp. 52–3).

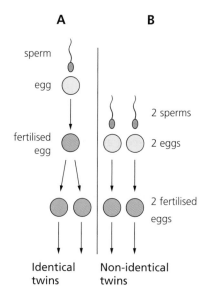

TWINS

Twins are either identical or non-identical depending on whether they come from one egg or two.

Identical twins (uniovular twins)

These develop when a fertilised egg splits into two parts (diagram **A**) and each develops into an individual. These twins are very much alike in appearance and are always of the same sex as they have inherited identical genes. Identical twins are more likely to be born to a younger mother.

Non-identical twins (binovular or fraternal twins)

These develop when two eggs are released instead of one. Each egg is fertilised by a different sperm (diagram **B**), so the twins will be no more alike than any other two children in the same family. They can be either the same sex or a boy and a girl.

The chance of having non-identical twins increases with the age of the mother, the number of pregnancies and when there is a history of twins in the mother's family.

Non-identical twins

Sextuplets

Questions

1 a (i) What are genes? (ii) What do genes link together to form? (iii) Where do a child's genes come from?

  b (i) How many chromosomes do the sex cells contain? (ii) How many chromosomes occur in all other cells?

  c (i) What does each chromosome contain? (ii) What does each gene contain?

  d Give examples of the effects of genes on the growth and development of the body.

  e What is the difference between 'dominant' and 'recessive' genes?

2 a Which sex chromosomes are possessed by (i) females, (ii) males?

  b (i) What decides whether a child is a boy or girl? (ii) Draw a diagram to illustrate this.

3 a Name three inherited diseases of the blood.

  b How many chromosomes are present in the cells of people with (i) Down's syndrome? (ii) Turner's syndrome?

4 (i) Who may opt for embryo screening? (ii) Give examples of diseases that can be detected by embryo screening. (iii) Describe the procedure involved in the process.

5 a (i) Name two tests which are carried out to detect genetic disorders in unborn children.

6 Twins can be of two types – identical or non-identical. Which twins:

  a develop from one egg

  b are also called 'fraternal' twins

  c are also called 'uniovular' twins

  d are always of the same sex

  e are more likely to be born to a younger mother

  f are more likely to occur with a fourth pregnancy than a first one?

Further activities

 Investigation

Study one family you know well, perhaps your own family or the family of the child you are studying. From your observations, list the ways in which a child in the family resembles each of the parents. Which of these resemblances do you think are likely to be due to the genes the child inherited from the parents?

 Discussion

Nature–nurture? There is a continuing debate about the relative influence of genes (nature) and environment (nurture) in determining a child's total development. For example, if a child in a musical family grows up to be a good musician, is it because he inherited his musical ability or because he was in the right environment? Is obesity inherited or due to living in a family where hearty eating is the usual pattern? Write a report of at least three pages on the difference between nature and nurture, and include examples of each. Say which you think is more important, giving examples to support your argument.

Weblinks

For a good introduction to 'what is a gene', search at:

http://kidshealth.org

For information on genes and their effect on human development and behaviour, visit the science museum website, go to 'online stuff', select 'current science' and then go to 'your genes':

www.sciencemuseum.org.uk

For more information on genetic counselling, visit:

http://genome.wellcome.ac.uk

CHAPTER 28

Growth and development

Growth is an increase in size, and **development** is the process of learning new skills. Growth and development go hand in hand and it is often difficult to separate one from the other.

All babies follow the same general pattern of growth and development, and the stages in which they learn to do things generally follow in the same order. This is because they need to reach one **'milestone' in development** before they can progress towards the next. For example, their legs have to become strong enough to bear their weight before they can stand, they have to be able to stand before they can walk, and to walk before they can run.

EACH BABY GROWS AND DEVELOPS AT HIS OWN PACE

Although all babies follow the same general pattern, each baby grows and develops at his own pace. The rate of development depends on a number of factors which include:

- the genes which the baby has inherited
- the amount of encouragement and interest shown by the parents
- the baby's state of health.

When a baby is said to be 'slow' or 'late' in doing something, for example walking, it is often because he is concentrating on some other aspect of development such as talking, in which he is said to be 'forward'.

MEASURING GROWTH

Growth can be measured in terms of **weight** and **height** (or **length** in the case of children under 3 years of age). Generally, as children grow taller they also become heavier, but not always, because weight also depends on how fat or thin the child becomes.

Gain in weight

This varies from child to child and from week to week. A weekly gain of 150–220 g is to be expected in the first 6 months. As the baby grows older, the rate of gain in weight decreases. From 6 to 9 months it is about 90–150 g per week, and it then slows down to 60–90 g per week from 9 to 12 months, and for the second year is about 40 g a week. Some gain more, some less.

As these figures show, a baby's increase in weight is greatest in the first 6 months and then gradually slows down. This is also true for increase in height. As a rough guide, the average baby doubles its birth-weight in the first 6 months and trebles it by one year.

Finding the average rate of growth

The average is worked out from measurements of a large number of children of the same age but differing body build and social background. Graphs showing the average weight and height of children up to 8 years can be found on pp. 138–9.

Individual variation

The photograph shows how greatly children of the same age can vary. These boys are all aged 5 years 9 months. Their measurements are spread over a wide range on either side of the average (see table).

A   B   C   D   E

Name	Weight in kg	Height in cm	Birth-weight in kg
A Ali	28.0	119.5	3.5
B Kenny	19.5	114.0	1.0
C Troy	20.0	118.0	3.0
D Ashley	22.0	119.0	3.5
E David	16.5	105.0	2.25

HOW TALL WILL A CHILD GROW?

The most important factors which affect growth in height are the genes and chromosomes inherited from the parents. Generally, short parents have short children and tall parents have tall children. It is usual for a child's adult height to be somewhere between the height of his mother and that of his father. This is called the child's **potential** or **target height**. If a child is not growing normally and is not as tall as he ought to be, this could be due to one of the factors in the diagram below.

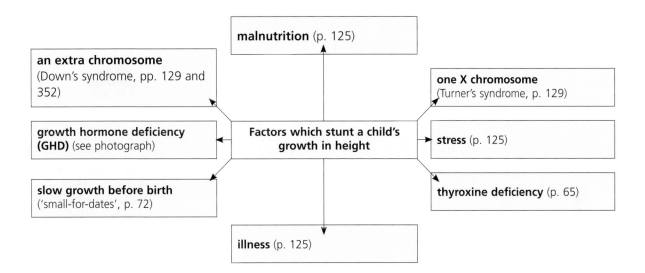

malnutrition (p. 125)

an extra chromosome (Down's syndrome, pp. 129 and 352)

one X chromosome (Turner's syndrome, p. 129)

growth hormone deficiency (GHD) (see photograph)

Factors which stunt a child's growth in height

stress (p. 125)

slow growth before birth ('small-for-dates', p. 72)

thyroxine deficiency (p. 65)

illness (p. 125)

Is the child's height normal?

It is possible to find out if a child is growing normally in height by using the 'centile' growth charts on pp. 38–9. To do this:

1. The child's height is measured, and the height plotted on the chart.
2. Preferably once a year (perhaps on every birthday) the height is again measured by the same person in the same manner. This measurement is also plotted on the chart.
3. The plots on the chart will show whether the child is growing normally. If the child's height is not increasing as it should, this may indicate a growth problem which needs to be investigated. Many growth problems (as with the girl in the photograph with growth hormone deficiency) can be corrected if treated early.

Which sister is the older?

The girl on the right is 4½ years old. Her sister, who is 6 years old, has growth hormone deficiency.

Children who are given doses of growth hormone before the age of 6 years may catch up and reach their full potential height.

Advice on height problems

Children who differ in height from their companions of the same age may have problems. Those who are much taller than average for their age may be expected by adults to behave older than their age, and they may fail to live up to adults' expectations. Those who are shorter than average may worry that they are not growing normally, and be upset when treated as being younger than their age. Parents may be able to obtain advice on growth problems from their family doctor. Assistance can also be obtained from the Child Growth Foundation (see p. 371).

PROPORTIONS CHANGE WITH GROWTH

As a child grows, the different parts of the body alter in shape as well as increasing in size. Some parts grow more quickly than others. This has the effect of changing the proportions of the body as the child gets older. For example, at birth the head is about a quarter of the total length of the body, but by the age of 7 years it is only about one sixth (see below).

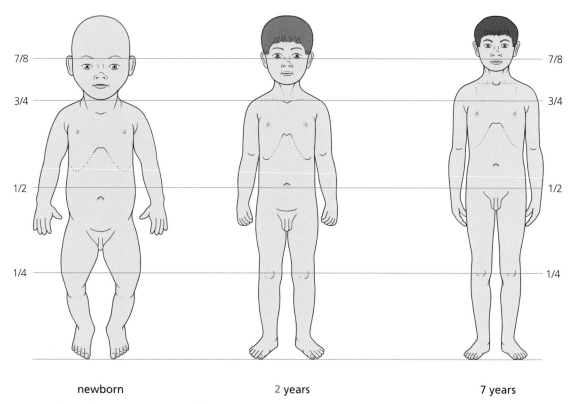

| newborn | 2 years | 7 years |

Source: Medical College of St Bartholomew's Hospital, London

Growth and development of the legs

In the early stages, a baby is bow-legged. This condition gradually disappears and is often followed by knock-knees at the toddler stage. By the age of 6–7 years, the legs have usually straightened.

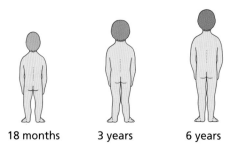

18 months   3 years   6 years

Questions

1 Explain the difference between growth and development.

2 Find the average weight and height of the children in the photograph on p. 134.

a Make a table to record the name, weight and height of each child.

Name	Weight in kg	Height in cm

b To find the average weight of these children, add all the individual weights together, then divide by the total number of children, i.e. five.

c In the same way, find the average height.

d Name the child whose (i) weight, (ii) height is nearest the average.

3 a (i) Which of the factors in the diagram on p. 136 was responsible for the slow growth of the smaller girl in the photograph below? (ii) Is there any treatment she could receive?

b (i) How can parents check that their child's growth in height is normal? (ii) If they are worried, who can they go to for advice?

4 Study the diagrams on p. 136 showing the proportions of the body.

a Why do the proportions of the body change as the child grows?

b At what age is the neck very short and not visible in front view?

c At birth the head is about ¼ of the total length of the body. Is the head proportionately larger or smaller at 7 years?

d On the newborn, the eyebrows mark ⅛ of the body. What marks ⅛ of the body at (i) 2 years, (ii) 7 years?

e (i) At 7 years, what proportion of the body is the lower leg? (ii) At 2 years, is the same part proportionately shorter or longer than at 7 years?

f At 2 years, the navel is at the mid-point of the body. Is the navel above or below the mid-point (i) when newborn, (ii) at 7 years? (iii) What has grown more quickly than the rest of the body to cause the level of the navel to rise?

Further activities

 Extension

1 Add pictures of children to your notes to show the three stages of leg development.

2 Growth charts can be used to compare the growth pattern of an individual child with the normal range of growth patterns typical of a large number of children of the same sex.

* The **50th percentile** is the **median** – it represents the middle of the range of growth patterns.

* The **91st percentile** is near to the top of the range (the greatest weight or height). If, for example, the height of an individual child was on the 91st percentile, in any typical group of 100 children, there would be 90 who were shorter and 9 who were taller.

* The **10th percentile** is near to the bottom of the range. If a child was on the 9th percentile, 8 children would measure less and 91 would measure more.

Weblink

For good information on children and physical growth, visit the site:

www.kidsdevelopment.co.uk and go to 'Physical Development 3+', on the sidebar, then select 'Children and Physical Growth'.

Boys' growth chart

Height (length) and weight charts for boys from birth to 8 years – showing 9th, 50th and 91st percentiles

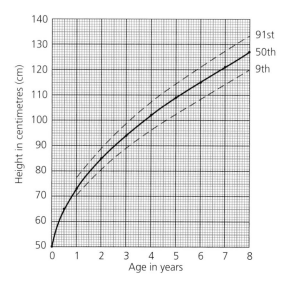

Calculating Body Mass Index (BMI)

Body Mass Index (BMI) is used to assess fatness. To find BMI, the body's weight in kilograms is divided by height in metres squared.

Example A child weighing 21 kg and who is 1.16 m tall:

$$\text{BMI} = \frac{\text{weight in kg}}{\text{height in m}^2}$$

$$= \frac{21}{1.16 \times 1.16}$$

$$= 15.61$$

When the child's BMI is plotted on a paediatric BMI chart it will indicate if the child is underweight or overweight.

Although in the majority of adults a BMI of between 18.5 and 24.9 is defined as being ideal, this range varies for children throughout their growing years. The adult definition of underweight, overweight and obese should never be applied to children.

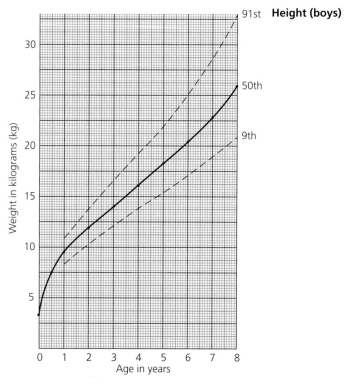

Source: Child Growth Foundation

Girls' growth chart

Height (length) and weight charts for girls from birth to 8 years – showing 9th, 50th and 91st percentiles

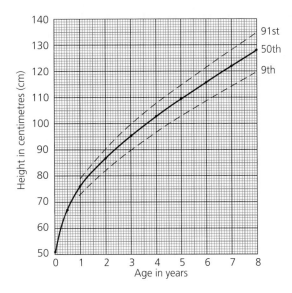

Height (girls)

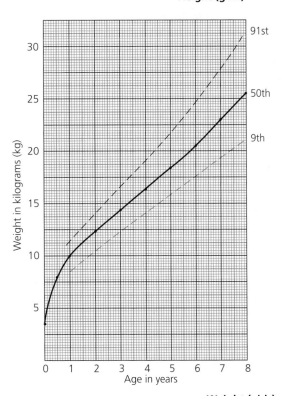

Weight (girls)

Source: Child Growth Foundation

Further activities (continued)

Table 1	Weight in kg	
Age in years	Boys	Girls
Birth	3.5	3.25
1	10.0	9.5
2	12.25	11.75
3	14.5	14.0
4	16.5	16.25
5	18.5	18.25
6	20.5	20.5
7	23.0	23.0
8	25.5	26.0

Table 2 Period	Weight gain (kg) per year	
	Boys	Girls
1st year	6.5	6.25
2nd year		
3rd year		
4th year		
5th year		
6th year		
7th year		
8th year		

Table 1 shows the 50th percentile weights for boys and girls. This information comes from the graphs on pp. 138–9.

a Use Table 1 to calculate how much weight is gained each year, then copy and complete Table 2.

Table 3	Height in cm	
	Boys	Girls
Birth	51	50
1	76	73
2		
3		
4		
5		
6		
7		
8		

Table 4 Period	Height increase (cm) per year	
	Boys	Girls
1st year	25	23
2nd year		
3rd year		
4th year		
5th year		
6th year		
7th year		
8th year		

b Copy and complete Table 3 using the 50th percentile information from the height charts on pp. 138–9.

c Use Table 3 to calculate how much height is gained each year, then copy and complete Table 4.

3 Copy the table on p. 134 onto a spreadsheet. Use the spreadsheet to draw charts to compare the weight, height and birth-weight of the group of boys. Include data on the median height and weight for this age group taken from the graphs on pp. 138–9. What can you say about the height and weight of each boy?

4 Use the weights given in Table 1 to convert kilograms into pounds with 1 kg = 2.2 lb. Use your results to draw a graph showing the average weight of boys and of girls from birth to 8 years in pounds weight.

 **Child study**

Measure the height and weight of the child. How do the child's measurements compare with the percentiles on the growth charts on pp. 138–9.

CHAPTER 29

Physical development

Topics 29 to 39 are concerned with different aspects of a child's development. All these forms of development are taking place at the same time, but it is easier to study them one by one.

This topic deals with **physical development**, that is, development of the body. Each of the diagrams is related to the average age at which the stage shown occurs. It is usual for most children to pass through the different stages of development within a few weeks either side of the average age. But it should be remembered that the age at which children sit up, walk and talk can vary a great deal.

MOTOR SKILLS

As physical development proceeds, the child acquires various physical skills – **motor skills** – which require co-ordination between brain and muscles. These skills often require a great deal of practice before becoming automatic. **Gross motor skills** use the large muscles of the arms, legs, hips and back such as when sitting, walking, catching, climbing, kicking a ball, throwing etc. **Fine manipulative skills** involve the co-ordination of the smaller muscles of the hands and fingers for pointing, drawing, doing up buttons, using a knife and fork, writing etc.

HEAD CONTROL

Movement of the head is controlled by muscles in the neck and in a newborn baby these are undeveloped and weak. Muscles need time to grow and develop. Also, the baby has to learn how to use them before gaining control over head movements.

Always support a newborn baby's head

Newborn

When the baby is picked up or lifted into a sitting position the head falls backwards because the neck muscles are very weak. (**A**). This is why the head must always be supported when the baby is being lifted, as shown in the photograph.

3 months

The baby is beginning to control her head (**B**): there is much less head lag when the baby is pulled into a sitting position. When the baby is held upright, the head is still liable to wobble.

6 months

The baby now has complete head control. There is no head lag and the baby is able to raise her head when lying on her back (**C**). When in a sitting position the baby can hold her head upright and turn it to look around.

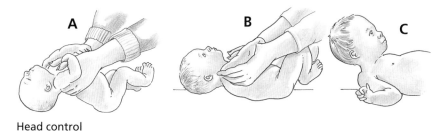

Head control

LEARNING TO SIT

Newborn

When a newborn baby is held in a sitting position she appears to roll up into a ball (**A**). The back curves over and the head falls forward because, as yet, the muscles of the neck and back are not very strong.

3 months

The baby still has to be supported when in a sitting position but the back is much straighter (**B**). Although the head is still rather wobbly, she can hold it steady for a short while.

6 months

The baby is now able to sit upright but still needs support from a chair or pram. She can also sit for a short while on the floor with her hands forward for support (**C**).

9 months

The baby can pull herself into a sitting position and sit unsupported for a short while (**D**).

1 year

The baby is now able to sit unsupported for a long while and is able to turn sideways and stretch out to pick up a toy (**E**).

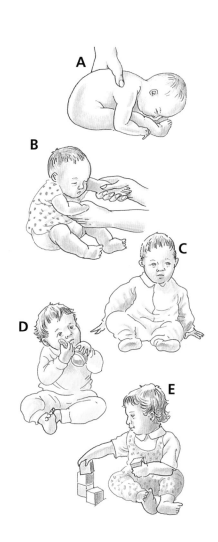

THE PRONE POSITION (LYING ON THE STOMACH)

Newborn

When a newborn baby is placed on her front, she lies with the head turned to one side and with the knees drawn up under the abdomen (tummy) (**A**). By 1 month old her knees are not drawn up so much and she is beginning to be able to lift her head.

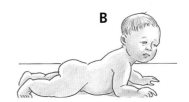

3 months

The baby now lies with her legs straight, and she can raise her head and shoulders off the ground by supporting the weight on her forearms (**B**).

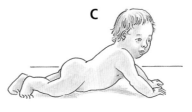

6 months

The baby uses straight arms to lift her head and chest off the ground (**C**). Usually by 5 months, the baby is able to roll over from her front on to her back. It takes about another month before she can also roll over from her back on to her front, and then she can easily roll off a bed.

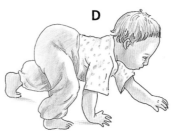

9 months

The baby can now move over the floor either by pulling or pushing herself with her hands or by rolling.

1 year

The baby crawls rapidly either on hands and knees, or like a bear on hands and feet (**D**), or shuffles along on her bottom. Although most children crawl before they can walk, some miss out this stage altogether.

LEARNING TO WALK

The legs of a newborn baby need time for further growth and development before they can be used for walking. The muscles of the legs, hips and back have to strengthen. In addition, the baby has to learn how to co-ordinate all these muscles and also how to keep her balance. All babies love the opportunity to kick, and kicking is an essential exercise in the development of the muscles of legs and feet.

Newborn

When a newborn baby is held upright with her feet touching a firm surface, she automatically makes walking movements, especially if her head is pushed back a little by holding a finger under her chin. This is known as the walking reflex (see p. 74). It disappears after a few weeks and it will be quite a while before the baby learns to make true walking movements.

3 months

When the baby is held in a standing position, the legs are beginning to be strong enough to take a little weight although they tend to sag at the knee and hip (**A**).

6 months

The baby can take her weight on her legs when being held (**B**), and enjoys bouncing up and down.

9 months

The baby can pull herself into a standing position. From now onwards the baby will start to walk, either sideways holding on to furniture (**C**) or when both hands are held by an adult.

1 year

The baby can walk with one hand held (**D**). At this stage she walks with feet apart and with steps of varying length, and her feet have a tendency to go in different directions.

15 months

The baby can by now walk alone. The average age at which babies first walk on their own is 13 months, but some walk much earlier and others much later. At first they are unsteady on their feet and tend to hold their arms up in order to keep their balance; they cannot stop easily or turn corners, and if they look down they fall down.

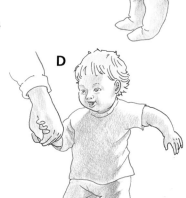

Once a child has learnt to use her legs for walking, she can acquire other skills. By 15 months the child is likely to be able to kneel and to crawl upstairs on all fours, but she does not yet understand that if she leans backwards she may fall down the stairs.

18 months

The child can walk upstairs by holding on to the rail and putting both feet on each stair.

2 years

The child can walk up and down stairs, two feet per stair, and can kick a ball without falling over. At 2½ years she can walk on tip-toe and jump.

Climbing stairs

3 years

The child can walk upstairs with one foot to each stair, but still places both feet on the same stair when coming down, and will often jump off the bottom stair. At this age the child can also stand on one leg.

4 years

By now the child places one foot on each stair when coming downstairs as well as when going up, and is also able to hop.

5 years

The child can skip.

USING THE HANDS

Newborn

A newborn baby keeps her hands tightly closed for most of the time. The baby also shows a grasp reflex – if anything is put in the hand, it is automatically grasped tightly (see p. 74). The automatic grasp reflex disappears after a few weeks and the baby will be able to grasp again only when she has learnt to control the muscles of her hands.

3 months

A

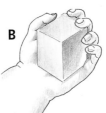

The hands are held open for most of the time now that the grasp reflex has gone. If the baby is given a rattle, she holds it for a few moments only. If her hands accidentally touch her clothes she pulls at them. This is the stage when the baby spends a long time looking at her hands (**A**).

In about another month the baby is able to clasp her hands together and play with her fingers; she learns what they look like, what they can do, and how to get them where she wants.

6 months

The baby can now grasp an object without it having to be put in her hand, and she uses her whole hand to do so (**B**).

B

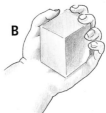

At this age, she picks up everything in her reach with one hand or two, passes it from hand to hand, turns it over, and takes it to her mouth. When lying on her back, she likes to play with her toes. She loves to crumple paper, and to splash water in the bath.

9 months

The baby is able to use fingers and thumb to grasp an object (**C**). She can also open her hands when she wants, and deliberately drops things on the floor.

C

D

By the tenth month she goes for things with her index finger and pokes at them, and can now pick up small objects between the tip of the index finger and the thumb (**D**).

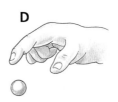

1 year

The baby can use her hands to throw things, and can point with the index finger to objects she wants.

Using hands

15 months

The child can take a cup or spoon to her mouth – but her judgement is not yet very good. She is likely to tilt the cup too far when about to drink and to turn the spoon over before the food gets to the mouth. When playing with bricks, she can place one brick on top of another to make a tower.

18 months

The child can feed herself completely, and make a tower of three bricks.

2 years

The child puts on shoes, begins to draw, turns door handles and unscrews jars. She can build a tower with six bricks.

2½ years

The child begins to be able to undress, builds a tower with eight bricks, and can thread large beads.

3 years

The child begins to dress herself but needs help with the buttons.

4 years

The child eats skilfully with spoon and fork.

5 years

The child dresses and undresses without help, and can use a knife and fork for eating.

RIGHT-HANDED OR LEFT-HANDED?

When babies start to use their hands, they use both hands equally. Many show some preference for using one hand or the other by the age of 18 months, and most have a clearly defined preference by the age of 3 years. Some are not obviously right- or left-handed until they are 4 years or older.

Most children are right-handed, but a few can use both hands with equal ease (they are **ambidextrous**). Others use one hand for some types of activity and the other hand for the rest, and about 10 per cent of boys and slightly fewer girls are left-handed. Left-handed children have more difficulty in learning to write, in opening doors, and in using equipment designed for right-handed people.

Handedness is controlled by the part of the brain which also controls language – speaking, reading and writing. If a left-handed child is forced to use the right hand, it may result in stuttering and in difficulties in learning to read and write.

LEARNING TO SWIM

Young children love playing in water and having fun with other people, and most enjoy being taught to swim. Swimming is excellent exercise as it develops muscles and co-ordination, and improves breathing. Being able to swim gives the confidence which comes from acquiring another skill, and is an important safety skill to learn.

Swimming for children with special needs

Swimming is high on the list of popular activities for these children. It gives them a sense of achievement in being like other children, develops courage and self-reliance, and improves stamina. Regular swimming sessions in a warm pool and with guidance from a qualified physiotherapist can be of particular benefit to those with certain disabilities, for example:

- learning disabilities – swimming encourages concentration and perseverance

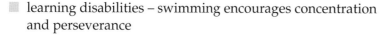

■ Down's syndrome – swimming firms up the floppy muscles, which aids digestion and breathing

■ cerebral palsy – swimming relaxes tight muscles, enabling a fuller range of movements

■ arthritis – the buoyancy and warmth of the water encourages movements of painful joints. Failure to move joints can affect growth and development.

Questions

1 What is meant by (i) physical development, (ii) motor skills, (iii) gross motor skills, (iv) fine manipulative skills?

2 Why should a newborn baby's head be supported?

3 Although the legs make walking movements, a newborn baby cannot walk. Why is the baby unable to walk?

4 What is the usual age at which babies become able to (i) roll off the bed, (ii) walk alone, (iii) play with their fingers, (iv) pick up small objects using the thumb and first finger?

5 a By what age do most children show clearly whether they are right- or left-handed?

b Name two possible consequences of forcing a left-handed child to use the right hand.

6 a Besides having fun, what other benefits are gained by learning to swim?

b (i) Why is swimming popular with children with special needs? (ii) Give examples of disabilities for which swimming is of particular benefit.

Further activities

 Extension

Describe the stage of physical development which will have been reached by a newborn baby in:

a head control

b the sitting position

c the prone position

d use of the legs

e use of the hands.

Draw pictures or find photographs from at least two different sources to illustrate each stage. Describe the progress made in A–E at 3 months, 6 months, 9 months and 1 year.

 Investigation

Carry out some research into left-handedness in children. For example, observe children in a playgroup or classroom. What percentage are left-handed? Are any of the children ambidextrous? Present your results in a pie chart. Does being left-handed cause any difficulties?

 Child study

Describe the child's stage of physical development. If a baby, what stage has been reached in head control, the prone position, sitting position and use of the legs and hands? If older, is the child right-handed or left-handed?

CHAPTER 30

Development of vision

Babies have some ability to see from the time they are born. As their eyes grow and develop and with experience, babies become able to:

- **understand** what is seen
- **alter the focus** of the eyes to see things more clearly at different distances
- **control the movements** of the eyes and use both of them together
- **recognise colours**.

STAGES OF DEVELOPMENT

Newborn

When newborn, a baby is probably only aware of vague shapes, darkness, light and movement. Babies of this age are very short-sighted because their eyes have a fixed focus of about 20–25 cm. They therefore see most clearly those things which are at this distance, with objects further away appearing blurred. When an object is placed about 20 cm in front of even the youngest baby, he will look at it for about two seconds. Babies look longer at patterns than solid colours – which indicates that they find patterns more interesting.

When a mother holds her baby in her arms, the distance between the eyes of mother and baby is the distance at which the infant can best focus. Babies are particularly interested in faces, and a few days after birth a baby is able to recognise his mother's face. Within a week or two, he will gaze at her face as she feeds or talks to him.

A newborn baby is sensitive to the intensity of light, and will shut his eyes tightly and keep them shut when a bright light is turned on. The baby also notices movement and will follow an adult or other large object for a moment. When an object, for example a bunch of keys, is dangled close to the baby, he will stare at it and will follow with short, jerking movements of his eyes if it is slowly moved from side to side.

3 months

Although still short-sighted, the baby now has a greater focusing range and therefore can see further. There is also much more control over the movements of the eyes. The baby is very interested in looking at everything around him and is able to follow people who are moving nearby. At this age, a baby spends much time in watching his own hands as he lies on his back.

6 months

The eyes now work together and the slight squint commonly shown earlier has disappeared (unless the baby has an eye defect).

1 year

The baby is able to focus on objects which are quite a long way away, and he can easily recognise people at a distance. The eyes are also able to follow a rapidly moving object.

2 years

The child can now see everything which an adult can see.

2½–5 years

A child begins to show sense of colour from the age of about 2½ years. From then onwards there is gradual improvement in the ability to recognise different colours. Red and yellow are usually the first colours to be known, and blue and green are the next. Most 5-year-olds know at least four or five colours.

EYE DEFECTS

The baby's eyes are examined soon after birth to make sure that there are no cataracts or major eye problems. At 6 weeks of age they are checked for squint and other defects, and again when the child starts school. Eye checks may also be given at 18 months and 3½ years of age.

Short sight

A short-sighted child can see near objects clearly but everything further away appears blurred. Short-sightedness develops most often between the ages of 6 and 10 years, and it can develop quite rapidly. Short sight interferes with school work; for example, a child who is unable to see what is written on the board at the front of the class may seem to be restless or slow.

Long sight

This makes objects near to the eyes appear blurred and fine details are missed. It is less common in children than short sight and may be more difficult to recognise. Long-sighted children have difficulty with writing and other close work and so they may seem to lack interest and be lazy.

Squint

A child has a squint when the eyes look in different directions. This means that the child is unable to use both eyes to look at the same object, so only one eye is used for seeing. If the squint is not treated, the child could go blind in the other eye (the 'lazy' eye).

A mild squint is normal in the first few weeks of life. Babies who have a persistent squint after the age of 6 weeks, or who develop a squint when older, should be seen by an eye specialist.

Before and after correction of a squint

Treatment for squint includes the wearing of glasses and exercises for the eye muscles. The photographs show a young child with a squint, and the same child wearing glasses to make him use his weaker eye to correct the squint.

Colour blindness

Colour blindness is the inability to see certain colours. It is much more common in boys than in girls. About 8 per cent of boys are affected to some degree compared with about 0.4 per cent of girls. There are different types of colour blindness, the usual type being red–green colour blindness; people with this defect cannot distinguish red from green.

Astigmatism

This defect of the eye makes things look blurred or out of shape. It can be corrected by glasses.

VISUAL IMPAIRMENT

The term **visual impairment** includes:

- **blindness** – the inability to perform any task for which eyesight is essential (very few blind people can see nothing at all)
- **partial sight** – vision is poor enough to be a substantial disability.

Blindness

Babies who are born blind, or who have become blind in early life, will grow in the same way as other children but their development will be hindered. Their lack of sight reduces opportunities for making contact with people and for play. This in turn reduces their opportunities for learning. Blind children will not be able to:

- make eye-to-eye contact with people (important in the emotional development of young children)
- gradually gain experience by seeing things and remembering what they look like
- reach out for objects which look interesting in order to play with them
- watch people and learn from watching
- seek out people – they will always have to wait for people to come to them
- move around on their own without being frightened or in danger
- understand the meaning of a green field, or red shoes, or a rainbow.

Blind children learn mainly through touch and hearing. They therefore need specialist help and training from the earliest possible moment to reduce, as far as possible, the effects of their disability. Parents also need to be taught how best to help their blind children develop.

Questions

1 a When a newborn baby uses his eyes, what will he be aware of?

  b As he gets older and gains experience of using his eyes, what will he become able to do?

2 a When does a baby become able to recognise his mother?

  b How can you tell that a baby is (i) sensitive to a bright light, (ii) aware of a movement?

3 a Give two ways in which a baby's vision develops between birth and 3 months.

  b By what age can the eyes (i) work together, (ii) follow rapidly moving objects, (iii) see everything which adults' eyes can see?

4 a Which colours are usually the first to be recognised?

  b Which is the most usual form of colour blindness?

  c Is it more common for boys or girls to be colour blind?

5 a (i) Why are babies' eyes not checked at birth for squint? (ii) When are they first checked for squint? (iii) Can a squint develop later?

  b (i) Why is the boy shown on p. 150 said to have a squint? (ii) What treatment is he being given, and what effect can you notice? (iii) Why is it important for the squint to be treated?

6 a Give two examples of ways in which eye defects can interfere with school work.

  b What is astigmatism?

  c At what age does short sight most commonly develop?

7 a What is meant by visual impairment?

  b Give reasons why the development of blind children will be hindered.

Further activities

 Investigation

Devise an experiment to discover what a baby finds most interesting to look at.

 Design

Design a mobile which you could make to hang above a baby's cot or in a 2-year-old's room.

 Child study

Use a graphics program to make an outline picture of an object with which the child is familiar, e.g. a train, car or teddy bear. Print several versions, each filled in with a different colour. Find out which colours the child recognises.

Weblinks

Search for 'development of eyesight' at:

www.childhealth.co.uk

For information on children's eyesight and how to recognise problems, visit:

www.mychild.co.uk

For information on taking care of children's eyesight, visit:

www.familiesonline.co.uk

and search for 'children's eyesight'.

CHAPTER 31

Development of hearing

By about the fifth month of pregnancy, babies' ears have developed sufficiently for them to hear, and they respond to a wide variety of sounds. While in the uterus, they can hear the mother's heartbeat and noises from her intestines. They also react to noises outside such as the slamming of a door or loud music. High-pitched sounds tend to make babies more active, and they are soothed by repetitive low-pitched sounds.

After the baby is born, the mother tends to hold her baby on her left arm. The baby can hear the mother's heartbeat, which is the same type of rhythm that was heard in the uterus, and which appears to have a calming effect.

CHECKLIST FOR DEVELOPMENT OF HEARING

The following checklist gives some of the general signs which show that the baby's hearing is developing normally.

Newborn

The baby is startled by a sudden loud noise (e.g. a door slamming) and blinks or opens his eyes widely.

1 month

The baby begins to notice continuous sounds (e.g. a vacuum cleaner) and pauses and listens to them when they begin. Young babies are often soothed by particular types of music and singing (e.g. lullabies).

4 months

The baby quietens or smiles at the sound of his mother's voice, even when he cannot see her.

7 months

The baby turns immediately to his mother's voice across a room, or to very quiet noises made on either side of him (if he is not too occupied with other things).

9 months

The baby looks around for very quiet sounds made out of his sight.

1 year

The baby responds to his own name and to other familiar words.

HEARING IMPAIRMENT (DEAFNESS)

Some children are born with hearing impairment. Others may become permanently deaf through meningitis or other causes. Temporary deafness can be due to 'glue ear' – a build-up of sticky fluid in the middle ear caused by infection. Glue ear can be treated by medicines or by surgery.

Hearing loss can be total or, more often, partial. Partial deafness means that some sounds are heard but not others. Sometimes only low notes are heard, and not those of a higher pitch. A baby cannot then make sense of the sounds people make when they talk to him. In other cases only loud noises or angry voices can be heard, but not normal speech or gentle voices. So these babies link noise with unpleasantness.

When deafness is unrecognised, a child may be wrongly labelled as lazy, difficult to manage, or as having a learning disability. In fact the child is confused and frustrated. He has great difficulty in understanding what is said to him and any slight changes or new instructions are a cause for worry.

Deafness prevents a child from learning to talk

Up to the age of 6 months, a deaf baby uses his voice to gurgle and babble in the same way as other babies. The parents may not realise that their baby has a hearing problem because the baby is responding in other ways. Babies respond to the vibrations of a slammed door as well as to the loud noise it makes. They respond to what they can see – facial expressions, gestures and the movement around them.

After about the first 6 months, speech development of a deaf baby does not progress any further. A child needs to listen to meaningful sounds in order to copy them, and a deaf child does not hear sounds which have any meaning. So he is unable to learn to talk. Instead of using his voice more and more like other children, a deaf child uses his voice less and the variety of sounds decreases.

SCREENING TEST FOR HEARING

A **screening test** for hearing is carried out on babies in the first few weeks of life. The aim is to identify the one or two babies in every 1,000 who are born with a hearing loss in one or both ears. The test is quick and painless and carried out while the baby is asleep or settled. A number of babies need to have a second test when the first test does not show a clear response from both of the baby's ears. This could be because the baby is unsettled, or there is background noise, or perhaps a temporary blockage in the ear.

It is extremely important to recognise deafness in children at an early age because the right training and treatment can then be given to reduce the effect of the disability. A child who does not hear sounds until the age of 3 years will be slow in learning new sounds. If a child cannot hear them by the age of 7, it will be very difficult or impossible to teach him/her the sounds.

Hearing test

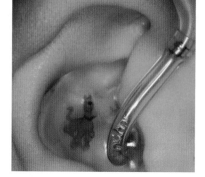

Child's hearing aid

Questions

1 a When is a baby first aware of sounds?

 b (i) Name four sounds which an unborn baby can hear. (ii) Which type of sounds are soothing?

2 a How does a baby indicate that he can hear (i) when newborn, (ii) at 1 month, (iii) at 4 months, (iv) at 7 months, (v) at 9 months, (vi) at 1 year?

3 a Why may parents not realise that their baby has a hearing problem?

 b Although a deaf baby can use his voice, why can't he learn to talk?

 c When a child's deafness is unrecognised, what may he be wrongly labelled?

 d (i) When are babies first screened for hearing? (ii) Why may they need a second test?

 e Why is it important for deafness to be identified early?

 f What is glue ear, and what effect can it have on hearing?

 g Is it more common for deafness to be total or partial?

 h How does partial deafness affect hearing? Give two examples.

Further activities

⏩ Extension

Try to get some idea of what it is like to be deaf by (i) wearing ear plugs for a while, (ii) turning the sound off when watching television. Suggest some of the difficulties which a deaf child will have to overcome and which a child who can hear well does not.

🔍 Investigation

Find out about the types of treatment and training that can be given to deaf children.

Weblinks

For a child hearing checklist, search 'hearing checklist' at:

www.medic8.com

For more information on hearing problems in children, visit:

www.safekids.co.uk

CHAPTER 32

Development of speech

Speech is an important means of communication. Talking enables people to exchange information, tell others about their feelings and discuss problems.

COMMUNICATION WITHOUT WORDS (NON-VERBAL COMMUNICATION)

Babies have an inborn desire to communicate with other people. Long before they are able to talk, they use other means of getting messages across, such as:

- using the eyes – contact with another person can be made in this way
- tone of voice – a cry, scream or gurgle all carry different messages
- expression on the face – this can indicate pleasure, anger, contentment etc.
- using the hands – babies try to make their wishes known by pointing, clinging, throwing, pushing away, pulling etc.

Before they have learnt to talk, some babies become very cross and frustrated when they cannot make adults understand what is in their mind or what they want to do. Much of this bad temper disappears when they can use words. Being able to talk also makes life much more interesting for the child.

HOW CHILDREN LEARN TO TALK

In order to be able to talk, children have to learn how to make the right sounds and to put them together in a meaningful way. This ability comes with lots and lots of practice over several years. The following activities all play a part in learning to talk.

1. **Other people talking to them** Most mothers, fathers and other adults seem to know instinctively that it is important for them to talk to a young baby. When they hold or look at

a baby who is awake, they nearly always speak or 'coo', often using a high-pitched tone of voice. It does not matter if the adults talk sense or nonsense at this stage. What is important to the baby is that someone is speaking to her.

2. **Listening** A baby is very aware of voices. She likes being spoken to, gazing up at the speaker and keeping quite still as she listens. As the child gets older she learns to make sounds which mean words. She does this by copying the sounds made by adults when they speak to her. A child cannot learn to talk merely by listening to the radio or television. She needs to be spoken to in a way that a young child can understand.

3. **Practising making sounds** Babies get pleasure out of using their voices and often spend hours making noises (babbling) to themselves. They also make noises to attract attention, and they enjoy holding 'conversations' (without words) with anyone whose attention they can capture.

4. **Copying sounds made by other people** Babies make a great variety of different sounds as they babble. Only some of these sounds are used when they reach the stage of copying the language of the people around them. If they are spoken to in English, they will copy English sounds and words. If they are spoken to in Chinese, Spanish or any other language they will copy the sounds and words of that particular language. If children hear a lot of swear words, then they will learn those too. If no one bothers to talk to them, then they will not be able to speak very well at all.

5. **Learning what the sounds mean** Young children understand the meaning of words long before they can say them.

PATTERN OF SPEECH DEVELOPMENT

Speech development follows a general pattern. However, there are great differences in the speed at which individual children learn to talk – greater than in any other field of development. Some children will be in advance of, and others much behind, the average ages mentioned here. Girls tend to talk earlier than boys.

Newborn

The baby uses her voice to cry. She also makes other noises when she hiccups, sneezes and 'burps'.

By the age of 1 month, the baby is making little sounds which come from the throat (**guttural** sounds). At 5–6 weeks she is beginning to use her voice (**vocalise**) to coo and gurgle in response to someone speaking to her.

3 months

The baby can make more sounds now that she is beginning to learn to control the muscles of her lips, tongue and **larynx** (voice box). She gurgles and babbles to herself, and also likes to hold

A

B

C

D

'conversations' with other people. A 'conversation' takes place when the baby makes a noise and then waits for the other person to make a noise.

6 months

A great variety of sounds can now be made such as 'goo', 'der', 'adah', 'ka'. Much time is spent practising these sounds. The baby also laughs, chuckles and squeals in play, and screams when annoyed.

9 months

The baby may say 'dad-dad', 'mum-mum' and 'bab-bab', often repeating the same sound many times. She also begins to copy the sounds made by adults.

1 year

The baby is beginning to understand that some sounds have definite meanings. It is usual, at this age, to say two or three words with meaning, for example, 'dad-dad', 'mum-mum', 'bye-bye'. As the baby comes to understand the meaning of words she can obey simple instructions, like 'Give it to Daddy'.

Babies' first words are nearly always labels for people, animals or things. For example, 'dog' can be used for all animals. The next words are likely to be for food and clothes.

During the next year the child continues to learn more words. She practises making the sounds by talking to herself, at times continuously. At this stage a child may use a language of her own (**jargon**), which no one but her parents can understand.

18 months

The child says 6–20 words.

2 years

She uses 50 or more words and may be able to put two or three together to form a simple sentence.

2½ years

She uses pronouns – I, me, you – and is continuously asking questions. (See also Topic 39.)

3 years

She can carry on a simple conversation and talks incessantly.

4 years

A child's speech is usually easy to understand at this age because most of the basic rules of grammar have been acquired.

PRONUNCIATION

Young children make many mistakes as they learn to speak. They may mispronounce words (say them incorrectly) because they have difficulty in making the correct sounds. They may substitute easier sounds. For example:

- th for s (yeth for yes) – this is called **lisping** and it is quite common in young children
- f for th (fin for thin)
- v for th (fever for feather)
- w for r (wed for red)
- l for y (lellow for yellow).

Difficulties in pronunciation have usually disappeared by the age of 5 or 6 years.

STUTTERING (STAMMERING)

Children aged 2–4 years may sound as though they are beginning to develop a stutter. Sometimes words or parts of words are repeated, almost as if the child is filling in time as she sorts out her thoughts. At this age there is much that children want to say, they are in a hurry to say it and they stumble over words as they try to do so. This is not a true stutter. It is a temporary stage that children pass through as they learn to speak.

Most children pass through this stage quite quickly. It is only likely to become a problem when parents make a fuss about it and try to correct the child's speech. The child then becomes self-conscious about talking and a real stutter may develop. A child who develops a longer lasting stutter may need the help of a speech therapist.

SLOWNESS IN LEARNING TO TALK

Slowness in learning to talk has many causes including:

- **inherited pattern of development** – it may be the family pattern to be late in talking.
- **concentrating first on other aspects of development** – learning to walk or use the hands may come first.
- **not enough individual attention from adults** – children learn to talk from adults rather than other children. A young child in a large family may not get enough attention from adults. This can also happen to twins and in families where young children are close in age.
- **lack of encouragement** – if no one shares the baby's pleasure in the sounds she is making, then the baby will not be encouraged to produce different sounds.

BARRIERS TO COMMUNICATION

Some children have great difficulty in communicating by speech for reasons which include:

- **deafness** (see p. 153)
- **a speech disorder** – this can be caused by a defect in any part of the body concerned with speech such as mouth, vocal cords, or damage to the part of the brain concerned with language
- **emotional** – reluctance to speak due to shyness, fear etc.
- **cultural** – differences in language, background, or accent.

COMMUNICATION THERAPY

This is treatment for people with communication difficulties, mainly problems with speech.
Speech and communication therapists give advice and help to children and their parents in cases of:

- **delayed language development** – slowness in learning to talk
- **speech defects** – the child does not speak clearly, because of physical or emotional barriers to communication.

Questions

1 Explain the meaning of these words:

   a babbling

   b guttural

   c vocalise

   d larynx

   e jargon.

2 (i) Give four ways in which babies communicate with people before they have learnt to talk. (ii) In what way is the baby in the photograph on p. 155 communicating?

3 Name five activities that must take place so that children can learn to talk.

4 **a** What is lisping?

   b Give four other examples of the ways in which children substitute easy sounds for ones they find more difficult.

5 **a** Give a reason why some babies become very frustrated at times before they have learnt to talk.

   b Which comes first, a young child's understanding of a word or the ability to say it?

   c (i) Why may a 3-year-old appear to be developing a stutter? (ii) When is it likely to become a real problem?

6 **a** Do girls or boys tend to be slower in learning to talk?

   b Give four other reasons for being slow to talk.

7 **a** Even when children know how to talk, they may have difficulty in communicating by speech. Explain why.

   b For what conditions are speech therapists consulted?

Further activities

 Extension

The drawings A–H on pp. 156–7 show children at different stages of speech development. Place the eight stages in the correct order of development, giving the average age at which each stage occurs.

 Discussion

Discuss 'Placing a child in front of the television for hour after hour is no substitute for a real live person to talk to'.

 Investigation

1 Observe a group of small children playing, and note the ways in which they communicate non-verbally.

2 Talk with children of different ages and stages of speech development. Record the conversations. Discuss and compare the results.

  a How many different words did each child use?

  b Set up a database of different phrases of (i) two words, (ii) three words, (iii) four or more words.

  c Sort out the words in your lists into nouns, verbs and pronouns.

 Child study

Talk to the child, listen carefully to what is said, then describe the stage which has been reached in learning to talk. Give some examples of what is said. Make a list of the words the child uses, adding more examples during the course of the study. Note any surprising statements the child comes out with.

Weblinks

Find out more about the National Literacy Trust's 'talk to your baby' campaign, to encourage parents and carers to talk more to children from birth to 3 years:

www.literacytrust.org.uk

They also have plenty of information on the impact of early speech, language and communication difficulties.

For information on speech therapy for children, visit:

www.kidsdevelopment.co.uk

and go to 'speech & language 3+' on the sidebar and select 'speech therapy for children'.

CHAPTER 33

Social development

Social development – **socialisation** – is the process of learning the skills and attitudes which enable individuals to live easily with other members of their community.

Social development follows similar patterns all over the world although social customs vary in different countries and even between different groups in the same country. Variation can be seen in eating habits, standards of hygiene, forms of greeting, attitudes to dress, religion and morals.

Activities which encourage social development are those which bring a child into the company of other people both inside and outside the home, for example:

- family outings
- parent and toddler groups
- playgroups and nursery schools
- opportunities to play with friends.

SOCIAL SKILLS

Children (and adults) are happier and healthier if they get on well with the people around them. It will be easier for them to do this if they are trained in **social skills**. These are skills which make a child's behaviour more socially acceptable to other people. They include:

- the ability to meet, mix and communicate with others
- knowing how to share, take turns, and accept rules
- having standards of cleanliness acceptable to others, e.g. washing, using the toilet
- eating in a manner which does not offend others.

Children are not born with a knowledge of these social skills. They gradually acquire them as they copy parents, carers and others with whom they come into contact. Parents and carers have an important part to play in guiding and encouraging them to develop acceptable social skills.

PATTERN OF SOCIAL DEVELOPMENT

Newborn babies are social beings right from the start. They have an inborn need for the company of other people. They cry if they are lonely and can be comforted by being held close to another person. The following stages occur in a baby's social development:

1. The baby begins to interact with other people

2 weeks
The baby watches his mother's face as she feeds and talks to him and he soon comes to recognise her.

4–6 weeks
The baby begins to smile. He will then smile to show pleasure when people look at him.

3 months
When an adult speaks to the baby, he will respond by making noises, and he likes holding 'conversations' with people.

6 months
The baby is beginning to understand how to attract attention, for example, by a cough. He learns how to make people do what he wants – at least on some occasions.

2. The baby learns that he is part of a family

9 months
He distinguishes strangers from people he knows, and needs the reassuring presence of a familiar adult to overcome shyness and anxiety.

3. The child learns to co-operate as a member of a group

1 year
He understands and obeys simple commands.

15 months
He copies and 'helps' adults in the house and garden.

2 years
He likes to play near other children, but not with them, and defends his possessions with determination. He will show concern for other children in distress.

3 years
He plays with other children and understands sharing.

4 years
He needs other children to play with but his behaviour is alternately co-operative and aggressive.

5–7 years
He co-operates with his companions and understands the need for rules and fair play.

LEARNING TO SAY 'THANK YOU'

When people say 'thank you' they are expressing their gratitude for something which has been done for them. Young children have no understanding of the efforts of others and it is not natural for them to say 'thank you'. But if they are taught to be grateful for what other people do for them, and to say 'thank you', it will make them more pleasant to live with.

LONELINESS

The child who does not have sufficient social contact, that is, does not have enough people and friends to talk to and play with, will feel lonely. There are also children who feel lonely even when they are being looked after with other children. Feeling lonely over a long period of time can make a child unhappy and slow down development.

Adults who are cut off from sufficient contact with other people can also feel lonely and perhaps depressed. This sometimes applies to mothers of young children. The remedy is for the mother to find ways in which she can meet and mix with more people. If these people also have young children, then her own child will benefit from more company as well as from a happier mother.

DEVELOPMENT OF SOCIAL PLAY

Between the ages of 1 and 5 years, children show gradual development from simple to more complicated forms of social play. Most children pass through the following stages as they learn to play together in groups.

1. **Solitary play** – playing alone.
2. **Parallel play** – playing alongside others but not with them (**A**).
3. **Looking-on play** – watching from the edge of the group as other children play (**B**).
4. **Joining-in play** – playing with others by doing the same thing as everybody else, for example, running around together, or playing with dolls as in **B**.
5. **Co-operative play** – belonging to a group and sharing in the same task, for example, doing a jigsaw together, or cooking, or playing with a rope, as in **C** and **D**.

A

B

C

D

Questions

1 a What is meant by social development?

b What is meant by 'social skills'?

c Give some examples of the social skills which children need to learn.

2 List the stages which come under the heading 'Pattern of Social Development'.

3 What is object permanence?

4 List the five stages in the development of social play.

Weblink

For more information on stages in children's social development, visit:

www.kidsdevelopment.co.uk and go to 'Social & Emotional 0–3' on the sidebar, then select 'General Stages of Social Development'.

Further activities

 Extension

1 List, in two columns, remarks which adults might make which would (i) bolster a child's self-esteem, (ii) discourage self-esteem.

2 a Use a camcorder to make a film of children playing (make sure you get their parents' permission first).

b Study your film. Can you identify (i) some or all of the stages in the development of social play listed above? (ii) some of the social skills mentioned on p. 161?

 Discussion

Discuss:

a 'How do children learn the necessary social skills?'

b 'The effects of loneliness on a child's development' (see also Topics 18 and 35).

 Child study

Describe the stage of social development which the child has reached. What social skills has the child already learnt?

CHAPTER 34

Emotional development

Emotions are feelings such as fear, excitement, affection, happiness, worry, sadness, anger, contentment, pride, jealousy, shyness, frustration, distress and disgust. Young children show all these emotions and many more. **Emotional development** – the development of a child's ability to recognise and control her feelings – is influenced by the child's inborn temperament (effects of her genes), her environment and her state of health.

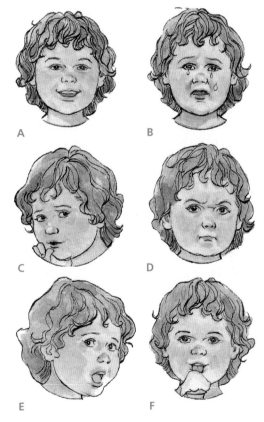

Inborn temperament

This depends on the genes the child inherits. Children vary considerably in the strength of their emotions. For example, some children are naturally very excitable, others less so. Some children are very shy, others are rarely shy. Some are great worriers, others seem almost carefree.

Environment

This means the surroundings and conditions in which the child grows up. Environmental factors which have a marked effect on emotional development include:

▥ **the home** – this includes the home conditions, the behaviour of the people in the house and the effects of the fortunes and misfortunes which occur as a child grows up.

▥ **training** – the type of training children receive from adults will affect the amount of control they develop over their emotions (**self-control**). For example, control over temper; whether they are able to overcome feelings of jealousy; how they learn to deal with worry and frustration.

▥ **children and adults outside the home** who influence the child.

State of health

There is a strong link between a child's state of health and her feelings. When a child is ill, she will have different feelings from when she is well. Long-term illness or handicap can have a marked effect on a child's emotional development. What sort of effect it will have depends on the child's inborn temperament and the care and training she receives.

BONDS OF ATTACHMENT

Emotional development will be affected by the extent to which infants form **bonds of attachment**, that is, strong feelings of attachment for the people who have the most meaning to them.

Being held close to another person gives a baby feelings of comfort and security. These feelings are strengthened by:

- **skin-to-skin contact** – as happens when the baby breast-feeds
- **eye-to-eye contact** – when the baby gazes into her parent's eyes
- **familiar smells** – a baby learns to recognise the smell of her mother's breast within a few days of birth
- **familiar sounds** – a baby soon learns to recognise the voice of her mother and responds more readily to it than to other voices.

As the infant becomes familiar with a person who stimulates feelings of comfort and security, a bond of affection develops. The baby's first emotional bond will be with her mother or the person who looks after her most of the time. The more the baby is cuddled and loved, the stronger the bond is likely to be.

LOVE

Love is one of the basic needs of every child (and indeed every adult). Babies thrive on an abundance of love. Parents who truly love their child accept her for what she is. They let her know they love her by cuddling and talking to her and by giving her their time, attention and companionship. Their love is continuous and undemanding.

Not all babies are loved and wanted. Lack of love and interest makes a child feel insecure and unhappy. Often, such children do not thrive physically or learn to deal satisfactorily with their emotions.

A loving family affects a child's emotional and social development because it allows strong bonds of attachment to be formed between her and other members of her family. She will not then be afraid to show affection for other people. Whereas a child who is not loved by her family may not learn how to love others because she is unable to form long-lasting bonds of attachment with them.

We buy her everything she wants and she's still not happy

'Smother' love

All children need plenty of love. They also need to be allowed to do things in their own way and to make mistakes so that they can learn from them. When they are over-protected and prevented from becoming independent as soon as they are ready, then the love becomes 'smother' love. Smother love may show itself in the following ways:

- not letting a child play as she wants and always interfering
- being over-anxious about every movement
- constantly worrying about the child's bowels and toilet-training
- constantly worrying about the amount she eats and sleeps.

SHYNESS

Children have phases of shyness, often for no apparent reason. At 6 months old, a child is usually still friendly with strangers but occasionally shows some shyness. By 1 year old she is likely to hide behind her mother when a stranger speaks to her, or cover her eyes with her arm (**stranger anxiety**). Even when older, some children may become silent and shy in the presence of people they do not know.

Some children are by nature much more shy than others. The shyness is increased when they are in a strange place with new people, whereas the presence of a parent helps them to feel much less shy.

Giving the child plenty of love and security and many opportunities to meet other children helps to prevent excessive shyness. Saying to a child 'Don't be shy' or 'Have you lost your tongue?', or teasing her about it, will make her more shy. Shyness usually disappears with time.

EMOTIONAL REACTIONS TO STRESS

Children often react very strongly to stress. Events which may cause stress in children include:

- starting at playgroup or school
- break-up of their family
- a new baby in the family
- death of a relative or a pet
- moving house
- child abuse (pp. 161–4).
- separation from a parent.

They do not understand what is happening and they have not yet reached a stage in emotional development which enables them to control or express their feelings. They may react by showing signs of distress in some of the following ways:

- regression (p. 159)
- temper tantrums (p. 223)
- jealousy (p. 172)
- bed-wetting (p. 186)
- nightmares (p. 174)
- aggression (p. 224)
- refusal to speak ('**elective mute**').

The stress can be reduced, and is less likely to be prolonged, when parents discuss the stressful event with their child or children in a way which helps them to understand.

SELF-ESTEEM

Self-esteem (self-respect) means valuing yourself as a person. You know that you are like other people in being able to do some things well, but not everything. Children with self-esteem have a positive self-image and this gives them:

- **self-confidence** – they know that they can cope easily with the people they meet and the situations in which they find themselves.
- **self-reliance** – they want to be independent. This comes when children are encouraged to do things for themselves, e.g. babies who are allowed to feed themselves, toddlers who choose what clothes to wear etc.

Factors affecting self-esteem

A child's self-esteem is affected by many factors:

most importantly:

- the way the child is encouraged and supported by parents and other adults who care for him.

Other factors are:

- the child's environment, e.g. poverty and deprivation
- discrimination because of race, gender, religion
- the child may be 'different', either because of:
  - disability, e.g. deafness, lameness
  - infection, e.g. HIV positive.

Encouraging self-esteem

Self-esteem develops more strongly in children who are:

- praised for what they can do, not criticised for what they cannot do
- encouraged to develop new skills
- given choices – perhaps about the clothes they wear or toys they prefer to play with
- encouraged to discuss their feelings and express their ideas
- given minimum assistance, so allowing them to feel that they have control over their own activities.

Low self-esteem (low self-image)

Signs of low-esteem may show as:

- often expressing dislike of herself
- trying too hard to please
- constantly belittling herself
- often saying that her wishes do not matter
- lack of pride in her origins
- trying to change her appearance.

A child with low self-esteem may need to be helped by social workers or others specially trained in this field to help prevent her from becoming emotionally damaged. When adolescent, low self-esteem can result in personality difficulties and problems with developing adult relationships.

Growing up to be emotionally healthy/unhealthy

Emotionally healthy

Emotionally unhealthy

praised and encouraged ⟷ faced with years of criticism

supported and encouraged ⟷ believing she is worthless; getting into trouble at home; getting into trouble at school

feels valued by family and friends, and more able to form long-term relationships ⟷ feels of little value to anyone and has difficulty in forming long-term relationships

Questions

1 a The six faces A–F on p. 165 show the emotions of happiness, fear, sadness, anger, contentment, and shyness. Sort out which face shows which emotion.

  b Other emotions are mentioned in this topic. Can you find ten more?

2 a Name three factors which influence emotional development.

  b What does the inborn temperament depend on?

  c Name three environmental factors which have a marked effect on emotional development.

  d What effect does the child's state of health have?

3 a With whom will a baby form her first bonds of attachment?

  b (i) What feelings are produced in a baby by being cuddled and held close to another person? (ii) What strengthens these feelings?

Questions

4 a How can parents let their child know they love her?

b How may a child who lacks love be affected (i) physically, (ii) emotionally, (iii) in learning how to love?

c Name four ways in which 'smother love' may show itself.

5 What may help to prevent excessive shyness in a child?

6 a Give some examples of events which may cause stress in a child.

b Give examples of ways in which children react to stress.

c What action may help to reduce the stress?

7 a What is meant by (i) self-esteem, (ii) self-confidence, (iii) self-reliance?

b (i) What is the most important factor affecting self-esteem in a child?

(ii) Give three other factors that can affect self-esteem.

(iii) Suggest more examples of disabilities that can cause a child to feel or be considered 'different'.

c Give five actions by parents and carers that encourage the development of self-esteem in children.

d (i) Give six signs of low self-esteem. (ii) What help can be given to children with low self-esteem, and for what purpose?

8 Describe in your own words why a child might grow up to be (i) emotionally healthy, (ii) emotionally unhealthy.

Further activities

 Extension

1 Draw or find photographs of children showing different emotions.

2 Look through this book and list illustrations showing situations which help a bond of affection to develop between (i) a child and her (or his) mother, (ii) a child and her (or his) father.

 Discussion

Consider the picture on p. 166 and discuss 'Can money buy love?'

 Child study

What different emotions (feelings) have you noticed in the child? For each emotion mentioned, describe the occasion when you noticed it. Suggest something which, in your opinion, may have produced the emotion. Describe ways in which the child is being helped to control his or her emotions.

Weblink

For a great many articles on various aspects of a child's development, visit:

www.kidsdevelopment.co.uk/

CHAPTER 35

Security and insecurity

A child's feelings may affect his development in many ways, and of special importance are the feelings of security and insecurity.

SECURITY

A secure child is one who **feels safe**. He knows that there is always someone who cares and always a place where he belongs. He feels safe not only from being hurt but also from being lonely, unhappy, rejected and afraid. Knowing that all is well with his world helps him to continue to develop normally.

INSECURITY

An insecure child is one who **feels unloved** and **unwanted.** In general, children who feel insecure will either become timid and withdrawn or (more likely) indulge in 'bad' behaviour in order to attract attention. Children soon learn that such inappropriate behaviour makes people notice them, while to be 'good' often results in being ignored.

Insecurity in children will be reflected in their behaviour. It may be expressed as (**list A**):

- jealousy
- fear
- rudeness
- spitefulness
- aggression
- destructiveness
- bad temper
- nervousness
- extreme shyness
- stuttering
- clinging to the mother
- stomach ache, headache, or other symptoms of illness
- toileting problems (e.g. wetting and soiling).

Insecurity may have many causes. The list below gives some suggestions (**list B**):

- loneliness and boredom
- excessive discipline and punishment
- too little discipline
- a new baby in the family
- the mother feeling depressed because she is unhappy or unwell
- fear of starting school
- too much worry on the part of the parents over such things as feeding, cleanliness, tidiness and toilet-training
- fears which an adult has passed on to the child
- low self-image.

SEPARATION ANXIETY

Separation anxiety occurs when children become anxious and distressed when separated from their mother or person who is most important in their life. They can see that their mother is walking away from them but do not understand that she will come back. It is a stage that many older babies and toddlers go though at various times and to varying extents, generally starting at about six months of age and declining at the age of three.

REGRESSION

Reverting to an earlier stage of behaviour is called **regression**. It is particularly likely to happen when a child feels insecure. For example, a child who is toilet-trained may revert to wetting his pants. It is no good scolding or smacking the child. What is needed is extra love and attention until he feels secure enough to go back to his normal behaviour.

JEALOUSY

Jealousy is a natural human emotion common to all children, but it is not a happy feeling. It can show in many ways including:

- hitting and biting another child
- snatching toys away from another child
- demanding attention
- moping (listlessness)
- reaction to a new baby in the family

A new baby in the family

Jealousy is often a problem when a new baby comes into the family. The feelings of an older brother or sister are likely to be a mixture of affection for the baby and jealousy arising from fear that the new baby is a rival for the parents' affections. Thus, the older child feels insecure. This type of jealousy is known as **sibling rivalry** (**sibling** means brother or sister).

The jealous feelings of the older child cannot be prevented. But, if the parents handle the situation well, jealousy can be kept to a minimum. It will gradually disappear when the older child no longer fears that the baby is a rival.

How parents can help

Parents can help to reduce the amount of jealousy in the older child by:

- preparing him for the new baby's arrival
- reassuring him often that he is loved and wanted (even when behaving badly)
- encouraging him to feel more grown-up and independent
- avoiding comparisons with the new baby in his hearing.

Preparing for a new baby

It is a good idea to prepare the child for a new baby's arrival. He will notice that his mother's tummy is getting bigger, and she can tell him that there is a new baby inside. She may let him pat her tummy and feel the baby kicking, but should explain that the baby needs to grow a little bigger before it is ready to come out. The mother should tell him that she will have to go into hospital for a little while when the baby comes. It will also help if the child knows what a new baby looks like and that he cannot expect a playmate.

Before the new baby comes, the parent should tell the child that when the baby arrives, it will need to be fed on milk, will cry sometimes, and will need to be looked after very carefully. The child can help to collect all the things the baby will need. The parents should try to make sure that the child knows and likes the people who will look after him while the mother is away.

FEAR

Fear is a natural response to danger, or to the thought of danger. Therefore it is quite normal for children to become frightened from time to time.

Young babies show fear by crying when there is a sudden noise or when they feel they are falling. Around 9 months old they may cry when strangers take notice of them. Between the ages of 2 and 3 years they develop particular fears, such as fear of the dark, thunder, dogs, spiders, 'nasty men', noisy machines, or even the plug hole in the bath.

These fears are very real to them. They come about because the child's imagination is developing and he is not yet old enough to understand. The natural fears of childhood can be increased when adults:

- **talk carelessly** in front of children about fires or burglars
- **make threats** – 'I will lock you in the cupboard', or 'I will run away and leave you'
- **let the child know that they themselves are afraid** – of the dark, thunder, or spiders.

NIGHTMARES

Some children have nightmares quite often, others rarely do. They may occur when an infection is just beginning, when the child is particularly tired, or following a heavy meal just before going to bed. The frightening dreams either wake the child up or the child appears to be terrified while still asleep and cries out with fear. An adult needs to go promptly to the frightened child to comfort, reassure and give security. Nightmares are no cause for worry unless they happen nearly every night. Then they are likely to be due to unhappiness or insecurity at home or school. The cause should be looked for and dealt with.

Questions

1 a What might an insecure child be trying to obtain by inappropriate behaviour?

b List some of the ways in which insecurity may show in a child's behaviour.

c Suggest reasons why a child may feel insecure.

d What is separation anxiety?

2 a What is a sibling?

b (i) When may sibling rivalry be a problem in the family? (ii) When will the older child's jealousy disappear? (iii) How can parents help to reduce this form of jealousy?

3 a Why is it normal for children to have fears?

b Suggest a reason for the development of fears in a 2-year-old.

c Suggest three ways in which other people may increase a young child's fears.

4 a (i) What is regression? (ii) Give an example.

b (i) What can parents do to help a child return to his normal behaviour?

(ii) What reaction by parents and carers is likely to be unhelpful?

Further activities

 Extension

1 How many types of behaviour in list A (p. 171) have you noticed in children? Choose four from the list. For each:

a name the behaviour.

b describe how the child behaved.

c in your opinion might the reason have been any of the suggestions in list B? If not, make your own suggestion.

 Child study

Have you noticed the child behaving in any of the ways in list A (p. 171)? How did you, or the parents, react to the behaviour? Does the child have nightmares?

Weblink

For more information on nightmares and night-time fears, visit:

www.healthvisitors.com and go to 'parenting', select 'baby sleep' and then 'sleep disrupters'.

CHAPTER 36

Discipline

Discipline (or the lack of it) will affect the ways in which children behave and their social and emotional development.

THE NEED FOR DISCIPLINE

Children need sufficient discipline to help them to understand:

- what is safe and unsafe to do
- what their parents and carers consider to be an acceptable standard of behaviour, and
- that there are consequences for misbehaviour.

The form of discipline will need to vary according to the stage of the children's development with the object of ensuring that, by the time they have become adults, they have learnt to control their own behaviour by self-control (**self-discipline**). Children show that they have self-discipline when they behave properly because they understand that they should, and not because they have been told or forced to do so.

Parents do not always find it easy to get children to co-operate with them, and children often resent being told what to do. But parents who provide a certain amount of the right kind of discipline can make life happier for all.

GOOD DISCIPLINE

Discipline which is **firm**, **kind**, **reasonable** and **consistent** benefits children because it:

- **makes them feel secure,** since they know what is expected of them
- **helps them to behave in a way acceptable to others,** who will like them better for it
- **teaches them what is safe and unsafe**
- **helps them to develop self-control.**

LACK OF DISCIPLINE

Insufficient discipline is often harmful. It results in a child who is likely to be:

- **insecure** – because no limits are placed on her behaviour
- **greedy** – she expects to get everything she wants

- **disobedient and unco-operative** – she never wants to do as she is told
- **rude** – she does not consider other people's feelings
- **selfish** – she always expects to get her own way
- **accident-prone** – she is not taught to be aware of dangers.

EXCESSIVE DISCIPLINE

Too much discipline is also harmful because, although it may stop a child from some types of poor behaviour, it can lead to others. Excessive discipline:

- **gives rise to continuous nagging by the parent** – 'Don't do this', 'Don't do that', 'Do as you are told'
- **demands too much of a child** – too much obedience, tidiness, good table manners
- **makes a child miserable** – there are so many things the child seems not to do right even when she tries.

No child is perfect

Excessive discipline makes it difficult for a close and loving relationship to develop between child and parent.

No child is perfect. A parents' efforts to try to make a child perfect are likely to lead to two types of behaviour. Either the child becomes timid and withdrawn; or the child rebels, in which case she will behave very badly by displaying one or other forms of antisocial behaviour, for example temper tantrums, biting, stealing, aggression.

WHEN SHOULD DISCIPLINE BEGIN?

There is no point in trying to discipline children until they are old enough to understand what is wanted of them. Discipline can only be applied gradually as their understanding develops and they come to realise that their parents are pleased by some things and not by others.

Young babies simply do not understand instructions. By 1 year old, most children have begun to understand the meaning of 'NO'. However, it will be quite a while before they understand what is meant by words like 'hurry', 'wait', 'tidiness' or 'quiet'. By 2 years of age they have more understanding of what they are being asked to do. By 3 years, they should have quite a good understanding of what they are expected to do and not to do, but there will still be times when they do not appreciate what is required of them.

A   B   C

HOW TO DISCIPLINE?

It is the parents' responsibility to discipline their young children. They may sometimes find it a difficult job. To make this task easier, parents and carers should try to:

1. **Set a good example**. Children learn a great deal by imitating adults, and copy both good and bad behaviour.
2. **Praise rather than criticise**. Rewarding good behaviour by a hug, a smile, or by showing interest in what the child does, is more effective than criticising bad behaviour.
3. **Be reasonable in what they expect**. A child needs time to learn, and if parents expect too much too soon it will only make them all unhappy.
4. **Be consistent**. When a rule is made, every effort should be made to keep to it. The child will then know whether she is doing right or wrong.
5. **Mean what they say.** A child will learn the rules more quickly when 'NO' means 'NO'. If parents do not mean what they say, then the child will be confused about the limits allowed. This can make the child feel insecure.
6. **Avoid battles they cannot win**. A child cannot be forced to eat or sleep or use the toilet, no matter how much parents shout and threaten.
7. **Say sorry when they have behaved badly**. All parents are at times short-tempered and unreasonable. If the parents can say sorry afterwards, it helps the child to learn to say sorry.

D   E

Questions

1 a Why do children need discipline?

  b (i)   What type of discipline benefits children?

    (ii)   Give four ways in which children benefit from discipline.

2 How may lack of discipline show in a child?

3 a Give three harmful effects of excessive discipline.

  b Give four examples of antisocial behaviour which may result from parents' efforts to make their child perfect.

4 a Why is there no point in trying to discipline a young baby?

  b (i)   Name one word which a 1-year-old will have begun to understand.

    (ii)   Name four words which the baby will not yet know the meaning of.

5 a Whose responsibility is it to discipline young children?

  b Give seven suggestions which make it easier to discipline.

Further activities

Extension

The drawings A–E on pp. 177–8 illustrate points made in the section 'How to discipline?' For each drawing, choose the point which you consider it illustrates best.

Discussion

'Some parents consider discipline is harmful because it limits a child's freedom to develop in his or her own way.' Use information from at least two other different sources to answer the following:

a What is your opinion of this attitude?

b Give other reasons why children may not be disciplined.

Child study

Give examples of occasions when the child was disciplined. How does the child react to discipline? Does the discipline have the desired effect?

CHAPTER 37

Teaching acceptable behaviour

During childhood, children need to learn the skills and behaviour necessary for adult life. Praise and correction will both have a part to play in this.

PRAISE

As mentioned in the previous topic, praise and encouragement are likely to be more effective than correction. For example, a baby who gets praised when he feeds himself learns faster than one who is scolded for making a mess. A toddler who is praised when he uses the potty will learn to be clean and dry more quickly than if he is told off for soiling his pants.

CORRECTION

Although praise is most important, children need occasional correction in order to learn that:

- antisocial behaviour results in unpleasantness
- parents and carers mean what they say
- some actions are unsafe.

At what age should correction start?

There is no point in correcting children until they are old enough to understand why they are being corrected. Otherwise they will learn nothing, and only become confused and insecure and more difficult to deal with.

For this reason, babies under the age of 1 year should not be corrected. When a baby is doing something that the parents or carers do not like, then it is up to them to prevent it. They can do this either by turning the baby's attention to something else (distraction), or by removing the cause of the trouble.

During the second year, children will begin to understand when they have done something wrong, although this stage is unlikely to be reached until at least the age of 18 months. If the right sort of correction is given now, it will help the child to be obedient. By the age of 3, children should be well aware of whether they are being 'good' or 'naughty'.

HOW TO CORRECT A CHILD

Showing displeasure
Often all that is necessary is for parents to show children that they are not pleased with what they are doing. Children who are given plenty of praise and encouragement when behaving well will soon notice when their parents are not pleased with them.

Parents can show that they are not pleased in a number of ways. For example, they can ignore the child for a little while. Or they can insist that the child has 'time out' by making him sit on the 'naughty' chair in the corner of the room (perhaps for about three minutes for a small child), or by sending the child out of the room for a set time.

Correction should be immediate
If it is necessary to correct a young child, then it should be done immediately so that the child knows what the correction is for. A young child will not remember what all the fuss is about if he has to 'Wait until Daddy or Mummy comes home'.

Linking correction with misbehaviour
For example, if a child scribbles on the wall then the crayons should be taken away. If a child deliberately hurts another child, he should be sent away to be on his own in a corner or another

room for a short while. If a child will not stop playing to come for his dinner then it should be cleared away. The child will not starve, but he will be ready for the next meal.

Threats

Threats should not be made unless the parent actually intends to carry them out. Empty threats will not teach a child to be obedient. Such a situation is shown in the drawing on p. 180.

PHYSICAL PUNISHMENT

Some parents believe that children should not be smacked under any circumstances. Others feel that giving a child a light tap on the hand occasionally helps to emphasise their displeasure at what the child has done. But it is **never** necessary to correct children by smacking them hard, shaking them or by other forms of physical punishment. The other ways of correcting a child which have already been mentioned are much more effective, and less harmful.

Smacking

Sometimes parents hit out in anger or frustration, particularly if the child cries a lot or has problems with feeding or sleeping. Such smacking can damage the child, especially when the child is hit on the head.

Shaking

It is always dangerous to shake a baby. The baby's head is big and heavy compared to the rest of its body and, unless supported, flops around because the neck muscles are not yet strong enough to hold it steady. Shaking makes the head move backwards and forwards very quickly and with great force. This may cause tiny blood vessels in the baby's brain to tear and bleed, which can result in blindness, deafness, fits, learning difficulties, or even death. The danger is greatest for babies under 12 months, but shaking can cause the same serious injuries in toddlers.

The law on smacking children

The Children Act 2004 states that it is unlawful for a parent or carer to smack their child, except where this amounts to 'reasonable punishment'. Whether a 'smack' amounts to reasonable punishment will depend on the circumstances of each case, taking into consideration factors like the age of the child and the nature of the smack. However, physical punishment will be considered 'unreasonable' if it leaves a mark on the child or if the child is hit with an implement such as a cane or a belt.

Punishment in schools, nurseries and child care

It is illegal for teachers, nursery workers and child care workers to smack another person's child. If a person is employed privately by a parent, such as a baby-sitter or nanny, the parent may give permission for that person to smack their child as long as it is reasonable and does not amount to an offence.

EFFECTS OF CORRECTION OR PUNISHMENT

The less often correction or punishment is given, the less severe they need to be in order to have an effect. The opposite is also true – the more often they are given, the more severe they have to be to have any effect. Also, constant correction and criticism can destroy a child's confidence and self-esteem (see p. 168).

List A	List B
Children behave badly more often when they are:	Parents tend to punish more often when they are:
• Hungry	• Cross and upset
• Worried	• Worried
• Tired	• Tired
• Unwell	• Unwell
• Bored	• Too busy
• Lonely	

Frequent punishment disturbs a child and can lead to troublesome behaviour – temper tantrums, bed-wetting, disobedience and so on. When parents are frequently punishing the child, they should ask themselves why.

- Are they asking too much of the child before he is able to understand?
- Is the child being punished frequently because he is copying the parents' behaviour? Do the parents often lose their temper, shout, argue, hit each other, or damage things?
- Is the child behaving badly because of any of the factors in list A on p. 181?
- Are the parents punishing frequently because of any of the factors in list B?

MORAL DEVELOPMENT

This is the development of moral values and standards of behaviour based on respect for other people. Babies are not born with a moral sense and have no understanding of 'right and wrong'. For example, they do not understand that hitting people is wrong.

By the age of 3–4 years, children begin to have some understanding and sympathy for the feelings of others. They learn that other people consider that some actions are 'right' and others are 'wrong'. As they gain more experience of life and become able to reason, they will judge for themselves what is right and wrong and this will lead to the development of their own moral values and standards of behaviour.

Questions

1 Is praise or correction likely to be more effective in training a child:
  a to feed himself, as in the picture on p. 179.
  b not to wet his nappy?
  Explain each answer.

2 **a** (i) Why should babies under 1 year old not be corrected? (ii) Name two ways by which parents can stop the baby from behaving in a way to which they object.
  b (i) By what age should children be well aware of being 'good' or 'naughty'? (ii) Give three reasons why children need occasional correction.
  c Why should correction be immediate for young children?

3 **a** Describe three ways of correcting a child.
  b When should threats not be made?

4 **a** What effect is frequent punishment likely to have on the child?
  b What questions should parents ask when they find they are punishing their child often?

5 When a baby is shaken (i) what happens to the head, (ii) why does it happen, (iii), in what way can the brain be damaged, (iv) what can such damage to the brain result in?

6 How does the law on smacking apply to (i) parents, (ii) nursery workers, (iii) nannies?

7 **a** What is moral development?
  b Why do babies not understand that hitting people is wrong?
  c By what age do children begin to learn right from wrong?
  d When will they begin to develop their own moral values?

Further activities

 Extension

1 a From your own experience, describe some occasions when a child has been corrected (perhaps yourself as a child). In each case, say what effect the correction had.

b For each, do you consider that any of the factors in (i) list A, (ii) list B, had any connection with the behaviour or punishment? You may consider that other factors were involved, in which case describe them.

 Discussion

Contribute to a class discussion on one of the following:

Do you agree or disagree that:

a 'Encouragement and praise are more effective than punishment in the training of children.'

b 'Children are most in need of love when they are behaving badly.'

c 'Smacking is never necessary.'

 Child study

What punishment is the child given, and what are the effects?

Weblinks

For a legal guide to smacking, go to:

www.childrenslegalcentre.com

and search for 'smacking.

For more information on encouraging better behaviour – a practical guide to positive parenting, visit:

www.kidsbehaviour.co.uk

and search for 'smacking'. You could also visit:

www.nspcc.org.uk and search for and download the pdf called 'Encouraging Better Behaviour'.

Visit the NHS website for a video about Attention Deficit Hyperactivity Disorder (ADHD):

www.nhs.uk

CHAPTER 38

Bladder and bowel control

The body produces waste matter which is stored in the bladder and bowel before being discharged. The **bladder** stores liquid waste called **urine**. The solid waste stored in the **bowel** has the technical name of **faeces**. Faeces are often called 'stools', 'the motion', or 'bowel action'. At intervals the outlet from the bladder or bowel opens and waste matter is released.

BABIES

When in the uterus, the baby's intestines contain a sticky, greenish-black substance called **meconium**. The baby gets rid of this during the first few days of life by passing greenish-black stools. The stools gradually change to a yellow colour as milk is taken and the baby's digestive system gets into working order.

It is common for babies to go red, grunt and strain when passing a stool, even a soft one. The stools of a baby fed entirely on breast milk are always soft. Bottle-fed babies have stools which are firmer, browner and more smelly.

Young babies are not able to control the outlet of either the bladder or the bowel, and the bladder in particular opens many times a day.

Using the potty

Some parents try to teach their baby to use a potty when the baby is a few months old. Usually they do not have any success because a baby of this age is still far too young to learn. However, a few babies will perform regularly on the potty. This is not because the baby has learnt what to do; the reason will be either that the cold rim of the potty triggers the outlet of bladder or bowel to open, or the baby has regular bowel or bladder movements at particular times of the day.

Who is likely to be potty-trained first?

Babies who use the potty in the early months may refuse to do so at 9–12 months old. A parent who then tries to force the baby to sit on the potty runs a real risk of starting a 'battle'. A baby of this age is not yet old enough to have any voluntary control over the bowel or bladder outlets. The parent should wait for a few months and then try again.

WHEN SHOULD TRAINING BEGIN?

There are no hard and fast rules. Some parents want their child to be toilet-trained as soon as possible, others don't mind how long the nappy stage continues (within reason).

There is nothing wrong in putting a baby on a potty after the age of about 12 months, and if successful it saves a wet or dirty nappy. Problems will only result if the baby is forced to sit on the potty against her will. This is the commonest cause of later difficulties.

Toilet-training can only start properly when the child begins to learn how to control the muscles which open the bladder and bowel. This rarely happens before the age of 15–18 months and often not until 2½–3 years old. There is great variation in the speed at which normal children develop; even children of the same family become clean and dry at quite different ages.

Some pre-school groups insist on children being potty-trained before attending. Putting the child under stress to speed up the potty-training process is likely to be much less effective than gentle encouragement.

Stress can also be avoided when a child starting at a playgroup or nursery school is aware that an accident in bladder or bowel control is natural and will be dealt with sympathetically and without embarrassment or reprimand.

DEVELOPMENT OF CONTROL

Bladder control

The usual stages of development of bladder control are as follows:

1. It begins when the child is aware of passing urine, and indicates to her parents she has a wet nappy (**A**).
2. She indicates when she **is** wetting her nappy (**B**).
3. Next, she indicates when she is **about to** do so (**C**).
4. Shortly after this stage is reached, she is able to tell her parents **in time** to be put on the potty or lavatory (toilet, loo, or whatever it is called) (**D**).
5. She becomes **dry during the day**. Most children are dry during the day by the time they are 2½ years, but a few may not be so until 4–5 years or even older. Girls tend to acquire control earlier than boys.
6. She becomes **dry during the night** as well.

A   B   C   D

Bowel control

This is likely to be learnt before bladder control, and is acquired in the same way.

RELAPSE OF CONTROL (REGRESSION)

It is quite common for a child who has learnt to control her bladder and bowel to stop doing so for a while, and to return to wetting and soiling her pants. The cause may be teething, illness, change of surroundings, insecurity due to the arrival of a new baby, or there may be no obvious reason.

The relapse is likely to be short if the matter is dealt with in a way which does not undermine the child's self-esteem and if she is given praise and encouragement on the occasions when she is clean and dry. But it will usually last for a much longer time if she is smacked or punished and made to feel unloved and insecure.

FORCING A CHILD TO SIT ON THE POTTY

Children who have been forced to sit on the potty against their will are those who in later months refuse to use it. They may:

- deliberately soil or wet their pants as soon as they get off
- withhold the motion and become seriously constipated
- become bed-wetters.

These problems are not likely to arise if the child is taken off the potty as soon as she wants to get off, whether she has passed anything or not. A child who comes to associate the potty with smacking and scolding will not want to use it.

USING THE TOILET

Some children may be afraid of the toilet, and special child seats help them to feel more secure on it.

BED-WETTING

Some children take much longer than others to learn control of the bladder. By the age of 5 years, one in ten children still wets the bed occasionally. They will eventually grow out of it.

How parents can help

Restricting the amount of liquid which the child takes before bedtime is not likely to make any difference to the problem. This is because the bladder tends to adjust to less fluid, and therefore holds less before feelings of fullness occur. But there are other ways in which parents can help:

- They should remain calm and patient so that the child does not feel worried or under stress about bed-wetting.
- They could have a star chart with small rewards for a certain number of dry nights (such as a treat at teatime or an extra bedtime story).

▓ Children should not be given fizzy drinks or drinks containing caffeine such as cola and tea and certainly not before bedtime as these stimulate the kidneys to produce more than average amounts of urine.

▓ A detector mat can be useful for children over the age of 7 years. The mat is placed under the sheet and it triggers a buzzer as soon as it becomes wet. Usually, with continued use, the amount of urine passed before the child wakes becomes smaller, and many children are cured within two to three months.

▓ Some medicines can be helpful. They are very powerful, are best used for children over 7 years, and should be used for short periods only, e.g. when away from home.

▓ Waking the child during the night so that she can empty the bladder can be helpful if the child is fully woken up and at a different time each night. Night-time waking should be stopped if the bed-wetting has not lessened after two months of this treatment.

Questions

1 a What is the liquid waste from the body called?

  b Give three names for solid waste.

2 a (i) Do babies have any voluntary control over the bladder and bowel? (ii) Give reasons which may explain why a baby may perform regularly on the potty.

  b At about what age do most children begin to learn to control the muscles which open the bladder and bowel?

  c By what age are most children dry during the day?

  d Is bowel or bladder control likely to be learnt first?

3 a List six stages through which children usually pass as they learn to control the bladder.

  b Give four reasons for relapse of control.

  c What type of treatment of the child is likely to increase the length of time of the relapse?

4 Name three possible conditions which may arise in children when they are forced to sit on the potty against their will.

5 a Give seven ways in which parents can help a child to cope with the problem of bed-wetting.

  b Why is restricting the amount of liquid the child takes before bedtime not likely to be of much help?

Further activities

 ### Discussion

Discuss problems which can arise in training children to be clean and dry, and how to deal with them.

 ### Child study

What stage has the child reached in bowel and bladder control? Describe the child's progress in 'potty-training'.

Weblink

For a video on how to potty train, visit: www.howto.tv

CHAPTER 39

Intellectual development

Intellectual development (mental development; **cognitive development**) is development of the mind. The **mind** is the thinking part of the brain – the part which is used for recognising, reasoning, knowing and understanding.

A child's mind is active from the time he is born. Day by day, as the child grows, the mind develops as he:

- learns about people
- learns about things
- learns new skills
- learns to communicate
- acquires more memories
- gains more experience.

As a child's mind develops, he becomes more **intelligent**. How intelligent the child becomes will depend on two main factors:

- **genes** – these control the amount of natural intelligence he has
- **environment** – the use the child makes of his intelligence will be very much influenced by the environment in which he grows up.

Throughout childhood, the genes and environment continuously interact to produce people whose minds develop in a great variety of ways. For example, children vary in their ability to remember, their artistic or musical talents, skill at languages or mathematics, academic ability (ability to study), cleverness with the hands, and whether they have a good understanding of people and their problems.

HOW TO ENCOURAGE INTELLECTUAL DEVELOPMENT

In the first year

Development of a baby's mind is helped when parents:

- talk to the baby
- play with him
- place him in a position where he can see what is going on around him
- provide toys and objects which he can handle and investigate, and which encourage him to concentrate
- allow him to practise new skills as soon as he is ready – e.g. feeding himself
- from the age of about 9 months, start to read to him, tell him stories and show him pictures.

After the first year

Development of a child's mind is helped when the child is encouraged to:

- talk
- practise new skills – dressing himself, drawing, playing games
- be curious and ask questions
- explore new places
- play with other children
- play with toys which stimulate his imagination
- be creative and make things
- listen to stories
- look at books, and eventually learn to read.

CONDITIONS WHICH HINDER INTELLECTUAL DEVELOPMENT

The following conditions can slow down the rate of development of a child's mind:

- lack of enough opportunities for talking and playing
- nothing of interest for the child to do
- constant nagging or bullying from other people
- deafness
- poor eyesight
- poor concentration
- frequent illness
- frequent absence from school.

If these adverse conditions persist for too long, they may prevent full development of the child's natural intelligence.

HOW CHILDREN LEARN ABOUT THE WORLD AROUND THEM

Using their senses

Young babies are far more aware of their surroundings than was once thought. From their earliest days, they use their senses to develop an awareness and understanding of the world around them. They are aware of stimuli from the environment in the form of light, sound, touch and smell, and they learn as they **look**, **listen**, **feel** and **smell**. Babies take most interest in what is new or different. They are more likely to be kept alert and happy by changing patterns of stimulation, whereas the repetition of sounds and movements will often send them to sleep.

Investigating and exploring

From the age of 3 months onwards, they want to touch objects and to handle them and put them in the mouth. They come to recognise an object by its shape, what it feels like, how it looks and behaves when turned in all directions, and how it sounds when it is moved or banged. They are gaining information all the while, and new objects interest them more than familiar ones.

When children are able to move around, they approach objects or places to explore them. Places which they find interesting will encourage exploration and will increase their information about the environment.

Exploring at the seaside

Asking questions

When children are able to talk, they start to ask questions. At 2½ years they ask 'What?' and 'Who?' At 3 years they ask 'Where?' At 4 years they want to know 'Why?', 'When?' and 'How?' Their questions are continual and demanding as they try to make sense of their world. Children who have their questions answered find out a great deal of information. They are now at an age when they can begin to understand about places and people they have never seen, and about events which have happened in the past or will happen in the future.

Using books

When adults encourage children to use books, they are helping to increase the children's knowledge and awareness. **Looking at pictures** with an adult helps in understanding pictures as representations of real things, and helps develop awareness of colours, shapes, sizes and numbers of objects. **Hearing stories** helps in learning to listen and to concentrate. When children can **read** (see Topic 43), they have the means of exploring a vast store of knowledge.

Acquiring basic concepts

Concepts are general notions or ideas. Children get ideas as they play, they test them out, and they ask questions. Gradually they come to understand more and more about how the world works, and they begin to understand basic concepts such as heat, light, gravity, living and non-living things, the change of state from solid to liquid to gas and back again, time (yesterday, today, tomorrow), distance, the meaning of right and wrong (moral development p. 182) and **object permanence** – realising that an object exists even when it cannot be seen.

Learning by imitation (by copying)

Children learn a great deal by imitating the behaviour of others. For example, they learn to:

- speak by copying sounds
- write by copying letters and words
- help in the house and garden by copying adults
- know the difference between right and wrong (provided that the people around them set a good example).

THE ROLE OF ADULTS IN EARLY EDUCATION

Children are naturally curious, showing great interest in new things and getting excited about new activities. They have a great deal to learn in order to acquire the knowledge and skills which they will need as they grow up and become adults. These are gradually acquired through ordinary daily activities and through play. The greater the child's ability to cope with life, the greater will be the child's self-esteem, self-reliance and self-confidence.

The early education of children is helped when they experience many different learning activities. These can be provided by the parents and carers, by childminders or pre-school groups. Children also depend on adults for their moral development; they need to be taught about right and wrong, good and bad, sharing, helping others, and being considerate towards others.

Children learn best when adults:

- **provide plenty of opportunities** to learn skills and reinforce the patterns of learning at the appropriate stage of development.
- **give them support and encouragement** when they need it, but **do not disrupt their play** by telling them how to do things – it is better to let children have the fun of finding out for themselves.
- **help them to understand** the information they receive through their sense organs, e.g. eyes, ears etc. (The interpreting of information received through the senses is called **perception**.)
- **tell them what is happening** and let them help in the planning of activities.
- **help them to recall** (remember) and predict.
- **set a good example** and show a strong sense of right and wrong in their dealings with the child and with others.

Questions

1 a The intelligence of a child depends on two main factors. Name them.

b How does each of these factors affect a child's intelligence?

2 a How can development of the child's mind be encouraged (i) in the first year, (ii) after the first year?

b List eight conditions which may hinder this development.

3 a (i) How do young babies learn about the world around them? (ii) How will they investigate things when they are 3 months old or more?

b How do children find things out when they can talk?

c Name three ways in which children can use books and say how each way helps to increase the child's knowledge and awareness.

d (i) What is meant by a concept? (ii) List at least seven basic concepts of which a child gradually becomes aware.

e Give some examples of what children learn by copying other people.

4 a What role can adults play in early education?

b Give six types of action which adults can take to create conditions in which children learn best.

Weblink

For more information on intellectual development in children, visit:

www.kidsdevelopment.co.uk

and go to 'Learning and Thinking 3+' on the sidebar and select 'Developing Intellectual Skills' or 'Intellectual Development in Children'

Further activities

 Discussion

Discuss the importance to a child's intellectual development of the example set by parents in their conversations, reading, choice of television programmes and hobbies.

 Investigation

Obtain some books intended for young children. List each title and:

a say what age group it is suitable for

b state briefly your opinion of the book

c give ways in which you think it would help a child's mind to develop, e.g. in imagination, general education, improving reading ability.

 Design

Record a story for children which will help their imagination to develop. You can use several voices and include sound effects.

 Child study

1 Encourage the child to tidy a kitchen drawer – check beforehand that it holds a selection of cutlery of different types and sizes for comparing, sorting and counting, and make sure there are no very sharp implements. Observe and record what the child knows about numbers, shapes, sizes, colours, names, purposes, safety etc.

2 What has the child recently discovered about the world around him or her? Give some examples.

3 List ten of the child's activities and, for each, name a concept which is being learnt.

4 Describe aspects of the child's behaviour that he or she has learnt by copying other people.

Exercises

1 (i) Find pictures to illustrate both of the lists under the heading 'How to encourage intellectual development' on p. 189. (ii) For each of the illustrations on p. 190, suggest a second question.

2 From your experience of child's play, describe one incident which illustrates each suggestion for how adults can best help children to learn (p. 191).

3 a Copy and complete the chart below.

Column 1: contains a list of some of the skills and knowledge which are learnt during childhood.

Column 2: for each of the items in column 1, select an example from drawings A to L opposite which provides a learning opportunity.

Column 3: explain why you chose each example.

Column 4: give another example not shown in the drawings which also illustrates each item in column 1.

b Describe the safety aspects which would need to be considered for three of the activities shown in the drawings A to L on p. 194.

ACQUIRING SKILLS AND KNOWLEDGE			
1 Skill	**2 Example**	**3 Explanation**	**4 Your own example**
Learning to ■ co-ordinate muscles ■ concentrate ■ remember (recall) ■ be self-reliant ■ exercise self-control			
Learning about ■ heat and cold ■ floating and sinking ■ solid to liquid ■ gravity ■ distance ■ living things and growth			
Learning the meaning of ■ time ■ right and wrong ■ consideration for others			

Exercises

Exercises relevant to Section 4 can be found on p. 383.

SECTION 5

Early childhood

CHAPTER 40

The importance of play

A

Children play because it gives them pleasure. They do not play when it is not enjoyable or if they are bored with the game. Play is also an essential part of their education because while they are playing they are learning. It is an important part of socialisation.

Children need opportunities both to play with other children and to play on their own. When two or more children are together, many different games are possible. Whatever the game, the children will be learning how others behave and how to mix easily with them. At other times, children need to play on their own and without interference in order to learn how to amuse themselves. If adults spend too much time playing with a child, the child will feel bored and miserable when left on her own. Then, instead of playing happily, the child will spend her time trying to demand attention.

B

BENEFITS OF PLAY

1. **Play enables children to find out** about themselves and the world. It allows them to:
   - **a** discover
   - **b** experiment
   - **c** create
   - **d** concentrate
   - **e** express ideas
   - **f** develop speech
   - **g** develop muscles
   - **h** invent
   - **i** learn new skills
   - **j** learn how other people behave
   - **k** role-play (pretend to be someone else)
   - **l** share possessions
   - **m** use the imagination
   - **n** co-operate with others
   - **o** show off (children like to let others know what they can do)
   - **p** act protectively towards someone less powerful than themselves.

C

D

2. **Play helps towards happiness**. A child who is absorbed in play is likely to be a happy child, as play produces feelings of satisfaction and achievement.

3. **Play helps prevent boredom**. Preventing a child from being bored is very important, as boredom can quickly lead to bad temper, irritability and destructiveness.

4. **Play can help reduce stress**. The acting out of stressful situations can help them to seem more familiar and therefore less frightening. For example, by playing 'schools' a child becomes familiar with the idea of going to school. This will help to reduce any nervousness about school which the child might have. In the same way, playing 'doctors and nurses' can help prepare a child for a stay in hospital.

5. **Play can help divert aggressive instincts**. Using a hammer to nail pieces of wood together to make a 'boat' is preferable to using the hammer to hurt someone or destroy property.

DIFFERENT TYPES OF PLAY

Children like variety and during the day will change from one type of play to another. Sometimes they use the same toy. More often they use different toys because changes stimulate different types of play. Six types of play can be recognised and each forms part of a child's total development.

E

- **Discovery play** (exploring play) enables a child to find out about things: what they are like – their size, shape, texture, colour; how they are made; what she can do with them, for example playing with water or sand. The child will also discover that things can be broken, and this can help to teach her to take care of her possessions.

- **Physical play** (exercise) takes place when a child is actively moving around – running, jumping, climbing, crawling, balancing, swinging, throwing a ball, and so on.

- **Creative play** is when a child expresses her own ideas and feelings to make something which is original, for example, a picture, an animal in modelling dough, a house in building blocks, and so on. A young child is able to express feelings and ideas more easily by painting and drawing than by using words. As the child becomes more skilled with words, she may then be able to write a story, poem or play.

- **Imaginative play** is 'pretend' or fantasy play. The child imagines that she is someone else or an animal such as a rabbit or dog. Children imitate the ways of adults when they play in a Wendy house or play 'shopping'. Attempting to behave like someone else helps the child to understand more clearly the ways other people behave.

F

- **Manipulative play** involves skilful use of the hands. During manipulative play the hands, eyes and brain are being trained to co-ordinate, that is, to work smoothly together. Babies become increasingly skilful with their hands as they play with rattles, soft toys and other objects. Later on, they benefit from playing with such things as modelling dough.

■ **Social play** takes place when children play together. It teaches them to co-operate, to share, and to be honest. It also teaches them that antisocial behaviour, like cheating, leads to isolation and loss of friendship. Children often quarrel and in doing so learn about each other's reactions.

At any one time, a child may be involved in more than one type of play. For example, when a baby plays with a rattle, she discovers what it is like as she learns to use her hands – this is both discovery and manipulative play. When a group of children play with bricks it could involve all types of play.

Questions

1 a Why is play considered to be an essential part of education?

  b Give a reason why children need to play (i) with other children, (ii) on their own.

  c List briefly five benefits of play.

2 What does play allow children to find out about themselves and the world? Give at least ten suggestions.

3 Play can be classified into six different types. Name and describe each type.

Weblink

For information on the importance of play in child development, visit:

www.child-development-guide.com

Further activities

 Extension

Study the six pictures A–F in this topic.

1 Each of the six pictures is intended to represent a different type of play. Decide which type of play each picture best represents. Give a reason why you consider it represents that type of play.

2 Take each picture in turn and say which of the items in the list on p. 196 are involved in that particular play situation.

3 (i) Some of the toys used by the children in the pictures are objects which have been found around the house and garden. Make a list of the objects which are being used as toys. (ii) Suggest other everyday objects which could be used as toys.

4 Make a database file on toys which can be bought for children aged 7 years and under. This could be a group activity. Here is a suggested layout for one record.

  Name: Bricks   **Cost**: £12.99   **Type**: Imaginative, manipulative
  Age (years): 1, 2, 3, 4, 5, 6, 7   **Comments**: Can be added to, very versatile.

  Use the file to find out (i) Which toys are suitable for children under 2 years? (ii) Which toys are suitable for creative play for children under 2 years? (iii) Which toys are suitable for more than one kind of play? (iv) Which toys for 5-year-olds cost less than £10.00? (v) Then think of some more questions you could ask.

 Investigation

Investigate the outdoor play facilities in your district, then write a report for your local council. Do you consider that children's needs are being met?

 Child study

Observe the child in a variety of play situations, for example when playing:

A on his or her own   **D** with a younger child

B with another child of the same age   **E** with a group of children

C with an older child   **F** with an adult.

State the occasions when you were able to identify each of the six types of play mentioned in this topic.

CHAPTER 41

Toys

As we saw in the previous topic, children play happily with many different objects which they find around the house and garden. They use these objects as toys. Nevertheless, toys which are specially made for children will also give them much pleasure and help to increase the variety and interest of their games.

CHOOSING A TOY FOR A CHILD

Toys come in many forms. Those which give pleasure will be used. Because they are used, they will provide the opportunity to learn. Toys sold as 'educational toys' will only be played with if the child finds them either fun or interesting.

A successful toy is one which a child both likes and uses often. Such a toy:

- **is right for the age of the child** – the child is old enough to enjoy it, but not too old for the toy to seem babyish. It can be dangerous for younger children to play with toys for older children
- **is strong enough for the child to use**
- **provides more than temporary interest** – it may:
  - give scope for the imagination
  - give scope for learning new skills
  - make the child think
  - have special appeal for the child

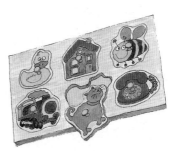

- **is safe to play with** – for example, the eyes of soft toys are firmly fixed and cannot be pulled out; there are no sharp edges or points; toy cars and tricycles are stable and will not easily tip over.

SAFETY REGULATIONS

CONFORMS TO B.S. 5665

Toys are governed by safety regulations. The 'CE' symbol on a toy shows that it meets the requirements of the European Union's Toy

Safety Directive and is safe for children to play with. Those with the 'Lion Mark' of the British Toy and Hobby Association (BTHA) meet the British legal safety requirements.

TOYS FOR CHILDREN OF ALL AGES

Many toys are used only during a particular stage of development. However, a few seem to appeal to children of all ages and are used over a long period of childhood. These include bricks, climbing frames, dolls and soft toys, and toys for bathtime.

Bricks

Bricks probably have the longest life of any toy. Building with bricks encourages children to concentrate, be patient, to invent and to be skilful with the hands.

When a young child first plays with bricks, he has difficulty in placing one brick on top of another. He has to learn:

- **to use the hands and eyes together**
- **to develop fine control** over the muscles which move the fingers
- **to concentrate** as both time and effort are needed to achieve a satisfactory result
- **to persist** and keep on practising until the bricks can be placed where they are wanted.

As the child gets older, more use is made of the imagination to arrange the bricks in different ways. There are a large number of games in which bricks can be used. For example, bricks can be made into walls, towers, steps, houses, roads, tunnels and patterns. They can keep one child amused or occupy a group of children playing together.

For bricks to be a really useful toy, there need to be enough of them. A few bricks are not much use except to a baby. Older children need many more. Hundreds of bricks require quite a lot of space, both for storage and when they are being played with. Parents must be prepared to have half-finished games left over a large part of the table or floor.

Interlocking bricks like Lego®, Duplo® or Sticklebricks® keep children happily occupied for many hours throughout childhood. Children can start to play with them as soon as they have the skill to lock them together and when they have grown out of the stage of wanting to put small things in the mouth. If a collection of bricks is begun when the child is young, then added to from time to time, it can be made to keep pace with his developing skills and imagination.

Climbing frame

This large and expensive toy can be erected wherever there is enough space, either inside or outside the house and, once put up, has to be left in place. The advantage of a climbing frame is that it can be used throughout childhood both for physical play and for many other activities.

A climbing frame is particularly useful for children who do not have a large garden or nearby adventure playground in which to play. It gives opportunity for children to use their muscles, gain control over their movements, test their skills and use up energy. A young child using a climbing frame has to decide where to put his hands and feet, how far to climb and how to hold the body to stay in balance. As experience is gained in moving around, the child will become more confident and adventurous. Adding objects to the climbing frame such as a rope, plank, hammock or blanket increases the interest and provides ideas for many imaginative games.

Dolls and soft toys

The favourite doll or teddy or cuddly animal becomes a sort of 'person' to whom the child can turn for companionship or comfort. Unlike people, they are always ready for play, do not make demands, can be talked to in confidence and then left alone until wanted again. Sometimes children prefer to share their grief, anger or pleasure with dolly or teddy rather than with people. Many children rely on them for comfort throughout childhood.

Dolls come in many shapes and sizes. Some are elaborately dressed and often appeal to grown-ups. However, children usually seem to prefer a simple doll or soft toy as there is more scope for the imagination and less to go wrong.

Toys for bathtime

Children love playing with water and have fun with toys which float, sponges for squeezing, and containers for scooping up water. One way of getting children to wash themselves all over or to have their hair washed at bathtime is a promise to give them time afterwards to play in the water, perhaps bathing a doll or washing its hair. Supervision of children in a bath continues to be needed at all times for safety reasons.

Sponge blocks float and can be squeezed; when wet they will stick to a flat surface

TOYS IN THE FIRST YEAR

Babies begin to play at 3 months or earlier. They love having objects to handle and to look at. They find new objects more interesting than familiar ones. It is therefore best if their toys are given to them a few at a time, then changed around for variety. They will then show renewed interest in a toy which has not been played with for a few days.

In general, babies prefer toys which are brightly coloured and which make a noise. Toys for this age group should be attractive, manageable, fun, unlikely to break, washable and safe. **Safe** means that the toy can be handled and put in the mouth without causing harm. It must have no sharp edges, or points, or small pieces which could be swallowed. Also it should be splinter-proof. Stuffing should be clean, and paint should not contain lead.

3 months

The baby's first toy is likely to be a rattle, which has to be placed in the baby's hand. The rattle should be light and with a handle or ring which is the right size for a baby to grasp.

4 months

The baby will get pleasure from waving a rattle about. He will also enjoy beads on his pram and a mobile above his cot. 'Baby gyms' provide a lot of fun and discovery – the baby handles and kicks the hanging mirrors, rattles and beads.

5 months

Now that the baby is able to pick up objects, a wide variety of toys will give him pleasure – in the pram, on the tray of his chair, on the floor, in the bath and in the garden. When the baby is able to sit up unaided, the range of toys that can be enjoyed is increased.

10 months

Babies of this age have better co-ordination. They can easily reach for, grasp and pick up objects. They enjoy putting things into containers (bags, boxes, tins etc.) and taking them out again.

1 year

Babies now begin to take an interest in books. Those shown on p. 210 are suitable for this stage.

Baby gym/activity centre

TOYS FOR CHILDREN AGED 1–2 YEARS

Most of the toys for children under 1 year old will still be used between 1 and 2 years. In addition, the children can now stack bricks and play with other toys requiring similar co-ordination skills. They like picture books with simple stories or nursery rhymes. 'Push and pull' toys are popular with children who can walk. Towards the age of 2, they are able to thread large beads, play with a ball, enjoy a paddling pool, and like 'helping' with the cleaning, cooking and other jobs with adults.

TOYS FOR CHILDREN AGED 2–3 YEARS

Children now have sufficient skill with their hands to manage large interlocking bricks, toys which unscrew, the 'posting box' with holes of different shapes, peg boards with pegs to hammer, blackboard and chalks, coloured crayons and poster paints, and modelling dough. They also like books with pictures and books in which they can draw and colour. Towards the end of the third year, they are able to use scissors to cut out shapes and pictures.

TOYS FOR CHILDREN AGED 3–5 YEARS

Children of this age group appreciate toys for imaginative play – drawing and painting materials, coloured paper to make patterns, and dressing-up clothes. They enjoy being active outdoors with toys like balls, climbing frames and tricycles. Their interest in books will be increasing, which helps in learning to read.

The big whale swam in the deep blue sea. He sang a song as he went along.

FROM 5 YEARS ONWARD

Children are now ready for jigsaws, card games, board games, computer games, sewing kits, and books which they are able to read for themselves.

HIGH-TECH TOYS

High-tech toys are electronic toys with computer chips. They are popular with children of all ages and include electronic books and games, toy cameras and dolls that learn to talk. They are considered good toys when, like other good toys, they encourage children to:

- use their imagination
- take exercise
- play together
- talk with each other or adults
- learn about things
- learn new skills.

This toy is operated by a remote which responds to a light touch by the elbow, foot or nose. When the remote is touched the little engine vibrates and plays a tune. The surfaces are also very tactile.

TOYS FOR SPECIAL NEEDS

Children with special needs (see Topic 73), like all other children, learn through play. They therefore need plenty of toys which they can use and which they find interesting and fun. When selecting toys for children with disabilities, some important points to note are:

Vibrating train

- Toys should match the child's ability; those which are too easy have little play value, those which are too difficult can lead to frustration and anger or withdrawal.
- Toys intended for use in training to overcome or lessen a disability will be more successful if they are also toys which the children enjoy.
- The right toy can produce an active response from an otherwise inactive child.
- Children who are physically disabled must be comfortably positioned for play.
- Children who cannot use ordinary toys may be able to use switch-operated or remote-operated toys.

Sound-sensitive computer game – the child has to make sounds in order to keep the game going. The sensitivity can be adjusted to encourage the child to speak louder. Deaf children with electronic hearing aids, or autistic children, may be encouraged to speak by using computer games such as this

Activity mat – offers a range of activities which can be explored. It includes squeakers, rattles, beads, and pockets in which various items can be placed. Children with **visual difficulties** (those who cannot see very well) can enjoy this toy. It has patterns with **high visual contrast** (large shapes and bright colours), can be explored with the hands, and makes noises

Ball pool – is useful for children with physical disabilities because it encourages movement, which strengthens muscles and improves co-ordination

Magnet blocks – encourages hand-eye co-ordination and therefore useful for children with **poor manual dexterity** (difficulty in using the hands)

Toys useful for children with particular disabilities

TOY LIBRARIES

These are places which parents can visit with their young children in order to look at toys, play with them, and borrow them for a short time. Toy libraries may be found in a variety of premises such as nursery and primary schools, Child Health Clinics, family centres and day nurseries, and also on mobile buses. They provide:

- opportunities for children, including those with special needs, to play with a wide variety of toys
- a friendly meeting place for parents and carers – there is often someone who will listen to worries and concerns and, perhaps, offer guidance
- informal support networks for parents who may be under stress
- information about other services
- support from visiting professionals.

Questions

1 a Give four points which make a toy successful.

  b Give four reasons why a toy might be of more than temporary interest.

  c Although illegal, unsafe toys can still be found on sale. To avoid buying unsafe toys, what two labels indicate that a toy meets legal safety standards?

2 a Name four types of toy which are used over a long period of childhood.

  b What are young children learning when they play with bricks? Give four suggestions.

  c Suggest four reasons why at times children prefer their favourite doll or teddy to people.

  d (i) What treat might be offered to a child who objected to being bathed?

     (ii) Describe the bath toys on p. 201 and how they could be used.

3 a (i) For which children is a climbing frame particularly useful? (ii) Name four opportunities it gives to such children.

  b Name four objects which can be added to a climbing frame to make it more interesting.

4 a At what age do children start to play?

  b When choosing a rattle for a baby, name six safety factors to be considered.

5 What is the average age at which children become able to:

  a enjoy beads on the pram

  b pick up toys

  c put toys in containers and take them out again

  d take an interest in books

  e walk along pushing a toy

  f unscrew the pieces of a toy

  g use scissors

  h enjoy dressing up

  i enjoy card games?

6 a For each of the toys on pp. 202–4, suggest one way in which a child could find it fun to play with.

  b Describe a toy which could be used (i) to help strengthen muscles, (ii) to encourage hand–eye co-ordination, (iii) to increase attention span.

  c Which toy would you select for a child (i) who has difficulty using his hands, (ii) with visual difficulties, (iii) who is being taught to speak?

Further activities

 Extension

1 Make a collection of pictures of toys which you consider will give children long-term fun and are value for money.

2 Choose three hi tech toys, each recommended for a particular age group.

3 Assess each toy against the following criteria by giving it a score out of 5 (a score of 1 is the lowest and 5 the highest).

  a suitable for the age-range

  b entertainment value

  c safe to play with

  d supports development of speech

  e gives opportunities for learning

4 Where is your nearest toy library? If possible, try to arrange a visit. Find out more about toy libraries, for example the history of the organisation, and their importance to both parents and children.

 Investigation

Write a report on one of the following activities:

a Watch a child playing with bricks. Then read the section on bricks in this topic. Comment on how the points mentioned in the topic relate to what you saw.

b Observe children playing on a climbing frame – many parks and schools have them. Describe how the climbing frame was being used and note the approximate age of the children.

c Compare the way in which boys and girls play with the same kind of toy. Do they use the toy differently?

 Design

Design a toy for a child. What age is it most suitable for? What would the child learn by playing with it? Have you considered the safety of the toy?

Further activities (continued)

 Child study

1 The child will almost certainly have a favourite doll or soft toy. Describe it, and observe when and how the child plays with it.

2 Play with the child. Describe the way he or she plays with different toys. Which are the favourite toys and which are never used? Where are the toys kept? Who puts them away when the child has finished playing with them?

Weblink

To find out about toys for special needs, visit: www.special-needs-kids.co.uk

CHAPTER 42

Learning to draw

DEVELOPMENT OF THE IMAGINATION

From an early age, a child begins to form pictures (images) in the mind. These pictures involve himself and the world about him, and also include other people and the way he sees them.

By 2 years of age, the imagination has developed enough for the child to be able to use **symbols** to represent real things. For example:

▥ dolls represent people
▥ small toy cars represent real cars
▥ words are used for objects and actions
▥ drawings describe events and express feelings.

At times, it is very hard for young children to separate the real world from their imaginary world.

DRAWING

Drawing is important as it helps children to express their feelings and imagination and to record their experiences.

Children love to draw. They are ready to do so as soon as they can hold a pencil or crayon, which is between the age of 12 and 18 months. The first drawings are scribbles. This is followed by 'big head' figures. The drawings gradually become more realistic as the child develops more control over the pencil, and as he comes to notice and understand more about the world.

STAGES IN LEARNING TO DRAW

Children pass through most or all of the following stages as they learn to draw. These stages often overlap, so when looking at a drawing made by a child, it may be difficult to place it in any one particular stage.

Stage 1 The child's hand moves backwards and forwards to produce a scribble.

Stage 2 The child becomes able to lift the pencil from the paper and move it in different directions.

Stage 3 He begins to scribble in circles.

Stage 4 He becomes able to draw round and round in circles.

Stage 5 He now starts to draw people and uses a circle to represent a face. Marks are put inside for eyes, nose, mouth.

Stage 6 Lines are added all round the circles as well.

Stage 7 The lines are arranged in bunches to represent hair, arms, legs.

Stage 8 The arms come straight out at the sides of the face. The legs come from a circle which is drawn below for the body.

Stage 9 The body becomes much more important and the legs have feet.

Stage 10 Clothes are added. The drawings also have trees, houses, animals, cars and other objects in the child's world.

WHEN A DRAWING IS FINISHED

Children generally like to have their drawings admired and sometimes pinned on the wall for everyone to see. However, sometimes after completing a drawing, they scribble or paint over it so that it can no longer be seen. This often seems to give them pleasure similar to that which they get from knocking over a pile of bricks or a sand-castle.

Questions

1 Name four ways in which children use symbols.

2 a When are children ready to start drawing?

  b What are the first drawings like?

  c What type of drawings follow next?

  d When do the drawings become more realistic?

3 Describe the ten stages which children pass through as they learn to draw. Accompany each stage with a simple drawing.

Further activities

Extension

The three pictures shown below were drawn by children – Laura Brend, aged 5; Claire Williams, aged 6; Elisabeth Cottam, aged 8. Which girl do you think drew which picture? Give your reasons.

Activity

Find some different types of drawing, colouring and puzzle books available for children of different ages. In what ways do they help children to learn about colour and shape?

Use this information and a graphics program to design an outline drawing for children to colour in. Print several copies, or make a few designs which can be made into a colouring book.

Child study

If the child is old enough, encourage him or her to draw a picture, but without saying what to draw or showing how to do it. When the picture is finished, ask the child to tell you about it. Have you learnt anything about the child's imagination or feelings?

Repeat this exercise every few weeks. Make a collection of the drawings and compare them.

CHAPTER 43

Learning to read and write

Children have to be taught to read and write by adults. These skills take years to learn. Some children learn more quickly than others, but they all make better progress when the learning process is an enjoyable experience.

PRE-READING ACTIVITIES

Parents and carers have an extremely important part to play in preparing children for the early stages of reading. Learning to read is made so much easier if children:

- have had stories read to them
- have had the chance to talk about stories, pictures and what happens
- know some nursery rhymes
- know that books are fun.

BOOKS FOR BABIES

From the age of about 9 months, or even earlier, children begin to enjoy books when they share the activity with an enthusiastic adult. They soon learn to:

- hold the book the right way up
- point to pictures
- listen attentively
- help to turn the pages.

Board book – sturdy and can withstand being put into the baby's mouth

Texture book – encourages a child to be aware of the sense of touch

Flap book – encourages a child to explore and predict

Cloth book – washable and strong

Bath book – waterproof

BOOKSTART

Bookstart is a free books programme run by the national reading charity Booktrust that encourages all parents and carers to enjoy books with their children from as early an age as possible. Free packs of books are given to every young child in England, Wales and Northern Ireland to inspire, stimulate and create a love of reading that will give children a flying start in life.

Bookstart packs

All Bookstart packs are now free to parents through different schemes in England, Wales and Northern Ireland. There are three different book packs for the different age groups.

- **Bookstart pack for babies** is for babies aged 0–12 months
- **Bookstart +** is for toddlers aged 18–30 months
- **My Bookstart Treasure Chest** for children 36–48 months

The Bookstart pack for babies is normally given to parents and carers by health professionals. They also often give out the Bookstart+ packs, or parents and carers are informed that the pack is available. My Bookstart Treasure Chest is distributed to parents and carers through libraries and Early Years settings.

Bookstart pack for babies   Bookstart+   My Bookstart Treasure Chest

Other Bookstart schemes

Booktouch packs aim to get blind and partially-sighted babies and toddlers 'bookstarted' and include two touchy-feely books. Booktouch packs are provided free to parents or carers of blind or partially sighted children up to (and including) the age of 4.

Bookshine packs aim to help deaf babies and toddlers to get 'bookstarted'. They are provided free to parents or carers of deaf children up to (and including) the age of four.

Welsh Bookstart packs contain books in both the Welsh and English languages.

Bookstart Book Crawl is an activity that encourages parents, carers and children to use the library.

LEARNING TO READ

Each child learns to read at his or her own speed. Starting to learn may be left until the child attends school at the age of 5, or the child may be ready to begin earlier. It is important for parents to encourage a young child's natural interest and ability without trying to force the pace. If a child is made to learn too soon, reading will not be an enjoyable experience, and the child may resist learning and begin to fail. Learning to read involves learning:

- to recognise letters and link them with sounds (**A**)
- that groups of letters or sounds make words that have meanings (**B**)
- that strings of words make phrases or sentences that have meanings (**C**).

Parents can encourage a child to follow the words as a story is being read out loud, and to begin to say the words at the same time as the reader. Gradually the child will learn to recognise words and even phrases, gaining clues from the context of the story and from pictures.

The child should be praised and encouraged, and not corrected every time a mistake is made. It is essential that the child does not get frustrated and lose interest.

When the child goes to school, a large part of each day will be concerned with reading and writing for several years, because the child has many essential skills to learn.

Sam enjoys:
- looking at pictures with his mum
- recognising objects
- talking about what is seen
- having his questions answered.

Cara enjoys:
- the comfort of being near her dad
- listening to the stories she likes over and over again
- following the words (she is learning that the words go from left to right across the page).

Local libraries welcome babies and young children, and the librarians will be able to recommend suitable books for borrowing

LEARNING TO WRITE

Before a child can write easily, a number of skills have to be mastered which require a great deal of practice:

- holding and controlling a pencil
- forming the letter shapes
- writing in a straight line with letters and words spaced neatly
- learning to spell
- 'joined-up' writing (a quicker way to write)
- using correct punctuation and grammar.

It is helpful if a child can at least hold a pencil correctly before starting school. Left-handedness should not be discouraged if it comes naturally to the child (see p. 146).

READING AND WRITING DIFFICULTIES

There are a number of reasons why some children have more difficulty than others in learning to read and write. These include:

- **lack of motivation** – no one is interested in the child's progress
- **the child is discouraged by repeated correction** when reading
- **the child's experience of language is limited** – the child has a small vocabulary and little practice in using it. (This may apply to children of ethnic groups who are being educated in a different language from the one they speak at home.)
- **poor eyesight**
- **poor hearing**
- **poor hand–eye co-ordination**, which makes writing difficult
- **dyslexia**.

Dyslexia

Dyslexia means 'word blindness'. Children who suffer from this condition find reading, writing and spelling difficult even though they are able to talk well and have none of the other difficulties listed above. These children may say that the letters are confused, or they are the wrong way round, or they move around on the page. Children who are dyslexic often have to work very hard indeed to overcome this condition, and they may need a great deal of individual help from specialist teachers and parents.

Questions

1 What pre-reading activities help to make learning to read easier for children?

2 (i) From about what age do children start to enjoy books? (ii) What can they learn? (iii) What types of books are suitable for babies?

3 (i) What does Sam enjoy about books? (ii) What does Cara enjoy about books?

4 a At what age do children start to learn to read?

  b Why is it important to encourage a child's natural interest in reading, but not to force the pace?

  c What does learning to read involve?

  d (i) What is Tracey learning about letters? (ii) What is Ben learning about words? (iii) What is Jane learning?

5 What skills are involved in learning to write?

6 a List seven reasons why learning to read and write is more difficult for some children.

  b What is dyslexia?

Further activities

Extension

1 If a child has a story read to her every day before she starts school, from her 2nd to her 5th birthday, how many stories would she have heard?

If another child, who did not have any stories read to him until he started school on his 5th birthday, then listened to the teacher read the same number of stories at the rate of one per day, 5 days a week, 40 weeks of the year, how old would this child be before he had had the same number of stories read to him as the first child had heard by the age of 5? In what ways do you consider the second child to be disadvantaged?

2 Make a series of 'flash cards' to help letter recognition, e.g. a card with an apple and the letter a. Use a computer for the letters and/or the graphics.

Discussion

Do you think that correct spelling is important? Give your reasons for and against this.

Investigation

Select three or more books for a particular child. Read each book to the child. Compare their suitability, for example:

a What was the story like – exciting, funny?

b Did the child understand the words?

c Did the language sound like the spoken language with which the child is familiar?

d Was the child's interest level high?

e Did the illustrations relate closely to the text?

Give a short illustrated talk to explain your findings.

Design

Use the computer to write a short story for children which could be used to teach road safety. Indicate the age range of children for whom the story is intended. Include illustrations and present it in the form of a book taking into account the following requirements:

a appropriate content for the age range

b attractive appearance

c originality of text and illustrations

d a suitable style of print

e care taken with suiting illustrations to text.

Use the book with a child of an appropriate age, and write a report on its success or failure.

Weblinks

Booktrust is an independent national charity which encourages people of all ages and cultures to discover and enjoy reading:

www.bookstart.org.uk

Talk To Your Baby is a campaign run by the National Literacy Trust to encourage parents and carers to talk more to children from birth to three to help them do well at school and lead happy, fulfilled and successful lives. To find out more visit:

www.literacytrust.org.uk/talk_to_your_baby/

CHAPTER 44

Learning about numbers

Numbers are part of a child's world. They are heard in:

▥ conversation

You can have two biscuits

3 years old today!

▥ stories, rhymes and jingles

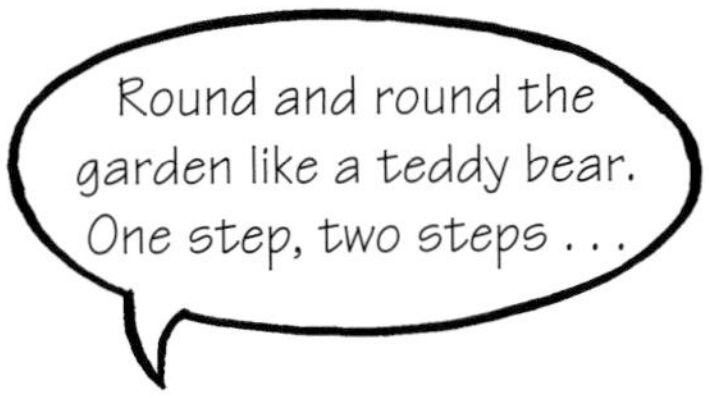

Round and round the garden like a teddy bear. One step, two steps . . .

Two-four-six-eight Mary shut the garden gate

STAGES IN THE DEVELOPMENT OF NUMBER CONCEPTS

Children gradually acquire the ability to put numbers in the right order and to use them to count, to compare and to measure. Various stages can be recognised in this development, which usually occur more or less in the order listed here:

1. **Repeating numbers** Many children are able to repeat numbers at 2 or 3 years, but the words mean very little and they are often said in the wrong order.
2. **Matching number words to objects**
3. **The correct order of numbers** The child learns that numbers have a definite order, for example, 1 is followed by 2, and then by 3.

Stage 1   Stage 2   Stage 3

4 **Learning the meaning of 'first', 'second', 'third', ... 'last'** These are called 'ordinal' numbers.
5 **Comparing numbers** The child comes to understand the meaning of 'more than' and 'less than' as applied to numbers. For example, understanding that with 5 toys here and 3 much larger toys over there, 5 is still more than 3, and 3 is less than 5.

Stage 4   Stage 5

6 **Understanding that the number of things is constant regardless of size or position** For example, 9 things are still 9 regardless of how they are placed. Before this important concept has been reached (usually between 4 and 7 years), a child may agree that there are 9 cubes on the table (**A**), but if these cubes are spread out (**B**), without re-counting he may say there are now more than 9, and if they are heaped up (**C**), he may say there are less than 9. This concept cannot be taught, but comes from many experiences.

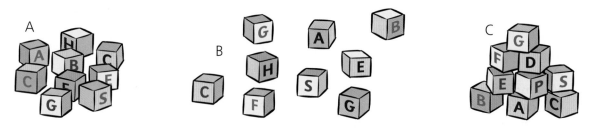

Stage 6

7 **Learning to recognise and write numbers** Children learn the figures (symbols) that are used for numbers, and how to write them.

Stage 7

8 **Manipulating numbers (doing sums)** Once it is understood that a certain number of things is always the same number (stage 6 above) the child is then ready to . . .

Stage 8 . . . add numbers together . . .   . . . take them away . . .

. . . share . . .   . . . measure

Questions

1 In what ways are numbers part of a child's world? Give examples.

2 List eight stages in the development of the concept of number.

3 a When children first start to repeat numbers, how may they do it?

 b Give an example of: (i) matching the right number to a given set of objects, (ii) understanding the meaning of 'more than' and 'less than' when applied to numbers, (iii) use of ordinal numbers.

 c Name four ways in which numbers can be used.

Further activities

 Investigation

1 Find some (i) songs and rhymes, (ii) games, which involve numbers and are suitable for young children. Use some of them with a small child and note the child's interest and understanding.

2 Carry out this problem-solving exercise with a group of three to five children aged 5 years. Using a heap of about nine toys, put the following questions, and note how the children tackle them: (i) How many toys are there? (ii) How many children are there? (iii) Are there enough toys to have one each – and another one each?

 Design

1 Make a simple 'matching number-to-number' game for 5-year-olds. For example, each child has a picture of a clown and six separate numbered pieces of clown. A die (1–6) is thrown in turn and the child who covers his clown correctly first is the winner.

2 Use a graphics or desk-top publishing program to design a booklet to encourage a child to count.

 Child study

Observe the child playing and note any occasions when number words are used. What stage in the development of number concepts do you think the child has reached?

Weblink

For tips on learning numbers through play, visit: www.topmarks.co.uk

CHAPTER 45

Learning through music

Children can enjoy music in many ways even when they are very young. From birth, babies seem to be comforted when parents sing to them in a soothing and rhythmical way (**A**). From a very young age they show an interest in objects which make pleasing sounds, for example a musical mobile (**B**). When they are a little older, they want to join in songs, or to clap their hands to music (**C**). From about 3 years onwards, they can play their favourite CDs on players specially designed for young children (**D**).

SINGING

From about 2 years of age, children begin to be able to imitate tunes more accurately and to sing with other children. Singing becomes more interesting for children when:

- they sing in groups
- the songs relate to what they know, e.g. daily activities, weather, time of year

- they do actions to accompany a song
- they are allowed to choose some of the songs
- words of a familiar song are adapted for a particular purpose
- new songs are introduced
- songs are accompanied by percussion instruments
- adults play the piano or guitar to accompany the songs.

As they sing, children learn:

- new words
- to develop their memory for words, sounds and music, e.g. 'Old Macdonald had a farm'
- about festivals, e.g. Christmas
- about past times, e.g. 'London's burning'
- about different cultures, e.g. folk songs, dances, rituals
- that other people sing in different languages, e.g. 'Frère Jacques'.

LEARNING ABOUT SOUNDS

Children can have difficulty in distinguishing between different sounds, for example between 'high' and 'low' notes and between 'loud' and 'soft' sounds. One way of overcoming this is to play a game in which the children respond to changes in the music by using different actions.

Pitch   Volume   Tempo (speed)

MUSIC AND MOVEMENT

Dancing and exercises to music help children to:

- develop movement skills (motor skills)
- listen and respond with actions
- extend their range of movements
- improve posture and balance
- learn about dances in other cultures
- use their imagination when they mime to music
- keep fit
- have fun.

MAKING MUSIC

Young children enjoy producing sounds with percussion instruments such as the home-made ones shown opposite. A percussion instrument is one which is used to produce sounds when it is hit, shaken or banged, such as bells, tambourines, cymbals, triangles, maracas and drums.

Maypole dancing

Music-making is usually a social activity and the children learn to co-operate with other players. At the same time, they are developing listening skills and co-ordination of movement.

Shaker

plastic food pot with lid – rice, split peas, paper clips etc. inside

saucepan and wooden spoon

Drums

wooden spoon

three layers of greaseproof paper or a layer of cling-film

elastic band

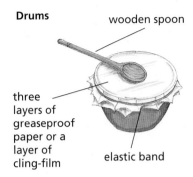

Home-made instruments

LEARNING ABOUT MUSIC

When children are ready, they can start a more formal training in music. For many children, early encouragement can lead to very satisfying hobbies and careers, for example playing the piano, violin or trumpet, singing in a choir, or being a member of a steel band or jazz group.

MUSIC FOR SPECIAL NEEDS

Children with special needs enjoy music and music-making as much as other children, and most of them can use the same instruments, including a keyboard. Those children with **poor manual dexterity** (poor control over their hands and fingers) may need specially adapted equipment or instruments, for example larger handles or touch boards.

Questions

1 a When are babies first aware of music?

   b In what ways are the children in drawings A–D on p. 219 enjoying music?

2 Give six things which the children in the drawing on p. 220 are learning.

3 Describe three home-made percussion instruments.

4 In what ways can early encouragement in music be of benefit to children as they get older?

Weblink

Visit the National Literacy Trust website for the pdf 'Communicate Through Music':

www.literacytrust.org.uk

Further activities

 Design

Make a list of songs that could be sung on a car journey with a young child.

 Extension

Suggest at least one song or piece of music for (i) lulling a baby to sleep, (ii) having fun with a toddler, (iii) singing with a group of children. Explain why you selected each of the songs or pieces of music.

 Child study

Describe the part which music plays in the life of the child.

CHAPTER 46

Behaviour in early childhood

All children behave 'badly' or are 'difficult' from time to time. This is a normal part of growing up. At one time or another they are all likely to show some of the types of behaviour discussed in this topic – saying 'No!', seeking attention, having temper tantrums, telling lies, hitting, and stealing. They behave in these ways because they have not yet learnt to control their emotions or are frustrated that they cannot make adults understand their feelings. Helping children to behave in a more acceptable way can best be done as part of a loving relationship rather than through strict discipline.

The point at which such behaviour will cause the parents concern varies from family to family. What seems 'very bad' behaviour in one family may be regarded as normal in another. The types of behaviour mentioned above only become real problems when they persist or are carried to excess and regarded as anti-social behaviour. Children then need to be helped to grow out of them or the behaviour may continue into adolescence or adult life.

THE NEGATIVE ('NO!') PHASE

It is normal for children between the ages of 9 months and 3 years, and especially at 1½–2½ years of age, to go through a stage of saying 'No!' to anything they are told to do. They want to do the opposite. Being tired, hungry or unwell tends to make them worse. Active, determined children are likely to be more troublesome in this respect than placid ones.

Children can be very difficult to manage at this stage. It helps parents to be more patient and tolerant when they realise that this negative phase is a normal part of a child's development and not just naughtiness, and that it will pass. Although there will be good days and bad days, the bad days get fewer as the child gets older. On the other hand, if the parents are determined always to make the child 'do as she is told', then long-term behaviour problems are very likely to develop, for example frequent temper tantrums or persistent bed-wetting.

ATTENTION-SEEKING BEHAVIOUR

It is normal for a child to want to be the centre of attention, especially between the ages of 1 and 3–4 years. Children of this age group feel important when they are noticed. As a result, they will do many things to show off and attract other people's attention, including:

- making lots of noise
- coughing
- refusing to eat
- eating earth
- holding their breath until blue in the face
- spitting
- biting
- head banging
- refusing to sit on the potty
- passing urine in the wrong place at the wrong time
- having temper tantrums.

All these tricks are aimed at making the child the centre of attention. If the tricks succeed, they are likely to be done repeatedly and to become habits.

Ignoring the habit (if possible) is usually the best way to stop it. Sometimes however, when the habit persists, it indicates that the child's basic needs are not being met – not enough notice is being taken of the child, or the child is not being loved and praised enough. So the child finds that the only way to get attention is to do something naughty.

TEMPER TANTRUMS

A temper tantrum is a period of uncontrolled rage. The most common age for tantrums is between 18 months and 3 years. This is the stage at which a child wants to do things her way, and loves to say 'No!' Tantrums are more likely to happen in determined children with abundant energy, and not to be a problem in those who are placid and easy-going.

When in a tantrum, the child screams and kicks and may deliberately throw things in order to damage them. She pays no attention when told to stop, and will not listen to reason. The reaction of parents may be to smack the child, but this rarely helps and is much more likely to make matters worse. The child is punished by no one appearing to take any interest in the outburst, although it may be necessary to prevent the child from hurting herself or others, or from damaging things.

Possible causes

A temper tantrum once in a while can be considered normal behaviour. But when a child has frequent temper tantrums the cause may be:

- **frustration** at being unable to do what she wants or to tell other people what she wants or feels. Often a child's feelings develop faster than the ability to use words to express them.
- **imitation (copying)** of older children or adults. She sees them lose their temper and does the same.
- **emotional needs** – the tantrum draws attention to the child's need for love and stimulation.

Trying to understand why a child has temper tantrums will help in knowing how to deal with them.

STEALING

Young children have a natural desire to take what they want and they have to learn that they cannot take things which belong to other people without asking first. A simple way of teaching this lesson is to allow children to have their own possessions and a place to keep them. A child will then know what it feels like if they are borrowed without permission. The good example of the parents is also very important in teaching children not to steal.

Stealing is not usually a problem during the first five years. It occurs more amongst school-age children.

TELLING LIES

It is natural for young children to use their imagination to play pretend games and to make up 'tall stories'. It takes time for them to understand the difference between what is real and what is make-believe. Therefore, truthfulness can only develop slowly. A child's greatest help in learning to be truthful is having parents who set a good example.

By the age of 5 years, most children understand that unless they speak the truth, people will never know when to believe them. One danger of punishing young children for untruthfulness is that they may continue to tell lies in order to escape punishment.

I have _not_ got teddy

HITTING AND BITING

The occasional hitting and biting of others is normal behaviour in young children. It must be expected when they are at the stage of learning to play together and do not yet fully understand the consequences of their actions.

A child who is **often** extremely quarrelsome and frequently attacks others by hitting, biting, kicking or shouting, is said to be **aggressive**. The cause of this aggressive behaviour needs to be found. It can then be dealt with in a way which will be of most help to the child in overcoming the problem. Causes for the aggression may include jealousy, a means of attracting attention, or imitation – if a parent frequently hits a child it will be natural for the child to hit others, especially someone smaller. The harmful effects of frequent physical punishment are discussed on pp. 181–2.

SLEEP PROBLEMS

Children, like adults, vary in their need for sleep. Some children regularly sleep for 12 hours, others seem to need much less. Some children continue to need a sleep in the middle of the day for several years, others do not. The amount of time a child sleeps becomes a problem when:

- it results in the child being tired and irritable during the day
- the parents are woken frequently during the night, and they themselves become short of sleep
- the parents expect their child to sleep much longer than the child needs
- the parents try to force a sleep pattern on to the child which is not natural to the child.

Getting to sleep

Sleep may not come easily if the child is:

- not tired, possibly because the child has not had sufficient exercise
- too hot or too cold
- thirsty or hungry
- uncomfortable – if the nappy needs changing, clothing is too tight, or the bed is not comfortable
- unwell
- not given a regular bedtime routine
- afraid of the dark – some form of night light may help
- worried
- wanting attention
- over-excited.

Broken nights

These may occur because the child:

- has developed the habit of waking up
- is hungry – some children are unable to go to sleep for a long stretch of time unless they are well fed beforehand
- is cold or too hot
- has nightmares
- wets the bed.

Sometimes there seems no obvious reason – it might be a stage through which the child is passing. If the problem seems to be loneliness, there is no reason why a young child should not sleep in the parents' room – provided both parents agree.

Waking early

The natural pattern is for young children to wake early, and they want to begin the new day as soon as they are awake. If this is earlier than the parents would like, interesting toys or books placed by the bedside may help to keep the child occupied for a while.

OVERACTIVITY

A healthy child is an active child. Many young children (18 months to 5 years) are described by their parents as being overactive, and this is often only because the child's level of activity is so different from the adults'. Young children:

- **can concentrate for only a short time**, 10–15 minutes perhaps, and they then need a new activity – a different toy or game, or a change of scene.
- **may find it difficult to sit still** for more than about 10 minutes – this makes them appear

restless. For example, eating a meal consisting of main course, pudding and drink may take too long for some young children.

▦ **can become troublesome when they are bored** – they are too intelligent to be satisfied with an uninteresting life.

▦ may rush around as a means of **seeking attention**.

Older children who are overactive may not have learnt, or had the opportunity to learn, to spend some of their time quietly. Overactivity in children of school age interferes with learning and social development at home and at school.

HYPERACTIVITY

This is a condition in which the affected child is overactive to a degree that is inappropriate to the child's age, and which interferes with family life and other relationships, and with learning.

Very few children are truly hyperactive and have an **attention deficit hyperactivity disorder** (ADHD). It is more likely to occur with boys who have had a difficult birth, who are slow to learn to talk, and who may have difficulties with reading, writing and tasks involving co-ordination of eyes and hands (tying shoe laces, playing ball games etc.).

FOOD-LINKED BEHAVIOUR

There is a growing understanding that some children are intolerant to certain foods which can affect their behaviour. Reactions to foods and additives have, in some cases, been linked with aggressiveness and hyperactivity.

Most foods cause most children no problems when they are eaten in moderation. Problems are more likely to arise when there is excessive intake of a particular type of food, for example four cans of cola a day (cola contains caffeine) or six packets of crisps (these can contain additives). Any type of food (including citrus fruit, dairy foods, eggs and cheese) can be the cause of health and behavioural problems.

Questions

1 List the first six types of behaviour discussed in this topic and say at which age or stage each is most likely to occur.

2 a What is meant by the 'negative phase'?

  b What may help parents to be more patient in dealing with a child who is passing through such a phase?

3 a Name some ways in which children attract attention to themselves.

  b When may these ways become habits?

  c Give two reasons why a child may want to attract attention.

4 a Describe a temper tantrum.

  b Name three possible causes of frequent temper tantrums.

5 a Why does truthfulness in a young child develop only slowly?

  b (i) What does a young child have to learn about other people's belongings?

    (ii) Describe one way of teaching this lesson.

6 a Why can occasional hitting and biting be considered normal behaviour in young children?

  b When is such behaviour said to be aggressive?

  c Name three possible causes of aggression.

Questions (continued)

7 a How much sleep do children need?

b Give four reasons for a sleep problem.

c Give ten possible reasons why a child may have difficulty in getting to sleep.

d Why may broken nights occur?

e (i) Is it natural for children to wake early?

(ii) How can parents try to keep them occupied?

8 a Give four reasons why adults may describe their young children as overactive.

b (i) Give a reason why an older child may be overactive. (ii) How may overactivity affect such children?

c What is meant by hyperactivity?

d (i) What is ADHD? (ii) In which children is it most likely to occur?

Further activities

💬 Discussion

Discuss 'Children need to be helped to grow out of behaviour problems or the problems may continue into adolescence or adult life'.

Investigation

a Carry out a survey, based on a questionnaire to find (i) the average number of hours per day that children of different age groups spend sleeping, e.g. 0–6 months, 6–12 months, 1–2 years, 2–3 years, 3–4 years, 4–5 years, 5–7 years, (ii) whether the parents think that their children have sleep problems, and what these are.

b (i) Use a spreadsheet program to calculate the average hours of sleep for each of the above age groups.

(ii) Draw a bar graph to compare the averages.

Child study

1 Describe an occasion when you have noticed any of the types of behaviour mentioned in this topic, either in the child you are studying or others. Say:

a what may have caused the behaviour

b how adults dealt with it

c what the child's reaction was.

2 Observe the child for one hour. How many different activities did you observe, and for how long did the child concentrate on each?

Weblinks

For more information on behaviour problems, visit:
www.kidsbehaviour.co.uk/

For sleep problems in children, visit:
www.netdoctor.co.uk and search for 'child cannot sleep'.

For more information on toddlers and sleep, search for 'toddlers sleeping' at:
www.bbc.co.uk

For an interesting article on 'the effect of diets on young children's behaviour', search at:
www.teachingexpertise.com

CHAPTER 47

Managing difficult children

The term **difficult child** applies to those children who are very hard to manage because they often show some or all of the following types of **antisocial behaviour**:

- persistent refusal to do as they are told (unco-operative behaviour)
- verbal abuse (shouting, swearing)
- physical aggression (pushing, hitting, biting, spitting)
- damaging property and other children's work
- frequent temper tantrums
- endless teasing or bullying
- deliberate disruption of activities and games
- self-inflicted damage, e.g. head banging
- unwillingness to be involved in new situations.

A difficult child often breaks the rules for behaviour at home and at school, and this makes adults cross. Adults who are often cross can make the child feel unwanted and unhappy. His difficult behaviour can lead to **social isolation** – other children will not want to play with him, and adults do not enjoy looking after him.

POSSIBLE CAUSES OF A DIFFICULT CHILD

Inborn temperament
Some children seem to be born with more determination to question and challenge than others. They need more careful handling than those who are placid and easy-going by nature.

Being 'extra special'
A child who is considered 'extra special' by his parents (perhaps because he was difficult to conceive, was premature or delicate as a baby, has been seriously ill etc.) can develop behaviour problems.

Lack of parental control and guidance
The reason for this may be one of the following:

- The parents do not know how to deal with their children in a way which encourages good behaviour.

- Stress caused by unemployment, lack of money, or cramped housing can make caring for children very difficult.
- A crisis in the family (e.g. the death of a relative or a divorce) has a very unsettling effect on the whole family.
- Most of the parents' time is spent on caring for a child or relative with disabilities, and the other children in the family feel neglected.

Wrong type of diet

Parents could try changing the child's diet to find out if there could be a link between food and behaviour. See also p. 258.

MANAGING A DIFFICULT CHILD

A young child who is very difficult to control will be feeling very frightened and insecure because he does not know how to behave. Such behaviour is a cry for help – the child needs adults to take charge and take control. To do this, they are advised to:

1. Give praise and encouragement when the child is behaving well (he will soon learn that when you become quiet and show no interest in him that you disapprove of his behaviour). See the illustrations below.
2. Cut down on commands (do not keep telling the child what to do – only give instructions when really necessary).
3. Decrease the number of times you say 'No' (reserve this for big issues involving safety and health).
4. Do not criticise (this gives rise to angry feelings of rejection).
5. Give the child a balanced diet and cut out additives (to help to find out if there may be a link between food and behaviour).

Ways of showing approval of good behaviour

Smiling

Cuddling and giving friendly touches

Enthusiastically describing out loud what the child is doing

Praising

Asking to play with the child or asking him what he would like to do next

Ways of showing disapproval of naughty behaviour

Looking away from the child's face

Not speaking to him

Looking uninterested

Not touching the child, except to keep him, or yourself, safe

WHERE TO OBTAIN ADVICE

- The family doctor (GP) or health visitor.
- Child Guidance Clinics and Child Psychiatric Clinics are run by the Health Service. Some are drop-in, others need a doctor's referral letter.
- The local library should have a list of all the local self-help groups – many people find it useful to share their feelings and ideas with other parents who have similar problems.

Questions

1 **a** What is meant by (i) a difficult child, (ii) social isolation?

   b (i) Give nine examples of antisocial behaviour. (ii) Why is a difficult child likely to be an unhappy child?

2 **a** Give four reasons why children may lack parental control and guidance.

   b Give three other possible causes of a child being difficult.

3 What advice is given to adults to help in managing a difficult child?

4 Describe how the father shown on p. 229 (i) encourages good behaviour, (ii) shows disapproval of naughty behaviour.

5 From where can advice on managing difficult children be obtained?

Further activities

 Discussion

Why are children naughty? Consider possible reasons and the different ways the naughtiness can be dealt with.

CHAPTER 48

Habits in early childhood

Habits are regular actions which are carried out without any, or with very little, thought. Examples of habits commonplace in children include the sucking of a thumb or dummy, nail biting, and the need for a 'comforter'. Habits of this kind are often used by children to comfort themselves when they are tired or unhappy. They are sometimes called 'comfort habits'.

As children grow older, these habits often fade away. In other cases, a great deal of willpower is required to break the habit. Occasionally, some habits persist into adult life.

THUMB AND FINGER SUCKING

All babies suck their thumbs or fingers, sometimes even before they are born. Some babies do this more than others. Many will stroke a doll, blanket or other material at the same time, or twiddle a piece of hair. They may do it when they are feeling sleepy, shy, bored, in trouble, or when a tooth is coming through. The skin on the thumb or finger may thicken or become sore or blistered by the sucking.

Thumb sucking is a harmless habit in a young child, and as it is harmless, no attempt need be made to stop it. If it is ignored, the child will be very likely to grow out of the habit naturally by the age of 4 years. On the other hand, if the parents try to stop the habit, the child will object strongly when her thumb is removed from her mouth. If they make a great deal of fuss, the child will do it all the more.

When thumb sucking continues after the age of 5, it may prevent the front teeth growing properly into place when the permanent teeth come through. Thumb sucking may need to be stopped for this reason, and by now the child should be old enough to understand.

SUCKING A DUMMY

Some parents have strong opinions about dummies. Some say that a dummy stops a baby crying because it soothes and keeps her contented. Others think that a dummy is a poor substitute for the love and attention that should be given when the baby cries. Another point of view is that dummies should not be used because they are difficult to keep clean and can pass on germs to the baby.

It is generally considered that dummies do not do much harm – unless they contain sweet substances for the baby to suck, which will encourage the front teeth to decay. Most children give up their dummy between 1 and 2 years of age – if the parents do not continue to encourage its use.

THE NEED FOR A COMFORTER

Most children have one favourite cuddly toy or piece of material which gives comfort and security, especially at bedtime. The child loves it however scruffy it gets, and will be very upset if it is lost. A child may even be very upset if it smells different after it has been washed. Some children need their comforters for several years.

NAIL BITING

So many children over 3 years old bite their nails that it can be considered a normal thing to do. These children bite their nails without realising what they are doing. It often happens when they are nervous or tense or deep in thought. Generally the only harm it does is to make the nails look unsightly, although it occasionally causes more serious problems. On the whole the most sensible course for parents is to ignore it. Nagging or punishing the child does not usually stop the habit because the child seldom realises when she is doing it. Some children just seem to grow out of the habit of biting their nails. For others it is an effort to stop, and a few still continue to bite their nails as adults.

HEAD BANGING, HEAD ROLLING AND BODY ROCKING

Some babies have the following rhythmical habits:

- **repeatedly banging the head** against something hard, perhaps the end of the cot. This may make a lot of noise but it does not seem to hurt the child. Padding the end of the cot, or using a cot bumper, helps both to reduce the noise and the possibility of bruising.
- **rolling the head from side to side**. The hair on the back of the head becomes rubbed off in the process.
- **rocking their bodies to and fro**. When a young child in a cot does this, the rocking action usually moves the cot across the room and it then bangs repeatedly against the wall. The cot may need to be fixed in some way to stop it from moving.

Babies are at least 6 months old before these types of habit appear. If ignored, the habits rarely continue after the age of 3 years. Efforts to stop them are likely to make the habits continue for a longer time. Some parents are worried by these habits. If seriously worried, they should discuss the matter with their doctor or health visitor.

HANDLING THE GENITALS

Babies discover their genitals in the same way as they discover their toes, and they will touch and explore in the same way. Because handling the genitals is a natural thing for young children to do, there is no reason why they should be made to feel naughty or guilty. After all, parents also touch these areas when the child is bathed.

A child is likely to play with the genitals less often if the parents ignore it or gently divert the child's attention to something else. Gradually, children come to understand that parents disapprove. From the age of 6 until puberty, children become less interested in sexual matters anyway.

Masturbation

This is handling the genitals for pleasure and only becomes a problem when done to excess. Excessive masturbation may be a sign that a child is deeply unhappy, bored, lonely, worried, afraid, or is being abused. Telling children that it is naughty or wrong to do it only makes them more unhappy – and guilty as well.

Questions

1 a What is meant by a 'habit'?

 b What habits are shown by the illustrations in this topic?

 c Why are habits of this type sometimes called 'comfort habits'?

 d As a child grows older, what may happen to these habits?

2 a Why is there no need to stop a young child from sucking her thumb?

 b If parents do try to stop the habit, what may be the result?

 c If a 6-year-old still sucks her thumb, why should the parent try to stop the habit?

3 a Give one reason for and one against the use of a dummy.

 b When might the use of a dummy encourage tooth decay?

 c (i) By what age will most children give up their dummy? (ii) What may encourage its use after that?

 d Give one reason why a child may be upset when her comforter is washed.

4 a Why may nail biting be considered a normal thing to do?

 b When are children more likely to bite their nails?

 c Is nail biting a harmful habit?

 d Why does nagging or punishing the child rarely stop the habit?

5 a Name three rhythmical habits of young children.

 b What is the usual age at which these habits occur?

6 a Are young children being 'naughty' when they touch their genitals?

 b (i) What is masturbation? (ii) When may it be a problem?

 c Give six possible causes for the problem.

Further activities

 Discussion

Should parents try to stop comfort habits and if so, how?

 Investigation

Choose one of the habits mentioned in this topic. Carry out a survey to find out how common the habit is in different age groups. If the habit has been discontinued, at what age did it stop?

 Child study

Describe any comfort habits the child may have.

CHAPTER 49

Pre-school groups

Pre-school groups include playgroups, nursery schools, nursery classes, and parent and toddler groups. Attendance is voluntary, so the parents can decide whether their child goes to a pre-school group or not.

A pre-school group does not take the place of home, but adds to it by providing a wider circle of people to mix with and a wider range of activities. A good pre-school group helps with a child's early education by providing:

- opportunities to socialise and learn how to mix with other children and adults and to enjoy their company
- facilities which include space to run around, apparatus to climb, toys, paints, paper, modelling dough etc.
- activities such as stories, music, dancing, singing and games
- activities which encourage early familiarity with letters and numbers, to help children acquire pre-reading and pre-counting skills.

Children who benefit most

A pre-school group is useful for almost all children, but it is particularly valuable for those who:

- are the only child in the family
- have little chance to play with others of their own age group
- live in a small flat
- live in a high-rise block
- have parents who find them difficult to manage
- have few toys at home
- are from overcrowded homes
- are neglected children – those whose parents do not talk or read to them or play with them.

When to start

A fairly independent 2-year-old may settle into a pre-school group without any trouble. However, at this age many children are still very dependent on their parents and timid with other adults and children. By 3 years of age, most children benefit from mixing with others of about the same age. This is a good time for a child to start attending a playgroup or nursery school. Many children will want their parents to stay with them for the first week or two, until they become used to being in a strange place and with a large group of people.

PLAYGROUPS

A playgroup is a group of young children aged from about 2½ to 5 years, who play together regularly under supervision. Many different play activities are provided for the children so that they can learn through play at their own speed.

Playgroups take place in hired halls or private houses. They may be run by parents who act as playgroup leaders or helpers, with one adult to every eight children. At least half of the staff should hold a relevant qualification – they may be teachers, nursery nurses, or mothers (and sometimes fathers) who have attended playgroup training courses.

Playgroups usually take place in the mornings for two to three hours, sometimes not every morning, and sometimes in the afternoon. The children attend on a regular basis, perhaps once or twice a week, perhaps every day. It is necessary for playgroups to charge fees to cover the cost of hiring a room, paying the helpers and buying equipment. Sometimes the Social Services Department pays the fees for children in need.

Many playgroups and parent and toddler groups are members of the Pre-School Learning Alliance (p. 372).

PARENT AND TODDLER GROUPS

Parent and toddler groups may be held in the same halls as playgroups, or in people's homes. They usually take place in the afternoons for about a couple of hours. Unlike playgroups, the parents must remain with their children, and young babies can be taken. A small fee may be charged to cover the cost of hiring the hall and for the equipment and refreshments.

This type of group is an ideal situation for parents to meet and chat while their children play. The youngsters can have fun exploring a world which is wider than home, and with different toys. At the same time, they have the opportunity gradually to get used to playing with other children. As the children get older and become happy to play without their parents, they may be at the right stage to attend a playgroup.

NURSERY SCHOOLS

These are schools for children aged 3–5 years, and the staff are trained nursery teachers or nursery nurses. Nursery schools are open on the same days as other schools and keep to the same term times.

Although the school day is from about 9.30 a.m. to 3.30 p.m., most children attend for only half the day, either in the mornings or the afternoons. There are not enough nursery schools for all children and some of the schools have long waiting lists. Nursery schools provide the same kind of activities as playgroups.

NURSERY CLASSES

A nursery class is a class for 3- to 4-year-olds in an ordinary school. It gives children the opportunity to begin school before the compulsory age of 5. Under the EYFS scheme, 3- and 4-year-olds are entitled to free nursery education for 15 hours per week at a pre-school group.

THE EARLY YEARS FOUNDATION STAGE (EYFS) 2008

The requirements for the care and education of pre-school children vary in the different countries of the UK. In England, the standards for care, learning and development for pre-school children aged 0–5 years are included in the EYFS framework (based on a government publication *Every Child Matters: Change For Children, 2004*). The aim is to ensure that every child makes progress, that no child gets left behind, and that a secure foundation is laid for future learning. This should enable 5-year-olds to move smoothly on to Key Stage 1 of the National Curriculum when they start school.

Free early learning
3- and 4-year-olds in England are entitled to a minimum 15 hours of free education per week for 38 weeks of the year, delivered flexibly over a minimum of three days. This is provided in both state (government funded) and private pre-school groups, who must all follow the EYFS standards, and include:

- reception and nursery classes in schools
- childminders
- day nurseries
- playgroups
- Sure Start Children's Centres
- after school and breakfast clubs
- holiday playschemes

The EYFS is based around four themes and six areas of learning

The four themes are:

A unique child
Recognises that every child is capable of learning from the moment it is born, and can develop to be resilient (able to recover quickly from difficulties), capable, confident and self-assured.

Positive relationships
Describes how loving and secure relationships with parents and carers helps children to learn to be strong and independent.

Enabling environments
Explains that a child's environment plays a key role in supporting and extending his/her development and learning.

Learning and development
Recognises that children develop and learn in different ways and at different rates, and that all areas of learning and development are equally important and inter-connected.

Six areas of learning

The EYFS identifies six areas of learning which are equally important and interlinked in a child's development. They are:

- physical development (PD)
- personal, social and emotional development (PSED)
- communication, language and literacy (CLL)
- knowledge and understanding of the world
- problem-solving, reasoning and numeracy (PSRN)
- creative development.

QUALITY OF CHILD CARE

The quality of care which children receive in a pre-school group will depend on a number of factors, including the size of the group, the resources available, whether the carers are trained or untrained and, most importantly, their attitudes. Children start to develop their own attitudes and opinions early in life and they will be influenced by the attitudes and prejudices of their carers – parents, relations, playgroup staff, teachers, etc. Children will receive high quality, sensitive care when they are treated with tolerance and consideration. Carers of children need to be aware of the following:

- **The multicultural nature of society** – children attending pre-school groups will mix with children who have different abilities and disabilities, and may come from different racial, religious and cultural backgrounds. Children need to be encouraged to respect and value differences in other people, and discouraged from making racist, sexist and antisocial remarks which are hurtful and upsetting.
- **Avoidance of stereotyping** – all children have their own likes and dislikes, manner of speaking, family customs and social background. A child should not be expected to conform to a **stereotype** – a pattern of behaviour which the carer considers to be standard for the particular group to which the child belongs (nationality, ethnic group, social group or gender). Meeting and mixing with others from different backgrounds widens children's knowledge and experience of people and is part of their education.
- **Equal opportunities** – boys should not be expected to behave in different ways from girls, and both sexes should be given the same opportunities to play with the full range of toys and to take part in all types of activities (see also pp. 8–9). Treating boys and girls differently is known as **gender stereotyping**.
- **Language and accent** – it is important to make sure that the children can understand what is said to them, particularly when a child comes from a different background from the carer. It is also important that the language which is spoken in the child's home is respected. Children who speak one language at home and another at school, and who move easily from one to the other, often seem to benefit and show increased creativity and flexibility of thought.
- **The importance of self-image** – each child is an individual and should be encouraged to develop a positive self-image (self-esteem, p. 168). This applies to all children, particularly to those who, for example, belong to a minority group or are socially disadvantaged or are disabled.

Questions

1 a Give four examples of different types of pre-school group.

  b What does a good pre-school group provide for young children?

  c Which children are likely to benefit most from attending a playgroup?

2 a Why are many 2-year-olds not ready to attend a playgroup?

  b What is generally a good age to start?

Questions (continued)

3 a What is a playgroup?

  b What do playgroups provide and for what purpose?

  c Which other type of pre-school group provides the same kind of activities as a playgroup?

  d Explain the difference between a nursery school and a nursery class.

4 Give the following information about playgroups and parent and toddler groups:

  a Of which organisation are these groups likely to be members?

  b Is attendance voluntary?

  c Which of the groups has to be registered, and with whom?

  d At which of these groups do parents remain with their children?

5 a When children start to form their own opinions, what will they be influenced by?

  b In what ways should child care workers be aware of (i) the multicultural nature of society, (ii) avoidance of stereotyping, (iii) equal opportunities, (iv) language and accent, (v) the importance of self-image?

6 a (i) What does EYFS stand for, (ii) what is its aim?

  b EYFS is based around four themes. What do these themes:

    (i) recognise (2 answers), (ii) describe, (iii) explain?

  c List the six areas of learning.

Further activities

 ### Investigation

1 Find out more about the Pre-School Learning Alliance. Information can be obtained from a local playgroup or parent and toddler group, or from the headquarters (see p. 372).

2 a Find out the whereabouts of pre-school groups in your area. Try to arrange to visit or help at one or more groups.

  b Observe the children at play at a pre-school group. (i) Draw a plan of the play area and mark in the various activities which have been set out for the children to use. (ii) Observe one child for a time (say half an hour). Map the child's movements on your plan, noting how long was spent at each play activity and what the child did. (iii) Observe another child in a similar way. Compare your results from the two children.

Can you suggest reasons for any differences in the ways the two children played?

  c Compare differences in stages of development and skills between two children in a playgroup, for example a 3-year-old who has just started and a child of 4½ who has been at the playgroup for a year or more.

3 Research the pre-school groups in your area. Prepare a PowerPoint presentation to inform parents about each of the pre-school groups you have researched. Explain where and how your information may be used. This could be a group exercise.

 ### Child study

If the child attends a pre-school group, talk with the child to try to discover what happens there and how the child feels about it.

Weblinks

For more information on pre-school groups, visit:

www.direct.gov.uk

For the 'Statutory Framework for the Early Years Foundation Stage' pdf, visit

www.nationalstrategies.standards.dcsf.gov.uk

CHAPTER 50

Starting school

Education in Britain is compulsory from the age of 5 years. Children are legally required to attend school full-time from the beginning of the term after their fifth birthday, or to receive a suitable education elsewhere, for example to be educated at home. Some schools take them earlier, either full-time or part-time.

CHANGES TO THE CHILD'S LIFE

For a child, starting school is the next stage in becoming independent and building up a separate personality. Children enter a new world alone and soon come to know more about it than their parents. They can decide what to tell them about it and what to keep to themselves. They find themselves in a large building with lots of unknown people. They join classes with other children of about the same age and they all share the attention of one adult. They are expected to keep to a timetable. New friends are made. The playground is shared with larger and older children. Some stay for dinner and must get used to school meals. All must abide by the rules and codes of behaviour necessary for the smooth running of large organisations. These are great changes to a young child's life, apart from the necessity of being away from home and parents for a large part of the day.

PREPARING A CHILD FOR SCHOOL

How can parents help?

Parents can help by talking to their child about school, and telling him what to expect, and by making it sound exciting. If the mother is sad at the thought of losing her child's companionship and of being left alone in the house, she should not show it. It may worry the child and make it difficult for him to settle at school. The child who is happy and secure at home is less likely to have difficulties at school.

Whatever the size of the class, the teacher will not be able to give continuous attention to one particular child. Therefore, children who have been encouraged by their parents to 'stand on their own feet' are likely to find it easier to adjust to school than those who are used to the continuous attention of their parents.

Attending a pre-school group can help

A child who has been to a playgroup or nursery school will be used to:

- being away from home
- being separated from his parents
- mixing with other children
- sharing the attention of an adult with other children
- the noise and movement created by a large number of children.

Schools can help

Infant teachers are well aware that all children, to a greater or lesser degree, worry about starting school. They understand the big step that children take when they move from the small social world of home to the much larger social world of school. At school, they have to face all sorts of new situations without the support of their parents.

Many schools try to help new children settle into school life easily and happily, and they do this in a variety of ways. For example, they may:

- invite new children to visit the school in the term before starting
- arrange 'staggered' starts so that only a few new children start on the same day
- allow half-day schooling in the first few weeks
- let parents stay in the classroom for a while
- encourage parents to talk to the teacher about matters which affect the child. It helps the teacher to know about the other members of the child's family and any health or behaviour problems. It is also helpful for the teacher to know if the child is left-handed.

USEFUL SKILLS

When children start school it helps them to fit into the new environment more easily if they have already acquired certain **self-care skills**. For example, the ability to:

- say their name and address clearly
- put on clothes
- do up buttons, zips and other fastenings
- tie shoe laces and fasten buckles
- blow their nose
- go to the toilet without help
- wash their hands
- eat with a knife, fork etc.

Children in this age group like to be able to do the same things as others in the class. If they have already acquired the skills listed above by the time they start school, it will help them not to feel inferior or different from the other children. It also gives a degree of independence as they do not continuously have to seek the help of the teacher.

HELPING CHILDREN TO DO THEIR BEST

Before starting school

Parents and carers help children to get a good start at school by:

- encouraging them to concentrate on activities for more than a few minutes
- encouraging them to share and join in activities with other children
- reading and talking about books with them
- encouraging them to look at books by themselves
- giving them plenty of opportunities to use pencils and crayons. If they are ready to write their name, show them how to use a capital letter followed by lower case letters (e.g. Peter)
- introducing them to as many new words as possible
- helping them count and use numbers in everyday situations.

When at school

Children do better at school when their parents:

- give them lots of love and security at home
- are interested in what they do and talk to them about it
- encourage them to enjoy all the activities
- understand and support them when they have difficulties.

BASELINE ASSESSMENT

When children first start school at the age of 4 or 5 they will undergo a **baseline assessment** which has two aims:

- to find out what children know, understand and can do. This enables teachers to plan effectively for each child's learning needs
- to help schools measure and monitor children's progress from the time they start school.

BULLYING

Although bullying takes place most often amongst school-age children, it may also occur in pre-school groups. By the age of 3 or 4 years, some children have already learnt that being aggressive helps them to get what they want. The bullying can take the form of:

- **verbal abuse** (name-calling, teasing, racial insults)
- **physical abuse** (punching, kicking, jostling, pinching)
- **extortion** (demanding money etc.)
- **threats**.

Bullying may be a sign that the child himself (or herself) is being bullied or neglected at home, or there may be other reasons. Whatever the cause, it needs to be stopped for the benefit of both the victim and the bully. Victims need to be comforted and helped to develop a sense of security and self-esteem. Bullies need attention and help in order to learn not to hurt other people or their feelings.

'GIFTED' CHILDREN

These are children with very high ability in many subjects or who are talented in a particular area, for example, music, mathematics or sport. If their ability is not recognised or catered for at school, they may become bored and frustrated. This can lead to a complete lack of interest in school work, or to disruptive behaviour or the development of social or emotional problems. Educational approaches for gifted children could be:

- individual work at a more advanced level
- being placed in a higher ability group that follows a specialised curriculum
- moving up a year at school; though this can be a disadvantage if the gifted child has not reached the same level of social and emotional development as the other children in the year group.

Questions

1 a At what age are children in Britain legally required to attend school?

b Name five ways in which children can be helped to settle into school life.

2 Name five ways in which attending a playgroup will help prepare a child for school.

3 Name eight useful skills to have learnt before starting school.

4 In what ways can parents help their children to do their best at school (i) before the child starts school, (ii) when at school?

5 (i) What are the various forms which bullying can take? (ii) Does bullying occur in pre-school groups? (iii) What type of help do the victims need? (iv) Why do bullies also need to be helped?

6 a Which children are regarded as gifted?

b How may these children behave if they are bored at school?

c Suggest three educational approaches for gifted children.

d When can being moved up a year at school be a disadvantage?

Further activities

 Extension

1 a Give ten examples of how a child's life will change when he starts school.

b How would you suggest that parents prepare their child for these changes?

2 Answer the following questions using information from Kidscape (see p. 371) or other sources.

a What signs may indicate that a child is being bullied?

b What factors may cause children to become (i) temporary bullies, (ii) chronic (long-term) bullies?

c Give some ways in which parents can help a child who is being bullied.

d Give some suggestions for dealing with bullies.

 Investigation

Visit an infant school (first school), if possible as a helper.

a Write an account of your visit.

b Watch the children arrive at school, leave school, and when they are in the playground. Observe their behaviour and note any interesting points. How did the children react when they were reunited with their parents after school?

CHAPTER 51

Children's clothes

Clothes for young babies were discussed in Topic 24. Once babies begin to move about, different types and a greater variety of clothes become desirable.

A list of requirements for baby clothes is given on p. 107. The same list applies to clothes for children of all ages, together with additional requirements.

Additional requirements for children's clothes

Children's clothes should be:

- loose enough for movement but not so big as to get in the way
- hard-wearing
- easy for a child to put on
- easy for the child to take off for toilet needs.

Shoes are required from the toddler stage onwards.

Different types of clothes are needed for daytime, night-time, and to wear outside in cold, hot and wet weather.

DIFFERENT TYPES OF CLOTHES

The following are some examples of different types of clothes for children.

Nightwear

A **sleepsuit (A)** keeps the child warm even when not covered by blankets. It may have feet attached, sometimes with soles made of a material which can be easily wiped. Then the child does not need a dressing-gown or slippers.

Pyjamas (B) have a tendency to part in the middle, but are easier to remove for the toilet than a sleepsuit.

A **nightdress (C)** does not keep the child as warm as a sleepsuit or pyjamas, but this can be an advantage in hot weather.

Points to note:

▦ Children's nightdresses, nightshirts, dressing-gowns and bathrobes (except bathrobes made from 100% terry towelling) *must* all pass a test for slow burning fabrics. These garments therefore do not need to carry a LOW FLAMMABILITY label.

▦ Children's bathrobes and pyjamas made from 100 per cent terry towelling must carry a permanent label showing whether or not the garment passes the low flammability test for slow burning.

▦ If the garment has passed the LOW FLAMMABILITY test it will be slow to burn and be labelled:

> | LOW FLAMMABILITY TO BS5722 | or | LOW FLAMMABILITY TO BS5722 KEEP AWAY FROM FIRE |

▦ If the garment probably has not passed the low flammability test and is not slow burning, it will be labelled:

> | KEEP AWAY FROM FIRE |

Daytime clothes

Romper suits (D) and **dungarees (E)** are practical for the crawling and toddler stages. They help to stop nappies from falling down and ensure that there is no gap between trousers and top.

Clothes for active children (F) need to be easy to wash and comfortable to wear.

For outdoors, a warm washable **jacket with a hood (G)** is a useful garment for wet or cold, windy weather. It needs to be loose enough to go over other clothing and still give freedom of movement.

LEARNING TO DRESS

When children are very young, they do not mind what they wear. By the time they reach the age of 3 years, they take an interest in their clothes, and often make a great fuss about what they want, or do not want, to wear. They are also starting to dress themselves. At this stage, dressing is a slow job, and the clothes are often put on inside out and back to front. Adults know they can do the job easily and quickly and will be tempted to do so. However, the children are likely to get very cross if adults interfere as they want to do it themselves. Battles can rage between parent and child!

Making it easier

Parents can make it easier for children to dress unaided by providing clothes that are simple to put on. This gives children the satisfaction of being independent and self-reliant at an earlier age. Dressing dolly or teddy gives practice in using the fingers to do up buttons, velcro fastenings, zips, hooks and eyes, press fasteners, laces, toggles and bows.

'Learning to dress' doll

DRESSING FOR PLAY

Children easily spill food or drink, and they love playing with water, or in a muddy garden or with paints. Parents will be happier if they accept that it is natural for children to get dirty, and the children will be happier if they are dressed in hard-wearing clothes which can be easily washed. Children who are nagged too much about keeping clean are likely to react by worrying. The worry will result in them getting far less enjoyment out of their play.

SHOES

Shoes and other types of footwear are a very important part of clothing and need particular attention.

Children do not need shoes until they are walking. They then only need them when it is necessary to protect the feet against damage, or to keep them warm. Going barefoot as much as possible allows the bones and muscles to develop in the natural way to produce strong, healthy feet.

Although we shall be talking mainly about shoes, much of what is said applies to other types of footwear.

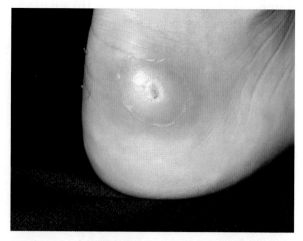

An abscess on a child's foot caused by ill-fitting shoes

The need for well-fitting shoes

Children's shoes need to be the right shape and size to allow the bones and muscles of the feet to develop properly. The bones in a young child's foot are very soft and rather like rubber. These bones can be easily deformed by badly fitting shoes. The bones harden as the child grows. If the foot is kept in perfect shape, the bones will harden in a perfect shape. If the feet are crushed into shoes which are too small, the bones harden into an imperfect shape, and the muscles will be poorly developed. The child rarely feels any pain when wearing tight shoes and therefore will not complain. Pain may come later, because many of the foot and back troubles which develop in later life are caused by ill-fitting footwear in childhood.

Toes and toenails may be damaged by the pressure of ill-fitting shoes. Corns, callouses and hardening and thickening of the skin are also caused by pressure. All these problems are avoided by wearing shoes that fit properly.

Rate of growth of feet

Feet grow about 2–2½ sizes each year until the age of 4 years. As a result, young children usually outgrow their shoes every 3 months. New shoes should be fitted to leave 12–18 mm growing space between the end of the longest toe and the end of the shoes, but not so loose that the shoes rub the heels and make them sore. The shoes also need to be wide enough to allow the toes to move.

The most suitable shoes for children are those which are made in whole and half sizes, and in several different widths to suit thin feet, fat feet and those in between.

Choosing shoes for a child

▪ **Measuring the feet** – when buying shoes for children, it is best that their feet are measured by a trained fitter in a shoe shop. Children should always wear socks and stand upright when having their feet measured and shoes fitted, as feet alter a little in shape when the full body weight is placed on them.

▪ **Uppers** –the upper part of a shoe may be made of leather or plastic. Leather is hard-wearing and stretches to take the shape of the foot. It also allows moisture to pass through. This means that sweat from the feet can escape and the shoes will be more comfortable to wear for a longer time. Shoes with plastic uppers are often cheaper and need less cleaning, but they do not stretch in the same way as leather or allow moisture to escape.

▪ **Soles** – soles which are light and flexible bend with the foot. This encourages a natural springy step which makes for easier walking. Soles which are anti-slip are safer. They also give greater confidence to a child who is learning to walk.

▪ **Points to check** – Shoes for children should:

1 be smooth inside and with no hard seams
2 have a firm fitting heel
3 have an adjustable fastening
4 have a low heel so that the foot does not slide forwards.
5 have soles which are light and flexible
6 have room for growth
7 be wide enough to allow the toes to move
8 give support and protection to the feet
9 have flexible uppers which bend as the foot bends

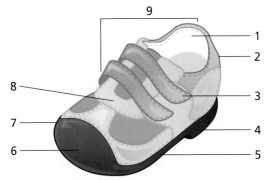

Type of shoe considered to be suitable for young children

Other types of footwear

▪ **Pram shoes (A)** are not meant for walking. They are sometimes worn when a baby is dressed for special occasions.

▪ **'Padders' (B)** keep a baby's feet warm and give some foot protection when crawling or toddling. Those with an antislip sole help to keep toddlers steady on their feet.

▪ **Sandals (C)** are useful for wearing in hot weather as they allow air to get to the feet, which reduces the unpleasant effects of sweating.

▪ **Plimsolls (D)** are lightweight canvas shoes with rubber soles which are useful for energetic games because they bend easily. As plimsolls are not usually made in half sizes or a variety of widths they are not usually a good fit.

▪ **Trainers or sports shoes (E)** are sturdy shoes made of leather, canvas or plastic, with rubber soles.

▪ **Wellington boots (F)** are made of rubber or plastic to keep water out. Water from sweat is also kept inside. When the boots are worn in hot weather, the feet quickly become hot and sweaty. This makes the feet uncomfortable if the boots are worn for a long period of time. When the boots are worn in cold weather, the feet quickly become cold unless warm socks are worn inside. The size of the boots should allow for this.

Socks and tights

These should be big enough to give a loose, easy fit at the toes. If too tight they can cause foot troubles in the same way as tight shoes. On the other hand, over-large socks or tights can be very uncomfortable to wear.

Questions

1 a What are the requirements for children's clothes in addition to those required for the layette?

b What label shows that a garment (i) has passed the low flammability test, (ii) has not passed the slow burning test?

c Why do children's nightdresses not need to have a low flammability label?

2 List the different types of clothing worn by the children in the drawings A–G on p. 245, giving one reason why each type of garment is useful.

3 a By what age do children take an interest in what they wear?

b How can parents make it easier for children to dress themselves?

c (i) Name four situations when children are likely to get dirty.

(ii) What clothes are most practical for children?

4 a Give two reasons for wearing shoes.

b Why is it important that shoes are the right shape and size?

c Why are the bones in a child's foot easily deformed?

d Why do children usually not complain when their shoes are tight?

e What caused the abscess on the child's foot in the photograph on p. 246?

Questions (continued)

5 a How much growing space needs to be left at the end of new shoes?

  b What is the advantage of having a choice of shoes in a variety of widths?

  c Give two advantages of having the uppers made of (i) leather, (ii) plastic.

  d Why are light and flexible soles considered to be an advantage?

6 a Name the types of footwear A–F shown on p. 248, and say when each would be of use.

  b Give reasons why socks and tights should not be (i) tightly fitting, (ii) over-large.

Further activities

 Extension

1 Copy the drawing of the shoe on p. 247 and match each of the numbers with one of the 'Points to check'.

2 Make a collection of pictures of different types of children's clothing, including shoes. Give your opinion of the usefulness of each garment.

 Discussion

Discuss the advantages and disadvantages of dressing identical twins in the same clothes.

 Investigation

Devise and, if possible, carry out an experiment to test the flammability of various materials commonly used for children's clothes. Only a small sample of each material needs to be tested. Say what safety measures were taken during this experiment.

 Child study

1 Measure the child's feet. Are they both the same size?

2 Discuss children's clothes with the mother. What are her views on the way children should be dressed? Has the child any views on the clothes which he or she wears?

Weblink

For safety measures to note when buying toddler shoes, visit

www.parentingtoddlers.com

Exercises

Exercises relevant to Section 5 can be found on p. 384.

SECTION 6

Food

CHAPTER 52

Food and energy

People take in food to satisfy feelings of hunger and because they enjoy eating and drinking. The body uses this food to provide:

- material for growth
- material to replace worn out or damaged tissues
- energy for the wide range of chemical activities that take place inside the body
- energy for physical activities
- heat to keep the body warm.

FOOD SUBSTANCES

All foods consist of one or more of seven types of substances:

| proteins carbohydrates fats minerals vitamins fibre water | **nutrients** (substances derived from foods that are essential for life) |

A few foods, for example sugar, contain only one of the substances (sugar is 100 per cent carbohydrate). The great majority of foods are a mixture of several substances.

A variety of foods needs to be eaten to provide the body with sufficient amounts of each nutrient in order to grow and develop properly, to be active, and to keep healthy.

PROTEINS

Proteins are used to build the body and keep it in good repair. They are particularly important in childhood for building the brain, muscles, skin, blood and other tissues in order to make a strong healthy body. Protein foods can be obtained from both animals and plants.

Animal proteins

Plant proteins

CARBOHYDRATES

Carbohydrates provide energy. Starch and sugar are both carbohydrates. Some of the more common carbohydrate foods are shown below. They have been grouped according to whether they contain mainly starch, mainly sugar or are a mixture of both. When more carbohydrate is eaten than the body can use, the remainder is changed into body fat and is stored until needed.

Sugary foods

Foods rich in both starch and sugar   Starchy foods

FATS

Fats may be in solid form like butter, or in a liquid form like oil, depending on the temperature. Generally, at room temperature animal fats are solid and plant fats are liquid and called oils. Margarine differs because, although made from oils, the oils are processed in such a way as to make a solid fat.

Fats provide energy. They have a much higher energy value than carbohydrates. That means, weight for weight, they contain more calories (see p. 256). Some foods consist almost entirely of fats, and many popular foods contain large amounts.

The body needs a certain amount of fat but when more is eaten than is used, the extra becomes stored as body fat.

Foods which contain fat

Fats and oils

MINERALS

Minerals are substances like calcium and iron which occur naturally in the earth. Fifteen minerals are known to be essential for the various chemical activities which take place in the body and to build and repair the tissues. They are obtained from:

- foods derived from plants which absorb minerals from the soil
- foods derived from animals which have eaten plants
- drinking water in which the minerals are dissolved.

Nearly all foods contain one or several minerals. The only minerals which are sometimes in short supply in the body are calcium, iron and fluoride.

Calcium is essential for strong bones and teeth. Chief sources include milk, cheese, white bread, yoghurt, green vegetables.

Iron is essential for the formation of red blood cells. Chief sources are red meat, liver, eggs, green vegetables, wholemeal bread. It is added to some breakfast cereals.

Fluoride helps to produce strong, healthy teeth. If it is not present in the water supply, it can be given to children in tablet form and in toothpaste.

Phosphorus has a wide variety of essential functions in cells and, together with calcium, is needed for strong bones and teeth. It is present in nearly all foods.

Other essential minerals include **potassium, magnesium, phosphorus, zinc, sodium** and **chlorine**. Sodium and chlorine are both obtained from salt (sodium chloride).

VITAMINS

Vitamins are complex chemical substances made by plants and animals. Generally, the human body cannot manufacture vitamins so they have to be obtained from food. They are needed for various chemical activities. Only a very small quantity of each vitamin is required for the body to keep healthy and active. Vitamins so far discovered include the following:

Vitamin A

This is found mainly in foods containing fat, for example, milk, butter, margarine, fish liver oils. Carrots and green vegetables also provide it. Vitamin A is essential for being able to 'see in the dark' and for a healthy skin.

The B vitamins

Vitamin B is now known to be not just one vitamin but a number of vitamins including **thiamin** (B1), **riboflavin** (B2), B6, **folic acid** (folate), and **niacin** (also called **nicotinic acid** but nothing to do with nicotine). These vitamins occur in foods like wholemeal bread, oats, milk, cheese and liver, and they are often added to processed breakfast cereals. An exception is B12 which occurs only in animal products and never in food from plants. Generally, the B vitamins enable the body to obtain energy from food.

Vitamin C

This is found in fresh fruits and vegetables. Small amounts occur in milk, particularly breast milk. This vitamin easily disappears when fruit and vegetables are kept for a long time or when they are cooked. Vitamin C keeps gums healthy and helps wounds to heal.

Vitamin D

This is obtained mainly from foods containing fat such as margarine, butter, oily fish, eggs. It can also be made in the skin when the skin is exposed to sunlight. Vitamin D is essential for healthy bones and teeth.

Figure 52.09 Foods which contain vitamin C

Vitamin E

Most foods contain vitamin E and, as it can be stored in the body, it is never in short supply except possibly in premature babies.

Vitamin K

This vitamin helps the blood to clot. Vitamin K is never in short supply in a healthy person because it is made by bacteria in the large intestine (the bowel). It also occurs widely in green vegetables. As there are no bacteria in the intestines of newborn babies, they are given vitamin K to protect them from a rare bleeding disorder.

DIETARY FIBRE

Dietary fibre (roughage) consists of plant material which cannot be digested. It is present in vegetables, fruit, wholemeal bread, pulses such as peas, beans, lentils, and cereals such as oats, wheat, and bran. Fibre is an important part of the diet because by increasing bulk it encourages the movement of food through the intestines, which helps to prevent constipation.

WATER

Water is the main substance in the body and accounts for about two-thirds of the body's weight. It forms part of all the body tissues and is the liquid in which the chemical activities in the body take place.

Water is continuously being lost from the body in sweat, breath and urine. The water that is lost needs to be replaced. It enters the body as part of solid food as well as in drinks.

ENERGY FROM FOOD

The body needs a continuous supply of energy to keep alive. Energy is used for breathing, circulation, growth and keeping warm, as well as enabling the body to move. The more active (energetic) the person, the more energy will be used. This energy all comes from food.

The amount of energy a particular food contains can be measured in either kilocalories (kcal) or kilojoules (kJ):

$$1 \text{ kcal} = 4.2 \text{ kJ (approx)}$$
$$1000 \text{ kJ} = 1 \text{ MJ (megajoule)} = 239 \text{ kcal}$$

In everyday language the 'kilo' part of kilocalorie is often left off. So, when the word **calorie** is used it usually means kilocalorie. The same often happens to the word kilojoule. It is technically inaccurate to use calorie and joule in this way and can be confusing.

Different foods contain different amounts of energy per unit weight, that is, they have different **energy values**. Foods which have a high energy value are those which contain little water and a high proportion of fat or sugar.

DAILY INTAKE OF ENERGY

The average daily intake for an adult woman is 8.1 MJ (1935 kcal), which increases by 0.8 MJ (191 kcal) per day during pregnancy. When breast-feeding, a woman requires, on average, an extra 1.9 MJ (454 kcal) during the first month, 2.2 MJ (525 kcal) during the second month, and 2.4 MJ (573 kcal) during the third month. The estimated daily average energy requirement for a boy of 0–3 months is 2.28 MJ (545 kcl) which rises to 8.24 MJ (1970 kcl) for a boy of 7–8 years. The estimated average energy requirements for girls are slightly less.

GENETICALLY MODIFIED FOODS

Genetically modified (GM) foods are foods that contain ingredients from genetically modified crops. **GM crops** are plants that have had their genes artificially altered in a laboratory. It is possible to alter a plant's genes to produce foods with new tastes and flavours, more protein, a longer shelf-life or a higher yield. Plants can also be designed to be poisonous to insects, which means that fewer pesticides are needed to grow the crop.

One of the most common GM ingredients in food is soya flour made from GM soya beans. GM tomatoes are also available. Soya flour and tomatoes are used in a wide range of convenience foods and ready-made meals. When a manufacturer knows that foods contain GM ingredients, the pack is usually labelled.

GM technology is still so new that any long-term effects (beneficial or disadvantageous) of GM crops on the environment, or GM foods on people's health, are still unknown.

Questions

1 a Give five ways in which the body uses food.
  b (i) Name seven substances found in food. (ii) Which are nutrients?
2 a What are proteins used for?
  b (i) Name some foods which contain animal proteins. (ii) Name some which contain plant proteins.
3 a What type of substance are starch and sugar?
  b (i) Name another type of food besides carbohydrate which provides energy. (ii) Which of these substances has a higher energy value? (iii) What happens to these substances when more is eaten than is used?
4 Of the following eight foods – olive oil, pastry, sweet biscuits, sweets, rice, butter, bacon, lentils – name one which is (i) liquid fat, (ii) solid fat, (iii) mainly sugar, (iv) mainly starch, (v) contains fat and protein, (vi) contains fat and starch, (vii) contains starch and protein, (viii) contains starch, sugar and fat.

Questions (continued)

5 a Name nine minerals.

  b Briefly, what is the difference between minerals and vitamins?

  c (i) Name three minerals which are sometimes in short supply in the diet. (ii) Why is each essential? (iii) From what sources can each be obtained?

6 a Which two vitamins are found mainly in foods containing fat?

  b Which vitamin is only found in animal products?

  c Which vitamin can be made in the skin?

  d (i) Which vitamin is found in fresh fruit and vegetables? (ii) Why do they have to be fresh?

7 a Why does the body need energy?

  b Where does this energy come from?

  c Name two units in which energy in food can be measured.

8 a What are (i) GM foods, (ii) GM crops?

  b For what purposes may a plant's genes be genetically modified?

Further activities

 Extension

1 Draw or find pictures to add to your notes of two or more examples of foods containing:

  a protein   **f** iron

  b fat   **g** vitamin A

  c starch   **h** B vitamins

  d sugar   **i** vitamin C

  e calcium   **j** vitamin D.

2 Study the information given on the right, taken from a packet of cornflakes.

  a Give the weight of an average serving in (i) grams, (ii) ounces.

  b Give the average energy value of an average serving in (i) kilojoules, (ii) kilocalories.

  c (i) Name the five vitamins of the B group listed in the ingredients. (ii) Give a function of these vitamins.

  d (i) Name the other vitamin in the cornflakes.

     (ii) Why is it important in the diet?

  e What reason is given for adding iron?

  f (i) How much dietary fibre is present in an average serving? (ii) Why is fibre important in the diet?

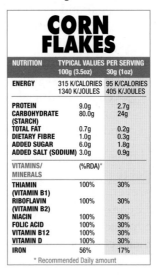

CORN FLAKES

NUTRITION	TYPICAL VALUES PER SERVING	
	100g (3.5oz)	30g (1oz)
ENERGY	315 K/CALORIES 1340 K/JOULES	95 K/CALORIES 405 K/JOULES
PROTEIN	9.0g	2.7g
CARBOHYDRATE (STARCH)	80.0g	24g
TOTAL FAT	0.7g	0.2g
DIETARY FIBRE	1.0g	0.3g
ADDED SUGAR	6.0g	1.8g
ADDED SALT (SODIUM)	3.0g	0.9g

VITAMINS/ MINERALS	(%RDA)*	
THIAMIN (VITAMIN B1)	100%	30%
RIBOFLAVIN (VITAMIN B2)	100%	30%
NIACIN	100%	30%
FOLIC ACID	100%	30%
VITAMIN B12	100%	30%
VITAMIN D	100%	30%
IRON	56%	17%

* Recommended Daily amount

3 From the information on the cornflakes label:

  a Draw a bar chart on graph paper or by using a spreadsheet program to show the typical amounts of protein, carbohydrate, fat, fibre, and sodium per 100 g of cornflakes.

  b What percentages of these cornflakes are sugar and sodium? Why do you think that sugar and sodium are added? Do you think they are necessary?

4 a For each of the essential nutrients mentioned in this topic, use a dietary analysis program or other data to find a selection of foods containing high amounts of the nutrient.

  b Find the recommended daily intake of energy for a 5-year-old boy in the table on p. 256. Using the food list which accompanies a dietary analysis program (or other data), plan meals for the boy for one day to give him food with the recommended amount of energy.

CHAPTER 53

Food additives

Additives are substances that are added to food to preserve it or to change it in some way. They can be:

- **natural** (obtained from nature), for example:
  - salt is obtained from salt mines or from sea water
  - sugar is obtained from sugar beet or sugar cane
  - carotene comes from green plants, carrots and egg yolk
  - vinegar and alcohol are produced by yeast
  - vitamin C (ascorbic acid) obtained from fresh fruit and vegetables
- **synthetic** (man-made by a chemical process), for example:
  - tartrazine and sunset yellow (artificial colours)
  - saccharin (artificial sweetener)
  - vitamin C (ascorbic acid); this natural additive is also produced synthetically.

Additives are controlled by government regulation and it is illegal to put anything in food which is known to injure health. However, a few additives can cause changes in children's mood and behaviour, making them hyperactive. If a child shows signs of hyperactivity or ADHD (p. 226), avoiding foods containing artificial colours might help to improve the behaviour. For example:

WHOLE ORANGE DRINK

NO TARTRAZINE OR SIMILAR ARTIFICIAL COLOURS

INGREDIENTS: WATER, GLUCOSE SYRUP, ORANGES, CITRIC ACID, FLAVOURINGS, PRESERVATIVES (SODIUM BENZOATE, SODIUM METABISULPHITE), STABILISER (E466), ARTIFICIAL SWEETENER (SACCHARIN), VITAMIN C, COLOUR (BETACAROTENE).

sunset yellow (E110), quinoline yellow (E104), carmoisine (E122), allura red (E129), tartrazine (E102), ponceau 4R (E124).

Food manufacturers are encouraged to find alternatives to these colours and, although their use is declining, they may be found in soft drinks, sweets, cakes and ice cream.

Additives are usually grouped according to their function. They can be identified by name or number, or both. Those with an 'E' (**E-numbers**) have been approved for use in food by the European Union (EU). Some examples are given below.

PRESERVATIVES

These protect food against microbes (bacteria and fungi). They prevent microbes from spoiling the food, which increases its storage life and also helps protect against food poisoning. Examples are:

- sugar, salt, vinegar and alcohol
- sodium metabisulphite (E223)
- sodium benzoate (E 211)
- potassium nitrate (E252)
- sulphur dioxide (E220).

ANTIOXIDANTS

These stop fatty foods from becoming rancid, and also protect vitamins contained in the food from being destroyed. Examples are:

- synthetic alpha-tocopherol (E307)
- lecithin (E322)
- L-ascorbic acid (vitamin C; E300).

EMULSIFIERS AND STABILISERS

Emulsifiers enable ingredients to be mixed together that would normally separate, for example fat or oil with water.

Stabilisers prevent substances which have been mixed together from separating again. Examples of substances which are both emulsifiers and stabilisers are:

- locust bean gum (E410), from carob beans
- gum arabic (E414), from acacia trees.

COLOURINGS

These are used to make food more colourful and attractive, or to change its colour. Examples are:

- tartrazine (E102) – yellow chemical
- curcumin (E100) – yellow extract of turmeric roots
- caramel (E150) – burnt sugar
- carotene (E160a) – orange-yellow colour obtained from carrots; becomes vitamin A in the body
- annatto – a yellowish-red dye.

FLAVOURINGS, FLAVOUR ENHANCERS AND SWEETENERS

Flavourings
There are about 3000 flavourings, but only tiny amounts are used compared with other additives. They are not at present required to be individually named on the packaging of foods. Flavourings include herbs and spices.

Flavour enhancers
These stimulate the taste buds and make food taste stronger. An example is monosodium glutamate (MSG, E621).

Sweeteners

These are used in low-calorie food products and in diabetic foods. Examples are:

- saccharin (E954)
- sorbitol (E420)
- aspartame (E951).

ANTI-CAKING AGENTS

These stop lumps forming in powdery foods. An example issilicon dioxide (E551; silica).

VITAMINS AND MINERALS

These replace naturally occurring vitamins and minerals that are removed by processing.

Questions

1 a What are additives?

   b Explain the difference between natural additives and synthetic additives, and give examples of each.

   c Are additives subject to any form of control?

   d Give examples of additives that can cause changes in children's mood and behaviour.

   e (i) How can additives be identified?

   (ii) Which additives have an E-number?

   f In which order are the ingredients in a food required to be listed on the label?

2 a Why are colours added to food?

   b (i) About how many different flavourings are there?

   (ii) Is it essential for them to be named on the packaging of food?

   c (i) What type of additive is monosodium glutamate?

   (ii) Why is it added to food?

   d Which types of food might contain an additive such as E551 and why?

3 The label from a bottle of orange drink is shown on p. 258. What additives does the drink contain?

Further activities

 Extension

1 Look at the information given here, which comes from a margarine carton.

> Sunflower oil, Vegetable oils; Whey; Salt; Emulsifier E471; Lecithin; Colours (Curcumin, Annatto); Flavourings; Vitamins A, D & E

   a (i) The ingredients include 'whey' – find out what whey is.

   (ii) Which vitamins does this margarine contain?

   b (i) What type of additive is lecithin? (ii) Give two reasons for adding lecithin to margarine.

   c (i) Which emulsifier has been added to the margarine? (ii) Why are emulsifiers added to food? (iii) Name three ingredients in this margarine which can be combined together by an emulsifier.

   d Name the two colours which have been added to the margarine, and the colour each gives.

2 a Why does the orange drink label on p. 258 state 'No tartrazine'?

   b (i) Which stabiliser has been added to the orange drink? (ii) What is the function of stablisers?

   c Name an ingredient other than sugar which gives the drink sweetness.

   d Name the two preservatives in the orange drink and give the E-number of one of them. (ii) What is the function of preservatives?

 Investigation

Study the labels on a variety of different foods commonly eaten by young children. List the additives and try to identify their purpose.

CHAPTER 54

Diet

Parents and those who care about children will want to feed them well to give them a good start in life. Sensible feeding begins during pregnancy when the expectant mother eats sufficient protein, fresh fruit and vegetables, to supply enough nourishment for herself and the developing baby. After the birth, the baby is fed entirely on milk for the first few months, then is weaned on to other foods. The child will then get nourishment from a variety of foods containing different types and amounts of nutrients. A child who is to grow into a healthy adult needs a balanced diet. To ensure that all children can benefit from a healthy diet, the government has introduced the **Healthy Start** and **Nursery Milk** schemes (p. 357).

A BALANCED DIET

The word diet means the usual type of food that is eaten. For example, a young baby has a diet of milk, whereas the diet of an older child is a mixture of foods. 'Going on a diet' is rather different. When someone 'goes on a diet' that person is restricted to eating certain foods, perhaps because of a disease such as diabetes, or in order to lose or gain weight.

A diet made up from suitable proportions of these food items would be balanced

A **balanced diet** is one which contains enough of all the necessary food substances. This does not mean that every meal has to be 'balanced', or that the right amounts of each of the seven substances listed on p. 252 have to be eaten each day. It means that over the course of several days, the body needs to take in enough of the right kinds of food substances to grow and to stay healthy.

Children who eat a balanced diet are more likely to:

- develop a strong, well-formed body
- have energy to keep warm and active
- keep healthy
- grow to their full potential height (the height which their genes will allow)
- maintain a suitable weight for their height and age.

A rough guide to a balanced diet

Parents do not need to worry too much about giving their child a balanced diet. If they offer a variety of food during the day, the child will eat what his or her body needs. Generally speaking, a child should have each day:

- some milk
- protein foods, e.g. meat, poultry, fish, cheese, an egg, beans
- vegetables – raw or cooked
- fruit
- bread, wholegrain cereals, potatoes, pasta, or rice.

Variations – likes and dislikes

The list given above is only a rough guide. A good diet can be obtained in a number of ways. For example:

- A child who doesn't eat meat or fish can get sufficient protein from milk, eggs, cheese, beans, peas and nuts.
- Some children do not like vegetables. They will come to no harm as long as other foods containing minerals, vitamins and fibre are eaten.
- Other children do not like fruit, but they may like home-made fruit smoothies or fruit juice drinks such as blackcurrant or orange.
- Children who do not like drinking milk can be given it in the form of milk puddings, custard, yoghurt, cheese etc.

The cost of good food

Good eating does not have to be expensive. Nourishing foods are often less expensive than the high-calorie foods mentioned (p. 265). When a parent knows which foods are nourishing (i.e. supply proteins, vitamins and minerals), good meals can be served which may well cost less than meals of poorer quality.

AN UNBALANCED DIET

The diet can be unbalanced because of shortage of food, too much of certain kinds of food, or lack of essential substances in the food. Children whose health could be improved by more food or better food are suffering from **malnutrition**. Such children fail to thrive, lack energy, and are less able to resist infections.

CULTURAL AND RELIGIOUS PRACTICES

The food which a child thinks is the 'normal' diet depends on the part of the world in which the child lives and the cultural background to which the family belongs. For example:

- Most children in Britain will be used to bread and potatoes as their main source of carbohydrate, whereas in Italy it will be pasta and in Asia it will be rice.
- Orthodox Jews do not eat pork or shellfish. Meat must be 'kosher' (prepared in accordance with Jewish religious law), and milk and meat are not eaten at the same meal.
- Muslims do not eat shellfish or pork, and other types of meat must be 'halal' (prepared in accordance with Muslim religious law).
- Hindus are mostly strict vegetarians.
- Sikhs do not eat beef.
- Asians living in Britain who retain their traditional diets may have a low intake of vitamin D. The amount of this vitamin made in the skin may also be low, especially in women and children due to customs of dress. To prevent rickets in childhood and softening of the bones in adults, the inclusion in the diet of foods rich in vitamin D, or vitamin supplements, will be necessary.
- **Vegetarians** do not eat meat or fish, but their diet can contain milk, milk products and eggs. Care should be taken to provide young children on a vegetarian diet with enough energy foods, protein, iron, calcium, vitamin B12 and vitamin C.
- **Vegans** do not eat any food that comes from animals. A vegan diet consisting mainly of cereals, fruit, vegetables, peas and beans can be very bulky. Young children on a vegan diet may have difficulty in eating enough of these foods to obtain the energy and nutrients they need for growth. These can be provided by the foods shown below. Soya-based infant formula can be given to babies in place of milk, and should be continued until the age of two years to ensure the child's diet contains enough protein.

Foods which can provide energy and nutrients suitable for children on a vegetarian or vegan diet	
protein	Quorn® and other foods made from pulses
energy	vegetable oils, and nut or seed butters
iron	fortified breakfast cereals, tofu, dried apricots, figs, prunes
calcium	soya mince, soya drink, tahini paste (made from sesame seeds)
vitamin B$_{12}$	fortified breakfast cereals, vitamin B$_{12}$ supplement
vitamin D	sunlight or vitamin drops

MEDICAL DIETS

Certain medical conditions require a special type of diet, for example:

- diabetics need a regular amount of carbohydrate in meals and snacks
- those with coeliac disease need a gluten-free diet (see p. 270).

DEFICIENCY DISEASES

When particular items in the diet are absent or in short supply (are deficient), illnesses called **deficiency diseases** develop.

Shortage	Deficiency disease
Iron or Vitamin B_{12}	**Anaemia** The lack of red pigment (haemoglobin) in the blood results in a shortage of oxygen throughout the body and feelings of 'no energy'.
Calcium or Vitamin D	**Rickets** Children's bones do not form properly, are soft and weak and bend under pressure.
Vitamin C	**Scurvy** The gums become soft and bleed. Teeth become loose, and wounds fail to heal properly.
Vitamin A	**Night blindness** (not being able to see in a dim light). There is also reduced resistance to diseases, especially those affecting the skin.
Protein and calories	**Kwashiorkor** (pronounced (quosh-ee-or-kor). This is a disease of severe malnutrition. The starving children have pot-bellies which are swollen with water

HIGH-CALORIE FOODS AND DRINKS

There are some foods which are high in calories but have very little other nutritional value. They contain a great deal of sugar, starch or fat and include sweets, chocolate, cakes, biscuits, pastry and crisps. Children often love them because they like the taste and find them easy to eat. Many children also love high calorie drinks. These include squash, cola, some fruit juices, and many of the drinks marketed specially for children.

There is no reason why these foods and drinks should not be part of the diet in small amounts, but, when consumed in large quantities, a child has less appetite for more nourishing foods. Too much high-calorie food may also cause a child to put on too much weight, and sugary food can help to cause tooth decay.

Nourishing snacks

High-calorie, less nourishing snacks

OBESITY

When more high-calorie food is eaten than the body needs and the excess is stored as fat. This causes people to become overweight or obese (grossly overweight). Childhood obesity used to be rare but it is becoming increasingly common. Causes can include:

Diet
Poor eating habits and a taste for junk food that is high in calories.

Exercise
Lack of enough exercise, due perhaps to long hours spent in front of the television or playing on the games console rather than on the sports field.

Genes
The tendency to be overweight often runs in families. So does the tendency to give children lots of high-calorie food.

Effects of obesity
- Fat babies and children are often not healthy. They suffer from shortness of breath due to the heavy fat they have to haul around and their obesity makes them prone to diabetes.
- Fat children often have low self-esteem. Children feel ashamed about being overweight and can be teased about it. Their unhappiness can affect their school work and their willingness to join in games and other social activities.
- Fat children who grow into obese adults are more likely to suffer from backache, headaches and joint problems.

Questions

1 a What is the difference between 'diet', a 'balanced diet' and 'going on a diet'?

  b Give five reasons for giving a child a balanced diet.

2 a Suggest a rough guide for a balanced diet.

  b If a child does not like drinking milk, in what other forms can milk be given?

  c (i) What is the difference between a vegetarian and a vegan diet? (ii) What may be in short supply in these diets? (iii) What foods can supply extra energy and nutrients?

  d What can children who do not like fruit be given instead?

3 Give three ways in which a diet may be unbalanced.

4 a What causes a deficiency disease?

  b What items in the diet are in short supply when the following deficiency diseases develop (i) anaemia, (ii) rickets, (iii) scurvy, (iv) night blindness, (v) kwashiorkor?

5 a List (i) some nourishing snacks, (ii) some high-calorie, less nourishing snacks.

  b What are the disadvantages of giving a child large amounts of high-calorie food?

6 a Give three causes of obesity.

  b How can obesity affect children's (i) health, (ii) self-esteem, (iii) future?

Further activities

Extension

1 Copy and complete the chart below to show the types of food substances present in the eight meals illustrated. Information about the foods can be obtained from Topic 52. Place a tick in the appropriate column if the food substance is present.

2 Record all the items of food you ate or drank yesterday. Do you consider that your diet for the day was balanced or unbalanced? Give reasons.

Investigation

Find out more about kwashiorkor and the effects of starvation on children.

Design

Make up five menus for packed lunches for a 5-year-old for one school week, each providing a balanced meal.

Child study

Describe the child's diet. What types of food does the child like and dislike?

Further activities (continued)

Description of meal	protein	carbohydrate	fat	calcium	iron	vitamin A	B vitamins	vitamin C	vitamin D	fibre
A Cheese sandwiches, ice-cream										
B										

Weblinks

For more information on the 'Healthy Start' free vouchers, that aim to ensure that pregnant women on certain benefits and their young children can have a healthy diet, visit:

www.healthystart.nhs.uk/

For more facts on diet, behaviour and learning in children, search for the 'Diet, Behaviour and Learning in Children' pdf at:

www.bda.uk.com

For more information on childhood obesity, search at:

www.weightlossresources.co.uk/children/childhood_obesity.htm

CHAPTER 55

Weaning

'Weaning' is the gradual changeover from a diet of milk to a diet containing a variety of foods, both solid and liquid.

Milk is the perfect food for the first few months of life. As babies get older, they begin to need foods containing starch and fibre. They also need more vitamins and minerals, particularly iron, than are present in milk alone in order to continue growing and developing properly.

Salt should not be added to weaning foods as it can be dangerous to young babies.

WHEN TO START WEANING

It takes several months for a baby's digestive system to develop fully. For example, starch cannot be readily digested until the baby is a few months old. There is, therefore, no point in weaning a baby until she is able to make proper use of the food. The danger of weaning too early is that the baby may become too fat, develop allergies to food, or suffer from indigestion.

The time to begin weaning is when the baby is about 6 months old and still seems hungry and restless after a good milk feed, or wakes early for the next feed and starts to suck her fists.

WEANING SHOULD NOT BE A BATTLE

New foods should be introduced one at a time. Even at this young age, babies make it clear whether they enjoy the taste or not. Babies are like adults in preferring some foods to others. If they are forced to eat a particular food it can easily lead to a feeding problem (see pp. 275–6). When a baby appears not to like a food, it is wise to wait for a week or two before offering it again. By this time there might be a change of mind.

STAGES IN WEANING

Starting to wean

Young babies cannot yet chew. They also have difficulty in swallowing and digesting lumps. So solid food such as cereals, fruit, vegetables and meat needs to be liquidised to a purée, to remove the lumps. It is then mixed with baby milk or other suitable liquid to make a thickened liquid which can be given to the baby on a spoon.

A small amount of such food once a day is enough to start with. Soon the baby comes to expect a little with each milk feed and the amount gradually increases. Different sorts of food should be given so that the baby gets used to a variety of flavours. Examples are 'baby rice' mixed with baby milk, mashed potato with a little gravy, mashed banana, boiled or steamed vegetables or stewed fruit which have been made into a purée, or meat stew which has been put through a blender.

Giving solid foods

Most babies learn to chew at about 6 months, whether they have teeth or not. It is then important for them to be given hard foods such as crusts and low-sugar rusks on which to chew. A baby who is not encouraged to chew at this age may find it difficult do so a few months later.

A baby who is able to chew can be given solid foods such as sandwiches, toast, cheese, whole banana and a wide variety of other foods. There is no need to wait until the baby has a mouthful of teeth before giving such foods. However, the tougher foods such as meat should be cut into small pieces first.

Babies should never be left alone when eating or drinking, especially when they are learning to feed themselves, because of the danger of choking.

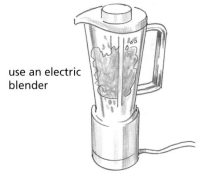

rub through a sieve

mash with a fork

use an electric blender

Ways of removing lumps from food

Reducing the amount of milk

As the amount of solid food increases, the need for milk decreases. Usually, by the age of 9 months to 1 year, babies have given up the breast or bottle (at least during the daytime) and are weaned on to a diet of mainly solid foods. They can then be eating food that is not very much different from the rest of the family. Milk is still needed each day, but it can be given in different forms such as milk puddings. Current medical opinion advises that babies should be given infant milk (formula) or follow-on milk to drink until 12 months old, and then they can have cow's milk.

Cow's milk given to children should be pasteurised whole milk until they are at least 5 years of age. Skimmed and semi-skimmed milks are not recommended because of their low energy and vitamin A content.

Drinking from a cup

Although breast- or bottle-feeding may continue until the baby is 9 months or older, the number of feeds becomes less and eventually stops. Cup-feeding usually begins about 5–6 months of age. Milk from a cup gradually replaces that from the breast or bottle.

It is quite common for babies suddenly to refuse to take any more milk from breast or bottle. Other babies are reluctant to give up the bottle. They may drink readily from a cup during the day, but still like a bottle of milk at bedtime. After the age of 1 year, the older the baby gets, the more difficult it becomes to give up the bottle.

WEANING FOODS

Tins, jars and packets of baby foods can be very useful for weaning. They are quick and easy to prepare, convenient when only small quantities are required, and very useful when travelling. These commercially prepared foods provide adequate nourishment and come in an increasingly wide variety, but are more expensive than home-prepared foods.

Commercially prepared foods should not replace fresh foods and home-prepared foods altogether. Babies can try most foods served to the rest of the family. This provides a greater range of tastes and textures than is found in the commercially prepared foods and so makes eating more interesting. More importantly, the baby gets used to eating the same food as other members of the family.

Gluten is a type of protein found in some cereals. A few babies are unable to digest gluten and this only becomes apparent when they are being weaned. These children have a condition called **coeliac disease**. They need to have a gluten-free diet, and cannot have foods containing wheat, rye, oats or barley. Alternative foods are rice, millet, potato flour and corn flour.

Commercially prepared weaning foods

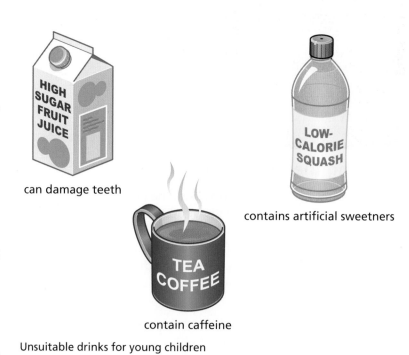

can damage teeth

contains artificial sweetners

contain caffeine

Unsuitable drinks for young children

Questions

1 a What is meant by 'weaning'?

b When is the right time to begin weaning, and what signs does the baby give?

c Name two food substances that babies need as they get older.

d What other food substances are needed in greater amounts than milk alone can supply?

e Name three possible dangers of weaning too early.

2 a Give two reasons why young babies should not be given lumpy food.

b Describe ways of removing lumps from food.

c (i) What is the advantage of giving babies a variety of foods? (ii) Name some suitable foods.

d (i) When may it be convenient to use the weaning foods in the photograph on p. 270 (ii) Give reasons why such foods should not replace fresh food altogether.

3 a By what age can most babies chew?

b Name foods that babies may be given when they can chew.

c Do babies need to have teeth before they are given the foods mentioned in b?

4 a At what age does cup-feeding usually begin?

b By what age is it usual for babies to be weaned on to a diet of mainly solid foods?

c At what age can babies be given cow's milk?

5 a (i) A few children need to be on a gluten-free diet; why? (ii) Which foods must be avoided? (iii) Name some alternative foods.

6 Give examples of unsuitable drinks for young children.

Further activities

 Extension

The table lists some do's and don'ts for parents weaning their babies. Take each item in the lists in turn and give reasons why it can be considered sensible advice.

Do	Don't
Give your baby a variety of foods for a variety of tastes.	Don't add salt or sugar to feeds.
Mash or sieve all your baby's food at first.	Don't give cereal at more than one meal a day.
Feed at your baby's pace rather than yours.	Don't give your baby food that's too hot.
Give extra water, especially in hot weather. There's no need to sweeten it/	Don't give sweet foods or drinks between meals.
	Don't leave your baby alone when eating or drinking.

Source: *Starting Your Baby on Solid Food*, Health Education Authority

 Investigation

Investigate the range of varieties of baby foods – those sold specially for babies. Choose at least three varieties of baby foods of a similar type, for example savoury foods or puddings. Compare their contents (for protein, fat, energy, sugar, salt, gluten, additives etc.) and then taste them. Present the information in a table.

Weblink

For an introduction to healthy eating habits from birth, visit:

www.nhs.uk/Start4Life

CHAPTER 56

Mealtimes

Mealtimes are more than just times when food is eaten. They should be social occasions as well.

FOOD AND EMOTIONS

A young baby is unhappy when hungry and happy when fed. When parents feed their baby they are providing happiness and love, so the baby comes to link food with happiness and love. These feelings help towards the development of a bond of attachment between parents and child.

Gradually, during weaning, babies want to feed themselves and, later, to decide what they eat. Children who are allowed to feed themselves and to eat as much or as little as they want, will continue to enjoy mealtimes and to link them with love and affection. However, if every mealtime is a battle over what is eaten or how it is eaten, then food will become linked with bad temper, wilfulness and fussiness. This can create a problem which may last throughout childhood and even longer.

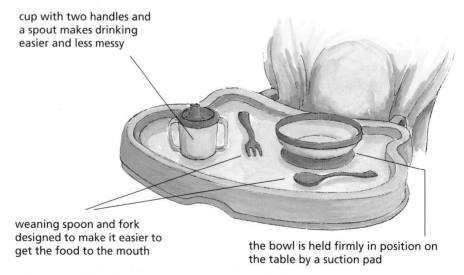

cup with two handles and a spout makes drinking easier and less messy

weaning spoon and fork designed to make it easier to get the food to the mouth

the bowl is held firmly in position on the table by a suction pad

Equipment which makes self-feeding easier and encourages self-reliance

Happy mealtimes

When mealtimes are happy occasions, children eat the food without a fuss, the parents and children will enjoy being together at this time, and they will have the opportunity to talk and listen to one another. Parents can encourage a young child to enjoy mealtimes by:

- serving food attractively
- varying the food
- serving small portions, with more to follow if wanted
- ensuring that the food is neither too hot nor too cold
- avoiding foods with very strong flavours
- setting a good example by eating proper meals themselves
- making mealtimes happy social occasions by all members of the family sitting at the table whenever possible.

'Fussy about food'

Encouraging a child to eat a variety of foods and not be fussy has three advantages:

- he is likely to have a balanced diet
- he will find it much easier to eat the food provided when away from home
- mealtimes will be happier occasions.

No one, apart from his parents, will have much sympathy for a child who is fussy about food and difficult to feed. He will be regarded as a nuisance.

TABLE MANNERS

When babies start to feed themselves, they have no understanding of table manners. At this stage, hands are used as well as spoons to get the food to the mouth. Food is also regarded as something to play with. Babies will undoubtedly make a mess.

During their second year, children learn how to use spoons and cups without spilling the contents. At this stage, they also come to understand that parents do not approve when they get food all over the place. They are now old enough to learn how to behave at the table. They will begin to copy the table manners of those around them, chiefly the manners of their parents and carers. These are the manners they will have throughout childhood and often for the rest of their lives.

SOME HINTS ABOUT FEEDING

- **Babies like to be with the family** at mealtimes. They enjoy company and they also learn how to behave with food.

- **Babies like to feed themselves.** It is messy, but much more interesting for the baby.
- **When everything is washable, there is no need to worry** about the mess. The chair, harness and tray should be easy to wipe and, if necessary, a plastic covering should be placed on the floor.
- **Bibs** save a great deal of mess.
- **Babies need to eat at their own pace.** This might be very slow and the parents need a great deal of patience!
- **Babies know when they have had enough** to eat, so never try to persuade or force the baby to eat more.
- **Young children may not want to eat large main meals**. They are happier to have smaller main meals with a snack between meals.

Bibs with sleeves are useful when babies start to feed themselves

A 'catch-all' bib is designed to catch any spills

Useful for older children who are eating at the table rather than in a high chair

Questions

1. How can parents encourage their child to enjoy mealtimes?
2. Give seven hints about feeding.
3. Name three advantages of encouraging a child not to be fussy about food.
4. **a** Why do babies make a mess when feeding?
   b When children become old enough to learn table manners, how do they learn?

Weblink

For tips for happy mealtimes, search under 'Special Interest' and 'Food & Recipes', then 'Fussy Eaters & Happy Mealtimes' at:

www.netmums.com

Further activities

Extension

Make a list of as many different table manners as you can think of. For each, decide whether you consider it to be 'good manners', 'bad manners' or whether it 'does not matter', and why.

Discussion

Are mealtimes social occasions or just the time for eating food?

Design

Use a graphics program to make a design to be used on a young child's bowl or plate.

Child study

Describe the child's behaviour at mealtimes. Comment on any examples you have come across where you think food and the child's emotions are linked.

CHAPTER 57

Refusal to eat

The commonest feeding problem in healthy children is food refusal. The child refuses to eat as much food as the parents think is needed. Consequently they become very worried about the child's 'poor appetite'.

Although this is a common problem in Britain, it does not occur in countries where food is scarce. Even in Britain, it is rarely a problem in homes where there are lots of children, nor in homes where no fuss about eating is made.

Children with this problem are usually between the age of 9 months and 4 years. It arises from a combination of factors including the following:

- Children of this age love fuss and attention and have a strong desire to feel important.
- The baby's rate of growth slows down during the first year and so does the rate of increase of appetite. This is the time of weaning and the mother is probably expecting the child to eat larger and larger quantities of food.
- Children go through a stage when it is natural for them to refuse to co-operate, and they have learnt to say 'no'.
- Children tend to dawdle over their meals and like to play with food. They have no sense of time and will not hurry so that the meal can be cleared away.
- Appetites vary. Some children (like some adults) have small appetites. The size of the appetite also depends on whether the child has been very active out of doors, or has spent time quietly indoors.

Do not try to force feed

It is unnecessary to try to force a child to eat and attempts will not succeed. No healthy children ever starve if left to please themselves how much they eat, but they will enjoy making a great deal of fuss if forced to eat.

Ways of trying to make a child eat may include:

- pushing food into the mouth
- coaxing
- nagging
- bribing
- threatening.

EXAMPLES FROM A DOCTOR'S CASEBOOK*

Worried parents consulted the doctor about the following feeding problems:

- A 10-month-old baby whose mother, father, aunt and two uncles crept about the room after him with spoonfuls of food, trying to get him to eat something.
- The child who would eat only when his father's car passed the window. As a result, the father had to drive the car backwards and forwards so that each time it passed the window, the mother could put a spoonful of food in the baby's mouth.
- One boy refused to eat unless he was given a toy motor car, and his mother said he had acquired nearly 300 cars in that way.
- A mother who said she never went anywhere without a bag of biscuits in her handbag, so that if her son ever said he would eat something she could give him one.

Advice to parents

In all the above cases, similar advice was given.

1. There is nothing wrong with the child's appetite. The problem lies with the parents.
2. When the child is given food, the parents must not appear to show that they care whether it is eaten or not. There should be no anxious looks at the plate, and no remarks about it.
3. A child who refuses to eat at mealtimes should not be given any food in between meals.
4. Healthy children never let themselves starve; they will quickly learn to eat if left alone to decide for themselves.

*These examples are from the book *Babies & Young Children*. Illingworth & Illingworth (Churchill Livingstone).

Questions

1 **a** In Britain, what is the commonest feeding problem in healthy children?

 b What is the usual age of children with this problem?

 c In what type of homes is this problem unlikely to exist?

2 Name five factors commonly involved in food refusal.

3 What advice was given to worried parents who consulted the doctor about feeding problems?

Weblink

For more information on toddler food refusal, search the term at:

www.nnuh.nhs.uk

Further activities

 Extension

Which of the ways of trying to make a child eat listed under the heading 'Do not try to force feed' is illustrated by each of the pictures A–E on p. 276?

 Child study

Have you come across a food refusal problem in a young child? (Do not confuse 'food refusal' with 'fussy eating'). Describe the problem. In your opinion, how many of the factors given in this topic, if any, were the cause of the problem you described?

CHAPTER 58

Food hygiene

Food hygiene is concerned with the care, preparation and storage of food in order to prevent food poisoning. Most food poisoning is due to eating food which has been contaminated by bacteria to such an extent that it upsets the stomach and intestines, causing gastro-enteritis. Gastro-enteritis is particularly serious in babies and young children (see p. 47) and food hygiene is therefore of special importance in child care. Four golden rules of food hygiene are:

- **keep food clean**
- **keep fresh food cold when being stored**
- **cook food thoroughly**
- **do not eat if past the 'use by' date.**

HOW BACTERIA GET INTO FOOD

Bacteria are too small to be seen with the naked eye and food which contains them may look, smell and taste good enough to eat. Bacteria get into food as a result of contact with:

- dirty hands
- dirty sinks and draining boards
- dirty work surfaces
- dirty dishcloths and sponges
- dirty towels and drying-up cloths
- dirty utensils – pots, pans, crockery, cutlery, glassware
- uncooked meat and poultry
- coughs and sneezes
- fingers or spoons which have been licked when preparing food
- flies
- septic cuts and sores
- rats, mice and their droppings.

Bacteria thrive in warm, moist foods particularly those containing protein, for example, both cooked and uncooked meat and poultry, gravy, egg dishes and milk. When such food is kept warm, any bacteria present quickly grow and multiply to become a possible source of food poisoning.

Bacteria multiply by dividing into two, and when conditions are right they can do so about every 20 minutes. The new bacteria grow quickly and 20 minutes later they are ready to divide again to produce more bacteria. After several hours, very large numbers will have built up in the food.

FOOD POISONING

The symptoms of food poisoning are diarrhoea, pains in the abdomen, and sometimes vomiting. Illness usually starts sometime between two hours and two days after eating contaminated food, although it can be almost immediate if the food is badly contaminated. The illness usually lasts for one to two days, but sometimes a week or more.

Treatment

Babies with food poisoning need medical attention quickly. Older children need medical attention if they are not recovering after 24 hours.

PREVENTION OF FOOD POISONING

1. Keep food cold

Low temperatures slow down the rate at which bacteria grow and multiply.

Refrigeration – The temperature at which refrigerators are usually kept is between 1°C and 5°C, which is too low for food-poisoning bacteria to grow. Some other types of bacteria and fungi are able to grow at temperatures as low as this, but only slowly. This is why food left in a refrigerator for a long time gradually turns bad.

Cooked food which is to be kept for the next day should be cooled as quickly as possible and then placed in a refrigerator. Any bacteria present will not then have a chance to grow and multiply to dangerous levels.

Freezing – When food is frozen, any bacteria it contains are unable to grow. However, they are not killed by the cold and when the food warms up they become active again. The recommended temperature at which freezers should be kept is minus 18 °C (–18 °C).

2. Keep food covered

Food needs to be covered to protect it from dust, dirt and flies. Dust and dirt are quite likely to contain food-poisoning bacteria. Flies can carry bacteria in their saliva and droppings as well as on their feet and hairy bodies, especially when they come from rubbish dumps and manure heaps in which they breed.

3. Hands should be washed and then dried on a clean towel before preparing food

Particular care to do this thoroughly should be taken after using the lavatory or dealing with nappies, because large numbers of bacteria capable of causing food poisoning live in the bowel.

4. Keep the kitchen clean

Floor, work surfaces, sink, cooking utensils, waste-bin, dishcloths, drying-up cloths etc. should all be cleaned regularly. Remember, food-poisoning bacteria can exist in dirt, and bits of leftover food lying around attract flies, mice and rats.

5. Cover any boils or septic cuts

Germs which cause these can also cause food poisoning. Cover them with a waterproof dressing.

6. Do not sneeze or cough over food
Food poisoning bacteria and other germs often live in the nose and throat.

7. Do not lick your fingers or smoke when handling food
This will prevent germs from the mouth reaching the food.

8. Keep raw meat separate
Uncooked meat, especially poultry, may contain food-poisoning bacteria. It therefore needs to be kept away from other foods to prevent them from being contaminated.

9. Cook food thoroughly
When cooking or reheating food, make sure that it is heated until it is piping hot all the way through in order to kill any food-poisoning bacteria. This applies in particular to 'cook-chill' meals (ready-cooked meals prepared in a factory and then kept cold but not frozen) and to frozen poultry (which should be thoroughly defrosted before cooking).

10. Keep pets away from food and food-preparation surfaces
Pets can be a source of dirt and food-poisoning bacteria.

11. Keep rats and mice away
Food-poisoning bacteria live in the intestines of mice and rats, and are present in their droppings.

12. Keep away from the kitchen when suffering from diarrhoea or sickness
The cause may be food poisoning and the bacteria could easily be passed on to other people if you handle food or utensils.

13. Check 'use by' dates
It is not always possible to tell if food is safe to be eaten by its look or smell. Therefore, foods labelled with a 'use by' date should be used by that date or thrown away.

14. Check labels for storage instructions
If foods are not stored properly they may not keep as long as the 'use by' date.

FOOD-POISONING BACTERIA

Several types of bacteria can cause food poisoning including the following.

Salmonella

These bacteria usually live in the bowel. They get into food from the excreta of humans or animals or from water which has been polluted by sewage. Illness is caused by eating large numbers of these bacteria. If food containing them is thoroughly cooked, the bacteria are killed and will not be harmful.

Staphylococcus

Bacteria of this type are found in many places including the nose, throat, boils and the pus from an infected wound. These bacteria produce toxins (poisons) as they grow and multiply in food. It is the toxins and not the bacteria which cause food poisoning. The bacteria are readily killed by cooking but the toxins are only gradually destroyed.

Clostridium

Spores of these bacteria are frequently found in human and animal excreta and they thrive when they get into the right types of food.

When conditions become unfavourable for the bacteria (for example, they become short of water) they produce spores. The spores are very hardy and can survive for long periods of time in dust, dirt and soil. They may even survive normal cooking processes. When they find themselves in warm, moist food, the spores turn into active bacteria again and multiply rapidly.

Clostridium welchii gives rise to a common type of food poisoning. Bacteria of this type produce toxins when they get inside the intestines. If the food is cooked thoroughly before eating, the bacteria will be killed and there will be no food poisoning.

Campylobactor

These bacteria can be found in milk, uncooked and undercooked poultry. The main symptom of this common form of food poisoning is diarrhoea containing blood. The bacteria are killed by thorough cooking and then do not cause harm.

E. coli (Escherichia coli)

These bacteria live in the intestines of humans and other animals and are usually harmless. However, some strains, for example, E. coli 157 can cause food poisoning when they contaminate food or drinking water.

Questions

1 a What are the four golden rules of food hygiene?
  b Why may food-poisoning bacteria be eaten accidentally?
2 a Name some types of food in which bacteria thrive.
  b What happens when these foods are kept warm?
  c What are the recommended temperatures at which refrigerators and freezers should be kept?
3 a What are the symptoms of food poisoning?
  b What is the treatment?
4 Name 14 ways of helping to prevent food poisoning, giving one reason for each.
5 Name five types of food-poisoning bacteria.

Further activities

Extension

1 A collection of 1000 bacteria is just visible as a tiny speck. If a speck of dirt containing 1000 food-poisoning bacteria got into a feeding bottle, and the feeding bottle was kept in a warm place, how many germs would be present after (i) 4 hours (ii) 8 hours?

2 Find some actual cases of food poisoning from newspaper reports or other sources. Then, using a desk-top publishing or graphics program, make a poster or leaflet to explain to parents how food poisoning can be caused and prevented.

Weblinks

For further information on food safety, visit: www.nhs.uk and search for 'food safety'.

CHAPTER 59

Teeth

Although the teeth of a newborn baby cannot be seen, they are already developing inside the gums. They usually start to appear some time during the first year, the average age being 6 months. The parents need not worry if their baby is late in teething. The teeth will come through when they are ready and there is nothing that can be done to hurry them up.

ORDER OF APPEARANCE

Milk teeth

There are 20 teeth in the first set which are called the milk teeth or baby teeth. The first to come through are usually the two teeth in the front of the lower jaw. A month or two later they are followed by the two teeth at the front of the upper jaw. All the milk teeth will have appeared by the age of 2½–3 years. The diagram shows the order in which the milk teeth generally appear.

Occasionally, a baby is born with a tooth that has already come through. It may need to be removed if it is so loose in the gum that it is in danger of falling out, being inhaled, and becoming stuck in the baby's windpipe. If the tooth is removed, there will be a gap in that position until the second set of teeth appear several years later.

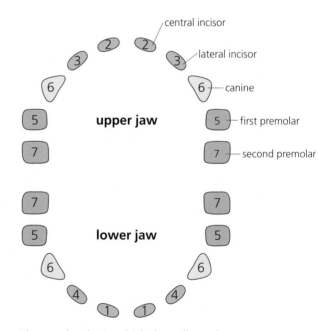

The usual order in which the milk teeth appear

From the age of 5 onwards, the milk teeth begin to fall out. Before they do this, their roots disappear.

Permanent teeth

The milk teeth are replaced by the permanent teeth. They start to come through when children are about 6 years old. The 20 milk teeth are replaced by larger teeth of the same type. In addition, there are 12 molars – 3 on each side of each jaw. When complete, the permanent set contains 32 teeth.

The first permanent teeth to appear are usually the lower incisors and the first molars. The latter are often called the '6-year molars'. Although the new teeth may appear looking crooked, they usually right themselves in time. Otherwise they may need to be corrected by dental treatment, e.g. the wearing of a brace.

The milk teeth can be seen developing inside the jaw.

The milk teeth are all through. The permanent teeth are developing underneath.

The milk teeth at the front of both jaws (the incisors) have been replaced by permanent teeth, and the first molars are also through. The roots of the remaining milk teeth are beginning to disappear.

The milk teeth are replaced by the permanent teeth

TEETHING

Some babies cut their teeth with no trouble at all. Other babies may be cross and irritable at such times. Babies may show one or more of the following signs that their teeth are cutting through the gums:

- **sore gums** – as a tooth grows, it has to pass through the gum. This process may cause the gums to become sore and painful, making the baby refuse food.
- **increased dribbling** – babies seem to dribble more than usual when a tooth is about to come through.
- **increased fist-chewing** – some babies seem to chew their fists and fingers more than usual when they are teething.
- **red cheek** – a bright red patch on one cheek is often a sign of a new tooth.

Help for teething babies

A baby who is troubled by teething needs to be cuddled and comforted. Efforts should be made to divert the baby's attention, for example, by giving her something different to play with, going for a walk, playing some music or, if old enough, telling her a story.

The baby may get relief from chewing something hard. For this reason, babies who are teething are given teething rings, crusts or rusks on which to chew. Teething jelly is unnecessary. It quickly washes off and, if too much is used, may poison the child.

The advice of a doctor is needed for a child who is in severe pain or very fretful at nights.

Teething does not cause illness. Although teething may make a baby feel wretched, it will not cause illness such as bronchitis, rashes, diarrhoea, fever or convulsions. If any of these conditions appear at the time that the teeth are coming through, they will not be due to teething and need the prompt attention of a doctor.

EFFECT OF DIET ON TEETH

Substances in the diet which build strong, healthy teeth are **calcium**, **fluoride** and the **vitamins A, C** and **D**.

Fluoride combines chemically with the enamel of the teeth, making them stronger and more resistant to decay. Children living in areas where the water supply contains fluoride have only about half as much tooth decay as those living in other areas.

When the water supply lacks fluoride, many doctors and dentists recommend that children should be given fluoride daily. Under the age of 3 the fluoride should be given in the form of drops. Older children can be given tablets, crushed if necessary. The use of toothpaste containing fluoride also helps to protect the teeth.

Chewing helps to keep the teeth and gums healthy. Therefore the diet should include foods which need chewing such as crusts, apples and carrots.

Eating sweet and sticky foods in large amounts encourages tooth decay. This is especially so when sugary foods are eaten between meals and in a form which sticks to the teeth. Tooth decay is also encouraged by the frequent sipping of sugary drinks.

TOOTH DECAY

The mouth always contains bacteria. However well the teeth are cleaned, some bacteria are always left in the mouth. The bacteria themselves do no harm, and indeed, they are essential to keep the mouth healthy. But

bacteria + sugar = tooth decay

When the bacteria in the mouth come into contact with sugar they produce acid. It is the acid which dissolves away the enamel and makes holes in the teeth. Sugar remains in the mouth for about half an hour after eating something sweet or even longer if a piece of food such as sticky toffee becomes caught up in the teeth. The longer the time that sugar is in the mouth the greater the chances of tooth decay.

The chances of tooth decay are reduced if sweets, chocolates, iced lollies and other sugary foods and drinks are given to a child only at mealtimes or on special occasions. It is also important for them to be eaten all at one go and not nibbled at over several hours.

CLEANING THE TEETH

Children can be taught to clean their teeth from the age of 1 year. They should learn to brush them up and down and not across. Also, the inner side of the teeth and the biting surface of those at the back need to be cleaned. The teeth should be brushed before going to bed and preferably after meals as well.

Although the milk teeth are only temporary, it is important to care for them because:

- tooth decay causes pain
- painful teeth may prevent a child from eating properly
- caring for teeth will become a good habit which will continue throughout life
- if milk teeth are lost prematurely, the permanent teeth may come through in the incorrect position.

VISITING THE DENTIST

Mothers are entitled to free dental care for a year after giving birth, and they can take their babies with them then. The baby can be registered with the dentist at this time, who can also give advice about the need for fluoride drops. If taken to the dentist regularly from an early age, children get used to the idea. They are then more likely to go happily when they are older and their permanent teeth have come through. Regular check-ups enable any problem to be treated before it becomes serious. Two words often used by the dentist are:

- **caries** – the name for tooth decay
- **plaque** – an almost invisible layer that is forming on the teeth all the time. Plaque is composed mostly of bacteria and materials from saliva. Cleaning the teeth removes plaque and leaves the teeth looking white and shiny.

Questions

1 a What is the average age at which teeth start to appear?

 b How many milk teeth are there?

 c By what age have all the milk teeth appeared?

 d Using information from the diagram on p. 282, complete and extend the following chart to show the usual order in which the milk teeth appear.

| 1 Central incisors of lower jaw |
| 2 |

2 a At what age do the milk teeth begin to fall out?

 b What part of a milk tooth disappears before the tooth falls out?

 c What are the '6-year molars'?

 d How many permanent teeth are there?

3 a Name four signs of teething shown by some children.

 b Name five types of illness which are not due to teething.

 c Describe ways in which a baby who is troubled by teething can be helped.

4 a Name two minerals and three vitamins which help to build strong, healthy teeth.

 b How does fluoride strengthen teeth?

 c If the water supply lacks fluoride, name two ways in which this mineral can be given to children.

5 a How is acid produced in the mouth?

 b What effect does acid have on the teeth?

 c How long does sugar remain in the mouth after eating something sweet?

 d How can the chances of tooth decay be reduced?

6 a How should children be taught to brush their teeth?

 b Why is it important to care for the milk teeth?

 c What are the advantages of taking young children to the dentist?

7 What is meant by (i) caries, (ii) plaque?

Weblinks

For facts on children's teeth and teething, visit:
www.netdoctor.co.uk and search for 'teething'.
For frequently asked questions about children's
teeth, find the leaflet at:
www.dentalhealth.org.uk by searching for
'childrens teeth' in the FAQS.

Exercises

Exercises relevant to Section 6 can be found on
p. 385.

Further activities

 Extension

1 The photograph below shows the milk teeth
of a 3-year-old girl who was very fond of
sweetened blackcurrant juice. Every time she
was thirsty or needed comforting, day or night,
she was given this drink.

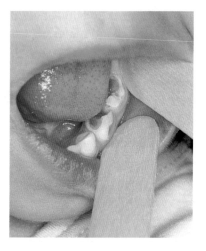

   a Describe the appearance of the teeth.

   b What might account for their condition?
   Give your reasons.

   c What advice would you give to parents
   to prevent this from happening to their
   children's teeth?

   d Are the teeth in the photograph incisors,
   canines or premolars?

2 Use a dietary analysis program or other data to:

   a calculate and compare the amount of sugar
   in drinks commonly given to children.

   b find foods which are major sources of
   calcium in the diet.

 Child study

Find out about the child's teeth. How many are
there? Has there been any teething trouble? Does
the child clean his or her own teeth? Does the
child go to the dentist?

SECTION 7

Health and safety

CHAPTER 60

Infectious diseases

GERMS

Infectious diseases are caused by certain microbes, called **germs** (or **pathogens)**. Some types of germ affect people of all ages, examples being those which cause the common cold, influenza, bronchitis, tetanus and tuberculosis. Diseases that occur mainly in childhood are given in the chart on pp. 290–1.

Germs can only be seen with the aid of a powerful microscope. They are usually either **bacteria** or **viruses**, but a few fungi and other microbes are also able to cause disease. The chart of infectious diseases indicates which are caused by bacteria (*B*) and which by viruses (*V*).

Bacteria

Bacteria are found almost everywhere – in the air, soil, water, food, and both on and inside the bodies of plants and animals. There are many different types of bacteria and each has its own special shape, size, and conditions in which it can live and grow. Only a small proportion of the total number of bacteria are able to cause disease in humans.

Each tiny bacterium consists of a single cell. After growing to its full size, it reproduces by dividing into two. In the right conditions, this may take place about every 20 minutes, so large numbers of bacteria can be built up very quickly.

Bacteria cause disease when they damage the tissues of the body in which they are living, or when they produce **toxins** (poisons). The toxins may travel in the blood stream to harm other parts of the body.

Viruses

Viruses are even smaller than bacteria. They only become active when they get inside the living cells of plants or animals. There are many different types of virus including those which can live inside human cells. When the virus gets inside the right type of cell, it feeds, grows and multiplies. The cell then bursts and the virus particles are released to infect other cells. As the virus spreads, it damages the cells and causes disease.

HOW DISEASES SPREAD

All the diseases in the chart on pp. 290–1 except tetanus can be spread by droplet infection and by contact. Passing a disease from one person to another is known as **cross infection.**

Droplet infection

Very tiny drops of moisture containing germs come from the nose or throat of an infected person when breathing, sneezing, coughing, singing and talking. If they enter the nose or mouth of another person they may give rise to infection.

Contact

It is possible to pick up infection by kissing or touching an infected person (direct contact), or by using towels, toys, or other equipment which have been in contact with the disease (indirect contact). Diseases that are spread by contact are called **contagious diseases**.

Tetanus germs are often found in soil, dust and manure. They can cause disease only when they enter the body through cuts or grazes in the skin. Some other types of germs, for example food-poisoning bacteria, can be transferred from one person to another in food, milk and water.

WHEN GERMS GET INSIDE THE BODY

The body reacts in various ways to try to destroy any germs which may get inside it. If these fail, the germs grow and multiply and eventually produce fever and other symptoms.

Incubation is the time between the entry of the germs into the body and the appearance of symptoms. **Symptoms** are changes in the body which indicate disease. The **onset** of the disease is the point at which symptoms appear.

The **infectious stage** is the time during which germs can be spread from one person to another. The patient becomes infectious either during the incubation period or at the end of it. Quite often, a child is infectious before anyone realises that he or she has the disease.

IMMUNITY

Immunity is the ability of the body to resist infection. Generally speaking, the infectious diseases of childhood are less severe in children than in adults. One attack usually gives long-lasting immunity to that disease, so it is rare to catch it for a second time.

When a person 'catches' the infectious disease, the body produces antibodies of the right type which eventually destroy the germs. The antibodies also give immunity against that disease and help to prevent the person from catching the same disease again. Another way to obtain immunity against some infectious diseases is by immunisation.

IMMUNISATION (VACCINATION)

Vaccines are available for certain diseases. A specific vaccine is required for each disease. One or more doses of vaccine make the body produce the right type of antibodies to destroy the germs which cause the particular disease.

The diseases for which immunisation is readily available are those marked with an asterisk on the chart on pp. 290–1.

Disease	Symptoms	Incubation in days	Infectious stage
*Diphtheria B	A white layer forms on the throat, which may block the airway; it also produces a powerful poison which damages heart and brain.	2–5	Usually for about 2 weeks after onset.
*Tetanus (Lockjaw) B	Muscles in the neck tighten and lock the jaw.	4–21	Cannot be passed directly from one person to another.
*Whooping cough (Pertussis) B	Long bouts of coughing which may end with a 'whoop'.	7–12	A few days before onset to 4 weeks after onset.
*Polio (Poliomyelitis) V	Infection of the spinal cord causing fever which may result in paralysis.	3–21	From 2 days after infection to 6 weeks or longer after onset.
*Hib (Haemophilus influenzae type b) V	Varies depending on the part of the body which is infected.	Varies	Varies.
*Meningitis Various B and V See also Hib above	Some/all of: fever (possibly with cold hands and feet), vomiting, rash. Also in babies: high-pitched moaning cry, blank expression, arched back, bulging fontanelle, difficult to wake. Children and adults may complain of severe headache, stiff neck, drowsiness, painful joints, dislike of bright lights, and have fits.	2–10	Continuous. Meningitis bacteria commonly live in the back of the nose and throat, only causing disease when they overcome the body's defences. Many viruses, for example Hib, can cause meningitis and they are widely spread.
*Measles V	Fever, severe cold, cough. 4–5 days later a red rash appears on the face and spreads downward.	10–15	From onset of cold symptoms until 5 days after rash appears.
*Mumps V	Painful swellings near the jaw on one or both sides.	12–28, usually about 18	Until the swelling goes down.
*Rubella (German measles) V	A mild disease with a red rash and usually with swollen glands.	10–21	From onset to end of rash.
*Tuberculosis (TB) B	Fever, sweating at night, cough with phlegm containing blood, loss of weight, continuous ill health.	28–42	Variable.
Chicken pox (Varicella) V	Small red spots which turn to blisters then scabs.	10–21	2 days before the spots appear until the last spot has formed a scab and flaked off.
Scarlet fever B	Sore throat, fever, bright red rash.	2–4	Up to 2 weeks after onset.
*Pneumococcal disease B	Symptoms vary depending on the part of the body infected.	Varies, usually 1–3 days	Variable.

*Immunisation is available to protect against these diseases: B = Bacterial infection; V = Viral infection

Other information	Immunisation
Although now uncommon, it is still liable to occur in children who have not been immunised.	Vaccines against five diseases – diphtheria, tetanus, whooping cough (pertussis), polio and Hib – are given together as a single injection at 2 months old, 3 months and 4 months. This injection is known as DTaP/IPV/Hib or 'five in one'.
Germs exist in soil, dirt and animal droppings, including those of horses and humans. They enter the body through cuts and scratches.	A further dose of Hib vaccine is given around 12 months of age.
Can be very dangerous in babies up to 1 year old. Whooping cough vaccine does not always prevent the disease, but it makes it much less unpleasant and the coughing less severe.	Before the child starts school, around the age of 3 years 4 months, or soon after, there is a single injection containing booster doses of vaccines against diphtheria, tetanus, whooping cough and polio (pre-school booster).
Immunisation has almost eliminated this disease from Britain.	
Hib causes a range of illnesses including a dangerous form of meningitis. The disease is rare in children under 3 months, rises to a peak at 10–11 months, declines steadily to 4 years of age, after which infection becomes uncommon.	Between the ages of 13 and 18 years, a single injection is given containing booster doses of vaccines against diphtheria, tetanus and polio.
Meningitis is inflammation of the lining (meninges) of the brain and spinal cord. It can be caused by several types of bacteria or viruses. They can spread rapidly and be confused with flu. Viral meningitis is more common. Bacterial meningitis is more serious with three strains – A, B and C.	Injections of Men C (against meningitis strain C) are given at 3 and 4 months. A further dose of Men C is given around 12 months old. When outbreaks of meningitis occur, students in school and colleges may be offered vaccination against groups A and C. No vaccine is available for group B.
Dangerous to the fetus in the first 4 months of pregnancy.	A single injection of combined measles, mumps and rubella vaccine (MMR vaccine) is given at around 13 months with a pre-school booster at 3 years 4 months, or soon after.
More serious in infancy than in older children.	
Mumps in males over the age of 11 may damage the testes and result in sterility.	
Most people who are infected by TB germs do not develop the disease. They do, however, develop natural immunity to the disease. The BCG vaccine does not give complete protection against the disease.	Immunisation against TB targets children who are at the greatest risk, especially those living in areas with a high rate of TB. The BCG (Baccillus Calmette Guerin) vaccine is best offered from birth but can be given at any time.
A mild disease in children. The virus can remain in the body and cause shingles in later life.	Although a varicella vaccine is now available in the UK it is not offered as part of the routine childhood vaccination programme but only to those with low immunity.
Scarlet fever causes tonsillitis and a rash. Usually clears up quickly with antibiotics.	
Children infected with the pneumococcus bacteria can develop serious illness, mainly pneumonia or meningitis.	Three injections of PCV (Pneumococcal Conjugate Vaccine) are given at 3, 4 and about 13 months.

The risk of harmful complications from any of these vaccines is extremely small – very much smaller than the risk of harmful effects from the disease itself. There are very few genuine reasons why a child should not be immunised.

Before an immunisation takes place, the situation should be discussed with the doctor or health visitor if the child:

- has a fever
- has had a bad reaction to any previous immunisations.

In most cases, there will be no reason to delay immunisation.

Benefits of immunisation

1. Almost all children get long-lasting protection from these diseases.
2. The more children who are immunised, the rarer the diseases become. This protects young babies and other children and adults as well. Polio is an example. Polio vaccine was introduced in 1957, and within five years the disease was almost wiped out.

EFFECTS OF IMMUNISATION

Usually there are no side-effects from immunisation. Occasionally, redness and swelling may develop where the injection was given, and then slowly disappear. A few children may be unwell and irritable and develop a temperature. Allergic reactions rarely occur and, if treated quickly, the child will fully recover.

IMMUNITY OF BABIES

Very young babies rarely catch the infectious diseases common in childhood because they are protected by antibodies obtained from the mother. When the baby is in the uterus, antibodies pass across the placenta from the mother's blood to the baby's blood. Because of this the baby is born with protection against the same diseases that the mother has had or has been immunised against. If the baby is breast-fed, the baby will continue to get supplies of these antibodies.

Antibodies from the mother survive in the baby for several months. All that time, the baby is growing stronger and becoming more able to withstand infection. The age of 2 months is the recommended time to begin immunisation. The baby will then begin to develop antibodies to take over from those of his mother, which gradually disappear.

Whooping cough is an exception. A newborn baby has no antibodies from the mother against this disease (whooping cough antibodies are too big to pass across the placenta). It is a very dangerous disease in babies and they should, therefore, be kept well away from anyone who is infectious. Even if the baby has been vaccinated against whooping cough it takes several months for the vaccine to become fully effective. It is useful to know that the cough lasts much longer than the infectious stage.

Questions

1 From the chart on pp. 290–1.

    a What is the technical name for (i) German measles, (ii) polio, (iii) whooping cough, (iv) lock-jaw, (v) TB, (vi) Hib?

    b Why is mumps a risk to boys?

    c Which disease may cause shingles in an adult?

2 **a** Which of the diseases in the chart are caused by (i) bacteria, (ii) viruses?

    b Name two ways in which bacteria can cause disease.

    c How do viruses damage cells and cause disease?

3 The DTaP/IPV/Hib injection contains vaccines against five diseases. Name them.

4 **a** How can disease be spread by droplet infection?

    b What is the difference between catching a disease from an infected person by (i) direct contact, (ii) indirect contact?

    c What is a contagious disease?

5 Give the meaning of the following terms when used to describe an infectious disease: (i) symptoms, (ii) incubation, (iii) onset, (iv) infectious stage.

6 **a** (i) What is the meaning of immunity?
       (ii) Name two ways in which immunity can be obtained.

    b For which of the diseases in the chart is immunisation available?

    c Before an immunisation takes place, what reasons might there be for discussing a possible delay with the doctor or health visitor?

    d Give two benefits of immunisation.

    e Are side effects from immunisation likely?

7 **a** (i) Why do very young babies rarely catch the infectious diseases common in childhood?

       (ii) Why is whooping cough an exception?

    b When is the recommended time to begin immunisation?

Weblink

For more information on childhood diseases and vaccinations, visit:

www.babycentre.co.uk and search for 'immunisation'.

Further activities

Extension

1 Use graph paper or a spreadsheet to produce a bar chart to show the duration of incubation of the infectious diseases of childhood mentioned on pp. 290–1 (excluding Hib).

2 Copy the timetable below and complete with the name of the disease for which the vaccine is given.

Timetable for immunisation

Disease	Injections
1 .... 2 .... 3 .... 4 .... 5	2, 3 and 4 months
6 .... 7	3 and 4 months
8 .... 9	around 12 months
10 .... 11 .... 12 .... 13	Around 13 months
14 .... 15 .... 16 .... 17 .... 18 .... 19 .... 20	3 years and 4 months or soon after
21 .... 22 .... 23	13 to 18 years

Investigation

Since the year 1900, the infant death rate in Britain has been reduced from about 25 per cent of all deaths in the whole population to about 2 per cent. This dramatic reduction has been due to the control and treatment of measles, diphtheria, whooping cough and other diseases. Find out:

a why each of the three diseases mentioned above is dangerous

b when the method of control became generally available.

Give a short talk to your class about your findings.

Child study

1 Has the child had any of the diseases mentioned in this topic? If so, how did they affect the child?

2 Has the child been immunised? If so, make out a timetable. If not, perhaps the parents would be kind enough to discuss the reasons with you.

CHAPTER 61

Parasites

The parasites discussed in this topic are head lice, itch mites (which cause scabies), fleas, threadworms and roundworms. These parasites obtain their food from humans and one or more are likely to affect all children at one time or another. There is no reason for parents to feel ashamed if their child 'catches' any of these because they so easily pass from one child to another. The treatment to remove them is simple and advice can be obtained from the doctor, health visitor or clinic.

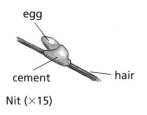

HEAD LICE

Head lice are tiny insects (each is called a **louse**) which live amongst the hairs of the head and look rather like dandruff which moves. The lice crawl around fairly rapidly and five times a day they pierce the skin for a meal of blood, leaving little red bite marks which itch.

The eggs (**nits**) are about the size of a pin head. Live eggs are grey/brown and are found glued to the hair, usually close to the scalp. They take seven to ten days to hatch, leaving empty egg shells. These are white and shiny and are found further away from the scalp, having grown out with the hair.

head with sucking parts to obtain blood

legs for crawling

claws for hanging onto hairs, etc.

Louse (×20)

How lice spread

When heads come into contact for a minute or more, lice can crawl quickly from one head to the other.

Treatment

Washing hair will not get rid of head lice. They are not affected by the water as both lice and nits are waterproof. Nor do they get washed away – the nits are cemented to the hair, and the lice have claws which enable them to cling very tightly. There is a choice of treatment:

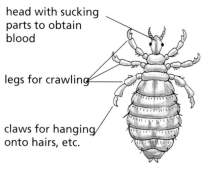

egg

cement

hair

Nit (×15)

▌ **Wet combing**. After washing the hair with an ordinary shampoo, apply lots of conditioner to make the hair slippery. The wet hair is then combed with a **detector comb** (fine tooth comb) to remove the lice. This process needs to be repeated every three to four days for two weeks to remove the lice as they hatch.

▌ **Chemical shampoos**. These kill the lice but not the nits.

▌ **Chemical treatments**. These kill both lice and nits and are considered safe, but should only be used in moderation. If more than two treatments are needed, advice should be sought from a pharmacist, nurse or doctor.

SCABIES

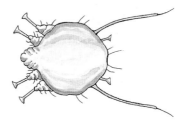

Scabies is also called 'the itch' as it causes extreme irritation, especially at night, and keeps the sufferer awake. It is caused by mites which burrow into the outer layer of the skin (the keratin layer) where they spend most of their life feeding on the skin and laying their eggs.

Itch mite (×50)

An irritating rash appears on the skin three to four weeks after infection. It looks like a scaly area with pimples and it may be possible to see the burrows of the mites. The rash makes the sufferer scratch, which can result in septic spots and boils. Scabies is most likely to occur on the palms, between the fingers, on the wrists, and sometimes armpits, groin and other places.

How scabies spreads

The main way that scabies spreads is by direct skin-to-skin contact for some minutes. This gives time for the mites to crawl from one person to another. For this reason, scabies spreads easily between members of the same family, especially if they sleep in the same bed.

Scabies mites do not survive very long away from the body and so do not spread easily in playgroups and schools.

Treatment

The doctor will prescribe a lotion which must be applied to all parts of the skin from the neck to the soles of the feet. The bed-linen and underclothes must be washed. The treatment only works if all the members of the family are treated at the same time so that all the mites can be killed.

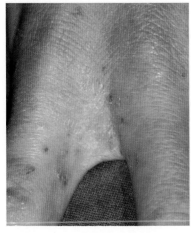

Scabies

FLEAS

Fleas are small wingless insects with long legs adapted for jumping. It is easy to become infested with fleas as they can jump long distances from one person to another. The type of flea which feeds on human blood lives in clothing next to the skin. The human flea does not carry disease, but when it pierces the skin to suck blood it leaves small red marks which irritate. Fleas lay their eggs in dirt in buildings, furniture, bedding or clothing.

Treatment

Cleanliness is important in the control of fleas. They do not live for long on clean people or in clothes which are regularly washed. The eggs will not survive for long in clean buildings or bedding.

thin body which enables flea to move easily amongst hairs

mouth parts for piercing skin and sucking blood

long legs for jumping

Flea (×25)

ANIMAL FLEAS

When young, children are often very sensitive (allergic) to fleas which live on dogs, cats, or birds. The fleas may be the cause of spots which persist for a long time. Pet animals with fleas need to be treated with a special insecticide available from pet shops and vets.

THREADWORMS

Threadworm (×2)

Threadworms are small white worms about 1 cm long. They look like small pieces of thread that wriggle. They live in the large bowel (large intestine), feeding on the contents and can sometimes be seen in the stools. It is quite common for children to have threadworms from time to time. They do little harm but are a nuisance as they cause itching around the anus (back passage). The itching occurs mainly in the evenings because this is the time that the female worms crawl out of the bowel to lay their eggs and then die.

Threadworms live for 5–6 weeks but before they die, the female lays about 10 000 tiny eggs. These stick to the skin and clothes or are caught in the finger nails. They become part of the dust of the room, and can survive for up to two weeks outside the body. If the eggs enter the mouth of a child on the fingers or in food, they pass down to the bowel where they hatch. The worms cannot multiply in the bowel, so the number of worms depends on the number of eggs that are eaten.

Treatment

A doctor or pharmacist will prescribe medicine to clear the worms from the bowel, but they will die out in time anyway – unless the child eats more worm eggs. It is therefore important for the home to be thoroughly cleaned and clothes, bedding and toys washed to remove all the eggs. The medicine should be given to all members of the family.

Helping to prevent infection

It is almost impossible to make sure that children's hands are washed before they put their fingers into their mouth or handle anything that they are going to eat or suck. But it helps to prevent infection if:

- children are taught to wash their hands every time they use the lavatory, and before meals
- the hands of the person who prepares and serves the food are washed before doing so
- fruit and raw salad vegetables are washed thoroughly before they are eaten.

PLEASE WASH YOUR HANDS AFTER USING THE TOILET

ROUNDWORMS (TOXOCARA)

These are the most common worms which infect dogs and cats, puppies and kittens. An adult worm is like a very thin, white earthworm about 15 cm in length. The worms lay large numbers of eggs in the intestine of the animal in which they are living. The eggs are then passed out in the animal's droppings (faeces) and can survive for two to four years in the environment.

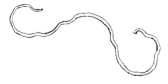

Roundworm (× 0.5)

Being sticky, the eggs can cling to fingers and if swallowed, particularly by a child, can hatch out and develop into worms, causing **toxocariasis**. Symptoms include fever, vomiting, and pain in muscles and joints. In some cases, eyesight can be damaged. Treatment is similar to that for threadworms.

Helping to prevent infection

- Encourage children always to wash their hands before eating and after playing with pets.
- Clear up dog droppings immediately, especially in places where children play.
- Fence off childrens' play areas from dogs and cats, and cover sandpits when not in use.
- Give dogs and cats regular doses of medicine to ensure that their intestines remain free from worms.

Questions

1 Copy and complete the chart opposite.
2 a What is the difference between lice and nits?
  b Why is it impossible to get rid of lice and nits by washing the hair?
3 a Where on the body is scabies most likely to occur?
  b Why is scabies also called 'the itch'?
  c Describe the rash.
4 Why should pets with fleas be treated with an insecticide, particularly in a household with young children?
5 a What can be done to help prevent infection by (i) threadworms, (ii) toxocara worms?
  b What are the symptoms of toxocariasis?

	Head lice	Itch mites	Fleas	Thread worms
Where they live				
What they feed on				
Where they lay eggs				
How a child becomes infected				

Further activities

 Extension

1 For each of the five parasites:

   a draw a diagram of the parasite

   b describe treatment to remove them.

2 Use the data available in Topics 60 and 61 to start a database of children's diseases and infections. This could be a group activity. A suggested layout of a record for measles is given below:

Name:	Measles
Part of body affected:	Respiratory system, skin
Symptoms:	Fever, cold, cough, red rash
Cause:	Virus
How it spreads:	Droplet infection, contact
Prevention:	Immunisation

 Investigation

Find out information about other parasites, for example bed bugs, tapeworms, malaria, bilharzia.

Weblinks

For facts about head lice, search at:
www.netdoctor.co.uk
For a fact sheet on toxocariasis, visit:
www.cdc.gov and search for 'toxocariasis fact sheet'.

CHAPTER 62

Skin problems

There are many different disorders of the skin. Some have already been mentioned. These include nappy rash (Topic 22), infectious diseases (Topic 60), and parasites (Topic 61). Other causes are dealt with in this topic and in Topic 63.

ITCHING AND SCRATCHING

The skin usually itches (irritates) when something is wrong with it. The natural thing to do is to scratch. If the itching persists, it makes a child irritable, restless and upsets sleep. There is also a chance that scratching will damage the skin and allow germs to enter and cause infection.

RASHES

Rashes of one sort or another are extremely common in children. If a rash is not a symptom of one of the usual diseases of childhood, a parent will want to know what caused it. Is it caused by an infection? Is it caused by something the child ate? Has the child been in contact with something she might be allergic to? Whatever the cause, if it worries the child and makes her scratch, or if she is obviously unwell, then prompt treatment by a doctor is required. It is much easier to deal with a rash at an early stage than later when it has spread and caused more trouble.

Urticaria ('nettle rash'; hives)

The rash is lumpy and usually white, with either lots of small spots or fewer, larger ones. It itches severely, but usually does not last long, and can be soothed by calamine lotion. It may be blamed on 'overheated blood', 'too rich food' or 'acid fruits', but these will not be the cause.

The rash indicates that the child is particularly sensitive (allergic) to something (see also Allergy p. 308). A number of substances are known to cause urticaria including:

- certain medicines such as aspirin or penicillin
- a particular food such as strawberries and shellfish
- sensitivity to insect bites such as those from the fleas of dogs or cats, or from bed bugs.

Urticaria is not dangerous, but if it occurs regularly, or persists for a long time, it needs to be investigated to discover the cause so that it can be avoided.

Heat rash

When babies get too hot, a rash may appear, particularly around the shoulders and neck. It is understandable for a rash to appear in hot weather or in hot countries – where it is known as **prickly heat**. It may also develop in cold weather if the baby is wrapped in too many clothes and kept in an overheated room.

Bathing the baby will remove the sweat – which is the cause of the rash. When the skin is quite dry, calamine lotion applied to the rash may be soothing.

Dressing the baby according to the weather will help to prevent heat rash. When it is very hot there is no reason for any clothes to be worn at all except a nappy.

Eczema

Eczema in varying degrees of severity is a fairly common complaint in babies. It tends to come and go during the early years, and most sufferers grow out of it by the time they begin school. It usually starts with patches of dry, scaly skin which become red and slightly inflamed and may weep. Eczema makes children want to scratch the sore places and it is very difficult to stop them.

Eczema is neither contagious nor caused by poor hygiene. Although the exact cause is unknown, there is often a family history of eczema, allergies, asthma or hay fever, and it tends to be worse when the child is emotionally upset.

SKIN INFECTIONS

Ringworm

This is caused by a fungus which infects the skin and grows outwards to form a reddish patch with a ring of little pimples at the edge.

When it affects the scalp, the hairs break off to leave a bald, round patch. Treatment with anti-fungal cream destroys the fungus, and the hair will grow again.

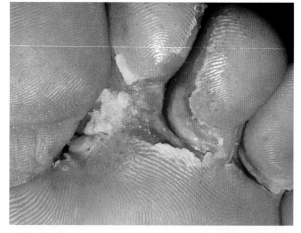

Athlete's foot

Athlete's foot

This is the name for ringworm which grows on the skin of the feet. It likes the warm damp conditions encouraged by shoes and socks, especially between the toes, where it makes the skin turn white and peel off.

Impetigo

This is a skin disease caused by bacteria. It starts as little red spots which develop watery heads and then brownish-yellow crusts. It spreads quickly to other parts of the skin, and can easily infect other people when, for example, they use the same towel. Impetigo can usually be cleared up quickly by antibiotics.

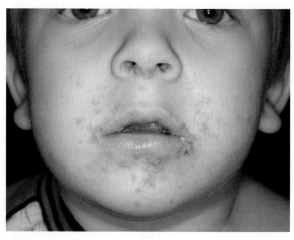

Impetigo

Warts

Although these do not cause itching and scratching, they are included here because they occur on the skin. Warts are caused by a virus infection which may spread to form a crop of warts. They are harmless and will disappear eventually without treatment.

A wart on the sole of the foot is called a **verruca** or **plantar wart**. Verrucas need to be removed because they are painful and contagious, being easily picked up in the warm, moist conditions of bathrooms and swimming baths. They can be treated by a chiropodist or with over-the-counter preparations sold in pharmacies. Like all warts, if left untreated, verrucas should disappear with time.

Questions

1 a Give four ways in which persistent itching may affect a child.

  b When is prompt medical treatment for a rash desirable? Why?

2 a Give two other names for urticaria.

  b Suggest some substances which might be the cause of urticaria.

  c Name a substance which can soothe the rash.

3 a Under what conditions may heat rash develop in cold weather?

  b What is the cause of eczema?

  c Is eczema catching?

4 Which of the skin infections mentioned in this topic is:

  a caused by a virus

  b caused by a fungus

  c caused by bacteria

  d called athlete's foot when it grows on the feet

  e called a verruca when it occurs on the sole of the foot

  f treated with antibiotics?

Further activities

 Extension

1 There are many different disorders of the skin. A number have already been mentioned in this book. How many can you remember? The first paragraph of this topic gives some clues. What treatment, if any, was recommended for each disorder?

2 Add to the database file of children's diseases and infections started in Topic 61.

Use the file to find out:

  a Which diseases and illnesses are caused by bacteria?

  b Which are caused by viruses? Then think of some questions of your own.

CHAPTER 63

First aid

This topic gives a list of equipment which should be kept in a first-aid box, and a brief description of treatment for the more common mishaps.

FIRST-AID BOX

Children often cut themselves or fall over, burn or scald themselves or get stung. Parents and carers have to deal with these first-aid problems and it is helpful to have all the necessary equipment handy in a special box. Suggested contents for the first-aid box are:

- **antiseptic wipes** – for cleaning wounds
- **plasters (low allergy)** – to cover small wounds
- **gauze dressing**, either in individual packs or a long roll – to cover wounds
- **bandages** of different widths – to hold dressings in place
- **adhesive tape**
- **safety pins** – to hold bandages in place
- **scissors** – to cut bandages and tape
- **crêpe bandage** – to support a sprained ankle or other joint
- **triangular bandage** – to make a sling to support a damaged arm
- **tweezers** – to remove splinters
- **eye dropper or eye bath** – for washing the eye
- **sterile eye pads** – to cover an injured eye
- **calamine lotion or cream** – for sunburn, chapped skin
- **anti-sting cream** – for insect bites
- **plastic gloves** – to prevent spread of disease through contact with blood
- **disposal bag** – for safe disposal of used dressings etc.

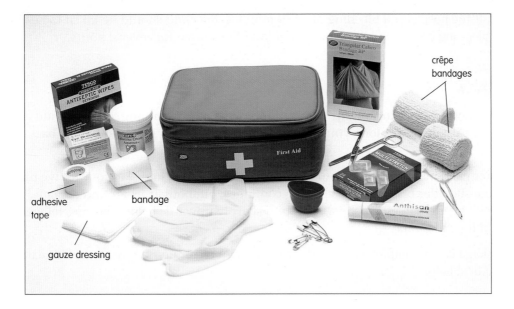

crêpe bandages

adhesive tape

bandage

gauze dressing

CUTS AND GRAZES (ABRASIONS)

Small cuts and grazes should be washed with clean water or soap and water and dried by patting with a clean towel. If necessary, they should be covered with a dry dressing, and the dressing held in place with a bandage.

Bleeding from a small wound soon stops of its own accord, and the scab which forms prevents infection. There is no need for a plaster unless the wound keeps opening up. Also, there is no need for antiseptic ointment as a child's natural resistance deals with nearly all infections, and the ointment makes the scab soft and delays healing.

Wounds with severe bleeding

When there is severe bleeding, the aim should be to stop the bleeding immediately and to obtain medical help urgently. To stop the bleeding, pressure should be applied to the wound with the fingers. A doctor may decide that a large or deep wound needs stitches. An injection against tetanus may also be necessary.

BRUISES

A bruise is caused by bleeding beneath unbroken skin. Firm pressure on the affected area will help to stop a bruise from developing. A bad bruise may be eased by a cold compress if it is applied at once. This is made by soaking some suitable material, e.g. cotton wool, in cold water and placing it on the bruise.

NOSE BLEEDS

These are common in young children. They are more of a nuisance than a danger – the sight of blood makes them appear worse than they really are.

There are many causes, but the treatment is always the same. Sit the patient upright and leaning slightly forward. Pinch the soft part of the nose for 10 minutes, then release the pressure. If the bleeding has not stopped, reapply the pressure for another 10 minutes. Repeat if necessary. If the nose is still bleeding after 30 minutes, the child should be taken to hospital. Once the bleeding has stopped, the nose should not be blown for several hours.

CHOKING

When a hard object gets stuck in the throat, it interferes with breathing, and the child chokes. In the case of a baby, lay him along your forearm, keeping his head low, and pat his back, four or five times.

For an older child, hold him over your knee, head downwards, and slap four to five times between the shoulder blades. If the choking continues, put both arms around the child's waist from behind, interlocking the hands. Then pull sharply upwards below the ribs, telling the child to cough at the same time.

If the blockage is not completely cleared, or the patient continues to have trouble breathing, seek urgent medical help.

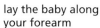
lay the baby along
your forearm

give five sharp pats
on the baby's back

keep the baby's head
low and support the
chin

How to deal with choking in a baby

bend the child over
your knees

give five sharp slaps
between the child's
shoulder blades

How to deal with choking in a child

ELECTRIC SHOCK

If a child is receiving a continuous electric shock, do not touch him with bare hands, or you will receive a shock too. Switch off the power if possible. If you cannot do this, push the child clear using a broom, cushion, or wooden chair – avoiding anything made of metal which would conduct electric current.

BROKEN BONES (FRACTURES)

Generally, the bones of a young child bend rather than break. If a bone does break, it is likely to crack on one side only. This is called a 'greenstick' fracture because it behaves rather like a bent green twig which refuses to break off. An X-ray may be necessary to discover whether a bone is broken or not.

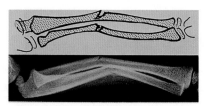

Greenstick fracture in the forearm

If a bone is obviously broken, it is important to keep the injured part still, stop any bleeding, and call an ambulance. Do not give anything to eat or drink in case a general anesthetic is needed.

SOMETHING IN THE EYE

When a particle of dust, an eyelash or other small object gets into the eye it can be removed with the corner of a clean handkerchief from the eyelid but not the eyeball. The eyeball itself should never be touched because of the danger of damaging the delicate surface. Rubbing the eye can also cause damage.

Dust or other small particles on the eyeball are best removed by washing the eye. Tilt the child's head so that the good eye is uppermost. Then pour some water into the inner corner of the affected eye so that it washes over the eyeball. If a little salt is added to the water (a teaspoonful of a salt to ½ litre water), the water will soothe rather than sting the eye (tears are salty). If the object cannot be removed easily, it needs to be dealt with by a doctor, or at the hospital. After the object has been removed, it will still feel as though something is there if the eyeball has been scratched.

When a chemical substance such as bleach gets into the eye, it should be washed out immediately by holding the face under cold running water from the tap.

BURNS AND SCALDS

A **burn** is caused by dry heat, for example from a fire or touching a hot cooking pan. A **scald** results from contact with moist heat such as steam or hot fat.

The skin of young children can very easily be damaged by heat and the scars may last for a lifetime. Burns and scalds are also very painful. Therefore, every effort should be made to prevent them from happening (see Topic 68). In young children, especially infants, even small burns or scalds should be regarded as serious and be given immediate treatment.

Small burn or scald

Hold the burnt area under running cold water or put in a bowl of cold water containing ice cubes to remove the heat and reduce the pain. It is important to do this for at least ten minutes. Pat dry and cover with a gauze dressing, cling-film or a clean plastic bag, but **not** a plaster. If the burn is on the face, or is larger than the size of the patient's hand, or has caused severe blistering or broken the skin, the child should be taken to hospital immediately.

- **NEVER** put ointment, cream, jelly, oil or butter on a burn – they delay healing.
- **NEVER** prick a blister – this lets in germs and encourages infection.

Severe burn or scald

Wrap the child in a clean sheet and rush to hospital without waiting to call a doctor.

SUNBURN

The sun's rays can easily burn the skin, so a child's skin should be exposed to the sun gradually, starting with a few minutes on the first day. The time can be slowly increased as brown pigment (melanin) develops in the skin to protect it. Those with fair skin burn very easily and need particular care, especially at the seaside, as the sun's rays are reflected from the water and this makes them extra strong. Babies and young children should always be protected by sun protection lotion (factor 30 for young babies) and should wear a suitable hat to shade the face and neck.

Sunburn only begins to hurt several hours after the actual burning has taken place. Severe burning needs medical attention. In other cases, cold water may help to soothe, as may calamine lotion or special creams or lotions sold for the purpose.

Excessive exposure to sun, particularly in those with fair skins, can cause skin cancer.

STINGS

Calamine, anti-sting or anti-histamine creams give relief when rubbed on to stings from insects and nettles. They help to reduce itching. If the sting is in the mouth, sipping cold water or sucking an ice cube or ice lolly helps to give relief while medical advice is sought. Medical advice is also required if:

- there is a known allergy to bites and stings
- shortness of breath or fever develop
- infection sets in.

POISONING

If a child has swallowed something poisonous

- **keep calm** – poisoning is rarely fatal in a matter of seconds or even minutes
- **do not try to make the child sick**

- **telephone your doctor or take the child to the nearest hospital**
- **take a sample of the poison with you** so that it can be quickly identified.

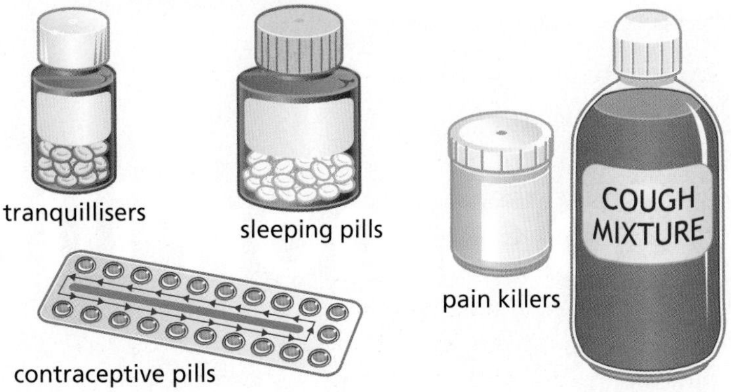
tranquillisers
sleeping pills
pain killers
COUGH MIXTURE
contraceptive pills

Common causes of poisoning in young children

Questions

1 List the items shown in the photograph of the first-aid box on p. 303. Give a purpose for each item.

2 a How does first-aid treatment for a graze differ from that for severe bleeding?

b Are sticking plasters or antiseptic ointments necessary for a small cut?

3 a What is the cause of a bruise?

b What treatment is necessary?

4 Describe how to stop a nose bleed.

5 What treatment is advised for (i) a baby who is choking, (ii) an older child who is choking?

6 If you have to deal with someone who is receiving a continuous electric shock, (i) what should you not do, (ii) what should you do?

7 How should a broken bone be dealt with?

8 How can something be removed from a child's eye?

9 a Give two reasons why every effort should be made to prevent children from being burnt.

b Describe the first-aid treatment for (i) a small burn, (ii) a bad burn.

c What should never be put on a burn and why?

d Why should blisters never be pricked?

e How can sunburn be (i) prevented, (ii) treated?

10 When is medical advice required for a sting?

11 a List the causes of accidental poisoning in young children shown above.

b What action should be taken when a child has swallowed something poisonous?

Further activities

Extension

Make a leaflet to fit inside a first-aid box giving emergency instructions for dealing with common accidents, such as the ones in this topic. Include a contents check-list to place inside the box.

Investigation

Check the contents of a first-aid box. Perhaps you have one at home. There will certainly be at least one in every school and college. Compare the items in the box with the list on p. 302. What items are missing? If there are any extra items, what are they there for?

Weblink

For more information on baby and child first aid emergencies, with animations, visit:

http://childrenfirstaid.redcross.org.uk

CHAPTER 64

Common illnesses

This topic gives a brief description of some of the more common illnesses from which children may suffer. They are placed in alphabetical order and not in order of seriousness or frequency.

An illness can be **acute** (short-term) or **chronic** (long-term). Depending on the severity of the illness it can be **mild**, **moderate** or **severe**. Details of illnesses should be recorded in the child's Health Record (see p. 67).

ADENOIDS

Adenoids consist of lymphatic tissue behind the nose which sometimes grows so large that it blocks the back of the nose. When this happens, the child has to breathe through the mouth. It may cause nasal speech, deafness, and sometimes a persistent cough. Common problems with large adenoids are a night cough, snoring and disturbed sleep. In such cases, the adenoids may need to be removed.

ALLERGY

Having an allergy means being unduly sensitive to a particular substance which is harmless to most other people. That substance may affect the body through the skin (e.g. detergent), or when eaten (e.g. strawberries, cow's milk, eggs, peanuts), or when breathed in (pollen, house dust etc.).

The allergy may show itself in one or more of the following ways: hay fever, asthma, eczema, urticaria ('nettle rash'), stomach upset, or other unpleasant symptoms.

Many people (adults and children) have allergies of one sort or another. A tendency to suffer from allergies often runs in families, although it may take different forms in members of the same family. For example, a parent with asthma may have a child who suffers from hay fever.

Little Paul Land is nuts about his granny but every time he gave her a cuddle he burst into tears and came out in blotches.

For months doctors were baffled but now allergy experts have discovered the cause.

Two-year-old Paul of Harlington, near Mexborough, South Yorks, is allergic to peanuts – and his granny, 63-year-old Mrs Ann Land, works in a nut factory.

Source: this news item appeared in the **Eastern Daily Press**

APPENDICITIS

Appendicitis is inflammation of the **appendix** (a worm-like extension of the large intestine about 8 cm long). It starts with pain in the abdomen (tummy) which becomes localised in the lower right side within a few hours. The pain is usually accompanied by fever and vomiting. An operation is necessary to remove the appendix and prevent peritonitis and the spread of the infection in the abdomen.

ASTHMA

This is difficulty in breathing caused by tightening (spasm) of the muscles surrounding the small air tubes in the lungs. It may be due to infection, allergy, or emotional upset, and may run in families. An asthma attack starts with a feeling of tightness in the chest and often a troublesome cough. This leads to 'shortness of breath' and noisy, wheezy breathing, which can be distressing to both the child and the parents.

Asthma is usually treated by inhalers (puffers) and tablets. In serious cases, a few days in hospital may be necessary to stabilise the condition.

COLDS

The common cold is caused by a virus infection. It spreads easily, either by droplets in the air that come from an infected person, or by contact with handkerchiefs or other objects recently used by an infected person. It is difficult to stop the germs from spreading between members of the same family. Colds are caused by a very large number of different viruses and as yet there is no known way of preventing them.

Young babies are more seriously affected by colds than older children. They are also more likely to suffer from complications such as chest infections. Therefore, it is wise to try to prevent anyone with a cold from coming into contact with a young baby. Babies have difficulty in feeding when the nose is blocked because they are unable to breathe and suck at the same time.

Children are particularly likely to catch colds in the first few months at playgroup or school. This is because they come into contact with a greater variety of different types of cold germs. By the time they are 6 or 7, they have usually built up more resistance to these germs.

CONJUNCTIVITIS ('PINK EYE')

This is caused by an eye infection. The eye looks red and there is usually a yellowish discharge which sticks the eyelids together. The infection easily spreads when other members of the family use the same towel or face flannel as an infected person. The eyes can be cleaned by wiping gently with cotton wool soaked in water, from the inner corner of the eye outwards. A fresh piece of cotton wool should be used for each eye. A doctor may prescribe antibiotic eyedrops or ointment.

CONSTIPATION

Constipation is the infrequent passing of very hard, dry stools. It is a common problem in children due mainly to not enough fibre in the diet and not enough fluids taken. Left to themselves, the bowels open when necessary, and usually according to a pattern. With some people (adults and children), the bowels may open once or more a day, or every other day, or once every three or four days, and any of these patterns is normal. There is no need for the bowels to open every day, or for the child to be given laxatives to make this happen. It is common for babies who are being breast-fed to go for several days without having a motion, and the stools are always soft.

Laxatives can be harmful if they are given regularly, as they interfere with the normal working of the bowels. Bowels should be kept open by diet not laxatives:

- for young babies – more water
- for babies being weaned – fruit purée
- for children – foods containing fibre such as wholemeal bread, cereals, fruit, vegetables.

COUGHS

It is essential to cough from time to time to remove phlegm from the windpipe or lungs, especially following a cold. There is no need to consult a doctor whenever the child coughs a little more than usual. If the child coughs a great deal, it can be due to a number of possible causes and needs a medical opinion.

Cough medicine will not cure a cough, but it might comfort the back of the throat. The instructions should be read before any cough medicine is given to a child, because some are not suitable for young children.

CROUP

Croup is a harsh, barking cough accompanied by noisy breathing and a hoarse voice. It occurs in children up to the age of 4 years, and is caused by **laryngitis** (inflammation of the larynx – the voice box). If it develops suddenly, a doctor needs to be consulted as soon as possible.

DIARRHOEA

Diarrhoea is the frequent passing of loose watery stools. To prevent dehydration children should be given plenty to drink, either water with a little sugar, or weak squash or weak fruit juice. A rehydration mixture available from a pharmacy can also be given. This will replace the essential salts lost during diarrhoea.

If the diarrhoea continues for more than 12 hours, or if it is accompanied by vomiting, medical advice should be sought.

EARACHE

Pain in the ears may be due to teething or a cold. If the earache persists, or if it keeps recurring, it needs to be investigated by a doctor in case an infection is present in the ear itself, e.g. 'glue ear' (see p. 153).

FEVER

Fever is when the body temperature is higher than normal. (Taking the temperature is discussed on p. 318.) A child with a fever will feel hot and sweaty. She needs to be allowed to cool off to reduce her temperature – not to be smothered in blankets. This can be helped by sponging the skin with tepid water, and lowering the heating in the room. Simple medicines such as infant paracetamol (e.g. Calpol®) may also help to reduce the fever.

Fever is usually a sign of infection, but not always. A high temperature on its own is not normally a reason for asking a doctor to call. However, if it remains high or is accompanied by other symptoms (such as headache), it is wise to ask the doctor for advice.

FITS (CONVULSIONS)

When a child has a fit, her eyes roll upwards, she loses consciousness and her limbs make jerking movements. Fits are caused by a wide variety of ailments, but not by teething. In many small children they are due to a high fever that occurs with infections such as tonsillitis or bronchitis.

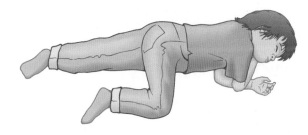

Recovery position

Once the convulsion has stopped, lay the child on her side in the recovery position. This prevents the airway to the lungs from becoming blocked by the tongue or by vomit. The doctor should be informed.

Should the fit continue for more than 10 minutes, or if the child remains unconscious for longer than this time, and a doctor has been unable to reach you, the child should be taken to hospital.

HEADACHES

Headaches are common in children and may be due to tiredness, worry, infection (e.g. tonsillitis), or migraine. On the other hand, pretending to have a headache can be used as an excuse for not doing something, for example not going to school. If having a headache is found to be an easy way of avoiding a difficult or a worrying situation it can quickly become a habit.

Whatever the cause, headaches need investigation so that the right treatment can be given to stop them.

INFLUENZA

Influenza ('flu') is caused by a virus. It is a more serious infection than the common cold. Symptoms include fever, chill, headache and dry cough. A runny nose and sneezing may also occur.

SORE THROAT

There are various causes of sore throat. Often it is the beginning of a cold. Sometimes the child may have tonsillitis. It is not necessary to consult a doctor every time a child has a sore throat. If it is accompanied by earache, a rise in temperature, or if the sore throat is still getting worse after two days, a doctor should be consulted.

STICKY EYE

A yellowish discharge from the eye sometimes gums the eyelids together. It may result from a blocked tear duct or an infection. To clean the eye, wipe gently with cotton wool and water; always wipe from the inner corner of the eye outwards, and use a fresh piece of cotton wool for each eye. A doctor needs to be consulted if the discharge persists.

STYE

Inflammation at the base of an eyelash caused by infection.

SWOLLEN GLANDS

There are many reasons why the glands in the neck swell, and a doctor should be consulted.

THRUSH

This is a fungal infection which causes white patches on the tongue and mouth. It occurs mainly in babies and makes them scream when feeding because the mouth is sore. Thrush can also occur in the nappy area as red patches with spots. The infection can be cleared up by antifungal cream or drops.

TONSILLITIS

Tonsillitis is an infection of the tonsils. The throat is sore, the tonsils are inflamed and it may be possible to see yellowish-white spots on them. Antibiotics prescribed by the doctor usually cure the infection.

There are two tonsils, one at either side of the back of the mouth. They normally enlarge at the age of 5–6 years and shrink after the age of 10 or so. Tonsils do not need to be removed just because they are large, but only if there are frequent bouts of tonsillitis which cannot be prevented by medicines.

VOMITING (BEING SICK)

It is quite usual for young babies to bring up a little milk after a meal. This is often curdled, and it smells sour as it has been mixed with the acid in the stomach. It is not a cause for worry.

Vomiting has to be taken seriously when a child is repeatedly sick. This applies to older children as well as babies, and the advice of a doctor is needed. Vomiting and diarrhoea are often symptoms of food poisoning (p. 279).

WHEEZING

A child with a wheeze should always be seen by a doctor. The wheeze may be caused by asthma, an infection, or by inhaling something. It can be very much helped by medical treatment.

Questions

1 Link each of these words with the correct description below: adenoids, asthma, conjunctivitis, constipation, croup, diarrhoea, fever, sticky eye, thrush, tonsillitis.

   a body temperature higher than normal

   b spreads easily when others use the same towel

   c noisy breathing with a harsh cough

   d white patches on the tongue and mouth

   e tissue which sometimes blocks the back of the nose

   f inflamed tonsils

   g yellow discharge which sometimes gums the eyelids together

   h loose, watery stools which are passed frequently

   i the infrequent passing of very hard, dry stools

   j difficult breathing.

2 What is the difference between acute and chronic illness?

3 a When a person has an allergy, what does this mean?

   b Name some substances which are known to cause allergies, and say how they get into the body.

   c What form may an allergy take?

4 a What causes the common cold?

   b How does it spread?

   c What particular difficulty do babies have when they suffer from a cold?

   d When children start attending playgroup, why are they particularly likely to catch colds?

5 a When can constipation become a problem in children?

   b When and why are laxatives harmful?

   c Give ways of encouraging the bowels to open regularly without the use of laxatives.

   d What should be given to children with diarrhoea, and why?

6 a Why should a child with earache be taken to the doctor?

   b What action is recommended when a child has a fit?

   c (i) What can cause headaches in children?

      (ii) Why may children have 'pretend' headaches?

   d What symptoms may indicate appendicitis?

Further activities

 Extension

a Use data from this topic to add to the database started in Topic 61.

b Use the database to find all the diseases that can affect the respiratory system.

 Child study

Has the child had any illnesses mentioned in this topic? If so, describe how the child was affected.

CHAPTER 65

The sick child

Parents can usually tell when their child is ill by changes in the child's normal pattern of behaviour. It is probable that the child will show one or more of the following symptoms:

- fever (looks flushed and feels hot)
- loss of appetite (will not eat)
- rash (spots or blotches on the skin)
- dark rings around the eyes, or the eyes look sunken
- vomiting or diarrhoea
- fretfulness
- unnaturally quiet and limp and shows no interest in anything
- unusual paleness.

With a baby, they will also notice that he cries differently.

CONSULTING THE DOCTOR

When parents feel that there is something wrong with their child, they have to decide whether to consult a doctor. There is no need to call the doctor every time the child coughs, or vomits, or has a raised temperature. These symptoms commonly occur in childhood and are often followed by a quick recovery. If the child does not recover quickly, or is more unwell than usual with these symptoms, or they recur frequently, then a doctor should be consulted.

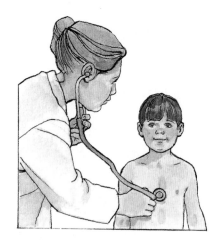

When parents need the advice of a doctor, they should phone or call at the surgery or health centre, preferably before 10 a.m. They will then be given advice, or asked to bring the child to the doctor, or told that the doctor will be calling to see the child.

EMERGENCIES

A child needs urgent treatment either from a doctor or the accident and emergency department of a hospital for:

- severe bleeding
- swallowing poison

- severe burns
- unconsciousness
- severe pain
- glazed eyes which do not focus
- severe blow on the head
- difficulty in breathing
- severe diarrhoea or vomiting (especially babies)
- any type of fit or convulsion
- swallowing a dangerous object like a button, battery or a safety pin
- broken bone
- electric shock.

CARING FOR A SICK CHILD

There is no good reason for keeping a child in bed unless he is happier there. The child will get better just as well in the living room as in the bedroom, so long as he is kept warm and comfortable. He is also likely to be less bored and feel less neglected if he is near other people in the family, and it is easier to care for him and keep him amused.

When a child has to stay in bed he needs to be kept clean, comfortable and occupied.

- Washing the face and brushing the hair and teeth help the child to feel fresh.
- A daily bath is unnecessary unless he is sweating a lot.
- The hands need to be washed before eating and after using the toilet.
- The bedclothes and nightclothes should be changed as often as necessary.
- The bed should be straightened several times a day and remade morning and evening.
- The room should be kept warm.
- The room should be kept ventilated to prevent it from becoming stuffy, especially when there is paraffin or gas heating. If the window is opened, the child should not be in a draught.
- A child who is old enough needs:
  - plenty of pillows so he can sit up comfortably
  - to be prevented from sliding down the bed by a pillow placed under the foot of the mattress
  - a bed-side table or tray for toys and play-things.

AVOIDING BOREDOM

Keeping a child happy and occupied throughout the day can be difficult at the best of times, but it requires extra thought and patience when the child is unwell. It can be helpful if parents keep some toys and play materials tucked away, ready to bring out when the child is ill or convalescing (getting better). Some of these things may have been given as birthday or Christmas presents, and then put aside for just such an occasion. The box in the drawing is kept by the family and taken out when a child is sick.

In addition to having new or different toys to play with, a child always loves having someone who will play with him, or will read or tell stories to him.

WHEN A CHILD HAS TO GO INTO HOSPITAL

Being a patient can be a big shock to children, especially if they have to be separated from their parents and are too young to understand. When children go into hospital they:

- will find themselves in strange surroundings
- will meet many people who are strangers to them
- may not understand what is happening to them
- may be ill or in pain
- may have to undergo unpleasant treatments or procedures.

In addition, they will have:

- a changed routine
- different food
- different bed, bath etc.

When ill, children need more love and support from their parents than usual. All hospitals now have some provision for parents so that they can stay with their babies or young children and help to nurse them.

When children are old enough to understand, then it should be explained to them what is going to happen, perhaps with the help of books, videos or pre-visits to hospital. They may even look forward to the event if told that:

- they can take some of their toys with them
- there will be more toys in hospital to play with
- there will be other children to play with
- their parents will be able to visit them or stay with them
- the doctors and nurses will look after them.

Questions

1 a How can parents usually tell when their child is ill?

   b What symptoms may the child show?

   c When is it advisable to consult a doctor?

2 Name 13 emergencies when the child needs urgent medical treatment.

3 How should a sick child be cared for at home?

4 a Name some changes which take place in a child's life when he goes into hospital.

   b How may hospitals make life easier for a young child?

Further activities

Extension

1 Look at the photograph of a child in hospital with a broken arm. How would the scene differ if a child was being cared for in bed at home?

2 Suggest a list of suitable items for the box in the drawing on p. 315.

Investigation

Try to arrange to visit the children's ward of your local hospital. You may be able to do something useful like play with a child who does not have any visitors. Write an account of your visit and what, if anything, you were able to do for the patients or the staff.

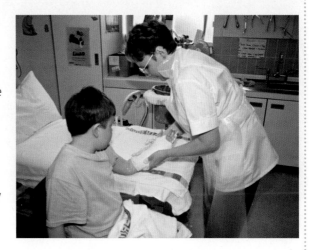

Design

Find out the kinds of toys which are useful in hospitals for keeping sick children amused. With the aid of a suitable graphics program, design and, if possible, make an item to keep a sick child amused.

Weblinks

For a useful article called 'Seven Ways to Stamp Out Boredom', search in the 'Kids 7 to 11' section at:

www.childrenfirst.nhs.uk

For amusing poems for children, visit:

www.funny-poems.co.uk

CHAPTER 66

Nursing a sick child

TAKING THE TEMPERATURE

It is natural for the temperature of the body to vary (see also pp. 78–9). Normal body temperature for children ranges between 36.0 and 36.8 °C (96.8–98.2 °F). The temperature of the forehead or armpit will be slightly lower than the mouth. A temperature above 38 °C indicates fever and below 35 °C **hypothermia**.

Different types of thermometer can be used for measuring body temperature.

Ear thermometer
This is placed over the ear with a small probe that detects body temperature. It is quick and easy to use, and is powered by batteries.

Mouth thermometer
This has to be held correctly and securely in the mouth and is unsuitable for small children.

Forehead thermometer
This is a strip of flexible plastic containing liquid crystals. When held against the forehead, and stripes change colour to indicate the level of body temperature.

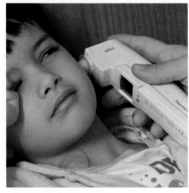

Ear thermometer

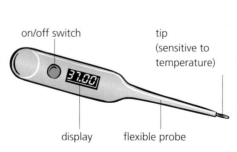

on/off switch

tip (sensitive to temperature)

display

flexible probe

Mouth thermometer

Forehead thermometer

GIVING MEDICINE

Medicines need to be used with care. When giving medicine to a child (or anyone else):

One for teddy, then one for you

- **Make sure it is the right medicine**. Before giving medicine, check that it is right for the patient.
- **Follow the instructions exactly**. The right dose needs to be given, at the right frequency. Most medicines have side-effects which can cause considerable harm if too much is taken.
- **Ask the doctor for advice** if the medicine does not seem to be doing any good, or if it seems to be causing troublesome side-effects.
- **Store the medicine in a cool place and out of reach of children**, preferably in a locked cupboard.

Medicine taken by mouth

Every effort should be made to get a child to take medicine willingly. Ways of persuasion include:

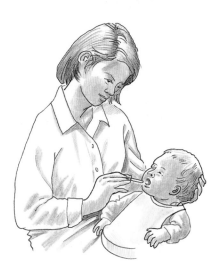

- making it into a game, e.g. by giving some to teddy
- pretending to have some yourself
- disguising the taste with jam or yoghurt.

When force is used to get the medicine into the mouth, the child will be certain to fight against it every time. It is dangerous to force medicine down a child's throat when she is crying in case she inhales it.

For babies, medicine can be trickled into the side of the mouth using a dispensing syringe instead of a spoon. They may find flavoured medicines easier to take.

Generally, children under the age of 5 years are unable to swallow tablets, in which case they need to be crushed first and then given in a teaspoonful of milk, fruit juice or jam.

ANTIBIOTICS

The drawing shows three of the many different kinds of antibiotic. Antibiotics are medicines used for treating diseases caused by bacteria and fungi. It is particularly important to follow the instructions that come with this type of medicine. It is also important to complete the course of treatment even if the symptoms have disappeared, as not all the germs may have been killed and the disease can start up again.

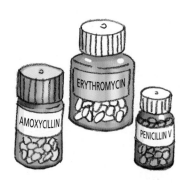

Antibiotics must never be stored and used later as they lose their effectiveness with time.

PREVENTING THE SPREAD OF INFECTION BY CROSS INFECTION

If a child is suffering from an infectious disease, the parents should try to prevent it from spreading by:

- general cleanliness
- keeping babies and other vulnerable people away from the infection.

A few serious infectious diseases may also require:

- **isolation** of the person suffering from the disease so that germs cannot spread to others
- **quarantine** of people who have been in contact with the infected person, because if they have caught the disease they may be infectious before the symptoms appear.

FOOD AND DRINKS

Children who are not feeling well often do not want to eat. It will do them no harm to go without food for two or three days. When better, they will make up for it by eating more than usual.

While there is no point in forcing food into children who are ill, they should be given plenty to drink, especially if feverish, to prevent dehydration. This might mean offering favourite drinks, or making special fruit drinks, iced lollies, using a drinking straw, or flavouring milk to make it into a milk shake.

ATTITUDES TO ILLNESS

Much of an adult's attitude to illness is learnt in childhood. Children learn:

- by how their parents deal with them when they are ill
- by the parents' attitude to their own health.

All children, at one time or another, have spells of not feeling very well – when they have a cut knee, a sore throat, a cold, a headache, and so on. If the mother or father becomes worried over every ache and pain, and keeps talking about it and making a great deal of fuss, the child will think it very important and learn to worry in the same way. If, instead of worrying too much, the parents put their energy into keeping the child happy and occupied, then she is unlikely to grow up to be over-anxious about her health.

Questions

1 a Describe in words or by diagrams three types of thermometer suitable for children.

  b Do children who are seriously ill always have a high temperature?

2 a What care should be taken when giving medicine?

  b Suggest ways of persuading a child to take medicine willingly.

  c What may result from forcing medicine into the child's mouth?

  d What is the usual age at which children become able to swallow tablets?

3 a What is an antibiotic?

  b List the different kinds of antibiotic shown on p. 319.

  c Why is it important to complete a course of antibiotics?

4 How can parents try to prevent the spread of an infectious disease?

5 Is food or drink more important for a sick child? Explain why.

Further activities

 Extension

What should a child who is unwell be given to eat and drink? Describe different ways of making drinks attractive.

 Discussion

Do you agree or disagree that much of an adult's attitude to illness is acquired in childhood? Give your opinion, backed up by examples, from your own experience.

CHAPTER 67

Prevention of accidents

Accidents are the biggest cause of injury and death of children over the age of one year. It is estimated that every year more than 1 million children in the UK require hospital treatment. Many more are treated by GPs and by carers.

TRAINING FOR LIFE IN A DANGEROUS WORLD

The world is a dangerous place and children have to learn to cope with the hazards.

Parents and carers are responsible for the safety of their children. At the same time, they are responsible for training them to become independent people who can take care of themselves. Throughout childhood, parents and carers have to judge between the amount of protection their child needs for safety and the amount of freedom the child needs and wants. Children need to be given freedom so that they can learn to make judgements for themselves. Children often want more freedom than is safe for them because it is a natural part of growing up to react against parents' and carers' wishes.

Learning about danger

During the first 18 months of life, babies have no understanding of danger and therefore need complete protection. However, during this time they are beginning to learn what is unpleasant and can hurt, for example a child will remember for a while touching a particular object which was hot.

By the time they reach the age of 18 months, children understand simple instructions. They can now start to be taught that there are some things that should not be done.

Between 18 months and 2 years, children are beginning to understand a great deal of what their parents and carers say and their memory is improving. They start to realise that certain actions have certain consequences. For example, if anything hot is touched it will hurt. They still need a great deal of protection but they are just beginning to learn to protect themselves.

The amount of supervision can be gradually relaxed as the children acquire more sense about what is dangerous and how to avoid it. At times, parents and carers have to take calculated risks when they allow children a little more freedom. But if complete protection continues too long, children suffer the consequences of over-protection.

The type and amount of supervision changes as the children get older. It gradually becomes less and less, but even as adults they will need to be protected by the Health and Safety at Work Act and other regulations.

WHEN ACCIDENTS ARE MORE LIKELY TO HAPPEN

Accidents and injuries to children are more likely to happen:

- **At times of stress** – these are the times when people (both adults and children) are more careless and forgetful. For example, when in a hurry, when afraid, during an argument, or when very worried, perhaps about health, friendship, jobs or money.
- **When parents and carers are less alert** – their senses may be dulled by medicines such as tranquillisers, or by alcohol, or by drugs, or perhaps because they are just very tired.
- **To children who are under- or over-protected** – children who are under-protected are not made aware of dangers, so fail to take care. Children who are over-protected may either be made so aware of danger that fear makes them nervous and unsure and therefore unsafe, or may rebel against their parents or carers by taking more risks than would otherwise be the case.
- **To children who are neglected or abused** – See Topic 75.

REDUCING THE RISK

All children have accidents, however safe the home and however careful the parents and carers. It is neither possible nor desirable to watch a child every minute of the day. Nevertheless, adults can help to reduce the possibility of accidents by the following means.

1. Set a good example – children copy the behaviour of adults.
2. Make the home and gardens as accident-proof as possible.
3. Teach children to be aware of dangers and how to cope with them.
4. Never leave children alone in the house.
5. Where possible, buy goods which have the appropriate mark or label showing that they have been approved for safety. Some of the marks are shown here.

Fire resistant – means that the covers and filling of the goods meet fire resistance regulations. Fire safety labelling must, by law, be attached to all new and secondhand furniture sold in shops

Low flammability – means that the garment has passed the test for low flammability, that is, it is slow to burn

Keep away from fire – means that garments carrying this label have not passed the test for low flammability. Extra care must be taken when anywhere near a flame or a fire

Labels to indicate fire-resistance qualities

Kitemark – the goods have been made to the correct British Standard

LOW FLAMMABILITY TO BS 5722

BS number – the number of the British Standard (BS) to which the goods conform

CE

CE mark – shows that the goods comply with European regulations

BEAB mark of safety – the goods meet government safety regulations for domestic electrical appliances (BEAB = British Electrotechnical Approvals Board)

Markings on containers of substances which can have harmful effects

Harmful/irritant – the substance is not a serious health risk, but may cause some ill health if inhaled or consumed or if it penetrates the skin; some of these substances will irritate the skin and the eyes

Toxic/very toxic – the substance causes a serious risk to health if swallowed, and in some cases if inhaled or spilt on the skin

Corrosive – the substance may cause painful burns and destroy living tissue

Labels which show that equipment meets safety standards

Questions

1 Why are accidents more likely to happen:
   a at times of stress
   b when parents and carers are less alert
   c to children who are under-protected
   d to children who are over-protected?
2 Name five ways that adults can help to reduce the possibility of accidents to their children.
3 a During what stage of life do children need complete protection?
   b When can the amount of supervision be gradually relaxed, and why?

Weblink

For detailed safety advice by age group, visit the parents section at:

www.capt.org.uk.

You can also find factsheets and quizzes by visiting their resources section.

Further activities

⇨ Extension

1 Collect or draw some labels that are used to indicate that goods or materials meet recognised safety and other standards.

2 Tables 1 and 2 show some statistics for home accidents to children under the age of 5 years. Answer the following questions.

   a Describe in words the figures shown in Table 1 and suggest reasons for them.

   b (i) Compare the types of injury of the two age groups shown in Table 2. (ii) For the age group 0–8 months, suggest one reason for each type of injury, and suggest an action which might have prevented it. Do the same for the types of injury to the older children.

3 Use a spreadsheet program with a graph-drawing facility to draw two graphs of the data in Table 2. Suggest reasons for the different shapes of the graphs.

TABLE 1 The age groups of the children (under 5 years) who attended hospital because of a home accident

Age group	Number per 1000 children who attended hospital
0–8 months	40
9–12 months	44
1 year	278
2 years	288
3 years	199
4 years	151
	1000

TABLE 2 Types of accident of the children taken to hospital

Type of injury	For every 1000 children 0–8 months	For every 1000 children 9 months–4 years
Cuts	100	373
Bruises	213	115
Dislocation/ fractures	48	59
Burns	76	38
Scalds	94	52
Poisoning	22	73
Concussion	57	21
Suffocation	5	0
Electric shock	0	2
No injury found	251	103
Others	134	164
Total	1000	1000

CHAPTER 68

Safety indoors

Homes are for people of all ages to use and to live in and it is impossible to make them completely safe for children. Nevertheless, much can be done to prevent accidents:

▪ Dangerous objects should be kept away from children.
▪ Children should be kept away from dangerous situations.
▪ Those items with which the child can have contact should be made as safe as possible.

Similarly, every reasonable precaution must be taken to ensure the safety of children in playgroups, nurseries and schools.

DANGEROUS OBJECTS

The following objects should be kept from children until they are old enough to use them sensibly.

Plastic bags

There is the danger of suffocation if a plastic bag is put over the head. Plastic material is airtight and clings to warm surfaces, therefore a plastic bag over the head will be very difficult to remove.

Small, hard objects

Sweets, peanuts, small pieces from a toy etc. can cause choking if swallowed. Choking is one of the commonest accidents of infancy because babies put everything into their mouths.

Medicines

These can be poisonous and should be locked in a cabinet which needs adult hands to open it. Pills and tablets in child resistant containers are difficult for a child to get at. Blister or strip packs make it less easy for a child to swallow a lot of pills at once. On the other hand, children may find these packs attractive to play with, especially if they see adults using them.

Poisons

Poisonous substances include cleaning materials, alcohol, weedkillers and other garden chemicals, and berries of a number of plants. Empty drink bottles should never be used to store poisonous liquids to avoid them being drunk by accident.

Sharp objects

There are quite a number of these in the average home, for example sharp knives and scissors, razor blades and needles. They should be kept out of reach of young children.

Inflammable items

Matches, lighters, petrol, paraffin, methylated spirits and fireworks should be stored where children cannot reach them.

DANGEROUS SITUATIONS

This section applies particularly to toddlers. At this stage, children are able to move around but are not yet old enough to understand about safety.

Safety barriers or gates prevent young children from wandering to a part of the house the parents or carers consider dangerous. Safety barriers are often fitted across the top and the bottom of the stairs and across the kitchen doorway (the kitchen is the most dangerous room in the house).

A safety barrier should have locks which children cannot undo and bars in which they cannot get their head, hands or feet trapped. It should be too high for a small child to climb over. If a child should climb over a barrier at the top of the stairs, the fall can be more serious than a simple fall down the stairs.

Electricity

Young children should be kept away from electrical equipment and supplies because of the risk of:

Socket cover

- **Electric shock** – if electrical equipment is damaged or live wires are touched, it can give rise to a shock. So too can a worn or damaged flex. Modern electricity supply sockets are designed to prevent tiny fingers or small objects from being poked inside, and safety socket covers are also available. Electrical equipment should never be touched when the hands are wet, as this increases the likelihood of an electric shock. Trailing flexes can be dangerous; coiled flexes are safer as they do not trail, and a child's pull is less likely to cause the electrical equipment to become disconnected from the live supply. (See also p. 304.)
- **Injury from moving parts** – items such as electric mixers can cause nasty accidents.
- **Fire hazards** – electric irons are examples of equipment which, if misused, can be the cause of fire.
- **Burns** – electric cookers, heaters, kettles and irons can cause very severe burns or scalds.

Fire

There are two good reasons for keeping children away from fires. There is the danger that:

░ they may burn themselves
░ some action by them, either accidentally or in play, may cause the furniture and the building to catch fire.

Fireguards should be put in front of open fires. A good fireguard:

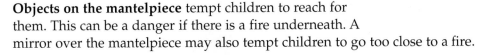

░ is strong and sturdy and has a cover on top
░ has no sharp edges
░ is firmly fixed to the wall by hooks which cannot be undone by a small child
░ has mesh small enough to prevent a baby pushing his arms or toys through
░ has a door (if there is one) that fastens securely.

When a fireguard is in front of a fire, it should never be used as a clothes dryer.

Objects on the mantelpiece tempt children to reach for them. This can be a danger if there is a fire underneath. A mirror over the mantelpiece may also tempt children to go too close to a fire.

MAKING THE HOME SAFE

There are some parts of any home which it is impossible to keep children away from or to keep out of their reach. The only thing to do is to try to make them as safe as possible.

Floors

Children can hurt themselves when they slip. To reduce this danger:

- always wipe up spilt grease or liquid
- it is safer to have a heavy mat than a lightweight one
- if floors have to be polished, use non-slip polish
- never polish under mats.

Windows

To prevent children falling out of windows:

- Young children should not be left alone in a room with an open window through which they could fall, unless there are safety bars.
- Catches need to be securely fastened on all windows that children can reach.
- Keep chairs and tables away from windows to help prevent children from climbing on to the window sills.

Toddlers have accidents with glass – windows and drinking glasses – because young children are unsteady on their feet and fall over easily. Older children are at risk when they play rough games. Ordinary glass is very brittle and breaks with sharp, jagged edges which can cause serious cuts. Therefore, in houses with children, it is safer to have toughened glass (safety glass) in any windows or glass doors which are in danger of being broken. Another way to make glass safer is to cover it with a film of clear plastic specially made for this purpose.

Cookers

Ideally, a cooker should have controls which are difficult for a child to reach and switch on. When the hob is in use, it can be made safer by a cooker guard. Turning the handles of pans inwards makes them more difficult to reach and tip over.

Tablecloths

These can be a danger; for example, the young child in the picture pulling at the tablecloth could be badly scalded by hot tea. Liquids do not need to be very hot to damage the skin of a young child.

cooker guard

Questions

1 Name objects which should be kept away from children because of the danger of

  a suffocation   **c** poisoning

  b choking   **d** injury.

2 **a** Name four possible dangers when children touch electrical equipment.

  b Give two reasons for keeping children away from fire.

  c What safety features will a good type of fireguard have?

  d Name three features which are essential for a good type of safety barrier.

3 **a** Give four ways of making floors safer.

  b Name three safety precautions which help prevent dangerous situations involving windows.

  c Name two ways of making the glass in windows and doors safer.

4 **a** Name three ways of making the cooker safer if there are young children in the home.

  b When can tablecloths be a danger?

  c Give one advantage and one disadvantage of having pills in a blister pack.

Further activities

 Extension

1 List the safety points you can remember from previous topics (or look them up), particularly the topics which dealt with clothing, nursery equipment and toys.

2 If a young child came to stay in your home, what would need to be done to make your home safer?

 Design

1 Design a fireguard or safety barrier suitable for use in your own home when a small child is present.

2 Use a graphics or desk-top publishing program to design a leaflet or poster to point out to parents particular dangers to a child at home.

CHAPTER 69

Outdoor safety

Children love to be independent, to explore and to experiment. This makes it difficult to foresee all the dangerous situations which might occur, especially when outside the home. However, there are precautions which parents and carers can take.

PLAYING OUTSIDE

Parents and carers can help to prevent accidents by making sure that:

- Children never play on the road.
- Young children, when playing outside, are supervised by an adult or a responsible older child.
- Children do not play with gardening or other equipment, e.g. tools, lawn-mowers, chemicals.
- Children are discouraged from eating plants, as many are poisonous to a greater or lesser degree.
- Children do not play in gardens where chemicals such as slug pellets, weedkiller, or rat poison have been put down.
- Dog droppings in the garden are cleared away, and avoided elsewhere, as they can spread worm infections (see also p. 297).
- Children do not have dangerous toys such as bows and arrows, air guns and catapults until they are old enough to understand the dangers and behave responsibly.
- Children do not run around with sticks or other sharp objects in their mouths – if they fall, they may perforate the palate (a hole may be made in the top of the mouth).
- Children do not play with fireworks.

Tetanus

When children play, they are likely to graze their skin occasionally. Those children who have been immunised against tetanus will be in less danger from tetanus germs in the soil.

SAFETY NEAR WATER

Special care is needed when children are near or on water because of the risk of accidental drowning. Parents and carers should make sure that:

- Paddling pools containing water are not left unguarded – babies have been known to drown in as little as 2.5 cm of water.

- Garden pools or swimming pools are completely fenced off or emptied when young children are around.
- Children are taught to swim as soon as they are old enough.
- Children always wear a life jacket when in a boat or canoe.
- Inflatable boats and Lilos® used on lakes or at the seaside are secured to the shore by a line to stop them floating away.

SAFETY IN CARS

A number of steps can be taken to help keep children safe in cars. These include:

- shutting doors with care to avoid trapping a child's fingers
- having child safety locks on the doors
- not letting children sit behind the rear seats of an estate car or hatchback
- keeping children under control so as not to distract the driver.

SEAT BELT LAW

- The driver is responsible for seeing that a child in the car wears an appropriate child restraint.
- A child **must not** sit on the lap of an adult travelling in the front of the vehicle.
- Rear-facing child seats should not be used on a front passenger seat if the car is fitted with a passenger airbag.
- All child restraints must conform to either British or European Safety Standards and carry the Kite Mark or the European 'E' mark.

Children under 3 years of age
When travelling in the front of the car, an appropriate restraint must be worn. When travelling in the back of the car an appropriate restraint must be worn if one is available.

handle allows a sleeping baby to be lifted in or out of the car undisturbed

harness is adjustable to allow for growth and thicker clothing

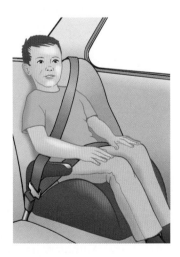

A Baby carrier (baby car seat)   B Child seat   C Booster seat

Children between 3 and 11 years old and under 1.5 m in height

In the front of the car, an appropriate child restraint must be worn if available. If not, an adult seat belt must be worn. An appropriate child restraint must also be worn in the back of the car if available. If not, an adult seat belt must be worn if available.

Children aged 12 or 13 or a younger child 1.5 m or more in height

If available, an adult seat belt must be worn in both the front and the back of the car.

CHILD RESTRAINTS

An appropriate child restraint may be a:

- **Baby carrier** (baby car seat). This can be used in the front or back seats of most cars. The baby is held in the carrier by a harness, with the carrier being held in place by a seat belt. When fitted to the front seat as shown on the previous page, the driver and baby can see one another. This type of car seat is available for babies from birth and until they weigh up to 13 kg (about 12–15 months).
- **Child seat.** This is suitable for a child weighing between 9–18 kg (about 9 months–6 years). It can be used in the front or back seat of the car and is held in place by a seat belt.
- **Booster seat**. This is suitable for children weighing 15–36 kg (about 4–11 years). It raises the child so that the seat belt is in the correct position, and also allows the child to see out of the window.

SEAT BELTS DURING PREGNANCY

Pregnant women, like everyone else, are required by law to wear seat belts. The correct way to wear a seat belt (whether pregnant or not) is for the strap to be flat and tight, going diagonally across the body and then over the thighs (A). When the lap belt is worn too high during pregnancy (B) there is the danger of injury to the unborn baby in the event of a crash.

Correct way of wearing a seat belt

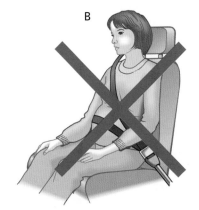
Dangerous way of wearing a seat belt

ROAD SAFETY OFFICER

Each Local Authority has a Road Safety Officer who can be consulted about the use of seat belts, child seats, or any other problems.

Questions

1 Give ways in which parents can help prevent accidents to children playing outside.

2 What five precautions can be taken against accidental drowning?

3 Name four ways of helping to prevent accidents to children in cars.

4 When travelling by car, describe a type of restraint suitable for a child weighing (i) 6 kg, (ii) 16 kg, (iii) 26 kg.

5 a Who is responsible for seeing that a child travelling in a car is restrained: the child, the parent, or the driver?

   b Is it legal for a child to sit on the lap of an adult who is travelling in the front seat of a car? Suggest a reason for this rule.

   c When should a rear-facing seat not be used on a front passenger seat?

   d What shows that a child restraint conforms to safety standards?

6 Compare drawings A and B on p. 332. (i) Apart from the black cross, what is the difference between them? (ii) Why is B dangerous?

Weblink

For more information about car safety for babies, young children and during pregnancy visit:

www.nct.org.uk and search for 'car safety'.

Further activities

Extension

1 How would you change the numbered items shown in the garden scene below in order to make it a safe place for children, and why is each action necessary?

2 Look outside your own home and make a list of the hazards for a young child. How would you recommend dealing with each if a young child came to stay?

Investigation

a Using information from the Internet, newspapers, and experiences of family and friends, carry out a survey about accidents which have happened to children aged 7 years and under. This could be a group exercise.

b Use the information from the survey to create a database file. An example of a record for the file could be:

Time:	Morning
Age of child:	2 years
Place:	Kitchen
Article 1:	Cup
Article 2:	Hot water
Injury:	Scald
Body part:	Arm
Description:	Pulled cup of tea from table, hot tea spilt onto arm

c Use the database file to find out: (i) What types of injury happened in the garden? (ii) During what part of the day did most accidents happen?

CHAPTER 70

Safety on the roads

Accidents on the roads are the most common danger outside the home. In 2006, 17 children under the age of 8 years were killed or seriously injured every week on roads in the UK. Many more were injured to a lesser degree.

HOW PARENTS CAN HELP

Parents and carers can help prevent their children becoming involved in road accidents when they follow these instructions:

- Set a good example by always crossing roads in a careful way.
- Use walking reins or wrist straps for toddlers – never rely on holding a toddler's hand as he can pull free in an instant.
- Do not let young children out on the roads by themselves.
- Insist that a young child holds the hand of an adult when crossing a road.
- Make sure the child can be seen – when out in the dark, children should always wear light-coloured or reflective clothing, or carry a reflective bag.
- Make sure their child knows the Green Cross Code – go through the code every time the road is crossed until the child knows it.

WHY CROSSING THE ROAD IS DIFFICULT FOR YOUNG CHILDREN

Young children cannot cross safely because:

- being small, they cannot see over parked cars etc.
- they do not remember instructions for very long
- they have not yet learnt to be good judges of distance or of the speed at which the vehicles are travelling
- they do not yet understand how traffic behaves
- their minds may be occupied with other matters, e.g. running after a ball.

LEARNING ABOUT ROAD SAFETY

Road safety education needs to begin at an early age. The majority of serious accidents to child pedestrians and cyclists occur on roads where the children live.

The under-5s

From the time that children can walk, they need to be taught that pavements are for people and roads are for traffic. Adults with children set a good example when they cross roads correctly. While doing so, they should talk to the children about stopping at the kerb, and looking and listening for traffic before crossing the road.

5–6 years

The risk of a road accident increases when children start school. They are not yet old enough to be out on the roads by themselves and should be taken to and collected from school. They have reached the stage when they can begin to learn how to cross quiet roads on their own. They will need to be taught and then be frequently reminded of the **Green Cross Code**.

GREEN CROSS CODE

1. **Find a safe place to cross, then stop**. Safe places include Zebra and Pelican ('green man') crossings or where there is a traffic island or school crossing patrol (lollipop lady or man). If it is necessary to cross near parked cars, stop at the outer edge of the cars and look and listen carefully before continuing across.

2. **Stand on the pavement near the kerb.** Do not stand at the very edge of the pavement; traffic often passes closer than you think.

3. **Look all around for traffic and listen.**

4. **If traffic is coming, let it pass. Look all around again.**

5. **When there is no traffic near, walk straight across the road**. If you are not sure, do not cross. Always walk, do not run.

6. **Keep looking and listening for traffic while you cross.**

Stand near the kerb but not at the very edge

Walk straight across the road and keep looking and listening for traffic

7–9 years

Children over the age of 7 should be able to cross quiet roads alone. They should now learn, understand and remember the Green Cross Code. When they have done so, they will be better able to cross busy roads safely.

SAFETY FOR CYCLISTS

Children need both the experience of riding a bicycle and training in road safety before they cycle on roads. It is therefore recommended that a child under 9 years of age should not ride on the road unless supervised by a responsible adult. Children over 9 years of age should be accompanied until they have successfully completed a cycle training course.

When cycling a child should:

- keep both hands on the handlebars except when signalling
- keep both feet on the pedals
- ride in single file on cycle tracks and lanes, and when in traffic
- not carry anything which may affect balance or get tangled up with the wheels or chain
- not carry a passenger unless the cycle has been adapted to carry one
- use front and back lights and a red reflector at nights and in poor visibility
- use a bell when necessary as a warning.

A cycle helmet protects the head from injury if the child falls off the cycle. The helmet needs to fit securely and be comfortable

Bright clothing and fluorescent belts enable the cyclist to be more easily seen

The cycle needs to be the right size for comfort and safety

The saddle and handlebars need to be adjusted to the right height

The brakes and gears must work correctly

Lights and reflectors need to be kept clean and in good working order

The bell should be used when necessary to warn other road users that you are there

Tyres should be hard and not flat

Questions

1 Calculate how many children under the age of 8 years were killed or seriously injured on the roads of the UK in 2006.

2 Name six ways that parents can help to prevent their children from being involved in road accidents.

3 Give five reasons why it is difficult for young children to cross roads safely.

4 Describe how a child under 5 can learn about road safety.

5 Read through the six rules of the Green Cross Code. Then close the book and see if you can write out the main points from memory, in the correct order.

6 a Before the boy on the bicycle on p. 336 cycles on the road, what advice should he be given?

   b Give two items of clothing he can wear for safety.

   c Name three conditions of his bicycle which should be checked.

Weblink

The Think! Children website includes information and advice for parents on road safety with games and activities for children, and can be found in the 'Education' section at:

http://think.dft.gov.uk

Exercises

Exercises relevant to Section 7 can be found on p. 386.

Further activities

 Extension

a Study the picture below showing Sally and her father waiting to cross the road. (i) What can Sally see? (ii) What can her father see? (iii) Suggest possible reasons for the flashing indicator on the car. (iv) Are Sally and her father standing in a good position for crossing the road? Explain your answer.

b Sally's father is making crossing the road into a game by letting Sally tell him when it is safe or unsafe to cross. Imagine a conversation between them.

 Investigation

What can be done to prevent accidents? Carry out research in one particular area, for example, baby safety, design of nursery equipment, child safety in the kitchen, safety at playgroup, cycling safety, safety on local roads, water safety. Information can be obtained from RoSPA (see p. 273) and from safety officers of your local council. You could then make a display of good safety advice.

 Design

Use a video camera to make a short film about crossing the road safely which could be shown to young children.

 Child study

If the child is old enough to talk to you, find out what he or she knows about road safety.

CHAPTER 71

Looking after other people's children

People who look after children have an influence on the way they develop. It is therefore important for parents to choose with care those they ask to look after their children.

Why child care is needed

Families use child care for a number of reasons:

- the parents are working or studying
- one parent is ill and the other is working
- they are one-parent families and the parent goes out to work
- the parents need a break from the demands of child care
- children benefit from more contact with other adults and children
- children need to be cared for out-of-school and during school holidays
- the child may have special needs and require specialist care.

OFSTED (OFFICE FOR STANDARDS IN EDUCATION)

Ofsted is the government department that regulates Early Years child care in England. Before a person or organisation can provide day care for children under the age of 8 years, they must register with Ofsted. Ofsted will check that they are able to meet the required standards, set out the maximum number of children of different age groups that the provider can care for, place any restrictions on the premises where the care is provided, and carry out inspections.

If the children are aged under 5 years, child care providers must work within the EYFS (Early Years Foundation Stage framework (pp. 237–8)).

Different types of child care are run by local authorities (councils), voluntary organisations, private companies or individuals. Children may be cared for full-time or part-time and, generally, parents pay for the services they use. Child care providers fall into two groups – those that need to be registered with Ofsted and those that do not.

REGISTERED CHILD CARE PROVIDERS

Child care providers that need to be registered include:

- childminders
- playgroups
- day nurseries
- crèches
- out-of-school care schemes
- holiday care schemes
- respite care schemes.
- Sure Start Children's Centres

Childminders

Childminders must register if they look after children who are not related to them for more than two hours per day. The children range from 0–8 years and are usually cared for in the childminder's own home. The childminders have to take a child care course, have criminal record checks, face inspections and meet targets for EYFS. They will be inspected by Ofsted every year to ensure that acceptable standards of childminding are being maintained, and they must have documents to show that they are suitable people to look after children.

A good childminder:

- likes children and gives them the love and care that all young children need
- is healthy
- has a clean home
- has a safe, warm place for children to play and to rest
- has adequate toilet and kitchen facilities for the children
- takes them outside regularly, or has a garden in which they can play
- follows the EYFS (p. 237).

People who enjoy childminding find that it gives them:

- the pleasure and interest of working with children
- the satisfaction of doing important work for parents
- the chance to meet other families
- the opportunity to earn some money.

Choosing a childminder

When parents are looking for a childminder, they should:

- consider whether the childminder needs to live near their home, or their work, or on their way to work
- go to see several childminders before selecting one
- ensure that the childminder is registered.

When a child is unwell

Before taking a child who is unwell to a childminder or any other type of child care, the parents need to take into account the nature of the illness, how serious it is, whether it is infectious, and how much attention the child needs. Children who are ill may well need to stay at home.

Day nurseries

Day nurseries provide full- or part-time day care for children up to 5 years old. A few may take children under 6 months old. They are staffed by trained nursery nurses and children attend on a regular basis. Day nurseries may be run privately or by the council. Large factories, hospitals, colleges and offices sometimes run a day nursery for the children of their employees.

Crèches

A crèche is a place where parents can leave their children safely while they are busy. Creches are found in shopping centres, sport and leisure centres, colleges, and at conferences.

OTHER CARE SCHEMES

Out-of-school care schemes

These offer care to school-age children from the end of the school day until their parents can collect them. They might also offer care before school starts.

Holiday care schemes

These offer full-day care to school-age children during the school holidays, and may include playwork schemes.

Playwork

Playworkers plan, organise and take part in play and leisure activities for 4 to 16 year olds. They work in various settings, such as breakfast clubs, after-school clubs, mobile playbuses and holiday playschemes.

Respite care schemes

Day and overnight care is provided for families with children with special needs, particularly those with severe learning difficulties or serious illnesses. This allows the parents a break (respite) from the demands of care.

UNREGISTERED CHILD CARE PROVIDERS

Child care providers that do not need to register with Ofsted include:

- relatives
- friends
- nannies
- 'mothers' helps'
- au pairs
- baby-sitters.

Relatives

Relatives are grandparents, aunts and uncles, brothers and sisters. A child who is looked after by a relative will usually be in the care of a person the child knows well. As a result, there are less likely to be problems of getting used to strangers and to different surroundings and ways of doing things. Nowadays, grandparents or other relatives are often not able to help. They may be very busy people with jobs, or may live too far away. So the parents have to find someone else to look after their child.

Friends

Friends can make arrangements to look after each other's children. But if a friend acts as a childminder without registering, the friend may be breaking the law.

Nannies/ 'mothers' helps'

These are employed by parents to care for children, usually in the children's own homes. Nannies and mothers' helps may or may not have relevant childcare qualifications.

Au pairs

An au pair is a young person from abroad who, in order to learn the language, lives with a family, helping with the housework and looking after the children, in return for board and lodgings. Au pairs are unlikely to have child care qualifications and may not have had experience of young children.

BABY-SITTERS

Baby-sitters are people who look after children in the children's own homes while the parents are out. Although called 'baby-sitters', they may be required to look after children of any age. The parents are usually only happy to leave their child or children when they feel that the baby-sitter can cope with any situation which may arise. A sitter for a young baby needs to be able to comfort a crying child, change a nappy and give a bottle. However, for an older child, it is better if the sitter is someone the child knows and likes, who understands the behaviour of the child's age-group, and is agile enough to cope.

There are no legal recommendations on the minimum age for a baby-sitter, but RoSPA (Royal Society for the Prevention of Accidents) recommends that no one under the age of 16 should be left to care for an infant. However, parents can be prosecuted for wilful neglect if they leave a child unsupervised in a manner likely to cause unnecessary suffering or injury to health.

Baby-sitters provide a useful service. They allow parents to have a break from their children for a short while. This helps to remind them that they are partners as well as parents. They are able to do things together and to go to places where children would not be welcome. Having a break from their children now and then often helps parents to enjoy their children all the more. The children can also benefit from meeting new people, especially when they enjoy the baby-sitter's company.

Instructions for the baby-sitter

It helps baby-sitters to look after children if they are given information which includes:

- the child's usual routine
- the words the child uses when asking for a drink, or a special toy, or to go to the toilet
- where to find the first-aid kit
- what to do in an emergency – how to contact the parents, the neighbours, and the telephone number of the doctor
- where to find refreshments such as milk, fruit juice, biscuits
- how to use the television etc.
- the approximate time the parents are expected back.

Most baby-sitting is done in the evenings, so the baby-sitter will need to know the **bedtime routine**:

- the time for bed
- whether a light is to be left on or off
- whether the bedroom door is to be left open or shut
- the need for a favourite cuddly toy, a drink, cleaning the teeth, and perhaps a bedtime story.

During the daytime, the baby-sitter needs to know about meals, the rules about watching television, where the children are and are not allowed to play, bathtime, and so on.

Questions

1 a Give some reasons why families use child care services.

  b (i) Who regulates Early Years child care services in England?

    (ii) What does Ofsted do?

    (iii) List eight types of child care that need to be registered and six that do not.

2 a (i) When must a childminder register?

    (ii) What are the conditions to become a registered childminder

3 a What makes a good childminder?

  b What points should parents consider when choosing a childminder?

  c Should a child who is unwell be sent to the childminder?

4 a For which children are day nurseries intended?

  b Where may a crèche be found?

5 Describe a type of care scheme which operates (i) after school, (ii) during school holidays, (iii) for children with special needs, (iv) for play and leisure.

6 a Describe a baby-sitter.

  b Give three requirements for a baby-sitter for (i) a young baby, (ii) an older child.

  c In what ways may the parents benefit from leaving their children in the care of a baby-sitter?

7 a What useful information can be given to a baby-sitter?

  b When the baby-sitting is done in the evenings, what may the baby-sitter need to know about the bedtime routine?

8 When may parents be prosecuted for neglect?

Further activities

 Extension

1 A mother is looking for a childminder for her 3-year-old daughter Jane. Below is a list of questions the mother will ask herself.

  * Is the childminder a warm, welcoming person?

  * Does she have a stable routine so that Jane will quickly get used to new surroundings?

  * Will she give Jane nourishing food?

  * Will the discipline be firm but kind?

  * Are there toys to play with?

  * Is the place clean?

  * Are the home and garden safe for young children?

  * Is the childminder registered?

In your opinion how many of the answers to these questions need to be 'Yes' for the mother to be able to leave Jane with confidence? Give your reasons in each case. Add to the list some more questions that Jane's mother could ask.

2 Describe any baby-sitting that you have done. Say why you were needed to baby-sit. What information were you given? What problems did you have and how did you deal with them? Give a short talk on your baby-sitting experiences.

Further activities (continued)

 Discussion

It is said that children of working mothers do not suffer provided that the child has a stable, continuous and happy relationship with the person who cares for the child during the mother's absence. In what ways do you think that (i) the child can benefit, (ii) the mother can benefit?

 Investigation

Visit a day nursery, crèche, or day-care scheme to watch how new children settle in. What difficulties do they have? How are they helped to overcome these difficulties?

Weblinks

For more information on how Ofsted checks childcare standards, and which childcare providers do, or do not, need to be Ofsted-registered, visit:

www.direct.gov.uk

and search for 'Checking childcare quality and standards'.

For plenty of information on what to look for when choosing a nursery, visit:

www.babycentre.co.uk

and search for 'work and childcare'.

For guidelines on using baby-sitters, visit:

www.rospa.com

CHAPTER 72

Local authority care, fostering and adoption

Sometimes children do not live with their natural parents but are looked after by other members of their family, foster carers, adoptive parents, or in special children's homes.

CHILDREN LOOKED AFTER BY THE LOCAL AUTHORITY

Under *The Children Act* 1989 the main duty of the authority (through the Social Services department) is to keep families together. If it is not possible to keep the children with their parents, the possibility of the children being cared for by relatives will be explored. If this is also not possible, the local authority will make arrangements for the children to be accommodated in foster homes or special children's homes. Any arrangements which are made will take into account the wishes of the child (when possible) and the parents. Responsibility for the child will be shared between the parents and the local authority.

The local authority is given the right to look after children in one of two ways:

■ By **voluntary agreement with the parents** – the child is placed in accommodation as part of a plan which all interested parties agree is in the best interests of the child.
■ By a **court order** (statutory care) – a court compels the parents to hand over their child to be looked after by the local authority.

Why children are looked after

There are a number of reasons why children may be looked after by the local authority. These include:

■ The parents are unable to look after their children because of illness, family problems or difficulties with housing.
■ The children have been neglected or ill-treated and are likely to suffer serious harm if they continue to live at home.

The length of time that children are looked after by the local authority depends on the reason for them being separated from their families.

FOSTERING

Fostering is an arrangement for children to live in other people's homes. It is usually on the understanding that the children will return to their own homes to live as soon as possible. The foster carers are paid an allowance for food, clothing and general care, but they do not have any legal parental responsibility for the children.

Children stay with foster carers for varying amounts of time. It may be only for a few weeks while the mother is in hospital, or it may be for many months or even years. In some cases it may be considered appropriate for children to remain in their foster homes until they are grown up. When the children are with foster carers for a long time they can become very attached to the family. It may then be hard for them to part when the time comes for the children to return to their own homes.

The Children Act requires Local Authorities to be mindful of children's needs in respect of race, religion and culture when placing them in foster care or for adoption.

ADOPTION

Adoption is a legal process by which adults become parents of children not born to them. In all cases, adoption must be because it is in the best interests of the child, not the adults involved. The adoptive parents gain parental responsibility for the child, whom they are expected to support completely, although, in certain cases, financial support is available through an Adoption Allowance. The natural parents relinquish all parental responsibility.

It is becoming more common for adopted children to continue to have some contact with their natural parents and siblings even after they are adopted. Adoption agencies may act as a 'post box' so that letter-contact between adoptive and birth families can be facilitated but, at the same time, remain confidential.

Children offered for adoption

Few newborn babies are available for adoption these days, the reasons being:

- wider use of contraception and of termination of pregnancy mean that fewer unplanned babies are born
- changes in attitudes and increased help from the state have made it easier for single parents to bring up children on their own.

There are about 5,000 children across the UK needing adoption every year. These children are from a great variety of ethnic and religious backgrounds. Many are of school age and over half of them are in groups of brothers and sisters who need to be placed together. Some of the children have learning difficulties or are disabled, some will have been abused or neglected. All will have experienced distress and uncertainty and their resulting behaviour may be challenging. For this reason, many adoption agencies have Post Adoption Services that can help, advise and support adoptive families.

Why adults adopt

People may wish to adopt because:

- They are unable to have children of their own.
- They have children of their own but wish to enlarge their family and to help a child needing adoption.
- They are the grandparents or other relatives of a child whose parents are unable to bring them up because of death or other reasons.
- The mother marries a new husband and they jointly adopt her child so that all the family share the same surname.
- They are foster carers who apply to adopt a child they are fostering.
- They are a same sex couple who want a child.

Adoption agencies

People who wish to adopt usually do so through an adoption agency. There are a number of different agencies, and they each operate slightly differently and with their own priorities. Most agencies are part of the local authority's Social Services department but some are run by voluntary organisations.

The adoption process

People who want to adopt must be over 21 years of age, and can be heterosexual or gay, married or single. There is no upper age limit, but they do have to be able to look after a child throughout childhood and into adult life. They will be interviewed by the adoption agency to make sure that they are healthy, happy, have a stable relationship and really want to adopt a child.

When a child has been chosen, there is a probationary (trial) period to give the child and potential parents time to get to know each other. A social worker from the adoption agency visits the home from time to time to make sure the arrangement is working well. If the probationary period has been satisfactory, the adoption can then be made legal. From that moment, the adoptive parents have parental responsibility for the child. The natural parents no longer have any legal rights over the child.

Adopted children are entitled, if they wish, to see their full birth certificates when they reach the age of 18 years (or 17 years in Scotland). They may seek to make contact with their natural parents, but this is not always possible; for example the natural parents may refuse to have any contact, or their whereabouts may be unknown or they may have died.

Information about adoption can be obtained from the local Social Services department, or from British Agencies for Adoption and Fostering or from any of the adoption agencies.

Questions

1 a If it is not possible to keep families together, who may take care of the children?

   b Give the difference between a voluntary agreement with the parents and a court order.

   c Why may children need to be looked after by the local authority?

2 a What is the difference between fostering and adoption?

   b Which is a temporary arrangement?

   c Which involves legal rights over the child?

   d Which are the financial arrangements in both cases?

3 a Give five reasons why people may wish to adopt a child.

   b Who can apply to adopt?

   c Give two reasons why there are fewer babies for adoption these days.

   d What children are needing to be adopted?

4 a Why are people who wish to adopt interviewed first?

   b What happens during the probationary period?

   c What happens when the probationary period has been satisfactory?

Weblinks

For more information on local authority services for children in need, visit:

www.adviceguide.org.uk

For more information on the BAAF – British Agencies for Adoption and Fostering, visit their website at:

www.baaf.org.uk

Further activities

 Discussion

Discuss the 'tug-of-love' case below from the point of view of

a the child

b the foster parents

c the natural parent.

Tearful Debbie aged 7 clung to her foster parents Joan and Geoff Taylor before being taken by car from the house in Balesham Road which has been her home for the last four years. 'We are heartbroken – it's so cruel,' said Geoff, 'especially as we were hoping to adopt her soon, and this came out of the blue a month ago.'

Debbie was taken to her new home with her mother Sue Neil who had to give up Debbie when she lost her job and became ill. 'It was a very sad time, but all that's in the past,' she said. 'I'm now in a steady job and have a nice flat. Having Debbie back completes my happiness, and I think I can be a mum she will be proud of.'

The social worker dealing with Debbie's case said, 'We are confident Sue Neil can give her a good home and upbringing. It is her legal right to have Debbie back.'

Yesterday evening Mr and Mrs Taylor contemplated life without Debbie: 'She was such a joyful child, we can only hope she doesn't lose that. We're keeping her room just as she left it.'

CHAPTER 73

Children with special needs

Children with special needs are those who suffer from disabilities which affect their development by interfering with growth or the normal functioning of the body or the ability to learn. Disabilities can be the result of accidents or infections, or they can be congenital.

CONGENITAL ABNORMALITIES

A **congenital abnormality** is a disability which is present at birth. In some cases the disability is obvious from the moment the child is born, for example Down's syndrome or spina bifida. In other cases such as deafness or mild cases of cerebral palsy, the abnormality becomes apparent only when the child fails to develop in the normal way. Congenital abnormalities can be due to:

- **Abnormal genes or chromosomes** which the child inherits from the parents or which occur in the fetus for the first time. Examples include Down's syndrome, haemophilia and muscular dystrophy.
- **Abnormal development** in the uterus. Examples include 'hole in the heart', cleft palate and cleft lip, damage caused by the rubella virus, or by the effects of drugs, smoking or alcohol taken by the mother.
- **Brain damage** during development in the uterus or during birth. This may be caused by insufficient oxygen (**anoxia**) or a number of other reasons. The disability which results depends on the part of the brain which is damaged. For example, if the part controlling movement is damaged this results is cerebral palsy. If the part controlling intelligence is damaged, this results in learning difficulties.

DEVELOPMENTAL DELAY

Disabilities can delay development. For example, children who lack mobility will not be able to explore their environment to the same extent as they would if they could move around freely. Those who cannot communicate easily will fail to receive and understand the necessary information for their mental development.

A child with special needs may have one particular disability which affects development, e.g. deafness. More often, there is a combination of conditions which include physical disabilities and learning difficulties.

PHYSICAL DISABILITIES

A physical disability affects the body. Normal growth and development are prevented and the result is a physical disability, for example:

- cerebral palsy
- muscular dystrophy
- spina bifida
- cleft palate and cleft lip
- 'hole in the heart'
- congenital deformities involving the limbs such as a dislocated hip and club foot
- communication difficulties due to deafness or blindness
- damage to the body caused by accidents
- **dyspraxia** – clumsiness due to imperfect co-ordination of muscle movements by the brain.

LEARNING DISABILITIES

Children with learning disabilities are those whose brain fails to develop normally or is damaged by accident or infection. The condition results in a level of intelligence which is lower than average, and the child has difficulties in learning. The disability can be mild, moderate or severe and may be due to:

- congenital conditions such as Down's syndrome
- brain damage in the uterus by rubella or other viruses
- brain damage during birth
- brain damage caused by a blow to the head
- infection in childhood, e.g. meningitis.

Rebecca* (who has Down's syndrome)

*The names of the children on pp. 351–3, have been changed.

Intelligence Quotient (IQ)

One way of measuring people's intelligence is by their IQ. This is worked out from the results of intelligence tests. The average IQ is 100. People with an IQ of less than 70 will have learning difficulties.

Training

Much can be done to help people with learning difficulties by proper care and training. The training is aimed at developing as much independence as possible. Those with a mild or moderate disability can learn to lead independent lives. The more severely affected will always need to be cared for to some degree by the community.

SENSORY DISABILITIES

A sensory disability affects the sense organs, principally the eyes and ears. For example:

- visual impairment (see p. 150)
- hearing impairment (see p. 153).

LESSENING A DISABILITY

Most babies are born perfectly healthy and with no serious problems, but disabilities do occasionally occur. It is important to know about them because it may be possible to:

- **prevent them** – e.g. rubella damage, Rhesus damage
- **have surgery to repair them** – e.g. 'hole in the heart', cleft palate and cleft lip (at birth the top of the mouth and lips are not joined together in mid-line)
- **have treatment to improve the condition** – e.g. some cases of spina bifida
- **control the condition** – e.g. epilepsy
- **lessen the effects of the disability by early training** – e.g. Down's syndrome, cerebral palsy
- **prevent the development of a secondary disability** – e.g. early treatment of children with hearing loss will make it possible for them to speak.

CHILDREN WITH DISABILITIES

Down's syndrome

Rebecca* (p. 351) has Down's syndrome. She is very small for her age and, although she is growing slowly, she will not reach full adult size. Her intelligence is limited and learning is a slow process. Rebecca is much loved by her family. The care and training they give her means that she will learn to do far more than if she was in a family where they had no time or love for her.

Spina bifida

Chloe* was born with spina bifida. Her backbone did not develop properly, so part of the spinal cord was left unprotected and became damaged. This means that Chloe can walk only with the aid of crutches.

Muscular dystrophy (MD)

This is a group of genetic disorder that gradually weaken the body's muscles, and there are various forms. Michael* has Duchenne muscular dystrophy – a severe form that only affects boys, although girls can be carriers of the faulty gene that causes the disease. Signs started to appear when Michael was a toddler with the muscles used for walking being the first to be affected. They are now so weak that he needs a wheelchair. Muscles that are used to move the arms and hands and those that are needed for breathing are also now being affected.

Autism

John* is autistic – a disorder that develops in early childhood. People with autism have difficulty communicating with other people and engaging with the outside world. They have a limited range of activities that are carried out rigidly and there is resistance to any changes in daily routine and familiar surroundings. **Asperger's syndrome** is a less severe form of autism.

Chloe*

Michael*

John*

Cerebral palsy

Joanne* has cerebral palsy. This condition is a result of damage at birth to the part of the brain which controls muscle co-ordination. The problems which it causes depend on the extent of the damage. They range from very mild stiffness of one arm and leg to severe movement problems in all four limbs together with learning difficulties, vision and hearing difficulties.

Joanne*

EFFECTS ON THE FAMILY

Most children with special needs are cared for at home by their families. Generally, this is the best place for them as they have the same need for a happy family life as other children. They need to be treated in the same way – that is, cuddled, smiled at, talked to, played with, taken for outings, given opportunities to meet people, and so on.

When there is a child in the family with a disability it can mean a great deal of extra work and expense for the parents, especially if the child is unable to eat without help, unable to be toilet-trained, unable to move around unaided, or requires special equipment. Other children in the family will be less likely to feel neglected if they themselves are involved in helping to care for the special needs of their brother or sister.

Support for families

Families with a child with disabilities may need outside help including:

- practical advice for day-to-day care
- advice on helping the child from babyhood onwards to lead as full a life as possible
- advice on education
- contact with other families with similar problems – to find out how they overcome difficulties
- financial support for special equipment and other necessary expenses
- help with the ordinary domestic jobs
- childminding help so that the parents can have a break
- transport for outings
- help with holidays
- respite care.

The help can come from relations, friends, neighbours, health visitors, the family doctor, social workers, schools and teachers. There are also a large number of voluntary organisations which help children with disabilities and their families. A list of some of them is given on pp. 171–3.

CHILDREN WITH SPECIAL EDUCATIONAL NEEDS (SEN)

These children have learning difficulties that are significantly greater than those of their **peers** (other children in the same age group). *The Special Education Needs and Disability* Act 2001 asserts the rights of children with SEN to be educated in mainstream schools if the parents request it, and the interests of other children can be protected. This allows all children to have contact with each other, and for those with disabilities to be accepted as part of the community. If a mainstream school cannot provide all the help that a child needs, the local authority may carry out an assessment to find out what the child's needs are and how they can be met. The 2001 Act also protects SEN children against disability discrimination in schools and other educational establishments.

Special schools

These are for those children who require more individual care than is available in a mainstream school, or who require specialised teaching. Special schools differ from mainstream schools in that they have:

- **teachers specially trained** to teach children with disabilities.
- **assistants specially trained** to care for children with disabilities.
- **a higher ratio of teachers to children** so that the children can have more individual attention.
- **physiotherapists** to help children with physical disabilities to make as full a use of their muscles as possible – this helps mobility and increases independence.
- **occupational therapists** to help with training in the skills for daily living activities – dressing, feeding, personal care and hygiene.
- **speech and language therapists** to help those with speech and hearing difficulties.
- **suitable buildings** – corridors and doorways wide enough for wheelchairs, no stairs, specially designed chairs, lavatories, washing facilities and so on.

Questions

1 Who are children with special needs?

2 a A disability which is present at birth is called a – – – abnormality.

  b Give three ways in which such disabilities can occur, and name one example of each.

3 a Give two examples of the ways in which disabilities can delay development.

  b Can a child with special needs have one or more than one disability?

  c (i) Describe the difference between physical disabilities and learning difficulties.

    (ii) From the list of physical disabilities on p. 351 choose at least five and say which parts of the body they affect.

    (iii) What is the aim of training those with learning difficulties?

    (iv) Name two sensory disabilities.

4 Name types of disability which can be (i) prevented, (ii) treated, (iii) lessened by early training.

5 Describe the types of help which families with a child with disabilities often need.

6 In what ways will a special school differ from a mainstream school?

Weblinks

The ACE Centre helps children with disabilities to communicate by using technology – you can find out more about their work at:

http://ace-centre.org.uk

For advice, information and support for parents of disabled children, visit:

www.cafamily.org.uk/

For information on care, education, therapy and rehabilitation for children with multiple disabilities, complex health needs and acquired brain injury, visit The Children's Trust at:

www.thechildrenstrust.org.uk

Further activities

 Extension

1 For each of the five children with disabilities in the photographs on pp. 351–3.

  a Describe the disability.

  b Is the disability a physical disability or a learning disability or both?

  c Do you think the child will benefit more from attendance at an ordinary school or a special school? Give your reasons.

2 **a** Use a telephone directory and other sources of information to find out which of the voluntary organisations listed on pp. 371–3 have a branch in your district. If not, find the nearest branch. Say what each organisation does.

  b Add any other voluntary organisations that you know of to your list.

  c Which of the voluntary organisations you have listed aim in particular to help children with disabilities?

 Investigation

Where are the special schools in your district? Find out as much as you can about one of them. Comment on the ways in which the special school differs from a mainstream school that you know.

CHAPTER 74

Help for families

A great deal of help is available to parents in the form of advice, assistance and money from many different sources.

- Social Security benefits provide financial help through Jobcentre Plus.
- National Health Service (NHS) provides health care.
- Social Services give advice and assistance, but not money (except in rare cases).
- Sure Start.
- Voluntary organisations. Some are listed on pp. 371–3.

Jobcentre Plus provides help and advice on jobs and training for people who can work and financial help for those who cannot. This includes benefits and services for families

SOCIAL SECURITY BENEFITS FOR FAMILIES

Child Benefit

This is a cash payment for people looking after children. It is paid for each child under 16, or under 20 if still in full-time education. It is also paid for those aged 16–17 if they are registered for work, education or training.

Income Support

This benefit is given to those aged 16 and over who are on a low income and are either unemployed or working less than 16 hours per week on average – for example, lone parents responsible for children under 12, or people who are unable to work because they are ill or disabled.

Child Tax Credit

This benefit can help to pay for childcare for parents who are in work but on a low income.

Disability Living Allowance

This benefit for disabled people includes children with a severe physical or mental disability who need personal care or have trouble with walking.

MATERNITY AND PATERNITY BENEFITS

Statutory Maternity Pay (SMP)
Pregnant women who have worked for the same employer continuously for at least 26 weeks up to and including the 15th week before the baby is due can claim SMP. To qualify they must earn enough to pay National Insurance (NI) contributions. SMP is paid for up to 39 weeks. The employer must be informed at least 4 weeks before the mother plans to stop work.

Statutory Paternity Pay (SPP) and Paternity Leave (SPL)
May be available to husbands or partners who take time off work to support a new mother and baby.

Maternity Allowance (MA)
Working pregnant women may be able to claim this allowance if they do not qualify for SMP.

Sure Start Maternity Grant
If the mother or her partner are on a low income they may be able to claim this grant to help with the costs of buying things for the baby before or after it is born.

OTHER TYPES OF BENEFIT

Housing Benefit and Council Tax Benefit
These are paid by local councils to people on low incomes who need help to pay their rent and/or council tax.

Help with NHS costs
- Women who are pregnant or who have had a baby in the previous 12 months are entitled to free dental treatment and doctors' prescriptions.
- Children under 16, and those under 19 who are still in full-time education, are entitled to free dental treatment, prescriptions, eyesight tests.
- Families on low incomes may also be entitled to some help.

Jobseeker's Allowance (JSA)
This benefit is for unemployed people over the age of 18 who are actively seeking work. Those receiving Jobseeker's Allowance for 12 months (or after six months in some cases) must take part in Flexible New Deal. If you do have to take part and refuse, you may lose benefits.

New Deal
There are a number of New Deal programmes aiming to help people who are out of work to get a job including:
- New Deal for lone parents – a voluntary programme for people who are bringing up children on their own and are interested in working.
- New Deal for partners – the partners of parents who are on benefits may be able to join this voluntary programme and receive a range of help.

Free milk, infant formula, fruit, vegetables and vitamins
- The **Healthy Start** scheme provides vouchers for women who are pregnant or have a child under four years old, and are on low income. The vouchers can be used to buy liquid cow's milk, infant formula milk or fresh fruit and vegetables. Free vitamin supplements are also available.
- The **Nursery Milk Scheme** provides free milk for children under 5 for each day they attend approved day care facilities for 2 hours or more.

NATIONAL HEALTH SERVICE (NHS)

The NHS is a government-funded service which aims to help people keep well and to care for them when they are ill. The NHS provides a number of services specially for parents and children, for example:

- antenatal clinics
- preparation classes
- midwives
- maternity services
- Child Health Clinics
- family planning clinics
- genetic counselling
- Healthy Start scheme
- school health service.

School health service

School nurses provide the link between health and education services. They work with school children, their parents and teachers to detect health and social problems, and to help children develop a healthy lifestyle. They:

- organise health checks to identify any problems early
- arrange further help from other specialist agencies if needed
- complete immunisation programmes
- support teachers in providing health education within the national curriculum
- provide health advice to individual children and parents about any health problems, which may affect their schooling.

SOCIAL SERVICES

Every local authority has a Social Services department which provides a range of services for children and families. For example, they:

- provide fostering and adoption services
- supervise children in care
- deal with cases of child abuse
- provide housing for families.

SURE START

Sure Start is a government programme that aims to give the best start in life for every child. It covers children until they reach the age of 14, and up to the age of 16 for those with special needs. Sure Start is organised from Sure Start Children's Centres. There are about 3500 Sure Start Centres in England and every community has access to one. Wales, Scotland and Northern Ireland have similar schemes.

Sure Start Children's Centres

These are places where children under 5 years old and their families can receive integrated services and information from pregnancy until children start school. Many of the services are free. Child care has to be paid for, but help may be available through Tax Credits.

In cities and towns
Sure Start Centres are situated in places that are easy to reach by people living in the area, and the full range of services, or most of them, will be available there.

In rural areas
When people are widely spread over a large area, the Sure Start Centre will be an office which organises those services which are needed in the villages and small towns. A team of health visitors, midwives, family support workers, playworkers, child care workers, childminders, speech and language support workers, teachers and business support staff will visit the different places. An outreach service will be offered to those living in isolated areas.

What Sure Start Centres do

They provide integrated services for:

- health care
- child care
- early education
- parent and family support.

The service providers come from the statutory sector – NHS, Social Services and Early Education, as well as voluntary, private and community organisations and the parents themselves.

The facilities offered include:

- child and family health services, ranging from health visitors to breast-feeding support
- either high quality child care at the Centre, or advice on local childcare options
- advice on parenting
- advice on early education
- access to specialist services such as speech therapy
- healthy eating advice
- help with managing money
- help parents to find work or training opportunities through Jobcentre Plus.
- drop-in sessions and other activities for children and carers at the centre.

Other services that might be offered, depending on the need for them, are:

- dental treatment,
- physiotherapy
- advice from a dietitian
- a 'stop smoking' clinic
- expert advice for children with learning difficulties or disabilities
- parenting classes
- a Citizens Advice centre
- English language lessons.

Questions

1 a Name five sources of help for parents

 b What is the main difference between the help given by the Social Services and by Social Security

 c How are the voluntary organisations financed? See p. 371.

 d For each of these six sets of initials: CGF, CPAG, NSPCC, RoSPA, RNIB, ASBAH, give (i) the full name of the organisation, (ii) a purpose of the organisation, (iii) a drawing or description of the organisation's logo (use the web addresses on pp. 371–3 to find the logos).

2 a Who can claim the following benefits? (i) Child Benefit, (ii) Income Support, (iii) Working Tax Credit, (iv) Disability Living Allowance, (v) Housing Benefit, (vi) Jobseeker's Allowance, (vii) vouchers for milk, fruit and vegetables.

 b (i) What is the purpose of New Deal? (ii) Name two programmes to benefit families.

 c Give the meaning of (i) SMP, (ii) NI, (iii) SPP, (iv) JSA, (v) NHS.

 d Who may be able to claim a Sure Start Maternity Grant?

3 a List nine services which the NHS provides specially for parents and children.

 b What is the purpose of the School Health Service, and what does it do?

4 List ways in which Social Services can help children and families.

5 a (i) What is the purpose of Sure Start, (ii) what is the age group of the children?

 b What age group is catered for in a Sure Start Children's Centre?

 c Name the four services that are integrated in all Sure Start Centres.

 d (i) Name three statutory (state) service providers, (ii) four other types of service providers.

 e How does Sure Start Centre in a city differ from that in a rural area?

Further activities

 Extension

1 Some of the different places where parents may go for advice are shown in the drawings in this chapter. For each suggest the types of services for parents and/or children.

2 Read the extract below from a report of one case dealt with by the NSPCC.

 a What does NSPCC stand for?

 b Suggest reasons why (i) Mary was dejected, (ii) her children demanded constant attention.

 c What advice might the inspector have given Mary and Joey about applying for help from (i) Social Security benefits, (ii) Social Services, (iii) National Health Service?

 d Can you suggest any other voluntary organisations (see pp. 371–3) which might be able to help this family?

When the local inspector first called on Mary, he met a dejected young woman, seven months pregnant and who could not have weighed more than 6 stone.

Her three young children (aged 4, 3 and 2) by a much older man, demanded constant attention – something Mary just could not give them.

Help was desperately needed – for Mary's sake as well as the children's. The father of her next child, a man named Joey, was serving a six month jail sentence. Meantime, Mary had just moved into a house for which she was paying an exorbitant rent even though it was very damp and in poor repair. She had no friends or relations nearby and lived in constant fear of eviction.

Though the odds were very much against the family staying together once they were reunited, their trust in the inspector in helping them build up a home and plan for the future was such that after two years all is well. Joey has not returned to prison, and the children are all fit and happy. Mary has put on some weight and smiles once more.

Weblinks

For advice on benefits for pregnant women, families and children, visit:

www.adviceguide.org.uk

To search for the Sure Start activities available in your area, visit the Sure Start section at:

www.direct.gov.uk

For information on the Change4Life campaign that aims to help children and families to keep healthy, visit:

www.nhs.uk/Change4life

CHAPTER 75

Child abuse

Although most children grow up in happy, loving homes, some are abused – harmed – by their parents or other people. They may be deliberately hurt by the adults around them, or suffer neglect in families that cannot cope with their problems. Child abuse may happen in any kind of home and any type of family, rich or poor, black or white.

TYPES OF CHILD ABUSE

There are various types of abuse. They are:

- physical abuse
- neglect
- sexual abuse
- bullying
- emotional abuse
- domestic violence.

Most sexual abuse is carried out by men, but women are as likely as men to abuse children physically, emotionally or by neglect. The degree of abuse ranges from mild to severe, and an abused child usually suffers from more than one of the types listed above. For example, a child may suffer from harsh physical punishment (physical abuse) accompanied by neglect or indifference (a form of emotional abuse). Sexual abuse will undoubtedly involve emotional abuse.

PHYSICAL ABUSE

Physical abuse occurs when the child is deliberately hurt. It is also called **non-accidental injury** (NAI) and may be bruising, burns, bites, abrasions (grazes), or damage to the mouth region. It may also include broken bones or internal injuries caused by severe shaking.

Physical abuse occurs most often to children who cannot defend themselves – mainly babies and pre-school children, and also to older children with disabilities. Babies may be abused because they cry continually. The adult, unable to stand the noise any longer, loses self-control and shakes, beats or burns the baby. A toddler may be attacked because he has been 'naughty' and is being 'taught a lesson'. The adult suddenly loses control, lashes out and beats the child because she has wet her pants or soiled her clothes.

Signs of physical abuse

▪ Delay by the parents in seeking medical help when it is clearly needed.
▪ Injuries to the child for which the explanation given by the parent or child does not make sense. For example, a baby with small round burns on her bottom that are said to have been burned by a heater, when the burns are clearly inflicted by a cigarette.
▪ Injuries to areas of the body which are normally well protected, e.g. the armpits, the anus, behind the knees or on the inside of the thighs, may be signs of physical abuse.

SEXUAL ABUSE

Sexual abuse occurs when a child takes part in sexual activities. These include being:

▪ touched or fondled in a way that makes the child uncomfortable
▪ forced or lured to have sex
▪ encouraged to take part in sexual activities
▪ involved in pornography.

Sexual abuse of children is usually carried out by people the child knows – father or step-father, uncle, grandfather, or older brother, family friend or carer. Strangers are rarely involved.

Whatever form the abuse takes, the child is very often threatened or bribed to keep quiet, perhaps by being offered sweets or money. The adult may say, 'It's our little secret, and if you tell anyone, I will get into trouble'. The child may feel very guilty, and although anxious for the abuse to stop, is often afraid to tell anyone. The abused child may fear that the family will break up, the abuser sent to prison, that he/she will be blamed and removed from the family by the local authority.

EMOTIONAL ABUSE

Emotionally abused children are those who lack love and security and the company of friendly people – sometimes described as conditions of high criticism–low warmth. Such children feel so rejected and unhappy that their health and development may be affected and they fail to thrive. Examples of emotional abuse are:

▪ **when children are constantly ignored** – the people around them show no interest in them
▪ **when children are in constant fear** because of:

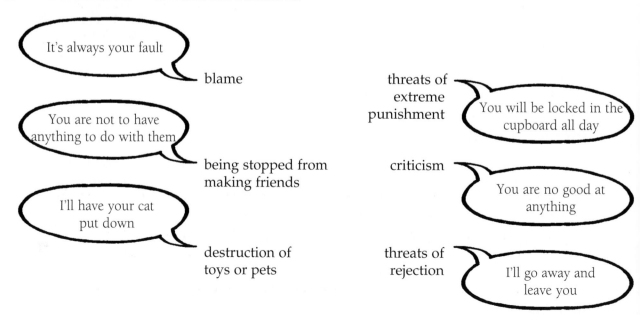

Emotional abuse is difficult to detect, but it may be suspected when a child fails to grow and develop properly for no obvious reason. The child's behaviour may indicate emotional disturbance, for example when her behaviour towards other people, particularly adults, is unnatural for the child's age.

CHILD NEGLECT

Child neglect can be physical and/or emotional. Children are neglected when they are not fed adequately, or not kept warm or clean, or when they are left alone for long stretches of time. Child neglect can be deliberate, for example locking a child out of the house, or keeping the child locked in the house on her own. More often, it is due to ignorance of how to bring up children, for example a mother not realising that children need to be fed at regular intervals because she herself only eats when she is hungry.

BULLYING

Bullying is being hurt, frightened or teased and can take place face-to-face, by mobile phone or on the Internet. It may be carried out by other children in school or outside of school. It may also be carried out by family members and by other adults. Children who are bullied may suffer health or sleeping problems, or not want to go to school, or pretend to be ill, to avoid for example:

- being called names or teased
- being pushed, hit, kicked or physically hurt
- having rumours spread about them
- being ignored and left out
- being threatened or intimidated
- having money and other possessions removed from them.

Bullying can also be part of other forms of physical, emotional and sexual abuse.

DOMESTIC VIOLENCE

Domestic violence happens in the home between adults who are family members or their partners. Children who witness domestic violence become distressed and their behaviour is affected. They may:

- become upset or withdrawn
- lack confidence and struggle at school
- suffer from health or sleeping problems
- become aggressive or show other behaviour problems.

WHERE TO GET HELP

A child or young person who has been abused, or is in danger, and wants to tell someone can:

- **Speak to an adult they can trust**, e.g. a teacher or youth leader.
- **Telephone CHILDLINE**: 0800 1111 (a freephone number). The line is open 24 hours a day every day of the year. The child does not have to give his or her name, and no action will be taken if the child does not wish it.
- **Log on to the website www.childline.org.uk** for a one-to-one chat with a counsellor or to send an email.

Parents, relatives, neighbours or others who suspect that a child is being neglected or abused should contact:

- **The NSPCC Child Protection HELPLINE:** telephone 0808 800 5000.
- **The local Social Services** – social workers investigate cases which come to their attention.
- **The police** – in cases of emergency where a child is in imminent danger.

ADVICE TO CHILDREN

Children should be warned not to go off with strangers, or to accept lifts or gifts from them. However, as most children who are abused already know their abusers, it is important for children to be taught to say '**NO**'.

Children need to be made aware that their body, and particularly their private parts, belong to them and not to anyone else. If anyone tries to touch them in a way which confuses or frightens them, children should say '**NO**'. They should then tell an adult whom they trust about what has happened.

Various books, videos and publications are available from Kidscape (p. 371) and the NSPCC (p. 372) to help in teaching young children about self-protection against abuse.

Questions

1 a Name six types of child abuse.

  b Who are the abusers likely to be?

2 a (i) Which type of abuse is also called non-accidental injury? (ii) Describe the form which this abuse may take.

  b To which children does physical abuse most often occur?

  c Give an example of an occasion when a baby may be abused.

  d Given an example of an occasion when a toddler may be abused.

  e Name three signs of physical abuse.

3 a (i) Who are most likely to be responsible when children are sexually abused? (ii) Name four forms which the abuse can take.

  b Why may abused children be threatened or bribed?

  c Why are they often afraid to tell anyone?

4 a (i) Describe emotionally abused children. (ii) How do they feel?

  b Give two main forms of emotional abuse.

  c Describe six things which a child may be in fear of.

  d When may emotional abuse be suspected?

5 a When may children be said to be neglected?

  b Give two reasons why child neglect may occur, with examples.

6 a (i) What is bullying, (ii) who may do the bullying, and how can bullying affect children?

  b Give examples of bullying.

7 (i) What is domestic violence, (ii) how does it affect children?

8 a Who can children contact to discuss their problems? Give three suggestions.

  b Who can parents or neighbours contact if they suspect that a child is being neglected or abused? Give three suggestions.

  c Describe the advice which children should be given to help protect themselves against abuse.

Further activities

 Extension

Watch a video for teaching children about self-protection. Write a report (i) describing its contents, (ii) giving your opinion of its usefulness in getting its message across.

 Discussion

The extensive publicity in recent years concerning child sexual abuse could make young children defensive against loving gestures from adults, and adults afraid of cuddling their children. To what extent do you think this is likely, and how can the correct balance of attitudes be achieved?

 Investigation

Study newspaper reports of at least two different cases of child abuse.

a In what ways did it appear that the children involved were abused.

b Who was the abuser(s)?

c What judgments were reached, and do you think they were fair?

 Design

Make an illustrated booklet for 4- to 7-year-olds to teach them about possible dangers from adults, and how to protect themselves. Use a suitable computer program to help, e.g. a word-processing and graphics program.

Weblinks

For information on the NSPCC, visit:

www.nspcc.org.uk

For advice on abuse and safety issues, such as emotional, physical and sexual abuse and also neglect, visit:

www.childline.org.uk

CHAPTER 76

The family and the law

There are some aspects of family life which are regulated by law. These include marriage, divorce and the legal duties of parents. In any 'domestic' proceedings which come before a court of law, the court's main concern will be the welfare of any child or children involved.

MARRIAGE

Marriage is a legal contract between two people of opposite sex. It seems to fulfil deep-felt human needs. This is shown by the fact that most people marry, and many of those who become divorced re-marry.

A marriage starts off with a ceremony – a wedding – during which a man and a woman are joined in a special kind of relationship – personal, legal, social, and sometimes religious.

Reasons for marriage

The reasons why people marry vary, but usually it is a combination of factors such as:

- love for each other
- the desire to share the future as a partnership
- the wish to have children within marriage
- financial benefits – two can live almost as cheaply as one
- legal considerations – marriage gives legal rights to the partners and their children, specially relating to property
- cultural reasons – to conform with the cultural pattern
- religious beliefs – to give the partnership a spiritual basis
- social status – to be recognised as a couple
- the romantic idea of a wedding
- because a baby is on the way.

Skills needed in a marriage

When two people live together they need to be able to:

- communicate with each other – listen to what is said, understand what is meant, and respond
- co-operate and reach decisions together
- care about and consider their partner
- modify their own behaviour so that it is acceptable to their partner.

Stress in marriage

No two people will agree all the time, and every marriage has its times of disagreement and stress. When there is a strong clash of personalities or the stress is continuous, one or both partners may feel that they should separate.

Reconciliation

When a marriage is in difficulties, a couple may wish to discuss their problems with, for example, a marriage guidance counsellor, in an attempt to hold the marriage together.

DIVORCE

Divorce is the legal ending of a marriage. This is a stressful time for the family, especially the children, who find the breakdown in the relationship between the parents distressing.

Divorce in England and Wales is granted on the basis of the irretrievable breakdown of marriage. There are currently five grounds for divorce which can be used as evidence:

- adultery
- unreasonable behaviour
- desertion
- two years' separation with consent
- five years' separation without consent.

The divorce court must be satisfied that the marriage has broken down irretrievably, and that both husband and wife have had sufficient time to consider whether the marriage can be saved. Couples are actively encouraged to seek counselling if there is a possibility of the marriage continuing. If this is not possible, they are advised to use a mediation service to help negotiate a settlement.

Divorce settlements

When a couple with children divorce there are a number of matters which need to be settled legally, such as:

- Who the children should live with.
- Who the children should have contact with. This includes arrangement for visits, and contact with grandparents.
- Division of property, including who should live in the marital home.
- Maintenance; financial support for the children is arranged, and financial support for the spouse is considered.

Civil partnerships

A civil partnership is a legal contract between two people of the same sex. It gives them equal treatment to married couples in a wide range of legal matters.

Cohabitation

Some couples prefer to live together (cohabit) without going through any form of ceremony. Cohabiting couples do not have the same legal rights and responsibilities as people who are married or have formed a civil partnership. Such couples may marry later, possibly when they intend to have children.

Child maintenance

Child maintenance is the amount of money that non-resident parents pay regularly as a contribution to the upkeep of their children. A non-resident parent (absent partner) means a parent who does not normally live with the child or children concerned. The parents can have a voluntary agreement on the amount of maintenance to be paid, or it can be arranged and administered by the Child Support Agency (CSA).

THE CHILDREN ACT 1989

This Act brought together for the first time nearly all aspects of the law relating to children. It came into effect in 1991. The main principles of the Act are:

- The welfare of the child is paramount (the most important factor) when any decisions are made, including court cases.
- Wherever possible children should be brought up and cared for within their own families.
- Children should be safe, and be protected by effective intervention if they are in danger.
- When dealing with children, courts should ensure that delay is avoided, and may make a court order only if it positively benefits the child.
- The views of children should be sought according to their age and understanding and they should be kept informed about what is happening to them.
- Parents with children in need should be helped to bring up their children themselves. This help should:
  - be agreed with parents
  - meet each child's identified needs
  - be appropriate to the child's race, culture, religion and language
  - be open to effective and independent representations and complaints procedures

 – be based upon effective partnership between a local authority and other agencies, including voluntary agencies.

Parental responsibility

Parental responsibility is defined as 'all the rights, duties, powers, responsibilities and authority which by law a parent of a child has in relation to the child and his property'. Examples of what is expected of parents include:

- not to harm, neglect or abandon their child (or children), i.e. to care for and show interest in the child
- to arrange appropriate education when the child is of school age
- to be financially responsible for the child
- to give physical and moral protection to the child
- to be legally responsible for the child's actions
- to maintain contact with the child.

Parents continue to have parental responsibility for their child, even when they are no longer living with them or are in care. The parents should be kept informed about their children and participate in decisions made about their child's future.

Official guardians

If a child is left without parents, an official guardian will be appointed to take on the role of the parents. Sometimes parents will have nominated someone to take on this role in their wills. The official guardian may be a relative, a close friend of the family, or Social Services, and must comply with the legal responsibilities of parents listed above.

THE CHILDREN ACT 2004

The Children Act 2004 places a duty on services to ensure that every child, whatever their background or circumstances, has the support they need to:

- be healthy
- stay safe
- enjoy and achieve through learning
- make a positive contribution to society
- achieve economic well-being.

THE CHILDCARE ACT 2006

This is the first piece of legislation dedicated solely to early years and child care. It is committed to give every child the best start in life and parents greater choice about how to balance work and family life. The Act places the following duties on local authorities in England:

For all children under 5 – high quality early learning and care and better access to early childhood services achieved by:

- the free offer of care and learning for parents of 3 and 4 year olds
- the new Early Years Foundation Stage which establishes a framework to support children's development and learning from birth to 5.

For working parents – a choice of a wide range of child care where they can be confident that their children will thrive and be well cared for, enabling them to have greater choices about balancing work and family life.

For local authorities – to secure, in partnership with the private and voluntary sector, sufficient child care for all parents who choose to work or are in training to:

- improve the well-being of young children, and reduce inequalities between them
- secure sufficient child care to enable parents to work
- provide information to parents about child care
- ensure that local child care providers are trained
- support the introduction of the Early Years Foundation Stage (EYFS) – a 'learning and development framework' for under-5s
- improve the outcomes of young children by providing better joined up and accessible early childhood services through Children's Centres.

CHILDREN'S PLAN 2007

In 2007 the government published the first ever *Children's Plan*. It recognised that parents bring up children, not the government, but that sometimes families needed extra help and support. The *Plan* is a vision for change to make England the best place in the world for children and young people to grow up. It put the needs and wishes of families first, setting out clear steps to make every child matter.

Questions

1 **a** What is a marriage?

   b Give some reasons for marriage. Place them in what you consider to be their order of importance.

   c Suggest some skills needed in marriage.

2 **a** What is divorce?

   b What are the grounds for divorce?

3 When divorce takes place, which four matters need to be settled legally?

4 What is meant by (i) a civil partnership, (ii) cohabitation?

5 What is child maintenance, and who administers it?

6 What does *The Children Act* 1989 say about:

   (i) the welfare of the child,

   (ii) where children should be brought up,

   (iii) safety,

   (iv) the views of children.

7 What is meant by parental responsibility?

8 When is an official guardian appointed?

9 What is the purpose of the (i) *The Children Act* 2004, (ii) *The Children's Plan* 2007?

10 **a** Who is *The Children Act* 2006 dedicated to, and why?

    b What are its aims for: (i) children under 5, (ii) working parents?

    c What duty does it place on local authorities?

Further activities

 Discussion

Discuss possible causes of stress in a marriage.

 Investigation

Find out about the work done by the counselling organisation Relate p. 372.

Exercises

Exercises relevant to Section 8 can be found on p. 387.

List of voluntary organisations

There are a large number of organisations dealing with particular aspects of child welfare; some of them are listed below. Each organisation has its own aims and rules and most are financed by voluntary contributions although, in some cases, the government may give a grant or subsidy towards running costs.

Association for Spina Bifida and Hydrocephalus (ASBAH)

www.asbah.org

ASBAH serves people with spina bifida and hydrocephalus and their families in the UK through a network of professional advisors.

Booktrust

www.booktrust.org.uk

Booktrust encourages people of all ages and cultures to discover and enjoy reading.

British Agencies for Adoption and Fostering (BAAF)

www.baaf.org.uk

Gives information and advice on adoption and fostering.

Child Growth Foundation (CGF)

www.childgrowthfoundation.org

An organisation that offers help and advice to parents with a child who has a diagnosed or suspected growth problem.

Child Poverty Action Group (CPAG)

www.cpag.org.uk

CPAG is the leading charity campaigning for the abolition of child poverty in the UK and works for a better deal for low-income families and children.

CHILDREN 1st

www.children1st.org.uk

CHILDREN 1st works with children and families in Scotland to help them change their lives for the better.

GINGERBREAD

www.gingerbread.org.uk

This organisation for one-parent families supports single parents and their children.

ICAN

www.ican.org.uk

ICAN supports children with communication difficulties by helping in the development of speech, language and communication skills.

Kidscape

www.kidscape.org.uk

Kidscape works to keep children safe from abuse. It offers a variety of resources dealing with bullying and child sexual abuse for use by parents, students and child-care workers.

Muscular Dystrophy

www.muscular-dystrophy.org

This organisation supports those with muscular dystrophy (MD) and other muscle diseases, and funds scientific research.

The National Autistic Society (NAS)

www.nas.org.uk

NAS provides individuals with autism and their families with help, support and services that they can access, trust and rely upon and which can make a positive difference to their lives. NAS provides day and residential centres for the support, education and training of children and adults with autism.

The National Childbirth Trust (NCT)

www.nctpregnancyandbabycare.com

NCT offers antenatal and postnatal courses, local support and reliable information to help all parents though pregnancy, birth and the early days of parenthood.

National Childminding Association (NCMA)

www.ncma.org.uk

NCMA works with registered childminders, nannies and other individuals and organisations to ensure that families in every community in England and Wales have access to high quality home-based child care, play, learning and family support.

National Children's Bureau

www.ncb.org.uk

An organisation dedicated to improving the health and well-being of all children and young people.

The National Deaf Children's Society (NDCS)

www.ndcs.org.uk

NDCS provides services for deaf children and campaigns to break down educational and other barriers that they face.

National Society for the Prevention of Cruelty to Children (NSPCC)

www.nspcc.org.uk

The NSPCC works to end cruelty to children in the UK by listening to them, by helping them and by standing up for their rights. (p. 364 re HELPLINE)

PLAYWORK

www.skillsactive.com/playwork

Playwork aims to improve the quality and quantity of play provisions for children and young people in the UK by providing information, training and support to individuals, groups and organisations.

Pre-School Learning Alliance

www.pre-school.org.uk

This organisation provides practical support to Early Years settings and involves parents and families in all aspects of their work.

Relate

www.relate.org.uk

Relate offers advice, relationship counselling, sex therapy, workshops, mediation, consultations and support face-to-face, by phone and the website.

Royal National Institute for the Blind (RNIB)

www.rnib.org.uk

RNIB offers advice and practical support for anyone with a serious sight problem to help them lead independent lives.

The Royal National Institute for Deaf People (RNID)

www.rnid.org.uk

RNID supports people in the UK who are deaf or hard of hearing.

The Royal Society for the Prevention of Accidents (RoSPA)

www.rospa.com

RoSPA is actively involved in the promotion of safety and the prevention of accidents in all areas of life – at work, in the home, on the roads, in schools, at leisure and on (or near) water.

Save the Children

www.savethechildren.org.uk

Save the Children works to improve children's lives in the UK and across the world.

SCOPE

www.scope.org.uk

Provides services for children and adults with cerebral palsy including care, education and training. Promotes public awareness of attitudes to disability. Their vision is a world where disabled people have the same opportunities to fulfil their life ambitions as non-disabled people.

Glossary

Abuse the deliberate ill-treatment of other people. Abuse can be physical, emotional, sexual or neglect

Acute lasting a short time

Additives substances that are added to food to preserve it or to change it in some way

Adenoids patches of lymphatic tissue behind the nose

Adoption the legal process by which adults become parents of children not born to them

AIDS (Acquired Immune Deficiency Syndrome) a disease caused by infection with HIV

Allergy reaction by the body to a particular substance

Ambidextrous can use both hands with equal ease and ability

Amniocentesis a procedure for obtaining a small sample of amniotic fluid to test for abnormalities

Ammonia dermatitis a cause of nappy rash

Anaemia a shortage of haemoglobin – the red substance in blood which carries oxygen

Antenatal care care of women during pregnancy

APGAR Score used to assess the health of a new-born baby by evaluating 5 vital signs: Appearance, Pulse, Grimace, Activity, Respiration

Antibiotics medicines for treating diseases caused by microbes, usually bacteria, some fungi, but not usually viruses

Antibodies substances in the body that can destroy germs

Antisocial behaviour behaviour that is harmful or annoying to others

Asperger's syndrome a less severe form of autism

Asthma a lung condition with wheezing, shortness of breath and coughing

Athlete's foot fungal infection of the feet

Autism great difficulty with communication and social relationships

Balanced diet a diet that contains appropriate amounts of all the necessary food substances for health and growth

BCG vaccine protects against tuberculosis

Blindness the inability to perform any task for which eyesight is essential; most blind people have some awareness of light

BMI (Body Mass Index) a guide to a healthy weight

Bonds of attachment strong feelings of attachment that children develop for the people who have the most meaning to them

Bookstart a national programme that provides books for babies

Caries tooth decay

Carrier a person who can pass on a disorder to others without showing symptoms of that disorder

Cerebral palsy a result of damage at birth to the part of the brain which controls muscle co-ordination

Child abuse any form of neglect or physical, emotional or sexual maltreatment of a child

Child Benefit a cash payment for people looking after children

CHILDLINE – 0800 1111 a free, confidential helpline for use by children and young adults in the UK who have been abused or are in danger

Childminder a person who cares for children 0–8 years old and who is not a close relative

Child neglect when a child is not fed adequately or kept warm, clean and safe, or is left alone

Children with special needs those who have disabilities which handicap their development, growth or normal functioning of the body or the ability to learn

Chromosomes thread-like structures in the nucleus of the body's cells that contain genetic information (DNA) for the development and functioning of the whole body

Chronic lasting a long time

Circumcision the removal of the foreskin of the penis by surgery

Coeliac disease the inability to digest gluten in wheat and some other cereals

Cognitive development (intellectual development; mental development) development of the mind – the thinking part of the brain used for recognising, reasoning and understanding

Colic abdominal pain which comes and goes; it is a common cause of crying in the first three months

Colostrum yellowish milky fluid secreted by the breasts immediately before and after giving birth

Congenital abnormality a disability which is present at birth

Conjunctivitis an eye infection

Contraception the deliberate prevention of pregnancy

Convulsions fits

Cot death (Sudden Infant Death Syndrome; SIDS) sudden unexpected death of an apparently healthy baby for which no cause can be found

Croup a harsh cough and noisy breathing; it occurs in children up to the age of 4 years

Culture the way of life of a group of people including their language and customs

Deficiency disease due to the shortage or absence of a particular item in the diet

Dehydration a shortage of water in the body

Delivery giving birth to a child

Development refers to an increase in abilities (what a child is able to do)

Diagnostic test to find out whether a person has a disease or not

Disability difficulty in carrying out or inability to carry out normal everyday activities because of physical or mental problems

Disability Living Allowance a cash benefit for disabled people, including children, who need personal care or have trouble with walking

Doppler a hand-held ultrasound machine

DNA deoxyribonucleic acid, the material of which genes and chromosomes are composed

Down's syndrome a disorder caused by having 47 chromosomes instead of the normal 46

DTaP/IPV/Hib the 'five-in-one' vaccine against diphtheria, tetanus, whooping cough (pertussis), polio and Hib (Haemophilus influenzae, serotype b)

Dyslexia difficulty in reading, writing and spelling

Ectopic pregnancy when a fertilised egg becomes implanted in a Fallopian tube

Eczema patches of dry, scaly skin which become red and slightly inflamed and may weep

EDD estimated date of delivery

Embryo a developing baby during the first seven weeks after conception

Emotional development learning to control feelings

Emotions feelings

Environment the surrounding conditions

Epidural anaesthetic an injection into the lower part of the spine to stop pain

Ethnic group people with the same racial origins and cultural traditions

Extended family a large family group which includes grandparents, parents, brothers, sisters, aunts, uncles and cousins

EYFS (Early Years Foundation Stage) standards for care and learning for children aged 0–5 years

Faeces (or faeces; stools; motions) solid waste which comes from the bowel

Family a group of individuals who live together and are related by blood, marriage or adoption

Family planning (birth control) taking action so that only wanted babies are born

Fertilisation when a sperm and an egg join together

Fetus (or foetus) a baby from 7 weeks until birth

Fever higher than normal body temperature

Fibre (roughage) indigestible matter in food; important for normal functioning of the intestines

Fits convulsions

Folic acid one of the B vitamins, particularly important in the baby's early development

Fontanelle soft spot on the top of a baby's head

Foster families families who care for children who are not related to them

Fostering an arrangement for children to be cared for in other people's homes

Fracture a broken bone

Full-term a baby born after 38 weeks of development

Gastro-enteritis inflammation of the stomach and intestines resulting in vomiting and diarrhoea

Gender (sex) male or female

Gene a tiny section of a chromosome that affects a particular part of the body. Genes are inherited from parents

Genetic counselling giving expert advice on the likelihood of a disease being passed from parents to children

Germs (pathogens) mainly bacteria and viruses

GIFT (Gamete Intra-Fallopian Transfer) a fertility treatment

Gifted children those with high ability in many subjects or who are talented in a particular area

Gluten a type of protein found in some cereals which a few babies are unable to digest

Green Cross Code six simple rules to help children learn to cross roads safely

Growth an increase in size

Gynaecologist a doctor who specialises in the functions and diseases of the female reproductive system

Hearing impairment deafness

Heartburn a strong burning sensation in the chest due to stomach acid passing up into the oesophagus (gullet)

Hib (Haemophilus influenzae type B) causes a range of illnesses including a dangerous form of meningitis

HIV (human immunodeficiency virus) a virus which breaks down the body's immune system, often leading to AIDS

Hormone a substance produced in one part of the body and carried in the bloodstream to affect another part of the body; hormones are produced in endocrine glands

Hot cot a crib used to keep premature babies warm

Hypothermia low body temperature

ICSI (Intra-Cytoplasmic Sperm Injection) a fertility treatment

Immunisation injection with a vaccine to protect the body against an infectious disease

Immunity the ability of the body to resist infection

Income support a benefit given to those aged 16 and over who are on a low income or are unemployed

Incubator a crib in which a premature baby is kept in a controlled environment and protected from infection

Infertility inability to produce children

Intellectual development development of the mind

Kwashiorkor a disease of severe malnutrition

Lanugo a fine layer of hair that may cover the skin of a baby who arrives early

Learning disability difficulty in learning and remembering

Listeria a bacterium in some uncooked foods that can cause a dangerous disease (listeriosis) if it occurs in pregnancy

Malnutrition a condition caused by insufficient food, too much food or an unbalanced diet; it leads to obesity, starvation or deficiency diseases

Manipulation using the hands

Masturbation handling the genitals for pleasure

Maternity Allowance pregnant women who are in work may be able to claim this allowance if they do not qualify for Maternity Pay

Maternity Grant for families on low income to help with the costs of buying things for the baby

Maternity Pay for pregnant women who have worked for the same employer continuously for six months

Meningitis inflammation of the membranes covering the brain and spinal cord

Menopause the stage when menstruation ceases and pregnancy is no longer possible.

Menstruation a 'period' – a discharge of blood from the uterus that takes place about once a month unless pregnancy has begun

Midwife a nurse who is specially trained in pregnancy and childbirth

Milia small, whitish-yellow spots on the face of newborn babies, particularly the nose

Minerals substances like calcium and iron which occur naturally in the earth; fifteen are essential in the diet

Miscarriage (spontaneous abortion) the fetus is expelled from the womb before it is able to survive on its own

MMR a vaccine to protect against Measles, Mumps and Rubella

Moral development the development of moral values and standards of behaviour based on respect for other people

Multicultural society contains people of many different ethnic groups – people of differing races or countries of origin.

Nausea feeling sick

Neonatal from birth to 4 weeks

Neonatal audiological screen test used for babies at high risk of deafness

New Deal programmes to help people who are out of work to get a job

NHS (National Health Service) provides health care to help people when they are ill and keep them well

Non-accidental injury (NAI) physical abuse

Non-verbal communication communication without words

NSPCC (National Society for the Prevention of Cruelty to Children) a charity specialising in the protection of children

Nuchal translucency scan measures the amount of fluid in the nape of the neck of a fetus to test for abnormalities

Nuclear family consists of parents and their children

Nutrients substances derived from food that are essential for life

Obese fat

Obstetrician a doctor who specialises in pregnancy and childbirth

OFSTED (Office for Standards in Education) regulates and inspects the care and education of children and young people

Ovum egg; plural – ova

Paediatrician a doctor who specialises in the care of children from the time they are born
Parasites organisms that live on or in the body and obtain their food from it
Parental responsibility all the rights, duties and responsibilities which, by law, parents have for
    their child
Paternity Pay and Paternity Leave time off and pay for men with new babies
Peers other children in the same age group
Pelvic floor the floor of the abdomen
Perinatal from the 28th week of pregnancy to 1 month after birth
Pertussis whooping cough
Physical abuse harm caused by physical mistreatment such as punching, kicking, jostling,
    pinching
Physical development development of the body
Physical disability any problem with the body that has an adverse, long-term effect on the
    ability to carry out day-to-day activities
Pinard a type of ear trumpet that magnifies sounds made by the baby's heart
PKU (phenylketonuria) a rare disorder that damages the brain and results in learning difficulties
Plaque an almost invisible layer that forms on teeth
Pre-conception care aims to increase the chances of having a healthy baby
Pre-eclampsia (toxaemia of pregnancy) a condition that occurs only in pregnancy and can be
    fatal to the baby and the mother
Pregnancy the process that occurs between conception and birth
Premature see pre-term
Pre-school the stage before children attend primary school, usually the age-stage 2½ to 5 years
Pre-term (premature) a baby born before 37 weeks
Prone lying face downwards
Pro-social behaviour behaviour that involves others with sharing, helping and caring
Puberty the stage during which the sex organs mature

Race Relations Act 1976 makes racial discrimination unlawful in employment, training and
    housing, education, and the provision of goods, facilities and services
Rash an outbreak of red spots or patches on the skin
Reflex actions movements that are inborn and made automatically without thinking
Regression reverting to an earlier stage of behaviour
Relationships personal links with other people
Rhesus factor a substance that individuals may, or may not, have in their blood. Important in
    blood transfusion and in babies who are rhesus incompatible with their mothers
Rickets a disease where the bones of children are soft and imperfectly formed due to a lack of
    vitamin D
Rubella German measles

Scabies (itch mite) a parasite that lives in the skin and causes extreme irritation
Screening test a routine test carried out on a large number of people to find those individuals
    who have a particular disease or are at risk of developing that disease
Self-concept 'who you think you are' – a combination of self-esteem and self-image
Self-confidence believing that you can cope easily with people and situations
Self-esteem (self-respect) means valuing yourself as a person
Self-image a mental picture of what you think you look like and how you behave
Self-reliance not needing outside help or support

SEN (Special Educational Needs) refers to children who have learning difficulties or disabilities that make it harder for them to learn or to access education

Sensory disability a disorder of one of the senses – sight, hearing, smell or taste

Shared-care families families where the parents live in separate homes and the children spend part of the week living with one parent and the rest of the week with the other

SIDS (Sudden Infant Death Syndrome) see cot death

Social development (socialisation) learning to mix easily with other people

Social Security a system that gives financial help in times of unemployment, illness or old age

Social Services services that offer advice and assistance, but not money

Social skills skills that make behaviour acceptable and pleasing to other people

Special schools for those children who require more individual care or specialised teaching than is available in a mainstream school

Spina bifida congenital disease where the backbone is not fully developed, leaving the spinal cord unprotected and liable to damage

Statutory service – a service provided by government laws, e.g. the NHS and Social Services

STI sexually transmitted infection

Stools (faeces; the motion) solid waste which comes from the bowel

Sure Start a government programme that aims to give the best start in life for every child

TB tuberculosis

TENS (Transcutaneous Electrical Nerve Stimulation) a method of relieving pain

Temper tantrum a period of uncontrolled rage

Termination of pregnancy abortion

Tetanus also called lockjaw, a disease due to an infection

Thrush a fungal infection which causes white patches on the tongue and mouth

Toddler a child from 1 to 2½ years old

Toxocara roundworms which infect dogs and cats: can be dangerous to children if they become infected

Toxoplasmosis – a rare disease that can be caught from cat faeces and soil contaminated by faeces; can be dangerous to unborn babies

Urticaria ('nettle rash'; hives) a skin rash

Vaccination giving a vaccine

Vaccine a substance that gives temporary or permanent immunity to a disease

Varicella chicken pox

Varicose veins veins which have become stretched and swollen

Vegans people who do not eat any food that comes from animals

Vegetarians people who do not eat meat or fish, but their diet can contain milk, milk products and eggs

Verbal abuse name-calling, teasing, racial insults

Vernix a greasy, white substance that covers an unborn baby's skin and may be present at birth

Verruca a wart on the sole of the foot

Visual impairment blindness

Vitamins substances essential to keep the body healthy; needed in very small quantities

Voluntary organisations (charities) those financed by donations of money

Vomiting being sick

Weaning the gradual changeover from a diet of milk to a diet containing a variety of foods, both solid and liquid

Working tax credit a benefit to help pay for child care for parents who are in work but on a low income

Exercises

SECTION 1 FAMILY AND HOME

1. a In general, during the last 60 years families in Britain have become smaller. Suggest **two** reasons for this. [2]

   b Suggest **four** factors which a couple should take into account before starting a family. [4]

   c Give **two** ways in which watching television can help a child's speech development. [2]

   d Give **two** ways in which watching television can hinder a child's speech development. [2]

   e Explain the difference between kinship and friendship. [2]

   f Give **four** reasons why a family may be unhappy. [4]

   g Give **four** factors which can help to make family life happy. [4]

   h List **five** responsibilities of parenthood. [5]

   i List **five** rewards of parenthood. [5]

2. Contraception[1]: by method used:

Great Britain	Percentages			
	1976	1986	1996	2003
Non-surgical				
Pill	29	23	25	25
Male condom	14	13	18	23
IUD	6	7	4	4
Withdrawal	5	4	3	3
Injection	-	-	1	3
Cap	2	2	1	1
Safe period	1	1	1	1
Spermicides	-	1	-	-
Surgical				
Female sterilisation	7	12	12	11
Male sterilisation	6	11	11	12
At least one method	68	71	73	75

[1]By women aged 16 to 49, except for 1976 which is for women aged 18 to 44.

Source: Family formation Survey and General Household

Survey: Office for National Statistics © Crown copyright material is reproduced with the permission of the Controller of HMSO and the Queen's Printer for Scotland

Use the information in the table to answer the following questions.

a Since 1976, which two methods have remained **(i)** most popular, **(ii)** least popular? [4]

b (i) What is meant by the 'safe period'? (ii) Give **one** advantage and **one** disadvantage of this method. [3]

c (i) What was the percentage increase between 1976 and 2003 in the use of contraception? **(ii)** What percentage was not using any method of contraception in 2003? **(iii)** Suggest three reasons for not using contraception. [5]

d Were more men using contraception in 2003 than in 1976? Explain how you arrived at your answer. [5]

e Give **four** possible problems caused by unplanned parenthood. [8]

3. a Describe **three** ways in which having a baby might change the parents' lifestyle. [3] AQA

4. A family is the basic unit of society.

   a Give **three** factors a couple could consider before starting a family. [3] OCR

Note: OCR questions are from OCR Home Economics: Unit B013: Principles of Child Development Specimen Paper; for the specification for first teaching in 2009; AQA questions are from AQA Home Economics: Child Development Specimen Paper for the specification for first teaching in 2009

SECTION 2 BECOMING A PARENT

1 a Name **two** early signs which might indicate that a woman is pregnant. [2]

   b Give **two** reasons why an expectant mother needs a well-balanced diet. [2]

   c State **four** minor health problems which often occur during pregnancy. [4]

   d State **two** advantages of a mother having her baby in hospital. [2]

   e What is an antenatal clinic? [1]

   f State **two** reasons why a baby may need to be born by Caesarian section. [2]

   g Give **two** functions of the umbilical cord. [2]

   h Give **two** reasons for testing the blood of an expectant mother. [2]

   i Why is regular testing of urine of an expectant mother necessary? [2]

   j A pregnant mother is advised not to smoke. State **two** ways by which smoking can harm the unborn child. [2]

   k What is the most likely sign of a threatened miscarriage? [1]

   l How many chromosomes are there in **(i)** an unfertilised egg, **(ii)** a normal body cell? [2]

   m What is the difference between 'baby blues' and postnatal depression? [2]

   n Explain what is meant by **(i)** Rhesus factor, **(ii)** induction. [2]

   o **(i)** When is the postnatal examination held? **(ii)** Give two reasons why this examination is important. [3]

   p Name **three** ways in which the arrival of a baby changes the daily life of the parents. [3]

2 Describe how an egg from the ovary develops into a fetus in the uterus. [10]

3 a Name **four** benefits and services available to pregnant women. [4]

   b Describe the roles of the midwife and health visitor in the care of mothers and babies. [8]

   c In what ways can regular attendance at clinics benefit both the mother and her baby? [4]

4 a **(i)** Name parts 1–5 of the diagram below. **(ii)** State what happens to each of the parts during childbirth. [10]

   b **(i)** Are the twins identical or fraternal? Give a reason for your answer. **(ii)** How do the twins obtain food and oxygen while in the uterus? [4]

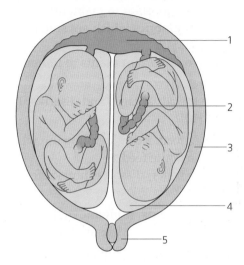

5 Hormones play a very important part in controlling the menstrual cycle, pregnancy, birth and breast-feeding.

   a **(i)** What are hormones? **(ii)** How do they move around the body? [2]

   b **(i)** Name **four** hormones and give **one** function for each. **(ii)** Which two hormones help in controlling the menstrual cycle? [10]

6 a What is the difference between pre-conceptual care and antenatal care? [1]

   b Explain how and why pre-conceptual care is important when planning a baby. [6]

   c Name **two** different types of drug-free pain relief. [2]

   d Suggest **three** ways a birth partner can help during labour. [3] AQA

SECTION 3 CARING FOR BABIES

1 a What is the usual cause of nappy rash? [2]
   b State **two** safety checks which should be made before buying a second-hand pushchair. [2]
   c How can a mother recognise 3-month colic? [2]
   d (i) What is a suitable room temperature for a young baby's bedroom? (ii) Why is it important to maintain this temperature? [3]
   e Select **four** fabrics which are suitable for baby clothes, giving a reason in each case. [4]
   f Give **two** important points to remember in preparing for baby's bathtime. [2]

2 Compare the advantages and disadvantages of disposable and towelling nappies. [10]

3 Preparing a feed. Add the following words to complete the instructions for preparing a bottle feed:
   boiled; cap; water; dissolve; hot; knife; milk powder; scoop; sterilising; teat; wash; wrist.

   (i) – – – your hands. (ii) Remove the bottle from the – – – solution. Rinse with boiled – – – (iii) Measure the required amount of warm, previously – – – water into the bottle. (iv) Add the required amount of – – -to the bottle, levelling off each – – – of powder with a clean, dry – – – (v) Place the – – – on the bottle and shake well to – – – the powder. (vi) Place – – – on the bottle. (vii) Before feeding, shake a few drops of milk on to the inside of your- – – to make sure that the milk is not too – – – for the baby. [12]

4 a Name **three** pieces of equipment essential for a newborn baby. [3] AQA
   b Suggest **three** factors to consider when buying large pieces of equipment for a baby. [3] AQA

5 a What is the average length and weight of a full term baby?
      Length ....
      Weight .... [2]
   b Describe the role of health visitors in caring for the mother and baby after the birth. [6] OCR

SECTION 4 DEVELOPMENT

1 a Give the approximate age (in months) at which children usually become able to: **(i)** walk with help, **(ii)** turn their head to watch something of interest, **(iii)** get into a sitting position unaided, **(iv)** take delight in dropping toys and other objects from the pram, **(v)** prop themselves up on their forearms when placed on the floor, **(vi)** point to an object they want, **(vii)** smile at their parents, **(viii)** know when they have done something wrong, **(ix)** start asking questions. [9]

b By what age should it be noticeable whether a child is right-handed or left-handed? [1]

c Describe **two** ways in which babies may move around unaided before they begin to walk. [2]

d If a 4-year-old child is not yet talking, there must be a reason for it. Give **two** possible explanations. [2]

e Who would be the right person to help a child who has difficulty in speaking? [1]

f State any **two** causes of deafness in a young baby. [2]

g Give **two** reasons why fresh air is important to a child's health. [2]

h Give **two** reasons why it is sometimes more difficult for an only child to mix with other children. [2]

i What is meant by parallel play? At about what age might children play like this? [2]

2 It has been claimed that one child in ten is hard of hearing and that many children are falling behind with their schoolwork when their only problems are minor hearing defects.

a Describe ways in which deafness in children can be detected. [4]

b Why may a child with a minor hearing defect be wrongly thought to be backward? [2]

3 a Using the information in Table 1 on p. 140, draw a graph of the 50th percentile weights of **girls** from birth to 8 years, like the one on p. 139. [3]

b On the same graph axes draw another graph to show the weight of a girl called Nina. To do this read the following and make a table of Nina's weight for each year, then draw the graph.

When Nina was born she was a strong, healthy baby of 3 kg. During the first year she gained weight steadily and on her first birthday weighed 9 kg. At 2 years she weighed 11.5 kg, 3 years – 13.5 kg, 4 years – 15.5 kg, and at 5 years – 17.5 kg. Then Nina started school and developed the habit of eating lots of sweets, chocolates, ice-cream and crisps. At 6 years her weight was 22 kg, at 7 years – 25 kg, at 8 years – 30 kg.

(i) Was Nina's birth-weight above or below the 50th percentile?

(ii) At what age did her weight equal the 50th percentile weight for girls?

(iii) By how much was her weight above the 50th percentile at 8 years? What may have been the cause of this? [12]

4 a Complete Table 3 on p. 140, using the growth charts on pp. 138 and 139. Draw the graph of the 50th percentile heights of **boys**. [3]

Height in cm at:								
	Birth	1 yr	2 yrs	3 yrs	4 yrs	5 yrs	6 yrs	7 yrs
Ben	56	79	84	88	103	113	118	125
Terry	43	68	82	91	100	109	112	117

b On the same graph axes draw **two** more graphs to show the growth in height of Ben and Terry, using a different colour for each boy. [8]

c Study the **three** graphs you have drawn and answer the following questions: **(i)** Terry was born 6 weeks prematurely. At what age did his height reach the 50th percentile height for boys? **(ii)** Ben was unfortunate in being severely ill for about a year. How old do you think he was when this happened? Was it followed by a time of 'catch-up' growth? [3]

d Who could be asked for help and advice if a child has a growth problem? [1]

SECTION 5 EARLY CHILDHOOD

1 a Give **two** reasons why play is vital to a child's development. [2]
  b Suggest **two** ways in which parents can encourage their baby to learn to use his hands. [2]
  c Suggest **three** suitable playthings for a 10-month-old baby, and give reasons for your choice. [6]
  d Give reasons why water is good play material. [3]
  e What is the value of a sand-pit in the garden to a 3-year-old child? [3]
  f Suggest two ways in which a 4-year-old can be encouraged to play with other children. [2]
  g The development of play follows a definite pattern starting with solitary play. Suggest, in order, **two** other stages through which play passes before group play occurs. [2]

2 a Suggest **two** hygiene rules to teach toddlers. [2]
  b Give **two** reasons why new shoes for a toddler should be fitted correctly. [2]
  c A child is likely to be jealous of a new brother or sister. Suggest **three** ways of helping the older child to accept the new baby. [3]
  d Why should you not scold or make fun of a young child for sucking her thumb? Give **two** reasons. [2]
  e Suggest **two** ways of encouraging kindness in young children. [5]

3 (i) What is Bookstart? (ii) Describe three Bookstart packs that are free to parents (iii) What is the purpose of Bookstart books? [3]

4 Many parents who work choose to send their children to a nursery. Suggest **four** points a parent should consider when choosing a nursery for their child. [4] AQA

5 a Name **two** types of pre-school group.
  b Give **four** points a parent/carer should consider when choosing a childminder for a two year old. [4] OCR

SECTION 6 FOOD

1 a Give **two** reasons why milk is good for growing children. [2]
   b Suggest **three** ways in which milk can be made attractive to a 4-year-old. [3]
   c At about what age do toddlers have all their milk teeth? How many of them are there? [2]
   d At about what age will a child's second set of teeth begin to come through? How many of these will there be? [2]
   e What is meant by a 'deficiency disease'? Give **two** examples. [3]
   f Assuming that a child has not much appetite, what arrangements would you make for meals? [3]
   g What is meant by **(i)** weaning, **(ii)** malnutrition, **(iii)** obesity? [3]

2 **Three feeding problems** with young children are:
   (i) refusing to eat, **(ii)** spitting out food, **(iii)** throwing food around.
   Possible causes of a feeding problem are that the child:
   – does not like the food
   – is not hungry
   – is bored
   – is tired
   – is unwell
   – has sore gums
   – wants to play
   – is being given food which is too hot
   – is being given food in large pieces
   – wants a change of flavour
   a For each of the problems, give what you consider to be the **three** most likely causes from the list above. [9]
   b Give **one** other cause of feeding problems not listed above. [1]

3 **Poor eating habits have led to an increase in obesity in children.**
   a What is meant by the term 'obesity'? [1]
   b Explain how obesity in young children can be avoided.
   c (i) Identify **three** good sources of protein for a baby aged 10–12 months. [3]
      (ii) Give one reason why the body requires protein. [1] OCR

SECTION 7 HEALTH AND SAFETY

1 a Give **two** ways infection may enter the body. [2]

b Give **two** ways in which infection can be passed on. [2]

c Name **three** precautions which can be taken to prevent an infectious disease from spreading. [3]

d Name a deficiency disease associated with shortage in the diet of **(i)** vitamin D, **(ii)** iron. [2]

e Name **three** diseases for which protection is obtained by the **(i)** DTP vaccine, **(ii)** MMR vaccine. [6]

f Name **two** diseases caused by **(i)** bacteria, **(ii)** viruses. [2]

g Name a disease for which a diet low in both fat and sugar is recommended. [1]

2 a List **eight** items which you would expect to find in a first-aid box and give a reason why each is included. [16]

b What treatment should be given for **(i)** a bad bruise, **(ii)** a baby who is choking, **(iii)** a nose bleed? [6]

3 Describe **five** types of accident which can happen to children under 1 year of age in the **(i)** home, **(ii)** garden. Suggest ways in which these accidents can be prevented. [20].

4 Study the chart below and answer the following questions.

a Identify the **two** blocks of time when road casualties involving children are at their highest. [3]

b **(i)** Give the approximate number of children that are involved in accidents between 3 o'clock and 4 o'clock in the afternoon. [1] **(ii)** Suggest one reason for this. [1]

c Suggest ways a parent might help children avoid road accidents. [3]

d Explain how you would **(i)** make a garden safe for a child to play, **(ii)** deal with a child who has a grazed knee. [2 1 2]

5 a Name the following childhood diseases

Description	Name
A fever, dislike of bright light and a rash that will not disappear when pressed.	
Painful swelling near the jaw on one or both sides.	
A fever, cough and runny nose followed five days later with a rash which spreads quickly.	
Small red spots that turn to blisters	

[4]

b Most of these diseases can be immunised against.

Explain how immunisation helps to protect against disease. [3]

c Describe **three** situations when a parent should call for a doctor or take a child to hospital. [3] AQA

6 Equipment can be bought to make a home safer.

For each of the following areas suggest **one** item that could be bought.

Explain how it might help to prevent accidents.

The first has been done for you.

Area of house	Safety item	How it prevents accidents
Stairs	Safety gate	Prevents children from climbing and falling.
Kitchen		
Bathroom		
Living room		

[6] AQA

SECTION 8 THE FAMILY IN THE COMMUNITY

1 a Give **three** ways of securing babies and children in a car. [3]
   b Suggest **two** causes of electrical accidents in the bathroom and ways of avoiding them. [2]
   c The Green Cross Code has **six** rules. Write down those you can remember. [6]
   d State **two** differences between fostering and adoption. [2]
   e Name **two** ways in which the Social Services may provide for the care of babies of working mothers. [2]
   f Name **one** disability known to be of genetic origin. [1]
   g State **two** ways a child may become disabled after birth. [2]
   h Give **three** ways in which a Special School differs from an ordinary school. [3]

2 a Explain what is meant by child abuse. [3]
   b What would make you suspect that a child in the nursery was being physically abused? [6]
   c What action should be taken in a case of suspected abuse? [6]
   d Why might some parents abuse their child? [5]

3 More grandparents are being asked to help with childcare.
   Give **three** advantages of using grandparents as a childcare option. [3] AQA

4 Study the table below which shows the number of babies placed for adoption in 1975 and 2000.

Year	Number of babies
1975	21,000
2000	4,000

(i) Describe **two** reasons why a couple may wish to adopt a child. [4; 2 points for each reason]
(ii) Give **three** reasons why a child could be taken into local authority care. [3] OCR

Index